STILL IN PRINT

STILL IN PRINT
The Southern Novel Today

Edited by Jan Nordby Gretlund

The University of South Carolina Press

© 2010 University of South Carolina

Published by the University of South Carolina Press
Columbia, South Carolina 29208

www.sc.edu/uscpress

Manufactured in the United States of America

19 18 17 16 15 14 13 12 11 10
10 9 8 7 6 5 4 3 2 1

Library of Congress Cataloging-in-Publication Data

Still in print : the Southern novel today / edited by Jan Nordby Gretlund.
    p. cm.
 Includes bibliographical references and index.
   ISBN 978-1-57003-943-0 (cloth : alk. paper) — ISBN 978-1-57003-944-7 (pbk. : alk. paper)
 1. American fiction—Southern States—History and criticism. 2. American fiction—21st century—History and criticism. I. Gretlund, Jan Nordby.
 PS261.S6175 2010
 813'.609975—dc22

2010015029

CONTENTS

Preface vii

Introduction: A Time of Excellence in Southern Fiction 1

PART I A Sense of History

Charles Frazier ~ *Cold Mountain* 19
   M. THOMAS INGE

Josephine Humphreys ~ *Nowhere Else on Earth* 29
   CLARA JUNCKER

Kaye Gibbons ~ *On the Occasion of My Last Afternoon* 43
   KATHRYN MCKEE

Pam Durban ~ *So Far Back* 58
   JAN NORDBY GRETLUND

Percival Everett ~ *Erasure* 73
   TARA POWELL

PART II A Sense of Place

Steve Yarbrough ~ *The Oxygen Man* 91
   THOMAS E. DASHER

Larry Brown ~ *Fay* 105
   JEAN W. CASH

Chris Offutt ~ *The Good Brother* 119
   CARL WIECK

Barry Hannah ~ *Yonder Stands Your Orphan* 135
   OWEN W. GILMAN JR.

James Lee Burke ~ *Crusader's Cross* 148
   HANS H. SKEI

PART III A Sense of Humor

George Singleton ~ *Work Shirts for Madmen* 165
    CHARLES ISRAEL

Clyde Edgerton ~ *The Bible Salesman* 174
    JOHN GRAMMER

James Wilcox ~ *Heavenly Days* 189
    SCOTT ROMINE

Donald Harington ~ *Enduring* 203
    EDWIN T. ARNOLD

Lewis Nordan ~ *Lightning Song* 216
    MARCEL ARBEIT

PART IV A Sense of Malaise

Ron Rash ~ *One Foot in Eden* 233
    THOMAS ÆRVOLD BJERRE

Richard Ford ~ *The Lay of the Land* 248
    ROBERT H. BRINKMEYER JR.

Cormac McCarthy ~ *The Road* 260
    RICHARD GRAY

Contributors 275
Index 281

PREFACE

We are eighteen experienced critics of southern literature with many publications behind us. Most of us are southerners, and six of us are Europeans. We are admirers of the great writers of the South and teach the works of Edgar Allan Poe, Mark Twain, Zora Neale Hurston, William Faulkner, Eudora Welty, Richard Wright, Flannery O'Connor, Walker Percy, Madison Jones, Alice Walker, and Lee Smith—in short, we deal with most of the classic southern writers on a daily basis and write about them. This means that mostly we work on literature by accepted and universally established authors and that nobody doubts the relevance of our writing about the southern classics.

But here we write about novels published from 1997 to 2009. The fact is many southern novels are published every year, but for the most part their shelf life is unreasonably short. Often a new novel—even an excellent one—appears in print, drops out of sight immediately, and is not heard about again. This is why my fellow critics and I have decided to stick out our necks and pronounce. We feel an urge to tell you about new novels that deserve to be kept in print.

Our goal was to make a useful book. We asked ourselves a few simple questions: Which good southern writers recently published novels? What can we do to keep those novels in print? What can we do to make people read these new novels? We thought of the lay reader, the guy lost before the screen or behind the sports pages, general readers both outside and within the academy. The eighteen novels we picked are good and should be better known than they are. Thus the idea behind every essay in the book is to convince a potential reader that this one novel is worth reading, that it deserves our attention, and that it is not necessary to have read other novels by the same author or other authors to appreciate that one book.

You may search this book for your favorite southern novel and ask why the editor chose the novels and novelists that appear here. But the critics picked the novels they wanted to write about, so the question should be why did the editor pick these critics to write about today's southern novel? A short version of my answer follows: I published my first essay on southern literature thirty years ago (it was on Allen Tate's "Ode to the Confederate Dead"); since then I have kept a keen eye on the literary criticism written on southern literature. I got to know critics by listening to them at conferences, by reviewing their work, and by editing and coediting volumes on Eudora Welty, Flannery O'Connor (two), Walker Percy, Madison Jones, southern landscapes, and the South in the 1990s, as well as two southern issues of periodicals. Just who the best critics are varies substantially from decade to decade; in the late 1980s and early 1990s women dominated both as novelists and excellent critics. Now, at the end of the first decade after 2000, men clearly dominate both as novelists and critics. I cannot explain the shifting gender distribution in literary achievement, but I know this will probably change again within a few years. As it is the essays in *Still in Print* have been written not only by prominent established critics but also by talented young critics, who will influence future criticism of the southern novel.

Let me add that the canon of the southern novel is *not* simply a local product; it is the result of an international collaboration. If you know your literary history, you know that both Edgar Allan Poe and William Faulkner could thank French critics for their lasting place in world literature. Today the European Union, with almost twice as many readers as the United States, is contributing substantially to the sale and study of the southern novel. Since 1988 there has been a very active and influential European Southern Studies Forum, which reflects the curious fact that more southern fiction is probably being taught at European universities than at American institutions. The reader will notice that *Still in Print* reflects this situation, as one-third of the essays on new southern novels are by critics from the Czech Republic, Denmark, Finland, Norway, and the United Kingdom.

We do not want you to get bogged down in the writers' biographies, but at the beginning of each essay there is a short biographical sketch of the writer, which you can read before you go to the essay, or skip and perhaps pick up again when you have read the novel discussed. The essays introducing the novels are also short but should offer you enough insight into the novels to enable you to decide whether you want to read them. The critic who wrote the essay thinks you should, as the novel deserves your attention and has potential to become a classic. There is, however, little chance of that happening, unless we can manage to keep the novel in print long enough for you and many others to notice it.

We hope teachers and students will note that many themes recur in the selected novels and that it would be easy to select five or six novels for a course or a thesis based on the essays. The arrangement of the essays is based on four overriding topics. The first topic, covering five titles, is "a sense of history," which could have been called "the past in the present," "the burden of prejudice," or even "a sense of justice" regarding both race and gender issues. The second topic, covering five titles, is "a sense of place," but it might as well be called "a sense of family and community." The third topic, covering five titles, is "a sense of humor," and it is about our incongruous everyday lives. Finally, what is immediately apparent as one reads the three titles within the fourth topic, "a sense of malaise," is an awareness of loss and despair, or alienation and homelessness, or even of a "sickness unto death."

Some readers will see entirely other potential constellations built into the book. If you rearrange the order of the novels, it is easy to focus on other topics, such as political and religious fundamentalism; identity in marriage; extended family and community relations; sex, violence, and crime; alcoholism; the rural versus the urbanized South, or the way we live now. Several of the novels are initiation stories, and the picaresque is often the style. No two readers will see the exact same topics in these novels, which is one reason the novels deserve our attention and should remain in print. To help you in the shaping of your own personal topic based on the novels considered, we have attached substantial Works Cited and Consulted lists to each essay.

When you ask leading figures in southern literary studies to choose a novel to advocate and nominate for survival, it is not for the editor to ask for discrimination based on race, gender, religion, or age. Many of the essays in this book would not have been submitted if I had not allowed the critics to choose their one novel freely. As a result it is very satisfying to note that the content of each essay turns out, as expected, to be decidedly politically correct on the topics of race, gender, religion, and age.

I thank the contributors to the collection for choosing such excellent novels, and for their ready cooperation, precision, and exactitude. I am indebted, once again, to the Institute for Southern Studies at the University of South Carolina for their help and hospitality. I also appreciate the continued support of the Department of Literature, Culture and Media, at the University of Southern Denmark, a university that encourages research in the humanities.

On behalf of all lovers of the southern novel, let me end the preface by expressing a profound sense of loss now that Larry Brown and Barry Hannah will no longer write novels that provoke, ridicule, shock, and entertain. Let us take comfort in the celebration of the very essence of living in their novels still in print today.

Introduction: A Time of Excellence in Southern Fiction

"The writer learns, perhaps more quickly than the reader, to be humble in the face of what-is. What-is is all he has to do with; the concrete is his medium; and he will realize eventually that fiction can transcend its limitations only by staying within them" (Flannery O'Connor, *Mystery and Manners*, 146).

From 1607 until today the South has been a center of literary creativity. But we have always had problems deciding just who is a "southern" writer. Should birth be the criterion? Or is it qualification enough for someone to have stayed and published in the South, however briefly? In the eighteenth century Joseph Brown Ladd of Rhode Island wrote some poems in Charleston then went home. Although he did not play a significant part in creating southern literature, he was awarded space in Rubin's *History of Southern Literature* (1985). Were he and, say, Caroline Howard Gilman southern writers? Is it their choice whether they should be claimed for the South? Or is it perhaps the critic's choice?

Many contemporary writers are regionalized, whether or not they like it. Some writers, such as Richard Ford and Maya Angelou, started out by disclaiming their southern background but later celebrated it. Some writers become southern through historical events. Mark Twain became "southern" in literary history in the 1950s, and his work does not appear in a southern literary anthology until 1970 (Gretlund 2008). Some writers from West Virginia, such as Jayne Anne Phillips, want to be, and yet do not want to be, southern. Anne Tyler, from the Baltimore / Washington, D.C., area wants to be southern and yet clearly is not. Ralph Ellison, who was from Oklahoma, is included in many southern anthologies with various explanations. Percival Everett is *not* included, although he was born in Fort Gordon, Georgia, and grew up in Columbia, South Carolina. Others, such as John Jakes, the fiction-writing historian, and Mickey Spillane, master of crime fiction, claim southernness because they stay in the South so often. What does regional branding reveal and to what extent is it political? Does literary regionalization matter?

It is obvious to me as a European that regional identity still matters in the lives of Americans. Academics may question the importance of the local and regional in their cosmopolitan world, but try having your Sunday grits in the Waffle House, attending service in the local Baptist church—followed by a dinner at the family-style Golden Corral—then shopping in a rural Wal-Mart or Piggly Wiggly. The people you listen to and talk with have no doubts about their identity as southerners. To seriously question the existence of a southern identity, you will have to be purblind to many facts about living in the South. The novels analyzed in this collection depend on these everyday facts as their material for fiction.

To call anybody a "southern writer" is more than to place the person geographically. In many readers' minds "southern writer" is a special category. The categorization is, of course, a qualification of "writer" and may even be understood as a limitation. But like most limitations it is also, as Flannery O'Connor wrote in a comment about Eudora Welty, "a great blessing, perhaps the greatest blessing a writer can have," because it serves as "a gateway to reality." What Welty always knew was that her imagination was bound to the reality of life in her southern state. Her fiction had come out of a particular landscape and was based on her familiarity with its people.

As editor I asked the authors of the essays in this book to choose writers who have spent most of their lives in the South and have published fiction after the year 2000. I also requested that they examine whether the subjects of their essays are faithful to the reality of the life they see about them today or if they cater to us with stereotypes and propaganda of the sort that belong in *Gone with the Wind* and *To Kill a Mockingbird* in both the novel and movie versions (possibly because they imagine their readers demand the two-dimensional world of the screen). Fortunately the southern writers of the new millennium are not homogenized mainstreamers and are not immune to the great changes in their region.

For more than a decade now *Inventing Southern Literature* by Michael Kreyling has had quite an impact among literary critics. The title of his book is *not* telling us that literature is invented, as that would surprise nobody. No, it is the adjective "southern" that is "invented." In spite of all the support for the idea of equating "southern" with fascism, racism, and gender discrimination, that idea is, I believe, nonsense. And the present collection on the contemporary southern novel bears me out. Kreyling wants to deny the South its culture, history, geography, and literature—in short, its identity—by appropriating the word "southern" for ideologies of the 1930s. Any sense of place and any sense of the past clearly show that the South has its history and literature, just as New England does, without our trying to identify achievement in that region with the ideology of one troubled decade in the seventeenth century. Southern literature had its first great year in 1835, long before Germany or Italy became unified nations, yet long after "German" and "Italian" literatures were celebrated the world over (Gretlund 1993). Should these two adjectives, "German" and "Italian," lose their right to exist because it is possible to identify them with fascist politics of the 1930s? Fortunately those adjectives are alive and well today, and so is the word "southern." Identity is always being created, lost, and reinvented; it is always looking for a new grounding, not only in ideology but also in ever-changing reality. Any expression of reality is created, and the world created is mediated through representations. There is no good reason to settle on a representation that mediates an exclusively negative "southern" identity—which never was the sum total of southern identity and which in today's South is hard to even recognize. I encourage a critical evaluation of the present demolition of past icons, as it will help us in the ongoing reinvention of the identity we daily identify as "southern."

The latest critical development in the South is called New Southern Studies. Let me try to sum up this development, as fairly as I can, on the basis of and using the vocabulary of Kathryn McKee and Annette Trefzer's excellent introduction to the special New Southern Studies issue they edited for *American Literature* in 2006: The New Southern Studies is based on the notion of an intellectual "global South," a term that embeds the U.S. South in a transnational framework. The argument is that this new global phase is a crucial turning point in the South and that transnational perspectives yield a fundamentally different field of study. The task is to provide models for how a globally inflected southern studies can productively defamiliarize texts and problems with which students of the U.S. South consider themselves familiar.

The New Southern Studies is *not* an argument about what is special about the U.S. South relative to the nation, and it is *not* an argument about the role race and gender play in setting the agenda of today's southern studies. Rather, it asks the following: What happens when we unmoor the South and it becomes a floating signifier in a sea of globalism? How is the South networked in global systems of culture and economy? What are the global gestures in literary texts that we formerly interpreted as regional or national issues? The dimensions of the global refer both to the importation of the world into the South and to the exportation of the South into the world. The idea is that these patterns of global cultural exchange can help us break out of habitual ways of seeing the South in opposition to the North. For many scholars of the U.S. South, the current integration of the region into larger global processes, it is suggested, constitutes a productive and fundamental change.

The field of southern literary studies, it is argued, is situated in the middle of a postmodern debate concerning the boundaries and sovereignty not only of its canonical but also its critical undertakings. In brief the social and theoretical contexts for the interdisciplinary study of southern literature are changing, and the fluid distinctions between the "global" and the "local" and between "contexts" and "literatures" reflect the tensions and the possibilities of this change.

In New Southern Studies a new approach to familiar questions is proposed regarding textual identity by asking: What new methodologies and theories are needed to think of the U.S. South and its literature as affected by and contributing to globalization? How can the integrative global identity of the U.S. South be illuminated by its literature and our new ways of reading it?

The South will then emerge, it is variously suggested, as an in-between space, a process, an agenda, an itinerary, a discourse, an idea, or a relational concept in a global context. It is predicted that this shape-shifting South, whose boundaries are so fluid, will also wash over the canon of southern literature, leaving it with increasingly blurry outlines.

One of the many challenges of a New Southern Studies is to figure out how to do it—how to make a set of reading practices that reshape curriculum and alter scholarly habits. The argument is not primarily about what belongs to and what should be excluded from New Southern Studies but about whether reading practices will change and texts gain new dimensions when the contexts take on global proportions. Advocates of New Southern Studies maintain that studying a place within its global context will not negate the value of the local; it will rather intensify that value by suggesting all that circulates through the region. The goal is to engage in the study of broadly defined Souths and their relation to the world and to organize transnational and multidisciplinary conversations that unmap, de-map, and remap the U.S. South.

New Southern Studies as it appears in this summary is a most praiseworthy effort. There is nothing wrong with idealism, although the real world will insist on a measure of realism. New Southern Studies *is* an idealistic undertaking, and the idealists behind it hope, of course, that it will come to encompass the future of southern literary criticism. But the southern literary world of 2010 does not in any tangible way reflect the somewhat naïve idealism of the academics behind this proposed paradigmatic shift. The critical essays of *Still in Print: Today's Southern Novel* reflect the reality of the contemporary South as regards to the novels, the writers, and the literary critics. If literary critics propose what novelists should write, it is putting the cart before the horse.

Alexander Hamilton's Federalist thesis and Thomas Jefferson's antithesis are both alive and well in southern literature of the twenty-first century. The struggle for centralized control, order, and unity is the essence of much writing by contemporary writers, and so is the Puritan idea that our passions are perverse and evil and must be restrained. On the other hand, faith in the ability of the individual to pursue happiness, and the right to manage our own lives with dignity without the intervention of authorities, is today characteristic thinking of many southern writers. In this sense the southern novel today expresses both the conforming, even stereotypical, life of the hamburger strip and the highly individualized, even grotesquely nonconforming, existence in the southern space and place.

The built-in constitutional problem of combining the advantages of unity and control with the right of the individual *not* to conform is obvious in the plots of the classics of the Southern Renaissance, such as William Faulkner's *Absalom, Absalom!* and Robert Penn Warren's *All the King's Men*. The clash between community control and individual desire is still offered the reader in new southern fiction, but, and this is my main argument, we are witnessing a sea change that, at least superficially, allows us to distinguish between "federalist" thinking and "agrarian" idealism according to racial and/or gender patterns.

The "typical" concerns of the region are, according to Roy Blount Jr., "dirt, chickens, defeat, family, religion, prejudice, collard greens, politics, and diddie wa diddie" (Blount 1994, 24). Although I am sorely tempted by the collard greens, not to mention the diddie wa diddie, the critics seem to focus on the prejudice. In the fiction they find a particular interest in the continuity—or lack of continuity—of the racial attitudes, assumptions, and values that used to inform the southern novel. But what if we look at new southern fiction placed not in the clay-eating and cross-burning southern past, but in the South, say, around the year 2000? What has happened to southern writers as the South has been changing? Does the suddenly superior, optimistic, and more prosperous South produce new voices, new topics, and less reliance on the topics of the past?

The humanism of Cicero and Erasmus is present in southern writing from the time of William Byrd to our own time. Man must make peace with his senses and his own basic nature; this is what culture is, as John Crowe Ransom also taught us. Contemporary southern fiction cannot be reduced to sensory experience, and the whole is still, as Richard Weaver pointed out, inscrutable and somehow greater than the sum of the analyzable parts. Is there still a sense of the past in the present, a sense of a place, a sense of a community, a sense of the grotesque aspects of everyday living, and perhaps even a sense of right and wrong in the southern novel? And if any one of these is missing today, is it then nevertheless present as a sense of something lost?

Is there still a pattern of ideas and conduct imbedded in the changing society we see reflected in the new novels? Do Nordan, Harington, Rash, Ford, Brown, Yarbrough, Hannah, Edgerton, McCarthy, Durban, Frazier, Singleton, Humphreys, Gibbons, Everett, Wilcox, Lee Burke, Offutt, and, add the name of your own favorite southern novelist, still see themselves in a specific southern place and see the past as a storehouse of values and guidelines for living? Or is the emphasis now more on an existentialist sense of "sickness unto death," as in *One Foot in Eden*, *The Lay of the Land*, and *The Road*.

Flannery O'Connor's southerners of the 1950s and early 1960s were intensely aware of being southern and acutely self-conscious about it. The writers of the mid-twentieth century seemed conscious of place, family, community, manifestations of religion and were keenly aware of the past in the present. They found history fascinating and wrote of an individual past that was involved with the regional past. The history of the South, its attraction and repulsion, from antebellum slaveholding over the Civil War to civil rights struggles in the twentieth century, is reflected in the region's literary history.

The myth of a stable permanent South in the past, which is often used by commentators on the South as a foil to the chaotic present, is arch-conservative. How present or how removed the past is has always been individual, but it is a mistake to believe that a changeless southern reality ever existed or, for that matter, ever dominated southern fiction. The South never cohered ideologically and culturally, and the community was rarely idealized. Change is always overtaking place and always has and this is why you cannot control the representation of southern identity. As southern fiction demonstrates most people do not stop changing long enough to realize that they are supposed to live in a changeless world. Since the 1820s the region has been forever changing, deconstructing, reinventing, refashioning itself, imbuing itself with its own meanings, and seeing the rest of the country as being aberrant and on the margin. There are still many Souths and one South, as the 2008 election demonstrated once again. The South is also struggling with its present, trying not to go spiritually and emotionally bankrupt, which is perhaps the clearest message of this collection.

Four novels considered in this collection, written by Charles Frazier (*Cold Mountain*), Kaye Gibbons (*On the Occasion of My Last Afternoon*), Josephine Humphreys (*Nowhere Else on Earth*), and Pam Durban (*So Far Back*, in part) are situated during and right after the Civil War. The pitfall in writing historical fiction is that after years of painstaking research in cultural and social history, and great efforts to get costumes, food, language, manners, interiors, and so on just right, the *material* for fiction may come to dwarf the fiction. The writer is easily tempted to overflow her narrative with lists of objects and enumerations of details of everyday nineteenth-century life. What is gained in historical depth is then lost in immediacy and characterization. History becomes a "straightjacket" and characters exist largely to speak quaint words of antebellum times, show old fashions and ways, and illustrate historical events. You could argue that their emotional development has been sacrificed on the altar of historical "accuracy." This is why Clark Gable's improvisation—"Frankly my dear, I don't give a damn"—at the end of the movie version of *Gone with the Wind* offers such relief. The added word "frankly" obliterates the historical opaqueness of what is really just another domestic scene. The historical novels by Frazier, Gibbons, Humphreys, and Durban manage to straddle the history pit and through their excursions into history say something significant about race and gender that is relevant for our present lives.

The eighteen novelists considered in this collection are, of course, individuals with highly divergent styles and different theoretical approaches, but they also have quite different southern backgrounds and personal histories. There is a pronounced out-of-life-into-fiction tendency in several of the novels treated here. All reading is, of course, the result of a desire to know a text. To know it fully is to *have control* of it. We are curious about the writer who wrote the text, because we believe that biographical knowledge will help us demystify the fiction. More than seventy years of New Criticism, or for that matter decades of structuralism, semiotics, and hermeneutics, have not succeeded in killing off our interest in the novelist.

Writers, publishers, teachers, and critics keep telling us that what we read is fiction, "a pure product of the imagination," and "pure" means untainted by the facts of private lives. Biography has been officially banished, but has anybody been convinced? Even critics read biographies. Maybe because we still suspect that all literature is in essence autobiographical. Impervious to all abstract reasoning, our interest in biography endures. Our reading of fiction is doubly oriented: we read it as one discourse that invokes another. Our focus is often on the fiction *and* on the author's involvement in her own fiction. To what extent, we ask, does the writer's life translate into fiction? If we are honest, we must admit that we ask this question frequently. As contributing critics to this collection, we have feared getting lost in the southern writers' interesting biographical backgrounds, so while the essays focus on one novel each, we have supplied a separate biographical sketch for each writer, and the main focus remains on the reading of one novel. We also include extensive bibliographies for those who want to read more fiction by an author or want to read more about the author.

Writers of highly divergent styles, techniques, and theoretical approaches seem to share an understanding of literature that confirms its traditional function and status in society, even in the everyday world of local communities. In general the contemporary southern novel is not a literature that reflects a modern feeling of homelessness and alienation, which does not mean that it offers characters wholly without problems—on the contrary. But the point is that it is a literature that does not try to separate itself from the southern context from which it emerges.

The interactions between the individual and the collective spheres remain crucial. Let us, as an aside, look at the ideas of "the family of man" and "the global village," which are still popular. But should they be? Not from a Jeffersonian point of view. The ideas offer no acceptable excuse for not knowing anything about where you are, the people who live and lived here, and what happened in their lives. We need to note that the most important element in the expression "the family of man" is the word "man," as in "mankind." The southern novel of today reminds us that the individual human being is always more important than anything as vague as "an idea." You have to be a member of a family, a particular concrete family—if you are not, create one as people do, also in southern fiction—then, and only then, you can try to be a part of something as abstract as "the family of man." In a similar way for a southerner the important element of the Emersonian expression "the global village" is the word "village." First you must belong to a village, be a part of a community—a local community, because all ideas and art, all history and literature, has its origin in a particular community. If you are of the village, then, and only then, can you be a member of anything as abstract and undemanding as "the global village" and other transcendental structures of meaning. The humorous fiction of Singleton, Edgerton, Wilcox, Harington, and Nordan show how the clichés function as distractions from the realities and needs of daily life, and that if they are not validated in the particular life in the community, the clichés remain just that. If we do not get to know the village and its individual members, any talk of the family of man and the global village is just a mental exercise. The novelists make sure we get to know that their characters are surrounded by their southern families and are totally engulfed in their communities.

The literature of a certain area is not, of course, obliged to reflect its origin; often it does not, which may actually be one reason we like to read it. But if history, literature, and all art, for that matter, are not grounded in local life, they may easily become superficial, ornamental, or "extra," as Flannery O'Connor would have said. And the teaching of history, literature, and art would be reduced to having a decorative function only and would *not* necessarily inform our lives—as they ideally should. As the essays on novels by Ron Rash, Richard Ford, and Cormac McCarthy make clear, the relationship between place and social place has, to put it mildly, weakened considerably. The disorientation and feeling of estrangement are results of a general cultural displacement, also in the South. The new southern novels imply that the social order is becoming impersonal and increasingly technological, and that a sense of self is no longer necessarily ingrained with a sense of family or community.

A sense of history and literature grounded in local life are excellent weapons against the wanton destruction of our natural or citified surroundings and the condemnation to oblivion of our cultural traditions. We also need a sense of continuity with our immediate environment, but a restless nomadic life in the world does not allow us the time to build up the memory and associations that will make us fit to live in one place. We do need a sense of place and a sense of history. Fortunately our southern novelists can help. Lewis Nordan, Donald Harington, Ron Rash, Clyde Edgerton, and James Wilcox show and explain the local life and its tradition in their place. These writers, and to some extent all the others considered here, have knowledge grounded in local life, and they bring common sense and new insight to old traditions. Their novels are also about the difficulty of being honest and unsentimental about the past and the people who represent it. And their fiction is about the necessity of coming to terms with the past, both the public myth of the past and the family past, and the role of the past in the present.

In one of her talks Flannery O'Connor said, "The novelist is required to open his eyes on the world around him and look. If what he sees is not highly edifying, he is still required to look" (O'Connor 1969, 177). The ideal is not only to look but also to pronounce—and that is what the novels and the critics selected for this collection do. One important question for the politicians and for southern writers is whether it is possible to urbanize and yet keep basic human values. Is it possible to avoid the creation of polluted areas and alienated people by simply emphasizing the old values of a sense of place, a sense of community, and an awareness of the history of a place?

The function of a contemporary literature is, among others, to express the meaning of contemporary culture in representations of actuality, that is, to show what we are doing right now. But often it also has an ethical purpose and a didactic goal, which is to help arrest the dehumanization inherent in our technological everyday. As readers we are looking to literature for ways to recover, restore, or reconstruct ourselves. Lewis P. Simpson pointed out that "the only meaningful covenant for the latter-day writer is one with the self on terms generally defined as existential" (Simpson 1975, 71).

Today's creative artist in the South has to look for the landscape behind a repetitive labyrinth of highways, motels, restaurants that do not serve grits, burger places, gas stations, and shopping malls. It is a modular world in which most of us are too easily at home, perhaps because things are everywhere the same. What the novelists have proved is that it is not merely pockets of virgin forests and overlooked, and therefore unpolluted, streams that awaken a feel for a place, but also citified areas. The city estranges us from the world only when it rapes and obliterates its site. Unfortunately this has happened in Charleston and Mount Pleasant, according to Josephine Humphreys. Consider whether this is also the future of other communities in the South: "I had studied the town of Herculaneum, buried by hot mud in the year 79 A.D. My town had been similarly engulfed, not by mud but by overflow from the city of Charleston" (Humphreys 1987, 11). The identification of writer and home ground is unmistakable, and it is obvious from the fidelity to every detail that there is a special relationship between the writer and her place. Her town and state are not only the geographical and sociological settings of her novels, they are parts of her interior landscape.

The decisive factors for our decisions are often values with their origin in the local community. But the traditional body of southern thinking, founded on a situatedness in place and community, has changed as the ethnic make-up of the South has changed, and the change is reflected in contemporary fiction. Faulkner's Native Americans of northern Mississippi bear little resemblance to Barry Hannah's cross-eyed Apache renegade called "Geronimo." And the presentations of the Chickasaws or Choctaws in Yoknapatawpha County and of the Western Apache are essentially different from Josephine Humphreys's portrait of the historic Lumbee Indians of Robeson County, North Carolina, in *Nowhere Else on Earth*. Just as Mark Twain's "outlandish" communities bear little resemblance to Cormac McCarthy's modern Mexicans in his border trilogy. And neither Twain's nor McCarthy's foreigners are much like Mary Hood's South Florida Cubans in her novel *Familiar Heat* (1995).

In the early part of the twentieth century the antebellum South was often romanticized and fetishized at home and abroad. But since the mid-1950s the

South has been considered a blemish on the national identity, a region spotted with a taint of guilt and a smudge of infamy. Some of the historical baggage is segregation, lynching, resistance to civil rights legislation, and exploitation, most of which rarely occurs anymore. But novels by Barry Hannah, James Lee Burke, Chris Offutt, Percival Everett, and Steve Yarbrough indicate that spiritual leftovers of hard-core conservatism, religious fundamentalism, celebrated agrarianism, romanticized myth, abject poverty, grotesque violence, and above all rampant prejudice—against: you name it—play an important part in the South and in discrediting the South.

Southern writers were born with a past of prejudice and racism. But is that something of yesterday only? Has the stain of past sins, in this postsegregation era of Dixie *resurgens*, faded so much that contemporary southern writers can write of other issues and without reflecting the racist burden of the past? Or is the stigma obvious also in southern fiction of today? And if, I say *if*, the stigma has been almost forgotten among the Ya-Ya girls in the beautiful K-Mart South, what are the topics and issues that have become crucial enough to obscure the old taint of guilt?

The southern culture of today is clearly the basis of new fiction and new thinking in matters racial, but there is still focus on the "human stain." The southern novels analyzed in this collection often express the national ambivalence over race. On this issue the South is *not* an exception, and surely there is no good reason to claim "exceptionalism" in that area. The southern pattern of racial engagement is a reflection of a broader pattern throughout the United States, but the South is often where the racial drama is performed. The South is not really so different. What the South has done and, to an extent, is still doing is to highlight essential national developments. Many American novels reflect the common racial assumptions and choices, but the southern fiction of today often distills the assumptions and choices precisely. The American obsession with racial interaction, the obvious integration efforts, and lingering divisive provocations are often, and strangely combined with, a denial of a biracial genesis and an awkward silence about interracial history. The progress is that most of the violent battles of today take place in the courtrooms, where they should have been all along.

What makes the narratives of new southern writers essentially different is the reclaiming of forgotten, or hidden, historical events, the claiming of ignored events in the present, and the acceptance and ready use of the ethnic reality of the South, or of the whole country, which *is* a reality of obvious, and sometimes less obvious, prejudice. An example of this can be found in Chris Offutt's novel *The Good Brother*, especially after the main character has had to leave Kentucky and is hiding out among well-armed radical dissidents in the West, but also in Steve Yarbrough's *The Oxygen Man*, Percival Everett's *Erasure*, and Pam Durban's *So Far Back*, all novels considered in the collection.

It is difficult not to note the human stain in the Western community. But its brand of open and unquestioning prejudice is not limited to white people in southern fiction; according to Percival Everett racism is also rampant in black communities. Thelonius "Monk" Ellison, the main character of *Erasure*, the best African American novel in decades, describes his situation: "The society in which I live tells me I am black; that is my race. . . . I am no good at basketball. I listen to Mahler. . . . I graduated *summa cum laude* from Harvard. . . . I am good at math. I cannot dance. I did not grow up in any inner city or the rural south." Thelonius is not, in other words, living down to our prejudicial notions of what a black man is, can be, or likes—seen from white or black points of view. His career as a novelist is suffering. He is writing retellings of Euripides and parodies of French poststructuralists, and after the seventeenth rejection of his novel, he is depressed: "'The line is, you're not black enough,' my agent said."

As James Cobb once pointed out, "the South's experience surely says that any identity—national, regional, cultural, or otherwise—that can be sustained only by demonizing or denigrating other groups exacts a terrible toll, not simply on the demonized and denigrated but ultimately on those who can find self-affirmation only by rejecting others" (Cobb 2005, 336). It is an old truth that the slaver ultimately enslaves himself. Steve Yarbrough's southerners are often encapsulated in time. He makes it clear that prejudice is not just a question of hate, that is, racial hate, but often prejudicial ideas are used to justify class issues and continued financial exploitation. Some of the white catfish producers in Steve Yarbrough's *The Oxygen Man* are aware of the correlation between prejudice and money. When they talk about what they are doing, they seem totally encapsulated in time, but Yarbrough is not talking about the past, he is writing about today.

The stain of racism is not ignored and has not been suburbanized away in new southern fiction. In the new millennium there are, fortunately, numerous southern writers who publish fiction discussing the present troublesome issues of racial segregation and exploitation. This is not only in bad novels full of literary clichés but also in some excellent fiction set in our time. Prejudice and racism still exist, and today's fiction, by Humphreys, Frazier, Gibbons, Durban, Everett, Offutt, Yarbrough and others in the collection, caters to our needs and realities by accentuating the issues. The contemporary southern novel mounts messages of potential change, which are of national and international concern, relevant for readers everywhere.

"At the bottom of Southern humor lies," according to Roy Blount, southern humorist, "the fundamental truth: that nothing is less humorous, or less Southern, than making a genuine, good faith effort to define and explain humor, particularly Southern humor" (Blount 1994, 21). After quoting Blount, the right, incongruous, and typical thing to do is to make a few remarks about it anyway. After all humor is the oldest tradition in southern literature. It goes back to the antebellum southwestern humorists, so called because Alabama, Mississippi, and Tennessee were also the West and the frontier at the beginning of the nineteenth century. The humorous tradition, created by David Crockett, Augustus B. Longstreet, Joseph G. Baldwin, Johnson J. Hooper, George Washington Harris, Mark Twain, and a host of others, is alive and well today.

It can be argued that the humor of the Old South is without the true wit of Cervantes, without the refined Swiftian existentialist satire, and lacks the intelligent stinging mockery of Alexander Pope. In fact a modern reader might think of old southern humor as that of a crude lower class, but he would be wrong. Not everybody could read in the nineteenth century, and those who could wanted their newspapers full of humorous stories. And they were. Some stories were even syndicated, such as Mark Twain's short "Jim Smiley and His Jumping Frog" story, which appeared in November 1865 and was brought in newspapers across the country. On its own that one story made Mark Twain, stand-up comedian, a household name. This should not surprise us in the twenty-first century, for we are still exposed to the old tradition through its direct inheritor: the American sitcom. When we watch *The Cosby Show*, *Cheers*, *Frasier*, *Everybody Loves Raymond*, *Friends*, and so on, we laugh at the short dialogues, continually. But when the show is over, most of us are unable to remember even the shortest of the humorous exchanges. We are not meant to, for the very essence of this type of humor is not intellectual; the purpose is enjoyment, escape, and immediate gratification.

Southern humor of today still encompasses local customs and speech and in this way reflects a place, a concrete place, such as George Singleton's town called Gruel, which does not really exist in South Carolina, stubbornly resisting any change. The place seems literal and physical and hardly ever abstract, and all conflicts are dramatized. The humor is oral, and a story must be told and told right; so it presupposes a conversing community, an audience, and the presence of specific individuals (whose lives are not abstracted for literary purposes). In spite of rapid social change, there is no discontinuity in this tradition. Southern humor, like country music, still depends on place and community not only for its kind but also for its survival. The drama presented is often confused, full of outrageous inconsistency and hard-to-believe grotesqueness, as in Edgar Allan Poe, William Faulkner, Flannery O'Connor, Barry Hannah, Lewis Nordan, Kaye Gibbons, Donald Harington, Ron Rash, Richard Ford, and Cormac McCarthy. Southern humor simply mirrors the incongruity and madness of everyday life. The particular vitality, dramatic (real) violence, and acidity of antebellum southern humor have survived in the ability of contemporary writers to recognize the ludicrous aspects of everybody. There is nothing subtle about it. It is like southern roadkill, fascinating in its variety from armadillo, possum, raccoon, and snake to squirrel and dog. Lots of big dead animals lying about. Nobody removes them but the buzzards, it seems. But actually some of it makes good reading.

Religion is always present in the South; *He* seems stuck there "like a rusty fish hook." As William Koon has pointed out, "No one knows just why the South produces such an abundance of Baptists hand-in-hand with such a large flock of genuflecting Episcopalians" (Koon 1986, ix). God is in the trailer parks and He is in the hills, ever present in Alabama via the state flower—the satellite dish. The poor whites people the churches and they sing, but they do not move their bodies with the music, not even their legs. To move would be to invite hell and damnation: "Look what happened to Elvis!" Southern writers still manage, without moving their legs, to expose religious hypocrisy and the greed of would-be evangelists. They place God in unexpected surroundings.

The unmistakable skepticism about us and the way we live our lives is refreshingly present and remains the sincere concern behind the pandemonium in humorous southern fiction. Clyde Edgerton, James Wilcox, Barry Hannah, Chris Offutt, Percival Everett, Kaye Gibbons, Steve Yarbrough, and George Singleton may try to fool you and pretend that they are just trying to be funny, and in the tradition of the good audience we must pretend to be fooled; but we realize that behind their humorous gyrations there is always the pity, consideration, and admiration for the simple endurance and survival of everybody. It is not easy to live peacefully and content in William Faulkner's southern world of misfortune, grief, and injustice, but humor helps.

Southerners in country and town, in fact everywhere, demonstrate an unwavering faith in a strong and united family. It is possible to see the whole family as a communal protagonist of much contemporary fiction. In all the sentimentality and broad comedy of the novels there is a serious note. Not only does the family matter, it is a defining part of ourselves. The family past demands attention, and its power over the present is reflected in the family legends. The characters are *not*, in any manner of speaking, living in the past; on the contrary, they live fully in the present. But for them the present moment always presupposes the presence of the past. In that sense the family, as an expression of the communal, is a weapon against changing times and so-called progress. The need, or even yearning, for a united family is very much alive, but it remains an ideal. There are no genuinely happy families in the contemporary southern novel, which is one reason why the characters are dissatisfied with their lives.

Family relations and kinship through blood are so important that you will accept suffering a good deal of abuse by your kin before you protest. A sheriff in Barry Hannah's *Yonder Stands Your Orphan* receives a phone call one afternoon and hears a "wild, high voice on the other end saying, 'My uncle put out cigarettes on my forehead for twenty years.' 'Why didn't you do something, or move?' the sheriff asked. 'What could I do? He was blood.' His uncle had just died, the man said. He wanted his uncle's corpse arrested" (2001, 133).

Much of the fiction by Brown, Hannah, McCarthy, Burke, and, to a certain extent, Rash, Offutt, and Yarbrough may appear to be preoccupied with violence and/or sex, through which they try to redeem people's fragmented and unhappy lives. But the lasting value of their fiction is not due to the prevailing atmosphere of callousness and desperation but to the writers' compassion for our constant suffering in our bourgeois situations. Their target is our calm complacency and smugness, which we are forced to realize and recognize because the truth is shown to us. Their compassion goes beyond the violence and sex and enables them to enter our closed-up private worlds. Today's southern novelists pity us and suffer with us because we hold on to sanity so hard that we are actually "insane." We are reduced to seeking redemption, or just a bit of relief, through the experience of sex and violence. The novelists describe our insane attempts at living so-called average, middle-class lives and suggest ways of restoring our distorted selves through rage, humor, and the arts. If the readers do not get the message, if the readers will not be corrected, if we will not leave the herd mentality behind and live out our secret fantasies, the writers will scorn the readers and insult us.

Contemporary southern fiction gives a positive answer to Allen Tate's despairing question in the "Ode to the Confederate Dead" about the capability of the modern individual to draw strength from tradition and to overcome emotional callousness by defining, reviving, and repossessing the past. Southern fiction of today shows how writers and readers may find a way out of our psychological isolation by facing our past and accepting it for what it can tell us about the subjectivity of life in time and place.

It is not that postmodernistic alienation is unknown to the southern novelists, but for them alienation is still an indication that something is wrong. They are, as a rule, not alienated writers looking for a better place to live and write. They are products of a time and a place, which became materials for their art. And in today's literary climate there is an obvious need to consider the historical and cultural background for their achievement. The strength of their fiction is identification in their fictional territories, with both their native area and its people.

The novelists, such as Ford, McCarthy, and Rash, are engaged in asking questions of how we can invest our world with comprehensible life and avoid living "a sickness unto death." The good southern novel is an attempt to probe the depths of the human condition, which matters more than any historical accuracy. It is the preoccupation with the human condition that gives southern fiction a place in world literature.

Today's southern novel shows a continued preoccupation with the past, with the clash between social classes, and with the survival of the community. But it is the writers' search for answers to existential questions that gives their fiction a place in the first order of southern literature. They are not sociologists trying to right social wrongs, they are not psychologists trying to explain the origin of psychoses, nor are they preachers choosing between vice and virtue. They are novelists offering their vision of how it has always been with us and of how it is with us now. They do not try to teach us how to behave, but they show us how we live and help us up to the point where we may be able to interpret and perhaps change our own lives.

The novelists write about the collective southern experience from the Depression until today. They deal with the historical, political, social, cultural, and ethnic landscape of their South by seeing it in the context of time. Their southern landscape contains ignorance, poverty, and political conservatism, but it is also a landscape of individuals who identify with their community and revere the traditions of their place. These contemporary novelists enable us to talk of a continuity of distinctiveness in southern fiction. They seem to experience life as being a very funny, very strange, and a very frightening affair. They often write about people who are down and out, suicidal, and cut off from their own humanity, but also people who try to regain their dignity and connect with the human race. Their protagonists, who are often also the narrators, are distressed and almost defeated but usually eloquent. There seems to be hope for a character who despises life from the moment he wakes up and yet does not commit suicide or go bowling but, in the tradition of Walker Percy, decides to tell his or her story instead. And the stories they tell are absurd and graphic in the rendition of every menacing detail, but often they are also full of humor and genuine emotion.

Outstanding contemporary southern novelists, such as Larry Brown, James Lee Burke, Pam Durban, Clyde Edgerton, Percival Everett, Richard Ford, Charles Frazier, Kaye Gibbons, Barry Hannah, Donald Harington, Josephine Humphreys, Cormac McCarthy, Lewis Nordan, Chris Offutt, Ron Rash, George Singleton, Steve Yarbrough, and James Wilcox write about love and separateness, about appreciating the local place and its part in their identity. They recognize the importance of the past in the present and look to the future with healthy skepticism, and above all their writings teach us to value, respect, and protect the individual. The novelists celebrate life's multiplicity and communicate the joy of living to their readers.

Works Cited and Consulted

Blount, Roy Jr. *Roy Blount's Book of Southern Humor*. New York: W. W. Norton, 1994.

Cobb, James C. *Away Down South: A History of Southern Identity*. New York: Oxford University Press, 2005.

Gretlund, Jan Nordby. "When Did Mark Twain Become a *Southern* Writer and What Do We Read by Him Today?" *Flannery O'Connor Review* 6 (2008): 147–56.

———. "1835: The First *Annus Mirabilis* of Southern Fiction." *Rewriting the South*. Ed. Lothar Hönnighausen and Valeria Lerda. Tübingen: Francke Verlag, 1993. 121–30.

Hannah, Barry. *Yonder Stands Your Orphan.* New York: Atlantic Monthly Press, 2001.
Humphreys, Josephine. *Rich in Love.* New York: Viking, 1987.
Koon, William, ed. *A Collection of Classic Southern Humor.* Vol. 2. Atlanta: Peachtree, 1986.
Kreyling, Michael. *Inventing Southern Literature.* Jackson: University Press of Mississippi, 1998.
O'Connor, Flannery. *Mystery and Manners.* New York: Farrar, Straus & Giroux, 1969.
Rubin, Louis D., Jr., Blyden Jackson, Rayburn S. Moore, Lewis P. Simpson, and Thomas Daniel Young. *The History of Southern Literature.* Baton Rouge: Louisiana State University Press, 1985.
Simpson, Lewis P. *The Dispossessed Garden: Pastoral and History in Southern Literature.* Athens: University of Georgia Press, 1975.

PART I *A Sense of History*

Charles Frazier ∽ *Cold Mountain*

M. THOMAS INGE

A Biographical Sketch

For several decades now numerous critics have announced the death of the novel; critical theorists have declared the writer himself irrelevant, if not defunct; and members of the New Southern Studies movement have suggested that not only is southern literature at an end, but the South itself never really existed, except in the fevered imaginations of New Critics, Agrarians, and Faulknerians. It is one of those historic ironies that in the midst of this grandiloquent nay-saying that someone such as Charles Frazier steps forward to publish a genuine masterpiece in the southern literary tradition and demonstrates that the funeral speech was premature.

Amazingly enough his novel, *Cold Mountain*, published on June 1, 1997, remained at the top of the *New York Times* best-seller list for forty-three weeks, rivaled in southern fiction only by Margaret Mitchell's *Gone with the Wind* and Harper Lee's *To Kill a Mockingbird*. By 1998 1.6 million copies had been sold. *Cold Mountain* won the National Book Award, the Book Critics Circle Award, and the Pulitzer Prize for fiction, and it served as the basis for a popular award-winning film released on December 25, 2003. It was that anomaly in American fiction in general, a beautifully written, profoundly thoughtful, but widely read popular novel. Over a decade later, *Cold Mountain* retains its appeal as demonstrated by continued sales in hardcover and paperback editions.

At the time of publication Charles Frazier was a forty-seven-year-old former professor of English who had left academe for free-lance writing and for being a home father to his daughter. He was born in Asheville, North Carolina, on November 4, 1950, and grew up in the small towns of Andrews and Franklin in western North Carolina, not far from the majestic Cold Mountain he would make famous in his novel. His parents taught him to value literature and to learn the folklore and family history of the region.

Frazier earned his bachelor of arts degree from the University of North Carolina at Chapel Hill in 1973, his master of arts from Appalachian State University in 1975, and his doctoral degree in American literature from the University of South Carolina in 1986. His dissertation topic was "The Geography of Possibility: Man in the Landscape of Recent Western Fiction," highly relevant research for the novel he would write. During these years he married, had a child, and coauthored two books. The first was a textbook in 1980 with Robert Ingram, *Developing Communication Skills for the Accounting Profession*, and the second, in 1985 with Donald Seacrest, was a travel guide for the Sierra Club based on his own journey through the several South American countries through which the Andes Mountains run, *Adventuring in the Andes*. Both he and his wife taught at the University of Colorado in Boulder before moving to North Carolina State University in Raleigh. Frazier produced a few short stories before leaving his teaching position to focus on a book he had wanted to write for years. Frazier and his family lived on a horse farm near Raleigh until the success of *Cold Mountain*. They now have a home in Florida and a summer residence outside Asheville near the life and culture that nourishes his fiction. In 2006 Frazier published *Thirteen Moons*, his second novel, which so far has not met with the public enthusiasm and critical acclaim that was and is accorded *Cold Mountain*.

Cold Mountain

Frazier knew from the start that he wanted to write about life in the Appalachian Mountains and the sturdy stock of people who settled there and somehow survived on minimal sustenance and primitive endurance. "I knew I wanted to write about those old folkways," he has said, "but I needed some point of access. I was given such an entry . . . when my father told me about an ancestor of ours, a man named Inman who left the war and walked home wounded. . . . The story sounded like an American odyssey and it also seemed to offer itself as a form of elegy for that lost world I had been thinking about. So I set out on Inman's trail and followed it for five years of writing" (Frazier, "Diary" 3).

While the novel belongs to the popular genre of Civil War fiction, it is not actually about that cataclysmic event. As he began work, Frazier says, "I was not then thinking about writing a Civil War novel, and though I am triply qualified for acceptance into the Sons of Confederate Veterans, I remain largely uninterested in the great movements of troops, the famous personality traits of the noble generals and tragic presidents." Rather he was interested in the ordinary people who "were caught in the crossfire of two incompatible economies" ("Diary," 2), that is, the agrarian slave-based economy of the South and the industrial-based capitalist economy of the North. Although Frazier's central character noted that "men talked of war as if they committed it to preserve what they had and what they believed," Inman found it to be a set of "new laws whereunder you might kill all you wanted and not be jailed, but rather be decorated" (Frazier, *Cold Mountain*, 218).

Thus *Cold Mountain* neither glorifies nor romanticizes the Civil War but shows its impact and meaning for the ordinary people who fought and endured it. This is human history at the ground level, how it appeared to those at the bottom of the economic and social ladder. Frazier's characters are mostly poor whites seeking to find some values by which to live, some principles in which to believe, something to give their lives meaning in these turbulent times. Like Faulkner's farmers and country people, they endure.

There are many very traditional and familiar elements that help account for the enormous popularity of the novel. In telling the story of an exhausted warrior returning home from a bloody war to his patient and waiting beloved, both readers and critics alike quickly picked up on the fact that the classic war epic, Homer's *Odyssey*, provided the novel's structure. Frazier told one interviewer how this happened:

> When my father told me the story of this ancestor, that was one of the first things I thought of—that there were certain parallels to *The Odyssey* that might be useful in trying to think of a way to tell this story. A warrior, weary of war, trying to get home and facing all kinds of impediments along the way, a woman at home beset by all kinds of problems of her own that are as compelling as his. So I reread *The Odyssey*—that was one of the first things I did when I really began working on the book. There was a certain temptation to write parallel scenes—to try to have a Cyclops scene, or whatever. But really quickly I decided that that would be pretty limiting and kind of artificial. So I just let *The Odyssey* stay in the back of my mind as a model of a warrior wanting to put that war behind him and get home. (Vintage 2003, 2–3)

In a thorough study of the classical parallels and references in the novel, which are numerous and plentiful, Ava Chitwood has suggested that "it is the familiar shape of the *Odyssey* to which most readers respond" (2004, 234).

Those familiar with the larger body of twentieth-century southern literature also recognize in the novel, Albert Way has argued, "a portrait of an agrarian-based society free of a hovering industrial complex": "As with [Wendell] Berry and the Agrarians, local knowledge is of primary importance to Frazier as well, and there is a genuine movement afoot today in some quarters for a return to a local knowledge-based system of land use. In writing a story set in preindustrial Appalachia, Frazier has projected on the past what many people want for the future" (2004, 36, 38).

Yet Frazier has avoided the trap of racial exclusiveness practiced by the Nashville Agrarians by presenting "a perspective more reflective of the post–Civil Rights era," as Ed Piacentino has suggested. By avoiding racial stereotypes and bigoted white characters, he is actually reporting "a viewpoint towards race common among Appalachian inhabitants who typically did not own slaves and who did not really support slavery, an attitude . . . that is consonant with historical plausibility" (2001–2, 100–101). The frequent cross-racial bonding then that appears in the novel as outlined by Piacentino, among whites, Native

Americans, and blacks, is not simply designed to appeal to modern readers but also to portray a likely historic reality.

Indeed a part of Frazier's project in the novel seems to be an eradication of common stereotypes, black and white alike. The blacks are mainly background figures but always helpful, kind, and humane, like the slave who gave Inman food and shelter after he was shot by the Home Guard. In his discussions with the old goat woman Inman encounters on his journey, he does not recall defending slavery as one of the reasons he joined the Confederate army. He never owned any slaves, he says, and "not hardly anybody I know did" (217). But she reminds him that he was doing so, no matter his intention.

In the harshness and brutality of war, the southern gentleman has given way to men involved in a base-level struggle for survival, as reflected in Frazier's quotation in his first epigraph from one of Charles Darwin's journal entries. The women, especially Ada and Ruby, are among some of the strongest, most resourceful, and enduring figures we have in southern literature. It is the stereotype of the southern mountaineer, however, that is most firmly debunked. Ada gives fullest expression to the nature of that image: "All of their Charleston friends had expressed the opinion that the mountain region was a heathenish part of creation, outlandish in its many affronts to sensibility, a place of wilderness and gloom and rain where man, woman, and child grew gaunt and brutal, addicted to acts of raw violence with not even a nod in the direction of self-restraint. Only men of gentry affected underdrawers, and women of every station suckled their young, leaving the civilized trade of wet nurse unknown. Ada's informants had claimed the mountaineers to be but one step more advanced in their manner of living than the tribes of vagrant savages" (42). Among the numerous mountain folk that populate the novel, a few are indeed malicious and cruel, but a far greater number are decent, civilized, and good-hearted people. God's variety is found among them as in every other branch of humanity in the South and elsewhere.

Other critics have recognized the pleasures of a classically balanced and aesthetically pleasing structure that can be found in the novel beyond the *Odyssey* influence. Bill McCarron and Paul Knole have explicated the transformation of the novel from a narrative about war to "a novel of peace and triumph in the best romantic literary tradition": "Frazier achieves this transformation through a masterful combination of parallelism (where characters, scenes, and symbols 'double,' prefigure, and are reduplicated by other characters, scenes, and symbols) and antithesis (where events and symbols demand dual, antithetical interpretation)" (273).

Not all critics, however, have been satisfied with exactly what Frazier does with the romantic literary tradition. Novelist Madison Smartt Bell, in an appreciation of another novelist he greatly admires, Cormac McCarthy, has accused Frazier of stealing from McCarthy:

> The prize-winning, best-selling *Cold Mountain* is a case in point. Here again the author (in terms of the style of the work) appears to be channeling Cormac McCarthy. In the storyline involving the wanderings of the wounded soldier Inman, not only the language but the content of the episodes is derived from McCarthy's work. Inman drifts around through a dark, inimical world, full of incomprehensible, unreasoning violence. He meets highwaymen and bushwhackers and other pilgrims with missions still more peculiar than his own and inscrutable but garrulous hermits who utter obscure but extensive discourses—in short he has all the adventures one would expect a Cormac McCarthy character to have. Except that these adventures do not have the same significance that they would have in a Cormac McCarthy novel. In fact, they don't have any significance. These episodes constitute a series of ornamental layers draped over the sentimental love story at the heart of *Cold Mountain*. In this respect the novel resembles a marshmallow elaborately wrapped up in barbed wire, and so, no doubt, deserves its great success. (Bell 1999, 28)

Bell's argument that Frazier had adapted the grim, lyrical prose of McCarthy is puzzling. Frazier's balanced, elegantly evocative prose is quite different stylistically from McCarthy's. That is not what actually seems to irritate Bell anyway. Rather it is that he reads the novel as at heart "a sentimental love story" wrapped in the coarseness of human experience. As if it were Margaret Mitchell's *Gone with the Wind* masquerading as Leo Tolstoy's *War and Peace*.

If *Cold Mountain* is to be read as simply a love story, then it has one of the most discordant endings of any such romance in literary history. Inman and Ada have but one night together, and rather than grant them any hope of a future life as a reward for all the cruel suffering and despair they both have witnessed and experienced, as one would expect in a romance, Inman is unceremoniously shot out of his saddle and killed by an unworthy opponent. Ada has not even the naïve certainty of Scarlet O'Hara that tomorrow is another day. There will be no other days. There will be only the consolation of a beautiful child left behind and the possibility of a lineage.

This unhappy ending is the very thing that irritates another novelist critic, who otherwise would have nothing but praise for what Frazier accomplished. Donald Harington has noted the following in an interview:

> One of the most beautiful novels in recent times is *Cold Mountain* by Charles Frazier. The prose is absolutely perfect. We are given a character that we immediately identify with, and we experience some of the most fabulous, excruciating adventures throughout the book. We really become him in a way we hardly ever do in a novel, regardless of whether we're male or female. Identification with the character is total. And then, in the end, the author rewards that absolute, total identification by murdering us. It's totally

unfair. It's a hideous thing to do to the reader. . . . I absolutely hated what Charles Frazier did when I got to the end of that book and felt so betrayed. . . . I'm sure somewhere out there there are people who like to have their books end so hideously. But I'm not one of them. (Hyde 2002, 98)

Frazier's fellow writers seem to want to have it both ways, each condemning the novel for what it is *not*. It may be a love story but one that turns the romance tradition on its head by thwarting any possible happy ending. It is a novel that offers satisfaction from another quite different tradition, one that values spiritual fulfillment over things of this world and detachment over materialism.

This is another major source of inspiration in *Cold Mountain* that has yet to be accounted for. The connection is found in the second of the book's two epigraphs, a quotation from an ancient Chinese poet about another place called Cold Mountain. A major symbol, indeed a major character in the novel, is the physical Cold Mountain itself, an actual mountain in the Blue Ridge range of western North Carolina, about twenty-five miles northeast of Asheville. It has an inaccessible and secluded summit of 6,030 feet inside Pisgah National Forest, which can be reached only by hiking along unmarked dirt trails and avoiding misleading dead ends. Only seasoned hikers can deal with the drops in temperature (ten degrees per one thousand feet of elevation) and help is not close at hand (there is no town of Cold Mountain as in the novel). Most people settle for viewing Cold Mountain and appreciating its dramatic and gorgeous vistas from afar, thus the promontory has long had a reputation as a remote but unspoiled jewel that remains just beyond our grasp (Whitmire 2004). Frazier's paternal grandparents owned a farm near the bottom of Cold Mountain, and he played and camped on the mountain as a boy.

In the novel, Cold Mountain becomes in the mind of Inman a spiritual sanctuary, a place where harmony and health might be restored, where the brutality and disappointments of the world might be ameliorated or burned away. It "soared in his mind as a place where all his scattered forces might gather" (17). His Cherokee friend Swimmer "believed Cold Mountain to be the chief mountain of the world. Inman asked how he knew that to be true, and Swimmer had swept his hand across the horizon to where Cold Mountain stood and said, Do you see a bigger'n?" (14). Here the particular serves not only as the universal but as the prototype.

There is another Cold Mountain, however, that lies behind this one. In the T'ien-t'ai Mountains in the northeastern corner of Chekiang Province, south of the Bay of Hangchow in China, there is a remote retreat named Hanshan, which means Cold Mountain in Chinese. These mountains, sources say, "famous for their wild and varied scenery, were from early times venerated as the home of spirits and immortals, and from the third century on became the site of numerous Taoist and Buddhist monasteries" (Watson 1970, 13).

In the late eighth or early ninth century, according to some scholars because knowledge of this man is very scant, a poet came to Cold Mountain in search of enlightenment and spent the rest of his days writing poems and inscribing them on rocks, trees, and the walls of houses. The name of this early graffiti poet has been lost to history, so we call him Cold Mountain or Han-shan, after the place of his retreat. Internal evidence in the poems suggests that Han-shan was a "gentleman farmer, troubled by poverty and family discord, who, after extensive wandering and perhaps a career as a minor official, retired to Cold Mountain. . . . In one poem he says he went to Cold Mountain at the age of thirty, and in another he speaks of having lived there thirty years" (Watson 1970, 9). Further research has indicated that he may have come from an educated family, although he was also familiar with the hardships of the farming life. A wife and son are mentioned several times in the poems, although he appears to have left them in pursuit of enlightenment (Hendricks 1990, 10–11).

Han-shan has traditionally been identified as a Buddhist poet of the Zen school, but if so, he seems to have lacked the confidence that came with Zen mastery because "in Zen, with its emphasis on individual effort and self-reliance, a man, once enlightened, is expected to stay that way" (Watson 1970, 14). Instead loneliness, doubt, and self-effacement are his usual themes, including the awareness that his rag-tag appearance evokes in others ridicule and laughter. As the poet says of himself in his most often quoted poem:

> When men see Han-shan
> They all say he's crazy
> And not much to look at—
> Dressed in rags and hides.
> They don't get what I say
> & I don't talk their language.
> All I can say to those I meet:
> "Try and make it to Cold Mountain."
> (Snyder 1965, 60)

Nor did he suffer the praise of those who approached him for wisdom or a blessing. When a court official of the T'ang Dynasty sought him out and found him in the kitchen of a temple, Han-shan shouted out crude taunts, ran out of the temple laughing, and hand-in-hand with fellow poet Shih-te disappeared into the mountains. This event gave rise to a longstanding tradition in art and painting that portrays the two poets as "two grotesque little men guffawing in the wilderness" and Han-shan as "the laughing recluse" (Watson 1970, 7–8, 14). All of this serves to underline the sense of humor and satirical spirit that resides in much of his poetry and the sense of detachment that moves him beyond the disillusionment and pain of the world.

Han-shan has been rendered into English by various hands, chiefly those of academic scholars. Among the most respected translators have been Arthur

Waley, Burton Watson, Robert G. Hendricks, and one who calls himself Red Pine, but the translations used by Charles Frazier are those by the Beat generation environmental poet, essayist, and activist Gary Snyder. Bringing his study of Chinese language to the task, as well as his own poetic sensibility as a poet in English, Snyder produced clear and concise renditions that capture the blunt simplicity and directness of the originals, as in the one from which Frazier quotes the first two lines as an epigraph:

> Men ask the way to Cold Mountain
> Cold Mountain: there's no through trail.
> In summer, ice doesn't melt
> The rising sun blurs in swirling fog.
> How did I make it?
> My heart's not the same as yours.
> If your heart was like mine
> You'd get it and be right here.
> (Snyder 1965, 42)

This poem captures much of the emotional longing Frazier's character Inman has for his home and the profound difficulties he has reaching it. There is indeed "no through trail," no direct route, to the mountain of his desire where his beloved Ada dwells. He makes it there because of the power of love in his heart. Others who wish to make the journey to their Cold Mountains can only do so if their hearts are in accord with his in its understanding of the transcendent power of love beyond the physical and the material.

The poetry of Han-shan, like Chinese poetry in general, is remarkably accessible to all readers. As Burton Watson notes in *The Columbia Book of Chinese Poetry*, the "Chinese poetic tradition is on the whole unusually humanistic and commonsensical in tone. . . . For this reason, even works that are many centuries removed from us in time come across with a freshness and immediacy that is often quite miraculous. The Chinese poetic world is one that is remarkably easy to enter because it concentrates to such a large degree on concerns that are common to men and women of whatever place or time" (1984, 3). Gary Snyder puts it another way when he writes, "Chinese poetry, at its finest, seems to have found a center within the tripod of humanity, spirit, and nature. With strategies of apparent simplicity and understatement, it moves from awe before history to—a deep breath before nature" (1995, 91).

In undertaking his homeward journey, Inman has turned away from his "awe before history," especially the degradations and cruel banalities of war, and he needs to take "a deep breath before nature" by returning to the cleansing and healing air of his spiritual center, Cold Mountain. Early in the novel, Frazier notes: "Inman did not consider himself to be a superstitious person, but he did believe that there is a world invisible to us. He no longer thought of that world as heaven, nor did he still think that we get to go there when we die. Those teachings had been burned away. But he could not abide by a universe composed only of what he could see, especially when it was so frequently foul. So he held to the idea of another world, a better place, and he figured he might as well consider Cold Mountain to be the location of it as anywhere" (17).

Had Inman lived to a ripe old age like Han-shan, he also would likely have expressed such thoughts as these:

> If I hide out at Cold Mountain
> Living off mountain plants and berries—
> All my lifetime, why worry?
> One follows his karma through.
> Days and months slip by like water,
> Time is like sparks knocked off flint.
> Go ahead and let the world change—
> I'm happy to sit among these cliffs.
> (Snyder 1965, 53)

Frazier could not have chosen a more appropriate poet in whom to seek inspiration than Han-shan, given his larger theme that mankind must set aside his individuality and place in human history and seek to merge with the cyclic life of nature and the universal life force itself. For Inman nature represents safety, freedom, spiritual peace, and escape into immortality, as it did for Han-shan. Ada's father, Monroe, was fond of quoting another student of Asian philosophy and poetry, Ralph Waldo Emerson, who merged Eastern and Western thought in Transcendentalism. The novel, in fact, is full of references to books: Homer, Shakespeare, Dickens, and so on. But Ada finds that literature does not prepare one for life itself. As Han-shan said in one poem, "Reading books won't save you from death; / Reading books won't save you from poverty" (Watson 1970, 74). They can indeed blind one to the natural world and human nature. But she learns that, and Inman already knows it. What instructs them all, Han-shan, Ada, and Inman, are their respective Cold Mountains, East and West. That such thoughts seem to match the sensibilities of so many modern readers no doubt contributes to the novel's spectacular success.

Works Cited and Consulted

Bell, Madison Smartt. "A Writer's View of Cormac McCarthy." *Chattahoochee Review* 19, no. 3 (1999): 21–33.

Chitwood, Ava. "Epic or Philosophic, Homeric or Heraclitiean? The Anonymous Philosopher in Charles Frazier's *Cold Mountain*." *International Journal of the Classical Tradition* 11, no. 2 (2004): 232–43.

Flora, Joseph. "Charles Frazier." *New Encyclopedia of Southern Culture*. Vol. 9, *Literature*. Ed. M. Thomas Inge. Chapel Hill: University of North Carolina Press, 2008. 275–76.

Frazier, Charles. *Thirteen Moons*. New York: Random House, 2006.

———. *Cold Mountain.* New York: Atlantic Monthly Press, 1997.
———. "Cold Mountain Diary." July 1997. http://www.salon.com/july97/colddiary970709.html/.
Gifford, Terry. "Terrain, Character and Text: Is *Cold Mountain* by Charles Frazier a Post-Pastoral Novel?" *Mississippi Quarterly* 55, no. 1 (2001–2): 89–96.
Hendricks, Robert G., trans. *The Poetry of Han-shan.* Albany: State University of New York, 1990.
Holt, Karen C. "Frazier's *Cold Mountain.*" *Explicator* 63, no. 2 (2005): 118–21.
Hyde, Gene. "'The Southern Highlands as Literary Landscape': An Interview with Fred Chappell and Donald Harington." *Southern Quarterly* 40, no. 2 (2002): 86–98.
McCarron, Bill, and Paul Knoke. "Images of War and Peace: Parallelism and Antithesis in the Beginning and Ending of *Cold Mountain.*" *Mississippi Quarterly* 52, no. 2 (1999): 273–85.
Peacock, Tony. "Charles Frazier." *Southern Writers: A New Biographical Dictionary.* Ed. Joseph M. Flora and Amber Vogel. Baton Rouge: Louisiana State University Press, 2006. 143–44.
Piacentino, Ed. "Searching for Home: Cross-Cultural Bonding in Charles Frazier's *Cold Mountain.*" *Mississippi Quarterly* 55, no. 1 (2001–2): 97–116.
Red Pine [Bill Porter], trans. *The Collected Songs of Cold Mountain.* Port Townsend, Wash.: Copper Canyon Press, 1983.
Snyder, Gary. *A Place in Space: Ethics, Aesthetics, and Watersheds.* Washington, D.C.: Counterpoint, 1995.
———. *Riprap and Cold Mountain Poems.* San Francisco: Grey Fox Press, 1965.
Vintage/Anchor Books. "A Conversation with Charles Frazier." 2003. http://www.randomhouse.com/vintage/frazier.html/.
Waley, Arthur. "27 Poems by Han-shan." *Encounter* 3, no. 3 (1954): 3–8.
Watson, Burton, trans. and ed. *The Columbia Book of Chinese Poetry: From Early Times to the Thirteenth Century.* New York: Columbia University Press, 1984.
———, trans. *Cold Mountain: 100 Poems by the T'ang Poet Han-shan.* New York: Columbia University Press, 1970.
Way, Albert. "'A World Properly Put Together': Environmental Knowledge in Charles Frazier's *Cold Mountain.*" *Southern Cultures* 10, no. 4 (2004): 33–54.
Whitmire, Tim. "For Book Purists, the North Carolina Mountain Is a Trip." *Richmond Times-Dispatch,* February 1, 2004. Associated Press release.

Josephine Humphreys
꙳ *Nowhere Else on Earth*

CLARA JUNCKER

A Biographical Sketch

On the first page of Josephine Humphreys's fourth novel, the so-called Queen of Scuffletown raises a question: What is history? And with her question she joins a long line of southern writers and characters who take upon themselves the burden of the past and offer up their interpretations of this elusive subject. In her fiction Josephine Humphreys has sought to dream up her own historical scenarios, at odds with established historical accounts. Her characters insist on self-narration and self-definition, as does Rhoda Lowrie, the narrator of *Nowhere Else on Earth* (2000). On November 3, 1890, Rhoda begins the account of her people and the place where they live. During the Civil War and its turbulent aftermath, she takes on the role of historian of the Native American community in Scuffletown, on the Lumbee River in Robeson County, North Carolina.

Josephine Humphreys's birth in Charleston, South Carolina, on February 2, 1945, links her to a rich historical heritage, which other Charleston writers, Mamie Garvin Fields and Pam Durban among them, have also explored. Humphreys earned degrees from Duke University, where she completed undergraduate work in 1967, and from Yale, where she received her master's degree in English in 1968. After completing her course work toward her doctoral degree at the University of Texas, Austin, she accepted a position at the present Charleston Southern University in 1971, where she taught until she decided to become a full-time writer in 1978 (Perry and Weaks 2002, 579). Her four novels all engage the history of the South, directly or indirectly, but *Nowhere Else on Earth* places the past at center stage.

Humphreys's first three novels prepare the ground, or the swamp, for the history of the Lumbee Indians in North Carolina that *Nowhere Else* presents. In *Dreams of Sleep* (1984), awarded the Ernest Hemingway Award for best first novel in 1985, Will and Alice Reese go through a marital crisis, which their babysitter Iris Moon, a lower-class, no-nonsense white girl, witnesses and helps bring to a tentative end. At one point in the rocky Reese marriage, Will escapes from his family and a sea resort to Bloody Marsh, where the Spanish were defeated, and to Fort Fredericia, where the English first settled in Georgia. History comforts him because it is alive and authentic, and his present place is not (76). In *Rich in Love* (1987), adapted to the screen by Metro-Goldwyn-Mayer, the historical echoes sound in the story unfolding around the seventeen-year-old narrator Lucille Odom, her collapsing family, and her brief affair with Billy McQueen, her brother-in-law. He is a historian looking for work in Charleston, where "history was in the making all around us" (53). Lucille ponders the function of history, "to *get it down on paper*; to be the official human memory" (52). She seems particularly enthralled by the Indian pottery hiding in the marsh. These "relics of ancient men" (130) reassure her and allow for a panoramic vision of her own adolescent struggles and joys. "Everything is history," as Billy explains when helping Lucille with her high school exams (215).

The Fireman's Fair (1991) revolves less explicitly around the southern past. It describes the existence of a single, thirty-something Charleston lawyer, Rob Wyatt, who in the aftermath of the Hurricane Hugo disaster reevaluates his life and his loves. As in other of Humphreys's novels, Rob must come to terms with his individual history before he may escape from loneliness, passivity, and indecision. But his post-hurricane surroundings, in which pianos rest desolately on flooded lawns and water invades houses and streets, suggest a world turned upside down and the hybrid nature of history that *Nowhere Else on Earth* explores. As with Charles Frazier's *Cold Mountain* (1997), *Nowhere Else* takes place in a remote region of the Civil War South, and it is Josephine Humphreys's most explicitly historical work. Like other southern writers, she explores how the history of the region is being altered and recovered.

Nowhere Else on Earth

As Gayle Graham Yates tells us in "The North Carolina Lumbee People" (2008), Lumbee Indians sided with the colonists during the American Revolution and were charged with pro-Union sympathies during the Civil War. The original Lumbees considered present-day Pembroke in Robeson County their home; in the nineteenth century it was called Scuffletown. Soldiers from both Civil War armies took cover in the Lumbee River swamps, and at the close of the war, Union soldiers, the Confederate Home Guard, and various Confederate groups murdered Lumbees freely for hiding enemy troops. From these conflicts rose the legendary Henry Berry Lowrie, a guerrilla outlaw, who avenged many Lumbee killings and raided those with smokehouses and corn in order to feed his tribe. Lowrie mysteriously disappeared after ten years of successful fighting. An oil painting of this hero of Robeson County now hangs next to one of Rhoda, his wife, in the museum of the Resources Center at the University of North Carolina–Pembroke (Evans 1971, 124). The couple and their impoverished but proud community figure prominently in Humphreys's historical novel, in which Rhoda tells her dramatic story.

Through the stage metaphor of Rhoda's first lines, Humphreys raises the question about how to get at history. She suggests that the past may forever remain the past: "What happened here twenty-five years ago could not have happened in any other place or age. Maybe it will be told in full someday, and all the secrets known. But my guess is nobody will ever roll back the curtain to show a true picture of us and our land" (1). Humphreys's narrator introduces a problem of representation, which includes the limited vision of actors on the historical stage and historians seeking to illuminate the past. The soldier can only describe a tree, a fence, his wounds, but he always longs for the whole scene, all its details and design, "revealed in a dazzling afternoon light" (1). The historian cannot roll back the curtain either and can never show Rhoda's "true picture." In fact Rhoda offers only a picture of the history she lived, not just because of the unknowable past but also because of her preference for art. She hides parts of her story by choice, just as she put an *X* instead of her signature on the first court paper she ever signed to hide her ability to read and write. "In those days I found it an advantage to hide many things," Rhoda writes (1–2). Her story suggests that the Queen of Scuffletown still prefers disguises. History may be spoken or written, but it remains representation, even performance. Ultimately Humphreys shows us that the best historian is an artist, a performer, or a writer of fiction.

Suspended between somewhere and nowhere, the title of *Nowhere Else on Earth* suggests the indeterminacy of historical endeavors. The initial map of Robeson County grounds the story of Scuffletown in geography and history, yet the title of the novel points toward negativity: it is here, not there, nowhere else, but where? It is above all a *remembered* place, elusive to those who seek to label and map. "Back then," Rhoda writes, "everything not pinewoods or fields was swamps, fifty of them labeled on the map and more whose names were never known to mapmakers" (2). Escaping categorization, the swamps of Robeson County shift from land to water, with bays that fill with rain and dry out in the sun, scattered cypress trees creating solid ground out of traveling streams, and vegetation unique to this hybrid space, including "one tiny bright green plant found nowhere else on earth, the toothed and alluring Venus flytrap" (2). With this echo of her title, Humphreys links Rhoda's remembered place to fluidity and liminality, and to feminine eroticism. The past is dangerous and careless. The Lumbee River carries off pigs, sheep, human beings, as it chooses one course and then, at whim, another. Its other name, Drowning Creek, suggests both death and flux. Rhoda's history of Civil War Scuffletown transcends categories of good and evil, past and present. As she herself puts it, "The result was a sodden, hard-to-travel territory of which our little part was always the worst (as they said, but we said the best), the hidden, tangled, waterlogged heart" (2). Her summary of place and space sets up a series of clear contrasts—worst versus best, they versus we—but she ends with the entangled heart. This trope suggests that the past remains mysterious, emotional, and embodied.

Along with her initial question about history, Rhoda poses a question about knowledge. Those outside the Scuffletown community fail to recognize the identity of its residents and cannot work out their history: Indian? Scottish? British? All of the above? "They declared we were a mystery" (12). The census takers, journalists, educators, ministers, and doctors who arrive in Robeson County represent traditional modes of knowledge, associated with linearity, formal education, measuring, and mapping. The government surveyor who climbed a tree to inspect Mr. Rafe's field ended up staying there till his dried bones dropped from the ancient oak. Obviously, established modes of knowledge cannot survive in Scuffletown. "Remember the bones," Cee, Rhoda's mother, keeps saying (11). Young Rhoda takes classes with Miss McCabe in science, the history of Scotland, and anatomy, but she quickly chooses other ways of knowing, as the older Rhoda explains: "I might say maybe I let the serpent of knowledge get my leg. If you have ever seen a milk snake eat a frog, you know it's not accomplished in one swift strike but is a long, slow, miraculous business. Sometimes, if the snake comes from behind, the frog's head and eyes are free to the last, and it struggles but can't see what is happening—how the snake keeps inching on, not so much swallowing as surrounding. I am in it now, moving as it moves" (69). In this rich passage, Rhoda suggests that knowledge comes slowly, even dangerously, when you cannot see it coming and do not expect it. It comes in pieces, out of the natural world, associated with movement and body. It is circular rather than linear, erotic, unconscious maybe, and ambiguously gendered.

Accordingly the history of Scuffletown must be oral and fragmented. The autobiographer becomes historian, not just because she lives history, but because she speaks it. Readers of Civil War history will recognize recorded events such as Mrs. Witherspoon dying from arsenic in the breakfast hominy grits her slaves served her in bed (187). Despite historical dramas enacted elsewhere, Rhoda's first-person voice and the voices of other Scuffletown characters dominate the text and make history out of sound as well as sight. Dr. McCabe might stand for hours counting the swamp parakeets, writing down flight and mating patterns in his green notebook, but his gold-tipped pages and the dead birds forgotten in his frockcoat pockets associate him with privilege and with dead history. Cee cannot read and write, but she remembers everything, her memory including not just her own lifetime in Scuffletown but also faces, names, and genealogies of a distant past (9–10). Historians such as her stress voice and memory as well as listening. "Listening," Rhoda explains, "was a Scuffletown talent, down to the dogs" (35). Listening makes the residents stay alert, tune in to news of war, and get access to power. The seductive Nelly, Cee's friend, crosses back and forth between army lines in her capacity as messenger and female companion. Rhoda herself collects fractured bits of the past, which may eventually yield a historical pattern. "From all the bits and pieces stored away, a knowledge comes," she argues. "It just does come, as little daily dawns collect, and months and years, until one day . . . you may see in the memories something that amounts to more than their accumulation" (71). Humphreys's history of Scuffletown includes a series of biographies—of Nelly, of the renowned Henry Berry Lowrie, of the runaway slave George Applewhite, who hid in the swamp. His story becomes the story of Scuffletown, hidden from history. "He was still a secret man," Rhoda tells us. "But then we all lived secretly, more or less. History would not recognize us or record us" (75).

The history of Scuffletown remains inconclusive, ongoing, like the frog moving inside the snake. The educated Miss McCabe writes in her journal and expects at the end of a week to find a conclusion. Rhoda finds her tutor overly impatient because a journal resembles history more than a grocery ledger does: "History won't tally like a column of figures. Sometimes years might have to pass—or decades and centuries—before it adds up to something" (44). Besides, Scuffletown cannot be summed up, or surveyed in a panoramic vision, except by God (146). It remains open to interpretation. At the end of *Nowhere Else*, Henry Lowrie has disappeared, Rhoda may or may not know his whereabouts, and loss is everywhere, as is the chance of recovery. Scuffletown hangs suspended in the last words of the novel: "We wait" (341). The town and its residents escape predictions and conclusions, like Humphreys's novel itself. Since established systems of knowledge fail in this environment, the historian of Scuffletown must rely on memory, which in *Nowhere Else* is related to the body. "No toil ages the spirit faster than the toil of too much memory," Rhoda makes clear at forty-one. "And the body, too, shows wear" (69). History, she argues, lives in the flesh.

Traditional historians such as McCabe hunt for the past in Scuffletown by measuring skulls and looking for land deeds or "Indian" words. The bodies living there complicate the historians' efforts by being too dark to be Indians, or too light, or not acceptable to distant Cherokees. They exist in a space of negativity, as non-Scots or non-Indians, but also in a space of possibility. McCabe declares Nelly part Portuguese, or Turkish, African, Gypsy, or related to pirates. She herself links ethnicity to place, "which covered all the possibilities" (36–37). Cee tells her children that "whoever's is here is one of us" (10). With these gestures, Nelly and Cee explode existing racial categories and insist on self-narration. So does the hickory-brown George Applewhite, who takes the name his wife picked "to throw in some more colors" (119). If history lives in the body, as in Rhoda's frog trope, the body cannot be forced into limited and limiting definitions of race. When a Philadelphia scientist examines eight-year-old Rhoda—her fingernails, teeth, limbs, and features—she returns his gaze and shrugs off his appearance and his method as "none too bright" (77). Instead she eventually speaks and writes the history of her people in a language of her own.

Rhoda's discourse of hunger records the Civil War as embodied history. She begins her story with an afternoon in the summer of 1864, as her family is hiding behind barred doors to avoid the Home Guard, out to conscript her brothers to forced labor in the Fort Fisher earthworks or the salt factory that supplied the Confederacy. Her experience is physical. She cannot breathe from heat and confinement; the smell of turpentine and sweat makes her gag, and she is famished (13–19). Hunger dominates her life and suggests a craving for more than regular food. Rhoda's belly wants "a food like fire, like iron, or earth itself in fistfuls" (19). At the beginning of her story, hunger means desire, for love and for independence. At fifteen she has yet to master her hunger, like Cee: "I hadn't yet learned how to kill hunger by force of will, as she could, or the even better trick of holding it and using it as a power" (19). At her wedding feast, just before her groom, Henry Lowrie, will be captured and jailed, Rhoda has accomplished her goal; she now has the resilience to resist for as long as it takes: "Hunger had become my driving force, and I didn't want to lose it. It strengthened me to look at that pie and that orange, and then to walk away" (261). Food and famine signal her initiation into womanhood and her new power and strength. The Civil War itself equals absence of food, while the community banquet signals the end of war, if not the fulfilment of desire. As Costas Canakis demonstrates in "Metaphors of a Body Meant to Die" (2003), the language with which we articulate and theorize the body shapes an era and its mode of thinking (26). The trope of hunger and its absence records the history of Scuffletown and the neighboring Hestertown, as individual and communal bodies strive for power and autonomy.

The discourse of hunger participates in the body rhetoric characteristic of *Nowhere Else* as a whole. The diary scribblings on which Rhoda bases her history of Scuffletown flow directly out of her herself, unconscious somehow, and replacing body parts and fluids. "One dog tooth is gone," she notes, "and my monthly flow has dwindled to a spatter." Her body evaporates as her writings accumulate, her wrists thin, her knuckles mere knobs. She pays this price for writing herself, "the frantic pen scratching past midnight, the hoarding of paper, the loneliness, the pages accumulating while I myself shrink down." Sometimes she wishes not to have taken on the role of historian and instead to have thrown herself "into the current of time and never taken up the job of considering the past" (70). Yet she finds that her writings, her rhymes and stories, surge from her own body "like bouts of hiccups I couldn't stop." When she holds a piece of paper, her hands itch and her skin begins to prickle. She combines writing with body, voice, and speech. She may wish for Dr. McCabe's gilt-edged pages and his controlled logic, but her own history remains disorderly. Her voice merges with other sounds, as Rhoda reads war news to her mother, who in turn voices opinions and edits for errors, based on stories heard from Nelly and the Lowries (84). This communal voice explodes the boundaries among reading, writing, speaking, and listening and constructs a history of bodies, dead and alive.

The discourse in *Nowhere Else* suggests the eroticized bodies of the Robeson County women. Like the snake and the frog moving together, inside and outside, back and forth in a shared if unconscious rhythm, Rhoda grounds her history in rhymes and earth. Especially her landscapes inspire the lyricism that propelled the author of *Nowhere Else* to fame (Perry and Weaks 2002, 579). In this passage Rhoda describes her place on earth: "The water was black where shaded by trees, in the open it could flash to green gold or silver, or any color the heavens lent. Fields and yards and ribbony lanes shimmered, and sometimes the sky in the water was more radiant, more bluely dazzling, than the sky above. Strangest of all were the ponds at nightfall, when the sky went black but the ponds for a moment shone white as milk" (84).

Her history becomes poetry, as words and colors dance across the page. It is a different place, inhabited by those marginalized and ostracized. "Armies couldn't fight on our ground" (84), Rhoda explains, thus placing her record in between Union and Confederate spaces. Her lyricism suggests a feminized, erotic space, removed from armies, contrasts, and conflicts. Milk, water, sky, and color open up a gendered space of possibility, hope, and change. In Robeson County houses may flood, get lifted, everything shifted, and relocated, "resulting in a new arrangement of life," as Rhoda wistfully writes, and a "refreshed perspective" (85). Her own poetic discourse rearranges rhetorical conventions and in the process makes visible new agents, new locations, and different Civil War histories.

Rhoda's history maps the journey of her own body through time and space. Her Scuffletown record begins when her body is aged fifteen and ends when, at the time of narration, it has turned forty-one. Rhoda's account charts the eroticized territory of her body, from its sexual maturation through impending menopause. *Nowhere Else* opens with Henderson, her childhood playmate, averting his gaze from the girl he has not seen recently: "I wanted to say, *It's just the same old me, Henderson*, but suddenly I wondered how true that was. Time had been at work on me since our childhood days" (17). Rhoda's bodily experiences determine plot. Her loss of virginity results in a break with Cee and in a "lifetime knot" tied with Henry Berry Lowrie, the mythical hero of Robeson County. Henry marks Rhoda's body in the sexual act and by taking her with him, only to witness the brutal murders of Allen and William Lowrie, his father and brother. Henry's gaze suggests ownership of a bodily terrain no longer innocent: "He must have seen my cuts and scratches, the mud and blood on me, the mark of his hand on my skin" (227). When Rhoda moves into the home he has built for her, the cottage becomes a body, as incomplete as Rhoda's own because Henry was arrested before their wedding night could begin. The house mediates between the bodies of the bride and the groom. Alone, Rhoda imagines his carpentry, "the shaved curls brushed slowly away as his hands lingered on the pine to test it, to learn its possibilities and what it needed. I knew that touch." She responds to the eroticized space they share: "I rested my face against the wall, and ran my hands over the boards" (269). Immediately afterward writing pours from her pen, an orgasmic, unconscious writing of the body: "Words flowed like a logjam breaking. Sentences streamed as fast as I could move my hand, and for the next few days I wrote and wrote. What for and who to, I didn't know" (270). Rhoda's free-writing maps the sexualized zones of her historical text: the female body, the swamps in which it moves, and the genre hybridity *Nowhere Else* demands: history as autobiography and autobiography as history.

Rhoda's pen suggests phallic power, while her submission to Henry's will and destiny does not. In her story, or herstory, she draws on a community of women, each with tools for subverting masculine dominance while seemingly confirming it. Scuffletown men assert their superiority through their control of guns and women, yet Rhoda's mother controls her own household, as well as her husband. Rhoda explains that her father remains "in the custody of a higher power. Hers" (5). She also notes that Cee brought her Scottish husband to Scuffletown to provide him with security and hope: "Daddy took it easy for a while, and she went back into turpentining" (6). Cee controls both economic and rhetorical terrain. Her friend Nelly uses a voluptuous figure to manipulate the men who turn into "mealmush" when she appears. Rhoda explains that "Nelly Gibson could please men or unman them as she chose" (36). While Nelly performs femininity to distract, to rob, or even to help murder evil men in town, young Rhoda performs masculinity to get her way, as when Steven Lowrie wants to recruit her brother Boss: "I drew myself up tall and swaggery. From watching my brothers I knew how to move like a boy, loose-jointed and wide-legged, rocking from the shoulders" (98–99). She demonstrates with her posture that masculinity may be performed, and subverted, outside of male bodies (Halberstam 1998, throughout). Rhoda also uses humor to minimize the power of the phallus. She first learns about sexual difference from Dr. McCabe's medical book but finds the real thing "less comical than the pictures." She still labels the thing "one of God's odder successes" (33). Still Rhoda Strong becomes Rhoda Lowrie and temporarily loses her independence: "I was starting my job as a helpmeet," she states without traces of irony after her first sexual encounter with Henry. She continues: "For the first time in my life I felt safe—with him, with that gun" (212–13).

Nonetheless she resorts to cross-dressing to gain control over Henry and his outlaws (291). Eventually Rhoda decides not to follow him out of Robeson County and into a future somewhere else. Instead she establishes a community of women and children without husbands, brothers, brother-in-laws, or soldiers. In postwar Scuffletown women enjoy a newfound tranquillity: "A sort of peace descended upon us, the peace of a beaten and ruined land where all the young soldiers are dead" (340). The list of dead or absent men with which her narrative closes stands as gravestones over Scuffletown men, their causes and their violence. With writing and endurance, Rhoda herself has become Queen of Scuffletown and its major historian. She grabs with her pen the power to control the historical record, and she introduces the necessary "refreshed perspective" that puts women center stage as they perform the femininity, or the masculinity, their situation demands.

Humphreys gives her story a twist. The female characters of *Nowhere Else* draw on their Indian heritage for inspiration so as to succeed in their struggles against dominant power formations. Rhoda puts on men's clothes when she wishes to gain access to gender-segregated terrain, and she rips off material from the front of her dress, lowering the neckline, when she wants to bewitch the jail keeper guarding her husband. She performs femininity, as she herself makes clear: "I rose into a new part, as if I had just stepped onto a stage. My real self dropped away, and all my fear" (274). Rhoda also becomes a shape shifter when the jailer tries to rape her, and she takes on an animal's strength: "—and then I bit. Bit hard, a dog's death-jaw clench, clamped on his tongue" (279). Lying on the floor she thinks of Margaret, her childhood friend imprisoned and repeatedly raped by the vile roadhouse proprietor, Brant Harris. Other women in her narrative represent female forms available for shape shifting. Margaret starts out as Rhoda's role model, a capable young woman proving to Rhoda that she might have ambitions and talents of her own. When Margaret becomes the victim of Harris's lust and power, another female shape, presumably the beguiling Nelly in disguise, helps in this new form to kill him off and they leave his body for others to find.

The indeterminate figures that fly in and out of Scuffletown homes and lives represent the trickster power of the female community, whose shape shifting suggest their feminine, and Native American, resources and craft. Though the older Rhoda invests the passage in which young Rhoda explains her secret powers with considerable irony, the young girl describes accurately her own subversive if youthfully overrated capacities: "I was a winter's witch, powered with icy spite. Barnes was a lost and troubled man, but something possessed me to bedevil him, and if it happened to drive him over the edge I wouldn't care. I *meant* to spook the wits out of him. And having done it I felt zesty, alive and energized. Everything around me shifted to a brighter liveliness: in the thin brown woods I saw a sudden lift toward purple, in the gray sky a silver wink" (164).

Like the shifting and winking landscape, Rhoda inhabits various figures and forms, energetic and resourceful. In the landscape alive with colors, animals, and possibilities, she rules: "I was filled with a new power. If I could be a witch, I could also be Nelly, or any other figures of magical endowment. I could take forms I never even thought of before" (165). As Anne Goodwyn Jones and Susan Donaldson argue in *Haunted Bodies: Gender and Southern Texts* (1997), discussions of race and gender intertwine in southern writings (3), and in her quest for influence and change, Rhoda must engage both her femininity and her ethnicity. Cee describes, in fact, the whole of Scuffletown as a community of shape shifters and tricksters. "They might know us but they don't *know* us," she tells Rhoda. "Even ones that should, by now, don't have no more notion of us than of so many yard birds. Everything they think we are, we aren't" (31). With the cunning of the trickster, Rhoda transforms femininity into magic and strength.

In *Dirt and Desire* (2000) Patricia Yaeger argues about southern women's writing that change erupts violently through images of ludicrous bodies articulating social arrangements or derangements. James Barnes's handicapped brother, Clelon, exists within a power matrix terrorizing the whole of Robeson Country, and he articulates with his deformed body this derangement. Clelon is defined by social convention, though Rhoda believes he may be "full-witted, or at least three-quarters" (59). She explains: "Blind or crippled, as so many were now from the war, a man still looks a man, and so he seems predictable. But a rolling head makes people think something lunatic and wild is going on inside it, such as a murder plot or a mad rampage. It looks too *different*" (59). Social norms, here represented with "people," have identified Clelon with pure difference, a nonman existing outside the masculine terrain of soldiers and veterans. His throwaway body signals insanity, chaos, criminality, and a world turned upside down and inside out. After Barnes has whipped his ox to death, Clelon harnesses himself to the plow in a gesture rich with meaning. He signals his status as mere animal, nonmale and nonhuman while simultaneously asserting the phallic power residing in the bull and its horns. Clelon, in short, articulates with his abject body the contradictions of the culture producing him.

Eventually he is locked up in a home for social outcasts, where he perishes in flames. He thus embodies the parts of history preferably forgotten. Young Rhoda decides not to remember him, as she has chosen to forget others found mutilated or dead: "I wanted to sweep trouble and threats and dangers out of my head with a stiff hearth broom, let them die into the cold ashpile of the past and never think of them again." As the metaphors of this passage indicate, her lack of memory links up with the performance of traditional femininity: "And so I made myself the know-nothing I had pretended to be" (69). With his abject body, Clelon dramatizes the conflicts within Rhoda and her community. Pauline Palmer writes in "Foreign Bodies" (2003) that a stigmatized body may reclaim marginality and empower bodies marked as monstrous outsiders (83). Clelon may be relegated to the cold ashpile of history, where marginal bodies reside, but his absence will ultimately inspire in Rhoda a desire for change and move her from domesticity into history.

James Barnes, the county postmaster, also articulates physically that history is necessary, and costly. As Rhoda ponders her shape-shifting capacities, she notices two boots, two legs, and a body on its back thrown in the woods. This dying body belongs to Barnes, presumably shot by Henry Lowrie and his men. His discarded body teaches Rhoda that words fall short of wartime realities, of living bodies dying: "A dying man, unlike the dead, is hard to tell about in words. The only part to be described is the wound, an incidental detail in view of what is *happening*, looming wordless, an enormity and a nothing" (167).

Barnes's body signals that history writes itself on the monstrous bodies that Patricia Yaeger associates with change. The corpse teaches Rhoda about ideals and reality, about witnessing the unspeakable, and about remembering it for the record: "There are some things you shouldn't see, because they are too strong to fade. I knew I would never forget that dark struggling thing" (167). With his abandoned heart and body, James Barnes embodies the injustice, and the history, that Rhoda cannot ignore.

Other discarded bodies speak the history of Scuffletown and the war. The evil Brant Harris has left behind written instructions about a mahogany coffin and a respectful wake, but his wife has other plans with her husband's corpse. As Catherine Harris tells the sheriff, "Find somewhere to store him . . . whether it's in the dirt or the river or some grand big fire. . . . If you bury him, I don't want to know where" (182–83). With her dismissive gesture, she sets herself free, along with all the other victims of Harris's lust and greed. As the sheriff realizes, the widow writes female liberation on the muddy body of her dead tormentor and thus destabilizes Robeson County hierarchies: "She had no fears, no desires, and nothing to lose—a dangerous woman. For the first time he was dealing with someone who didn't care if he was sheriff or not" (184). His description of Mrs. Harris would fit the woman Rhoda Lowrie ultimately becomes. She is Queen of Scuffletown, a woman alone—dangerous, free, and writing.

Certain aspects of war and history escape representation and may only be guessed. At the end of *Nowhere Else*, Henderson Oxendine, Rhoda's friend, faces execution for a crime he did not commit. She takes her two children to witness the hanging to ensure that this act of injustice will live on, unforgotten. Christianne Oxendine, Henderson's mother, wags her finger in Rhoda's face to commit the hanging to history: "You tell yours to tell Henderson's someday, what they saw here. And to their children too. Do you understand me? You *do* that" (311). In narrating the execution Rhoda describes the twenty-six-year-old prisoner as he steps onto the platform, his brave body strong and healthy, his long hair blowing freely. But the act of execution cannot be articulated; Henderson's body is absent from her record. A New York journalist scribbles his notes, a wasp lands on his hat along the brim, and Rhoda's son traces the contour of her ear. Seconds later Henderson's mother receives the contents of his pockets, his boots, and his clothes. Even Henry Lowrie is absent, though Rhoda imagines him somewhere near, ready to prevent history from taking its course: "I was the one who started hoping then, searching the trees and the rooftops, looking for my husband. He might be there in disguise or hidden behind a cart, ready to leap to the platform. Wasn't he there, wasn't he coming? But I couldn't find him" (314). The absent bodies of the hanged prisoner and the gunman who might have rescued him suggest a double horror, the unspeakable history enacted on the scaffold and the subjection of agents and witnesses. Henry Lowrie and George (Boss) Strong, Rhoda's husband and brother, proceed to fake their own deaths so as to escape from Robeson Country. They leave at the end with a train full of Federal soldiers, unknown and unrecognized. Their absent bodies haunt Rhoda's life and all pages of *Nowhere Else* and represent another loss she cannot word.

Henry Lowrie's shadow darkens moments of celebration or disruption and suggests his hidden monstrosity. When Rhoda finds the dying James Barnes and afterward meets a smiling Henry, she thinks: *"He didn't do it. Couldn't have killed Barnes and then smile it off so easy an hour later."* Yet Henry's shadow looms over the body in the woods: "It was not a simple killing done as an ordinary robber or rogue would think to do it, with a ball to the brain. It was deep murder. Whoever opened that breast and shot that face away—straight through the upraised hands—was a kind of man I didn't understand. He might smile or he might not, I couldn't know" (171). Rhoda's doubt and her parallel construction—he might smile or he might not—suggest a double vision, the body as well as the shadow behind it. This shadow lives in the public imagination and in the media, where Henry Lowrie gets credit for every criminal act committed in North Carolina and elsewhere: "He robbed a bank in Indiana, the paper said, and the next day he stole horses in Georgia. It was as if a ghost had sprung up, a double of Henry with a life and energy of its own, and it was growing" (289–90). This double also thrives inside of Henry, as Rhoda explains: "While the ghost grew, there were signs the real Henry was losing something of himself" (290). She no longer knows what her husband is or will be; the darker side of Henry has won the struggle. Rhoda cross-dresses and joins her husband and his outlaws, but her belief in change turns into disappointment. She decides that the hero is absent from Robeson County and that a ghost haunts the place she calls "nowhere else on earth." Rhoda dominates the novel because of her way with words, not weapons. Her husband casts his shadow across the pages she produces, but Rhoda stays in Scuffletown to witness and to tell.

Her history is local and communal. Humphreys links narration to the body, to the historical marks it carries, and to the place it lives. This place escapes categories and conclusions: "God's is the only eye that will ever see Scuffletown entire at a glance" (146). But the place offers a new vision of the Civil War and its heroes, as when Sherman slogs through North Carolina with his twenty thousand men. He stops to clean the Carolina mud from his fingernails and then, bored and depressed, he leaves Bethel Church and the state behind (247). Robeson County remains off center and decentered. "We belong here," Rhoda tells her children. She takes on the burden of home, history, and the place it all unfolds: "Overhead the wild grapes twined. About us was the luster of Robeson County, morning light stretched thin, black crow on fencepost, last year's broom grass red under this year's green. In my lifetime all my strongest urges of love and grief or wild fury had come to me in the out-of-doors, under this very sky. What flooded me now was not love and the other rages but *home*. There was nowhere else for me" (328). This passage makes it clear that living history begins and ends with place, with home, county, and land. As Jan Nordby Gretlund put it, the "landscape as observed by Humphreys is a fusion of human and natural order, and the result may offer a peculiar window on the whole" (Gretlund 1998, 228). History calls not for heroes with weapons and lost causes but for patience and endurance.

Rhoda becomes the historian of Robeson County and the hero of *Nowhere Else*. The past she explores is dangerous. Like the place itself, it is "more like a fishnet. Or a cobweb, a lacy swatch of tatting, a snare of mesh" (6). As she writes the history of her body and place, the past she enters is perilous and all-consuming. "Today," she notes, "the past is lively before my eyes, hot as coals." As she dances through, "the serpent of knowledge" bites her leg, and history invades her with its fire and ashes: "I am chewing red cinders and sparks" (69). To choose history takes its toll on body and spirit, as Rhoda finds out: "I have lost half my life to it, two decades turning the past in my head. No toil ages the spirit faster than the toil of too much memory. And the body, too, shows wear" (69). In *Nowhere Else*, Rhoda takes on the burden of history—a most heroic task because the past invades, consumes, and destroys. The past is, as Faulkner knew, not even the past.

Nor does the past ring true. Ultimately Humphreys writes a novel, not a history text, since the past must be imagined. Throughout *Nowhere Else* she stresses Rhoda's artistic sensibilities and her capacity for guessing, even smelling, the truth. Rhoda does not get at this truth through fact, through lived experience alone; she turns to art to represent history. In describing the Lowrie place, she introduces the problem of representation by concluding that "the whole place looked like a picture." She continues: "I loved pictures." Yet Rhoda rejects the idealized illustrations in Miss McCabe's *Illustrated News* depicting hunting scenes, battles, and ladies' fashion. From these pictures she concludes that "art is never true to life" (49). She knows, however, that she must speak and write in order to ensure that her place and its people enter history. Future generations will not remember without prompting: "It's not wise to count on them. We're at their service, not they at ours; and any scheme we make to bind them is a manacle of thread. Still we go about it, conniving one way or another to cast our will across the ages" (299). Only fiction will reach across generations and guess the history that Rhoda lived.

Josephine Humphreys dreams up the history of Robeson County and its Civil War in *Nowhere Else on Earth*. At the beginning of the twenty-first century, she explores how history may be lived and spoken across time and space. History is as hybrid and elusive as the swamp where it resides, so the historian must engage alternative modes of knowledge and reach toward the past with circular, even sensual, strokes. The past is slippery, though bodily contours emerge from the fluid landscapes of Robeson County. These bodies are sites for exploring southern history and politics, since women are often barred from public power but become central players in its symbolic scripts (Yaeger 2000,

121). In *Nowhere Else on Earth*, history surfaces on the bodies living and dying in this southern, marginalized space: racially indeterminate, hungry, and suffering. While female bodies and roles abound, hybrid constellations of ethnicity and gender live and speak in Humphreys's fourth novel, where the heroic Rhoda Lowrie usurps control. She inscribes the history of Scuffletown and its surroundings on the ludicrous, ostracized bodies of her people, who may appear only as absences or shadows. Her history of the place she knows and loves remains communal and local. As chroniclers of history Josephine Humphreys and Rhoda Lowrie employ an erotic, poetic discourse that ultimately transforms history into art. Both the Queen of Scuffletown and her author succeed in imagining the South and its past, and both bring to life a region and a history found nowhere else on earth.

Works Cited and Consulted

Canakis, Costas. "Metaphors of a Body Meant to Die." *Wrestling Bodies*. Ed. Zoe Detsi-Diamanti, Katerina Kitsi, and Effie Yiannopolou. *Gramma: Journal of Theory and Criticism* 11 (2003): 13–29.

Evans, W. McKee. *To Die Game: The Story of the Lowrie Band, Indian Guerillas of Reconstruction*. Baton Rouge: Louisiana State University Press, 1971.

Gretlund, Jan Nordby. "The Excitement and the Mystery of the Immediate: Interviews with Josephine Humphreys." *Chattahoochee Review* 22, no. 3 (2002): 33–55.

———. "Josephine Humphreys's New Southerner." *Frames of Southern Mind: Reflections on the Stoic, Bi-Racial and Existential South*. Odense: Odense University Press, 1998. 217–30.

Halberstam, Judith. *Female Masculinity*. Durham, N.C.: Duke University Press, 1998.

Humphreys, Josephine. *Nowhere Else on Earth*. New York: Viking, 2000.

———. *The Fireman's Fair*. New York: Viking, 1991.

———. *Rich in Love*. New York: Viking, 1987.

———. *Dreams of Sleep*. New York: Viking, 1984.

Jones, Anne Goodwyn, and Susan Donaldson, eds. *Haunted Bodies: Gender and Southern Texts*. Charlottesville: University of Virginia Press, 1997.

Palmer, Paulina. "Foreign Bodies." In Detsi-Diamanti et al. 80–93.

Perry, Carolyn, and Mary Louise Weaks, eds. *The History of Southern Women's Literature*. Baton Rouge: Louisiana State University Press, 2002.

Pitavy-Souques, Danièle. "Dancers and Angels: Communication in the Fiction of Josephine Humphreys." *The Southern State of Mind*. Ed. Jan Nordby Gretlund. Columbia: University of South Carolina Press, 1999. 185–200.

Yaeger, Patricia. *Dirt and Desire: Reconstructing Southern Women's Writing, 1930–1990*. Chicago: University of Chicago Press, 2000.

Yates, Gayle Graham. "The North Carolina Lumbee People as Seen through a Visit with Linda Oxendine." *Southern Ethnicities*. Ed. Youli Theodosiadou. Thessaloniki: Aristotle University Press, 2008. 115–29.

Kaye Gibbons ~ *On the Occasion of My Last Afternoon*

KATHRYN MCKEE

A Biographical Sketch

Kaye Gibbons was born Bertha Kaye Batts on May 5, 1960, into the small community of Bend of the River in Nash County, North Carolina. By her own account she survived a childhood children should not have to endure. The financial ups and downs that beset the farming family were only its most obvious challenge. In 1970, when she was ten years old, her mother, Alice, committed suicide. This was after a series of hospitalizations for manic depression and an open-heart surgery. Gibbons's subsequent life with her unpredictable and alcoholic father forced her into a premature independence that meant she was the most responsible member of her household. She even bought her own Christmas presents. Recognizing her home environment as unstable, Gibbons migrated among other relatives and at one point stayed in a foster home. She eventually landed with her older brother's family. Gibbons graduated from high school in 1978 and then enrolled at North Carolina State University, before transferring at the end of her sophomore year to the University of North Carolina at Chapel Hill. There she came under the tutelage of Louis D. Rubin Jr., to whom she showed the early versions of what eventually would become *Ellen Foster*. It was published in 1987 by Algonquin Books, the independent publishing company Rubin had created.

Kaye Gibbons's books were well received by both critics and readers from the start. *Ellen Foster* received the Sue Kaufman Prize for First Fiction from the American Academy and Institute for Arts and Letters. Following up on that early success, she published seven additional novels: *A Virtuous Woman* (1989), *A Cure for Dreams* (1991), *Charms for the Easy Life* (1994), *Sights Unseen* (1995), *On the Occasion of My Last Afternoon* (1998), *Divining Women* (2004), and *The Life All Around Me by Ellen Foster* (2006). Her work has been adapted for stage and television screen, and her fame is international; in 1996 she became the youngest recipient of France's Chevalier de L'Ordre des Arts et des Lettres. She has also received what is perhaps the highest recognition of popular success in the United States: two of her novels (*Ellen Foster* and *A Virtuous Woman*) were selections for Oprah Winfrey's book club. She also enjoys the high regard of the academic community and is a member of the Fellowship of Southern Writers.

Kaye Gibbons's personal life has followed a less steady course. After initially rejecting any idea of a correlation between her own life and that of Ellen Foster, the author eventually conceded that the novel, about a young girl's life with her alcoholic father after her mother's death, was semiautobiographical. A later novel, *Sights Unseen* (1995), also taps into her experiences with a mentally ill mother, but in writing the book Gibbons was able to draw not just on her mother's life but also on her own experience. First hospitalized in 1982 for what doctors then believed was manic depression, Gibbons has spoken openly about her mental illness, the medicines required to treat her, the various diagnoses, and the effect of her manic phases on the writing process. In 1995 she brought out *Frost and Flower: My Life with Manic Depression So Far* as a separate publication. It is an essay based on earlier addresses to mental health advocacy groups. In the essay she candidly describes her stays at Holly Hill Hospital in Raleigh and concedes that no magic cure can undo her illness. Even if such a panacea existed, its cost—her creativity—would be too high. "Things could be worse," she concludes, "I could go through life artistically mute—with a world of ideas in my head and no way to say them" (*Frost*, 20). But Gibbons has pursued her quest for mental health and her rich outpouring of fiction has continued unabated. She has been twice married and divorced and has three grown children who lend their names to the protagonist's daughters in *On the Occasion of My Last Afternoon*: Mary, Leslie, and Louise. The author resides in the Raleigh area of North Carolina, and the state remains the primary location for much of her fiction.

Without question her own life informs the central concerns of Gibbons's fiction. Among them are the process of defining "home," the ramifications for adults of unlived childhoods, and the power of individuals to endure and then overcome seemingly insurmountable odds. Her reliance on strong female characters has led many reviewers and critics to call her writing "woman-centered" and to point out that the men in her fiction are typically the greatest challenges the women have to overcome. Gibbons makes frequent use of the first-person narrator and she instantly plunges the reader into an unpredictable mix of humor and violence that demonstrates both the wide-ranging power of her language and the inevitable limitations of words to convey the full register of human experience.

On the Occasion of My Last Afternoon

On the Occasion of My Last Afternoon, Gibbons's sixth novel, is consistent with the themes and techniques evident in much of her earlier fiction. The novel is narrated in the first person by Emma Garnet Tate Lowell, a seventy-year-old woman writing in the year 1900 just as a new century dawns and she feels her own life ebb away. Her goal is to order and preserve the events of her life, and they are many. The novel divides into four chronological sections: Emma Garnet's childhood and adolescence until she marries at eighteen and leaves Seven Oaks, her father's Virginia plantation; the early years of her marriage to Quincy Lowell, son of the famous Massachusetts family, who takes her to Raleigh, where he is a doctor; the blur of years during the Civil War when she assists Quincy both in the hospital and in caring for the wounded in their own home; and the years of her life following Quincy's death during which she attempts to live into his legacy. Because her account is retrospective, time and nostalgia have probably tempered her recollections, but Emma Garnet tries to hold herself to the standard of unflinching honesty Quincy encouraged when she talked to him about her life: "*Face it all dry-eyed. Say it. Say it*" (273).

And some of what she has to remember and say is hard. Like Gibbons's first protagonist, Ellen Foster, Emma Garnet is born into an unsteady household overseen by an unpredictable and imperious father whose callous nature and unremitting self-absorption eventually result in her mother's death. The novel is shot through with violence. In the spirit of *Ellen Foster*, which begins "I used to think of ways to kill my daddy," *Occasion* unsettles the reader from its opening line: "*I did not mean to kill the nigger! Did not mean to kill him!*" Against the backdrop of the plantation's hog-slaughtering operation, its patriarch has slaughtered one of his slaves whose name he does not know nor care to learn. From this point forth the text periodically returns to the bloody violence done to bodies—at the execution of a man who wears the dried ear of his victim as a souvenir necklace, in the graphic description of Emma Garnet's brother's demise from syphilis, at her mother's deathbed, where she has been bled with leeches, and in the killing fields and bloody hospitals of the American Civil War. As in much of Gibbons's fiction, the body is vulnerable, under attack, and an insufficient barrier against the forces that would do it harm. Emma Garnet survives in order to give the reader this book, and although she is in some ways deeply flawed, she is also remarkably human in her desires and her shortcomings. Thus the reader becomes her ally in combating the forces of her nineteenth-century world.

In other signal ways *Occasion* represents a departure from Gibbons's other writing. Most obviously it is her only nineteenth-century historical novel; other books, *A Cure for Dreams*, for instance, have early-twentieth-century settings, but none are tied to particular historical events in the way that *Occasion* is. Actual battles—"Malvern Hill. Cedar Mountain. Groveton. Second Manassas. Chantilly. And, oh my God, Antietam" (218)—fuel Emma's hospital work, and she makes passing reference to the central figures of those events and their movements. Robert E. Lee, Varina Davis, the Lowells of abolitionist fame all cross the pages of this novel. But ultimately the book is far less about the historical event at its center than it is about Emma Garnet and this one woman's ability to survive the world time has given her. In this respect the novel underscores more broadly how all individual human lives are forced to play out in particular moments before fading into the next moment's backdrop unheralded, save for our efforts to capture experience with language.

The experience recalled in *Occasion*, however, comes from a different world than the one Gibbons most frequently gives us: Emma Garnet is an upper-class white woman, the sort of person who might have set out to rescue and reform Ellen Foster if she had lived later and had not been so preoccupied with Lavinia Dawes, this novel's "project" (120) from the white lower classes. Emma Garnet and Quincy take Lavinia in, see to her education—"She had to know that she need not fear stepping off the edge of a flat world" (119)—and in many ways consider her their daughter. "Clarice and Mavis and I made Lavinia over" (117), Emma Garnet recalls, presumably shaping the young girl into an object worthy of the privileges she receives. At eighteen, employed as a teacher and about to marry a lawyer, Lavinia writes to her benefactors that she hopes to replicate their happiness, concluding, "Thank you both for showing me this life" (122). By the next page Lavinia is dead, the victim of childbed fever and, upon closer examination, the victim of a great deal more, including the physical beatings of her husband. Her parents blame the Lowells for removing her from her proper sphere of life, and the implication lingers that perhaps Emma Garnet agrees with them—Lavinia could not flourish in soil so unlike her own. "To help my spirits," Emma Garnet reports, "Quincy bought the girls and me a mule." But "I was not ready, my heart was not ready, to train another creature to enjoy this life, and so I had Clarice trade her for a crate of rabbits," which she eventually sets free in the park (126). Lavinia's story is "the only blight" on these prewar years, otherwise filled with love, security, and comfort; the economic- and social-class standing can lull one into thinking life has guarantees.

This story of Lavinia—ending as it does with mules and rabbits proposed and rejected—blights something more, however. As Emma Garnet and Quincy consider Lavinia in such company, they require the reader to confront their paternalism as it seeps into other parts of the text, sustained most particularly in their relations with African American characters. In the case of Lavinia Dawes, Emma Garnet's "slaves" actually assist her in creating at least the external features of the white southern lady. This is but one indication that the complicated intersections of blackness and whiteness within the spaces of family and home will form the core of the novel. Gibbons offers an extended exploration of black labor in a white South, particularly in the character of Clarice. From the angle of historical fiction the novel delicately considers the white South's ongoing fascination and romance with the figure of the black woman in the white home.

Unquestionably Gibbons builds her novel with earlier accounts of the plantation in mind. Samuel Tate's estate is called "Seven Oaks," echoing Ashley Wilkes's well-known Twelve Oaks from Margaret Mitchell's *Gone with the Wind*, and in naming her protagonist Emma *Garnet*, Gibbons may well be invoking shades of Scarlett. Emma Garnet is opinionated and articulate, much more like Scarlett than Melanie, the alternate version of southern womanhood presented in Mitchell's novel. Emma Garnet's mother is beautiful and of an established old family, which has been rendered slightly shabby by bad finances but remains solidly upper class by all indications of culture and manners. She sees to her slaves when she is well enough to do so and not away visiting another plantation for solace from her boorish husband. But she provides no real model for how to survive the ravages of the world, confined as she largely is to the "candlelight and taffeta" of her memories, with her eyes "set on the make-believe past," according to Emma Garnet's own description (45). Largely ineffectual in life, her mother in death unsettles Emma Garnet even more. The daughter believes that had she not been so lost in loving her own life, she could have saved her mother. It is no coincidence, then, that Gibbons's mother and the fictional one she creates in *Occasion* share the name Alice. Although she is missing Scarlett's driving ambition and disregard for social conformity, Emma Garnet acts when she must. She and Quincy administer an overdose to her own father, an act that surely takes as much nerve as Scarlett's shooting of a ragged Federal soldier in her hall. When Emma Garnet is stung by a local woman, who broaches the subject of her brother's shameful death, she takes to her bed in a manic response that leads her to contemplate taking her own overdose. But in a scene that recalls Rhett and Scarlett's forced perambulations in front of their Atlanta home, Quincy sends her back out into the world to confront Raleigh society and to claim her place.

Emma Garnet's father recalls another narrative of the plantation, this time Faulkner's *Absalom, Absalom!* Samuel Tate is an imperious man—whenever it is possible to demand too much and think too little, he does, and his loud and unpredictable outbursts mean that his extended plantation household is in a constant state of anxious watchfulness. His callous disregard for the slave he kills in the novel's opening scene recalls Thomas Sutpen's wrestling with his "chattel." Although Emma Garnet does not actually witness her father commit murder, as Judith Sutpen watches her father wrestle his slaves, she is fully aware of his potential for cruelty. Like Sutpen, Tate has created himself to approximate the figure of the landed southern gentleman. He comes from poverty and outright abuse, but it is a past that he attempts to disguise beneath a veneer of high culture. He collects fine paintings and is exceedingly well read, and like Sutpen, Samuel Tate acquires in Alice the wife he believes will provide the final seal of social credibility. Samuel has also invested in the purity of his patriarchy and therefore banishes his son Whately for sexual indiscretions. But the tenor of their relationship has been so unrelentingly bitter that the reader suspects the source of the tension between them to be Samuel's dissatisfaction with the orientation of his son's masculinity. Samuel Tate's dark secret does not seem to be trips out back to continue his progeny, but rather a moment from his own childhood that finally and irrevocably gnarled his soul.

In harking back to these two well-known twentieth-century invocations of southern plantation life, Gibbons acknowledges their power and attempts to broaden the parameters of fictional representations of the period. First she centers the narrative consciousness in Emma Garnet so that the central female character guides the story. Readers certainly often hear from Mitchell's Scarlett O'Hara, but we do not always know what she is thinking. We know far less about Judith Sutpen in *Absalom, Absalom!*—a novel rendered largely through the speculation of shifting storytellers, none of whom is Judith. The second important shift in Gibbons's storytelling comes through the character of Clarice, who, like Mitchell's Mammy and Faulkner's Dilsey, guards the family's morality and supervises the production of its white womanhood. But Clarice is not a slave. In a world powered by slave labor and eventually at war in order to preserve that institution, Clarice is a free woman, which is an effort on Gibbons's part to complicate the plantation narrative. She is investigating the possibility of a bond between black and white women when one is not compelled to be in the presence of the other, when one holds no power over the other and when the connection between them is mutual affection. In this respect Gibbons joins other writers, particularly Ellen Douglas in *Can't Quit You, Baby*, in recognizing domestic space as a crucial testing ground for the boundaries of race relations between women. Yet where Douglas meditates on the power of one imagination to capture fully the experiences of another, the narrator regularly interrupts the text to insist on the limitations of her positionality as a white woman. Douglas does try to give voice to Tweet, the African American woman who has labored for many years in Cornelia's kitchen, and she works through the text to effect a moment when the two women can genuinely listen to and hear one another's stories. In Gibbons's *Occasion*, however, Clarice remains curiously silent; her relationship with Emma Garnet is rendered only from the latter's perspective. Yet she remains the novel's most compelling figure. Quincy Lowell is clearly an idealized, self-sacrificing character; Samuel Tate's evil become predictable; and Emma Garnet withholds little from the reader in her extended narration. Clarice is the text's enigma, key to nearly every event it records but frustratingly absent from any explanation of why it has happened.

Clarice acts as a dark and constant reminder of what Samuel Tate struggles to forget and as a quiet torment to his efforts at replacing the past with an elaborate screen of education, wealth, and the power of well-heeled whiteness. She appears on the novel's third page as witness to Samuel's protestations, and it is clear shortly after her introduction that she holds unusual sway in the household, especially as it relates to the patriarch: "She had known him when he was worth two acres, then two hundred, then two thousand, and she knew where his heart ached. . . . plus, she was free, not bound to him by any shackle other than her own unwillingness to tell all of her mind. In rare and necessary bursts, she would say there was something to tell" (5). But what intrigues the reader more, finally, than Samuel's secret, is why Clarice would keep it and how it could tether her to a man capable of the brutality in the novel's opening lines. Her eventual revelation that she witnessed him burying his own mother after being forced to shoot her by his sadistic father cannot finally explain why Clarice is drawn to him, instead of repulsed. When Emma Garnet marries, Clarice shifts her loyalty, leaving with her and making a parting speech aimed at Emma Garnet's parents: "Miss Alice, I worship the ground you tread and take your gifts to my heart. And you, Mr. Tate, you watch for her heart" (51). According to Emma Garnet Clarice's devotion is unshakeable, first to Samuel, then to Alice, and now to her.

Yet Clarice's loyalty is the most troubling element of the novel because it is the least explicable. The idea that a free woman would approximate the condition of slavery because she first saw up close the horror of Samuel's life and later became so attached to Emma Garnet that she could not leave her is not explanation enough. It satisfies Emma Garnet, apparently, who would no doubt have maintained, as do so many of the white women interviewed in Susan Tucker's *Telling Memories Among Southern Women*, that Clarice was a central member of her family. Earlier, at the moment of her brother Whately's dramatic departure, Emma Garnet observes of Clarice, who has taken off her apron: "Nobody's servant now, stripped of that emblem of servitude, she was another woman of the Tate household, crushed to see a son taking his leave. She kissed his cheek and pushed his hair from his forehead in the same way, the very same way, Mother had done" (79). On Clarice's tombstone, to be placed in the Lowell family plot, Emma Garnet plans the inscription *"Kind Mother"* (241).

Certainly for Emma Garnet, Clarice is an abiding maternal presence. From the novel's opening sequence, in which it is clear that there is a strong and particular bond between them, Clarice represents the idea of comfort to Emma Garnet. Even after she is married Emma Garnet knows how to cook only popcorn because Clarice runs the household, all "three floors, ten bedrooms, and Philadelphia plumbing!" (171). "My mother," Emma Garnet later muses, "had spoken of cooking as a mystery fathomable only by Negroes" (230). Later, exhausted from her long hours at the hospital, Emma Garnet collapses into Clarice's waiting arms, and when her sister, Maureen, later seeks refuge in the Lowells's Raleigh home, Clarice draws her bath and then "dried her body with the slow, loving care of a mare cleaning her foal of the gore of birth. She seemed to be trying, in her exertions, to massage years of woe from my sister" (206). More fully than Emma Garnet's own mother was ever able to, Clarice provides a safe mooring for Emma Garnet in an otherwise capricious world, and this is a relationship that extends beyond the white girl's childhood to her adult life. When Clarice herself is dying, Emma Garnet has the chance to reverse their customary roles. This time she sustains Clarice's feverish and failing body: "I held her up in the tub, as a mother would an infant, and poured water over her neck" (235). "She had worked for and loved all of us, been our constant guardian," Emma Garnet retrospectively surmises, concluding that "her mission was not to change history but to help both white and black prevail over the circumstances of living in that place, the South, in our time" (232). In this way, Emma Garnet suggests, Clarice lives into her particular moment of reconciliation, and the fact that she did not attempt to dismantle the institution of slavery singlehandedly is, in fact, only one more indication of her admirable wisdom.

Yet Clarice's role in the Lowell household so closely resembles that of a slave that outsiders believe she is one and readers have trouble denying it. The Lowell household, despite its ancestral roots in New England abolitionism, actually maintains a staff consisting of what appear to be three slaves in addition to the free woman Clarice, who is presented to them as their owner. Thus the Lowells themselves are not technically slaveholders, yet the slaveholding neighborhood is pacified in its anxieties about the dangers of free blacks. But Gibbons actually reserves something more damning for Emma Garnet and Quincy than being slaveholders in a slaveholding South. In fact, not only Clarice but also the other three servants, Mavis, Martha, and Charlie, are actually free as well; they were purchased by Quincy when they left Seven Oaks. The Lowells, and a complicit Clarice, just never get around to telling them until she makes the announcement on her deathbed. Overwhelmed, somewhat angry, and with a sense of betrayal, they stay long enough to teach Emma Garnet and her sister how to cook something before they leave. They share none of Clarice's sense of obligation to their white "family," making her persistent loyalty all the more puzzling and Emma Garnet and Quincy's denial of their liberty all the more troubling. The fact that they were paid small salaries hardly offsets the fact that their humanity was finally less of an issue for their "owner" than the Lowells' dependence on their labor and on their presence, in order to relieve the household of any obligation to explain its abolitionist leanings. "I feared that they would leave me at the mercy of my incapable self," Emma Garnet concedes, acknowledging that "the delusion of bondage [is] a condition no different from reality in its oppression on the soul" (237, 236). In the face of Mavis, Martha, and Charlie's muted outrage, Clarice sacrifices one more time, redirecting their accusatory stares from Emma Garnet to herself: "You listen to me. She did not go to do it. It was my notion. Let me be the one you blame" (237). They do not listen to her, nor do they believe her, coldly taking their leave of Emma Garnet in the kitchen after they give her a cursory lesson in administering it. Tossing a potato peel toward a trash can but missing it, Charles pointedly leaves it for Emma Garnet to pick up.

Loved *like* family members, and sometimes *actually* family members, African American figures such as the ones in *Occasion* haunt the margins of American literature, as Toni Morrison so eloquently explains in *Playing in the Dark*, and they constitute the white South's last great romance with its tortured past. All those black domestic workers in all those kitchens for all those years all across the South—all those women, both male and female white middle and upper-class southerners maintain, really did love us and love us still. They were part of our families. In large part silent themselves in the fiction written about their worlds—exceptions would include Sofia in Alice Walker's *Color Purple* and Tweet in Ellen Douglas's *Can't Quit You, Baby*—black female domestic workers constitute, at least for some white southerners, a lingering barrier to a full engagement with the insidious machinations of quotidian racism. If I mistook labor for love, this dimension of the white South reasons, if the woman who kept my house and made my lunch in the heart of my home did not see me, as I assumed she did, then what else about my own relation to race in America have I misunderstood? Neither Emma Garnet nor Kaye Gibbons is directly asking that question. In Clarice we have a dependable character who consistently shows her dedication to and love for Emma Garnet and her family, and Emma Garnet is genuinely devastated by her passing. In the wake of Clarice's death, we do not, however, find Emma Garnet pondering their relationship or wondering about the missing links in her history. That is left to the reader: where did Clarice come from and why did she stay, first with Samuel Tate and then with his daughter?

In Clarice, Mary Jean DeMarr maintains, Gibbons creates a fully rounded figure who "serves as a kind of moral compass for the protagonist's family" (23); she aligns *On the Occasion of My Last Afternoon* with (white) southern literature's longstanding inclination to center wisdom in African American women, who recognize from their marginalized social standing the misguided doings of the white people they serve. In many situations the black female teaches the white girls in her charge how to become women. In *Gone with the Wind* Mammy cinches Scarlett's waist and chastises her for showing too much skin; in *To Kill a Mockingbird* Calpurnia chides Scout for her boyish behavior; and in *The Sound and the Fury* Dilsey knows Caddy has gone too far to be redeemed. Clarice has Emma Garnet to educate into being a more effectual woman than her mother and a more decent human being than her father.

DeMarr maintains that Clarice does not belong to "the stereotype of the black 'mammy'" (138), by which she presumably means a comic grotesque of thoughtless devotion. Yet Clarice certainly occupies the *role* of "mammy"; she performs domestic labor in a white household intent on maintaining the *appearance* of slavery. By accepting this role she fits uneasily with the paradigm of black enslaved womanhood that Trudier Harris outlines in *From Mammies to Militants*. In many ways she does uphold the stereotypical mammy figure, what Harris terms "the basic historical conception from which other images and stereotypes [of black women] have grown" (4). Her life is consumed by tending to the patriarch and his children and later his grandchildren, and her service is rendered with full knowledge of the shortcomings of the Tates. Even if she is clearly more than a one-dimensional fictional construction, she demonstrates for the reader none of the double-edged discourse that delineates Harris's transitional phase between mammy and militant, and although she lives in a world saturated with violence, she never offers anyone more than a verbal lashing. With no access to her mind, readers are forced to accept Emma Garnet's explanation for Clarice's abiding presence: she loves Emma Garnet too much to be parted from her.

Recent studies, including Micki McElya's *Clinging to Mammy: The Faithful Slave in the Twentieth Century* (2007) and Kimberly Wallace-Sanders's *Mammy: A Century of Race, Gender, and Southern Memory* (2008), turn new lenses on the provocative and persistent figure of the mammy in American literature and mass culture. Wallace-Sanders in particular considers literary stylizations and rebuttals but also examines advertising campaigns (i.e., Aunt Jemima) and late-nineteenth- and early-twentieth-century efforts on the part of white women to memorialize the figure of "mammy." Her goal, she explains, "is to establish the differences between the literary character and stereotype mammy . . . and the actual African American women whose names were lost when they became 'Mammy.'" Visual artist Kara Walker, in her troubling and controversial silhouettes, especially of the recurrent figure of a "mammy," parodies white antebellum expectations for black slaves. At the same time Walker confronts the lingering power of such images in contemporary race relations and attempts to return to black women the ability to define their own bodies and their own sexuality. Actress and comedienne Michelle Nicole Matlock, whose touring performance "The Mammy Project" builds on the story of Nancy Green, the African American woman who embodied Aunt Jemima at the 1893 World's Fair in Chicago, also seeks to drive a wedge between disempowering stereotype and individualized experience.

Gibbons would seem to move tentatively in a similar direction, offering in Emma Garnet and Clarice the story of two women typically stereotyped—the white southern lady and the black mammy—but who resist the stifling images associated with them. Certainly Emma Garnet believes that she maintains a distance from the wheels of Old South mythology spinning in her lifetime, asserting "although I am a Southern woman, my life has not been cast in that romantic ideal of Scott's. Many fools I know have assumed possession of his language, and when I hear them drone on about chivalry and glory, I have wondered that we are of the same place" (62). Yet the one romance Emma Garnet clings to, the figure of Clarice, in her stoic wisdom and silent devotion, marks her kinship with the southerners she otherwise rejects. To say so is not to claim that black domestic workers never loved the families they worked for or that white families did not sincerely mean assertions of emotional kinship with the black women in their households. Nor is it, particularly, to indict Kaye Gibbons as somehow obtuse to the complicated interplay of race in domestic settings. Rather it is to suggest that Gibbons reveals in her novel one more time the white South's longstanding romance with this largely elusive, silent figure in the kitchen, whose centrally important story is nearly always told by someone else. Gibbons does not turn a particularly critical eye on that mythology, but her rendering of it suggests its vulnerability in subtle ways.

Emma Garnet's narrative voice, from its initial engagement with the reader, belies what it never consciously confronts—the unsettling nature of black-white relations in antebellum America. Taking the murder of a black man by a white man as its point of departure, the novel is fraught with the uneasiness of unresolved racial tension, stretching from Samuel's announcement that he did not intend to kill the man whose name he does not know, right into 1998, when Gibbons, perhaps unconsciously, recycles white America's lingering fondness for uncomplicated black/white relations within the domestic sphere. When she hears her father's protestations immediately following the murder, young Emma Garnet recalls knowing "that he had probably murdered with vile intent, and that all my night-fears of atrocities incited by the Turner rebellion would come true now—for vengeance, my family and I would be slit ear to ear in our sleep" (1). The historical reference here to Nat Turner is broadened by a rumor circulating among the children about a murderous "negro." It strikes fear into Emma Garnet's heart: *"The servants will rise, and they will cut our throats, and they will laugh and drink red whiskey and go about with our bloomers on their heads"* (2). An element of violence and callous disorder couples here with the threat of sexual violation: the whiskey may be red with blood, and if the bloomers are not being worn, then a body is somewhere exposed and implicitly violated in its most intimate parts. The body, then, is a site of sexualized anxiety from the novel's outset, and the home offers a potential staging ground for the sort of violence denied by narratives celebrating black and white relations within the domestic space.

Despite moments of paternalism Emma Garnet from childhood has a relationship with African Americans that is both transgressive in its insistence on viewing them as individual human beings and laced with fear at the specters introduced by their agency. As a child she wonders if she will go through all of her life "loving Negroes in secret, saying that I broke the rake handle to save Romulus from another slapping. Or, I thought as I fell down in the dark [of sleep], I could be kidnapped by Transylvanian Gypsies and buried alive" (29). The threat here of eclipsing, suffocating, and ultimately deadly blackness is of a piece with her fear of revolt, rebellion, and bloody death at the hands of murderous slaves, a linkage Patricia Yaeger explores in other texts in *Dirt and Desire*. Emma Garnet needs Clarice to counterbalance her fear, not of her father but of the world he has helped create in antebellum Virginia.

From its beginning *On the Occasion of My Last Afternoon* suggests that the trouble with blackness is not just its rebellious potential but also its unknown and potentially exotic origins. Many of Samuel Tate's slaves were purchased in a lot straight from Guinea in the market in Charleston the previous year (12). If the opening scenes of the novel take place in 1842, as the book's first page suggests, then Samuel would have purchased the slaves in 1841, a full thirty-three years after the United States officially ended its participation in the international slave trade. In this way Gibbons consciously locates the slaves as contraband. As Charles Joyner explains in *Down by the Riverside*, the illegal human trafficking persisted for decades after the U.S. ban, and it was centered in the port of Charleston and the sea islands off the South Carolina and Georgia coasts. Gibbons, then, intentionally laces the Tate slaves with markers, not of learned servitude, but of the exoticism of Africa itself. They speak a "mixture of field-hand English and Gullah" (12) that Clarice alone can decipher. The slave Jacob's "woman" is a particularly unsettling figure to Emma Garnet because she is a "trick Negress," capable of evoking some voodoo-laced retribution against the Tates. Whenever Emma Garnet heard that such a person was around Seven Oaks, she recalls that she "policed the grounds for piled bones, checked the thresholds for hairballs, huddled," and "wondered aloud about the tale, my pet nightmare, of the Negress who has squirted chloroform through a keyhole and killed five babies" (9). Such tales only heighten the plantation's already taut air and undermine comforting images of black nursemaids and mammies.

Yet Clarice counteracts such paralyzing fear. She alone seems able to navigate the troubling blackness that shadows her enslaved counterparts, although her own relationship to that blackness is at times difficult to discern. When the adult Emma Garnet reads aloud to her from Mungo Park's *Travels in the Interior of Africa*, for example, Clarice hands her a hat and sends her shopping, as it is a "better waste of time" (57). The nature of her objection is never made clear. Does she think knowledge of Africa useless? Or does she recognize Park's popular 1799 account as limited by his white imperialist gaze? Does she recognize the volume's veneer of romanticizing, linking it to Scott's portrayals of the U.S. South that Emma Garnet has earlier rejected? This would be irony heightened by the fact that Scott and Park became acquainted in the time between his two discovery missions to Africa. Clarice says no more. Although she clearly condemns Tate's murderous impulse in the opening sequence, she also goes out among his angry slaves, collecting their versions of what happened to the dead man and working to quell the unrest, finally suggesting that they accept the peace offering she will force him to send, consisting of "rat bait and flour and whole cloth and shoe leather" (14), lest they find themselves "up to the block" (15). It is Clarice, not Tate himself, who raises the specter of their being sold down river to be abused by someone worse, should they enact their righteous indignation. Literally invoking the tools of the master, Clarice aligns herself with an agenda of peaceful submission at the same time that she initiates a ceremony foreign to Emma Garnet, at least: "Now do his toes" (15). Each slave in turn then touches Jacob's exposed toes to avoid being molested by his ghost. Thus Emma Garnet positions Clarice in this early scene as her guide, her interpreter, and the primary translator of the hybrid world in which they both find themselves. Clarice makes the unfamiliar familiar and turns the exotic and alienating into something Emma Garnet can recognize and condone.

The roil of emotions Emma Garnet experiences upon receiving news of her mother's death highlights the intricacies of the black/white web in which she exists. When she hears Mintus and Ezekial, slaves she knows from Seven Oaks, quarreling outside, she is struck with a premonition of disaster; she characteristically vomits, then goes to the door to silence them by screaming "shut up." They have scarcely begun to deliver their news when Emma Garnet is overcome by a second wave of emotion. Looking at the aged Mintus, for whom she knows the journey has been arduous, she can only conclude, "But I despised him anyway. His alliance. His loyalty" (143). The qualities she so values in Clarice here repulse her. What she really despises, of course, is the fact that Mintus bears loyally the news that will irrevocably change her world; he cannot be turned aside from his errand. Emma Garnet naturally yearns for the maternal presence of Clarice, and she staggers into the yard calling for her. Overhearing neighbor boys chanting a "nigger" rhyme, Emma Garnet strips off her crinoline and scales two fences in order to silence their offensive language with her scream, now directing her animosity at the mere invocation of derogatory blackness. Emma Garnet's wild cascade of emotions—her high-handed treatment of Mintus followed by her literal stripping away of the vestments of ladyhood in order to silence a casually dispensed racial epithet—mirror her vacillations about blackness and its role in confirming and complicating her whiteness and the fragile balance of her nineteenth-century world. Clarice's response to the news of Alice's death is telling. Dry-eyed, with a heavy sigh and averted sight, Clarice says simply, "I am so sorry. So, so sorry" (148), offering measured condolences as one does to the bereaved, but not mourning herself, as we might have expected from one of the family.

In the end, of course, Clarice must have had her own family, must have come from somewhere, but the reader receives little information about her. The epigraphs Gibbons selects for *Occasion* point subtly toward Clarice's troubling presence in the novel. The author includes a short quotation from Allen Tate's much-cited "Ode to the Confederate Dead" about the dangers of being swallowed by the "ravenous past": "You hear the shout, the crazy hemlocks point / With troubled fingers to the silence which / Smothers you, a mummy, in time." The silence of Clarice's character, and of the many African American characters who precede her in white southern literature, runs parallel to the smothering blackness that Emma Garnet fears. What would the story have been if Clarice had told it? The relevance of that question is made plain in the lines quoted from Robert Lowell's "For the Union Dead," insisting as they do on the necessary interconnection of time and linking the Civil War, World War II, and the civil rights movement through the image of "the drained faces of Negro school-children [that] rise like balloons," embodied for the speaker on his television screen. He cannot begin to imagine what they are thinking. But, the poet suggests, he cannot afford to stop trying. The same is true for any reader of *On the Occasion of My Last Afternoon*, who should not content herself with Emma Garnet's narration as the final word on Clarice. Her enigmatic presence in the novel is key to both the stories the white South has retold and made into mythology and to the ones it has repeatedly failed to imagine, at its own peril.

Works Cited and Consulted

DeMarr, Mary Jean. *Kaye Gibbons: A Critical Companion.* Westport, Conn.: Greenwood Press, 2003.

Disheroon-Green, Suzanne. "Kaye Gibbons." *Dictionary of Literary Biography.* Vol. 292. Ed. Lisa Abney and Suzanne Disheroon-Green. Detroit: Thomson Gale, 2004. 126–34.

Douglas, Ellen. *Can't Quit You, Baby.* New York: Atheneum, 1988.

Faulkner, William. *Absalom, Absalom!* New York: Random House, 1936.

Gibbons, Kaye. *The Life All Around Me by Ellen Foster.* Orlando, Fla.: Harcourt, 2006.

———. *Divining Women.* New York: Putnam, 2004.

———. *On the Occasion of My Last Afternoon.* New York: Putnam, 1998.

———. *Sights Unseen.* New York: Putnam, 1995.

———. *Frost and Flower: My Life with Manic Depression So Far.* Decatur, Ga.: Wisteria Press, 1995.

———. *Charms for the Easy Life.* New York: Putnam, 1993.

———. *A Cure for Dreams.* Chapel Hill, N.C.: Algonquin, 1991.

———. *A Virtuous Woman.* Chapel Hill, N.C.: Algonquin, 1989.

———. *Ellen Foster.* Chapel Hill, N.C.: Algonquin, 1987.

Gretlund, Jan Nordby. "'In My Own Style': An Interview with Kaye Gibbons." *South Atlantic Review* 65, no. 4 (2000): 132–54.

Harris, Trudier. *From Mammies to Militants: Domestics in Black American Literature.* Philadelphia: Temple University Press, 1982.

Joyner, Charles. *Down by the Riverside: A South Carolina Slave Community.* Urbana: University of Illinois Press, 1984.

Lee, Harper. *To Kill a Mockingbird.* New York: Random House, 1960.

Makowsky, Veronica. "Kaye Gibbons." *The History of Southern Women's Literature.* Ed. Carolyn Perry and Mary Louise Weaks. Baton Rouge: Louisiana State University Press, 2002. 604–9.

Mason, Julian. "Kaye Gibbons." *Contemporary Fiction Writers of the South: A Bio-Bibliographical Sourcebook.* Ed. Joseph M. Flora and Robert Bain. Westport, Conn.: Greenwood Press, 1993. 156–67.

McElya, Micki. *Clinging to Mammy: The Faithful Slave in the Twentieth Century.* Cambridge: Harvard University Press, 2007.

Mitchell, Margaret. *Gone with the Wind.* New York: Macmillan, 1936.

Monteith, Sharon. "Between Girls: Kaye Gibbons' *Ellen Foster* and Friendship as a Monologic Formulation." *Journal of American Studies* 33 (1999): 45–64.

Morrison, Toni. *Playing in the Dark: Whiteness and the Literary Imagination.* Cambridge: Harvard University Press, 1992.

Snodgrass, Mary Ellen. *Kaye Gibbons: A Literary Companion.* Jefferson, N.C.: McFarland, 2007.

Tucker, Susan. *Telling Memories among Southern Women: Domestic Workers and Their Employers in the Segregated South.* Baton Rouge: Louisiana State University Press, 1988.

Wagner-Martin, Linda. "Kaye Gibbons' Achievement in *On the Occasion of My Last Afternoon.*" *Notes on Contemporary Writers* 29, no. 3 (1999): 3–5.

Walker, Alice. *The Color Purple.* New York: Harcourt Brace Jovanovich, 1982.

Wallace-Stevens, Kimberly. *Mammy: A Century of Race, Gender, and Southern Memory.* Ann Arbor: University of Michigan Press, 2008.

Wilson, Mary Ann. "'We Were Whole Again': Kaye Gibbons's *On the Occasion of My Last Afternoon.*" *North Carolina Literary Review* 8 (1999): 122–28.

Yaeger, Patricia. *Dirt and Desire: Reconstructing Southern Women's Writing, 1930–1990.* Chicago: University of Chicago Press, 2000.

Pam Durban ∽ *So Far Back*

JAN NORDBY GRETLUND

A Biographical Sketch

The author was born Rosa Palmer Durban in Aiken, South Carolina, on March 4, 1947, the daughter of Frampton Wyman Durban, a real-estate appraiser, and Maria Hertwig. The writer grew up in Aiken, where her family has lived for generations. In the family tradition she attended a Catholic grade school, St. Mary Help of Christians. She left her hometown to attend the University of North Carolina at Greensboro, from which she graduated in 1969. In the early 1970s she wrote as a free-lancer for *Osceola*, a newspaper in Columbia, South Carolina.

Durban worked as a journalist in Atlanta for *The Great Speckled Bird*, an alternative newspaper, and was also contributing editor for the *Atlanta Gazette*, 1974–75. In Atlanta she taped interviews with women in a textile mill community and published them as *Cabbagetown Families* in 1976. Portions of the book were made into a play called *Cabbagetown: Three Women*. She attended the Writers' Workshop at the University of Iowa and was awarded a master of fine arts degree in 1979. She married Frank H. Hunter, a photographer, on June 18, 1983. Their son, Wylie, was born in July 1987, and Durban received a Whiting Writer's Award the same year. She was a founding editor of the magazine *Five Points* and served as its fiction editor, 1996–2001.

Durban has taught creative writing at the University of New York at Geneseo, 1979–80; at Murray State in Kentucky, 1980–81; at Ohio University at Athens, 1981–86; and at Georgia State University, 1986–2001, where she was awarded a National Endowment for the Arts Fellowship in 1998. She is currently Doris Betts Distinguished Professor of Creative Writing at the University of North Carolina at Chapel Hill.

Throughout the early 1980s Durban published short stories in periodicals; her breakthrough came with "This Heat," published in the *Georgia Review* in 1982, and three years later she collected the story and six others in *All Set About with Fever Trees and Other Stories*. The stories are mostly set in the South, and the roots are evident in the attempts to find out who people are, how they got to be that way, and how they manage to go on. In the Faulknerian tradition

Durban tries to communicate the timeless and impressively experiments in storytelling. Several of the short stories look forward to her novels in idea, topic, and technique.

The Laughing Place (1993), her first novel, is a stylistic triumph with its graceful and poetical narrative voice. It is an amusing and depressing story of widowed Annie Vess's return to her native town, where she learns about her father's life and the family secrets. We know her well, as she is also the main character of the last three stories in the short-story collection. The novel is a complexly woven story of a family and a community's past and present. It is a major statement on the southern obsession with the past.

Prejudice is a topic in her second novel, *So Far Back*. Upon its publication in 2000, Durban said, "That book deals with what I see as some fundamental southern attitudes, and I realized as I was writing it that I'm very conversant with them all." *So Far Back* asks questions: Is there any point in trying to understand past injustice now? And to what extent is falsified history a part of our identity? The fact that the past proves *not* to be impervious to change gives the novel its depth. Upon its publication Durban was awarded the Lillian Smith Award for Fiction.

Durban is working on a book of nonfiction, primarily of a biographical nature, of which the sections "The Old King," "Veterans," "Clocks," and "A Southern Story" have already been published. She is also preparing her second collection of short stories, titled *"Soon" and Other Stories*, which will include the much praised stories "Gravity" and "The Jap Room." And Pam Durban has finished several drafts of her third novel, tentatively to be called "The Tree of Forgetfulness."

So Far Back

"Now it is my turn to trace the design, to tell the story and see where it ends, my turn to gather what I know, to take what I've read, what I've heard, what I've breathed in: to breathe it out, to go on with the story and leave a record for those that come after. I read that diary aloud, and when I came to the end, I said, 'The dress is yours, Diana, but what can I do about that now?'" (Louisa Marion in *So Far Back*, 187).

In her novel *So Far Back*, South Carolinian Pam Durban takes us back to the Charleston of 1837, a year of yellow fever, "deadly pestilence," racial unrest, and a cotton-market crash. Past and present are thoroughly intermingled, and the present is finally informed and improved by the past. But the past is also "changed" by what happens in the present. The whole hangs perfectly balanced between then and now, so that every element from the past is repeated or complemented by another in the present.

To help us see a world that far back in perspective, Durban places about half the narrative in the Charleston of 1989, a year of the final sit-ins, hordes of tourists, and Hurricane Hugo. The main characters are black and white women from the same two families, then and now; the focus is on interracial relations in both centuries and on what a blind allegiance to the ruling order can do to us. Pam Durban shows a black seamstress's rebellion and a white slave owner "enslaving" herself to uphold the system. *So Far Back* asks questions about the past: Can the record be set straight and can past injustice be helped? Is there any point in trying to understand it now? Are we willing to set free the true past and accept that the events of 1837 stay with us? And above all, to what extent is received and often *falsified* history a part of our identity?

So Far Back is a southern novel with an emphasis on the importance of remembering and what the loss of memory does to our sense of identity. The radical sense of displacement in the modern South, which seems unburdened by a memory of the past, is convincingly brought to life. The long form of the novel allows Durban, with her legerdemain, to juggle two patterns of time and two layers of meaning and keep them both vibrantly alive at the same time. She does this in the tradition of William Faulkner's *Absalom, Absalom!*, which shows how the past can be manipulated and altered. "The idea is," as fellow writer Mary Hood once put it, "that tragedy attacks the past as well. Imagine a bullet aimed at a photograph album, and it burns a hole through every page. Now that scar is on every page in the memory" (Gretlund 2001, 76). The stereo effect of seeing both past and present, at once—and the fact that the past is *not* impervious to present change—gives *So Far Back* its depth. For the reader there is plenty of "time and space" to cross, and it is the life of generations hinted at which makes the story.

In idea and technique some of Durban's short stories look forward to the novel. In "Notes toward an Understanding of My Father's Novel," collected in *All Set About with Fever Trees*, Durban comes upon a technique that she uses successfully in *So Far Back*. She looks for a way to bring an authentic source of the past into a situation in the present. In the short story she does so in the opening lines: "They say that history repeats itself. My father is history and he certainly does. In his book about the Second World War he is young, he fights in the infantry in the Pacific, comes home and we are born. In this book, which is never finished" (149). The daughter's life becomes layered in time through the constant awareness of her father's words about the past. By comparing her father's recorded thoughts to her own, she discovers patterns of time, place, and meaning. What is so well done is that the narrative is constantly forming in style and structure and always sounding its depth by sinking *lines* to the father's diary. In the dialogue with the past the theme is constantly forming, and so is the place: "The strength of this country, the low country, is that it is always forming. I count on that country, on that strength, that forming and dying and forming again" (170). Durban uses a similar technique in the title story of *All Set About with Fever Trees*, in which she uses a grandmother's letters from Africa to structure the story and to inform us of parallels to a granddaughter's existence. It is a story that leaps forward, bouncing through layers of more than twenty years. Layers of time and space, and patterns of meaning, are usually the materials of the novel.

Durban's first novel, *The Laughing Place* (1993), is an amusing and depressing story of widowed Annie Vess's return to her native small town. Vess is also the main character of three stories in the short-story collection. It is a complex tale of the past in the present in one South Carolina family.

"Keep Talking," a recently published story by Durban, was actually written after her first novel. It appears to be an old-fashioned short story, starting convincingly: "One day I saved a man's life, though I didn't really know him" (9). Then, after only three more pages, we are, as a total surprise, handed an alternative postmodern plot: "I had to know if I could have saved him because I knew I had not tried" (12). It turns out that the man was dead when she got there. Or maybe he was just dying, and hearing being the last sense to go, she told him about "*blackberries, sugar, cream, morning*" (13). And that is the point of the story, the power of words to kill or create. I mention the story because its main idea looks forward to *So Far Back*. Words can form a "net" to hold us a bit as we journey toward death, hence, "keep talking."

Among the six short stories Durban published after *So Far Back*, there is "Rowing to Darien," and like the novel it also has a nineteenth-century main character. If you are like me you are ready to despair once you realize this is historical fiction. The pitfall in writing historical fiction is that, after years of painstaking research in cultural and social history, and great efforts to get costumes, food, language, and manners just right, the material for fiction may easily come to dwarf the fiction. What is gained in historical depth is often lost in immediacy and characterization. *So Far Back* has some of the characteristics of the historical novel, but Durban's characters do not exist to illustrate history, and their emotional development is relevant for any reader at any time.

Durban does not tumble into the history pit. She uses her creative license, and in the manner of Charles Dickens on the French Revolution in *A Tale of Two Cities*, Durban builds on our knowledge of history. Frances Anne Kemble was a British actress and married to Pierce Butler, who owned a plantation in Georgia, and she wrote about her experience there in *Journal of a Residence on a Georgian Plantation in 1838–39*. Durban tells us, in her short story "Rowing to Darien," that Frances Kemble has just been in a situation that brought out the slave owner in her. In spite of all her abolitionist ideals, she was sorely tempted to strike a slave cook with a heavy kitchen tool. She did not, but she wanted to: "And as she thought of the respect that was being withheld from her, kept from her willfully, cunningly, with a great dumb show of humility, she found herself studying the tools that hung on the kitchen house walls— the pokers and the heavy tongs. It seemed that she could feel the weight of each one in her hand, feel it brought down hard to break this unrepentant silence" (27).

When she considered "the sorry-making weight of those tools that hung so close at hand" (27), she saw the Pierce Butler deep in herself and tried to row away from him. A flash impression of acute sensory detail, Mrs. Butler's looking at the kitchen utensils, assaying in her mind their individual heaviness, is one of the great moments in contemporary fiction. And who but a historian cares what those utensils were called at the time? In this short story the layers and patterns in time are obvious. The continuum from present to past is layered by the reader's thinking of antebellum times. Durban shows us that we can try to row away from the Pierce Butler in ourselves, but he will still be there. This lingering and, it seems, inherent prejudice is perhaps the main theme of *So Far Back*.

Some fiction has subtexts of a sociopolitical and perhaps propagandistic nature. In the best of fiction there may be parallel subtexts, and one may well be the author commenting on her own craft, as in *So Far Back*. The subtexts in question are not superimposed but thoroughly integrated in the narrative and are not necessarily noticed when first read. It is exactly that these subtexts are inextricable from the basic plot text that proves their essentiality. When the subtexts of the novel are sensed and the fiction is allowed to flaunt its bivalence, one finds that reading becomes more rewarding.

The social context is always present in *So Far Back*, as Flannery O'Connor said it should be, especially in fiction by a southern writer (O'Connor 1969, 198). It is, after all, the portrait of the racially divided society in Charleston, which early in the nineteenth century had been the largest port with regard to the importation of slaves, that makes the story about the missing seamstress so convincing. As O'Connor maintains in her advice on writing: "You can't cut characters off from their society and say much about them as individuals" (O'Connor 1969, 168). In 1837, when Diana, the slave, threatens to upset the social and racial balance by sewing too well and by planning to buy her freedom, Eliza Seabrook Hilliard's reaction reveals no uncertainty. She has the seamstress flogged and informs her that she could not legally buy her freedom in South Carolina, which technically is untrue as this right was still in the South Carolina Constitution in 1837. But in practice it had become difficult for a slave in Charleston to buy her freedom after the Denmark Vesey conspiracy was revealed in that city in 1822. In response to white fears of slave rebellions a municipal guard of 150 men was established in Charleston in an arsenal called the Citadel. In theory slaves could still be freed in Charleston, according to South Carolina historian Walter Edgar, but each case required an act of the legislature.

Even though the Stono Rebellion took place in 1739, a century earlier, people in Charleston had not forgotten that the site for the largest and bloodiest slave rebellion in American history was just about twenty miles southwest of their city. The rebellion led to permanent changes in South Carolina's slave codes, specified in the Negro Act of 1740. The bloody slave rebellion in Southampton,

Virginia, in 1831, led by Nat Turner, brought the Stono Rebellion and fear back to the Charleston mind and did nothing to improve a slave's chances to buy her freedom—on the contrary. The year 1835 was the last of Andrew Jackson's presidency. In spite of dramatic events such as the removal of the Seminoles and Cherokees beyond the Mississippi (as had been done to Choctaws, Creeks, and Chickasaws earlier in the decade) and in spite of the beginning of a revolution in Texas, Old Hickory's final year in office was a politically calm and a prosperous one for the twenty-four states of the Union. Public land disposal charts indicate that the prosperity of 1835 was not equaled until the year 1910.

In 1835 Americans were able to recollect the hectic years of the Revolution in war romances, and in the South nothing in politics seemed urgent enough to prevent writers from devoting their full energy to their art. Comparatively speaking the South was in a state of changelessness, and for the moment anyway, southerners chose to ignore that the rest of the nation was changing fast. It was as if southern writers ignored the present with its sectional politics, while remembering and recording became a vital act for them in an attempt to come to terms with history. For a short time it was alright to question and even to criticize local attitudes, and it was not yet an imperative that authors should use their art as a vehicle for glorifying or defending Dixie. Although this was also the year that North and South Carolina requested that other states control abolition activities, there was indeed a rare moment in 1835 of internal dialogue in the South; it was a moment when it was still possible to engage in an argument with one's neighbors without being accused of treason.

Today it is clear that in the short period from 1832 to 1836, with the year 1835 as a defining moment, there was a first flowering of southern writing. It was a period of grand achievement in southern art with promises of a great future for southern letters. But then a depression hit cotton planters. The Panic of 1837, caused mainly by President Jackson's order that all payments for public land be in gold or silver, meant that only plantations with large-scale economies based on slave labor could survive. By 1837 John C. Calhoun and other southern politicians were defending the institution of slavery, and the South's self-destructive preoccupation had begun. The westward advance of slavery across the South continued, and the increase in the number of slaves was dramatic from this time until the Civil War. In 1838, when some northern states passed laws to obstruct the Fugitive Slave Act and when the first antislavery party was formed the following year, the pressure on southern writers to become more politically oriented increased dramatically. This was the political and psychological atmosphere at the time when Diana hoped to get a chance to buy her freedom.

Miss Hilliard also has Diana's front teeth pulled—to make her more easily identifiable, it is claimed, but it is really lest anyone should start paying the pretty black woman too much attention (180). Clearly Miss Hilliard feels no obligation to her black "servants" as human beings; *her* moral obligation is to the social system as, she truly believes, God ordered it. She denounces the slave seamstress for upsetting "the order." And for Miss Hilliard this is much more important than a young black woman's suffering in captivity away from her children.

What frightens the slave owner is the potential of Diana's purchase of her own self, with money made from her skill as a seamstress, to be an indicator of the dissolution of all social, racial, and economic distinctions. The final word in the sociopolitical subtext is that the upholding of the social and racial order is considered vital for the existing economic stratification and racial division. Durban's style in *So Far Back* is that of the social satirist, and she satirizes a social order based on race. The main theme, relevant in any age, is what a blind allegiance to the accepted order can do to us, as Durban demonstrates with the story of Eliza Hilliard. Diana, the slave seamstress, is often nowhere to be found, and Diana becomes Miss Hilliard's growing obsession. She orders floggings left and right, at times three a week, to restore Diana to her "proper place" (181). Unlike Frances Kemble Butler, Miss Hilliard knows that the urge to kill and harm had been in her all along (186), and it is manifest in her dealings with Diana. The slave owner devotes all her psychological strength to thoroughly enslaving Diana, and in this way the enslaver herself becomes enslaved by the system.

If there is nobody to recreate a story such as Diana's, the facts in themselves will spark no enthusiastic reaction. It has to be told to really capture the imagination. If it is not told right, the events do not become a story and might as well never have happened, for they will not be remembered. In an almost postmodern way, Pam Durban repeatedly makes it clear that we are reading a story, and she invites the reader to join her in playing with fictional characters and situations. The point is that no matter how accidental and indeterminate the fiction, it quickly becomes obvious that there is a reality under the illusion, but the illusion created is not reality. The story of Diana is full of speculation and invention and there are many stops before it is fully told. What exactly *is* the story that Pam Durban is telling us about Miss Hilliard and Diana?

In her story "Everyday Use" Alice Walker writes about the difficulty of claiming the family "quilts" and producing authentic art. She does this by presenting her own art, the piercing of linguistic and literary intertexts, as quilt making with words. She "pieces" her literary quilts out of all that she has read and heard, and an apparently simple story becomes a profound examination of the life and background of an artist. We are invited to see the parallel between the quilts and her art of fiction. And the quilts are "intertextual" inasmuch as they contain scraps of past lives and embody the family history. In this way Alice Walker brings out a connection between quilt making and writing that increases our reading pleasure.

In *So Far Back*, writing, be it history or fiction, is also like sewing. The function of repeating a story, over and over, has its parallel in the repeated motion of sewing. When line is added to line, stitch to stitch, it becomes routine, and soon the outline of an image appears, and something has been created: an image or a story that can carry us out over the water, away from present life (17). When the novel is in the twentieth century, we are introduced to Louisa Marion's mother, Elizabeth Marion of the Hilliard family, who suffers from Alzheimer's disease. She remembers only one story, which is the story of Mamie's fear of the Cooper River Bridge, and she repeats it whenever she has the opportunity. Mamie Jones used to be her kitchen help. It was the only story that could still carry Louisa's mother away from the present life.

Louisa got involved with a priest, who offered escape from the bourgeois hypocrisy of her family and friends. But then he turned out to be the very essence of everything she hated about the world. To escape the world of perfect respectability, the everyday of the "little way," as Walker Percy called it, Louisa signed up for a bus tour of New England "to see the fall leaves." "To keep from talking [on the bus], she said she was a widow, too, and after that they left her to her knitting.... The pattern was very complicated and she had to keep strict count of the stitches.... Sometimes, if she got distracted and dropped a stitch or lost count, the square came out lopsided and she had to unravel it and start over. That was satisfying, too, in its own way; as though by knitting, then unraveling a square, she was making visible some hidden truth about the world, giving it shape and form" (*So Far Back*, 55–56). And like quilting, knitting is also like writing, and so is sewing.

When Hurricane Hugo hits Charleston, Louisa is finally forced to go to a shelter. As could be expected of a southern stoic, she sets a good example for the people in the shelter by "going through the familiar motions of charity," calmly smiling, and sewing. "She was grateful for it, suddenly, for the way sewing had carried her through her life. When she thought about important times in her life, it was what her hands had been doing she remembered—the movement of needle and thread through cloth, the growth of a design—and when she saw these needlework projects, even now, the weather and light and the feeling of those times came back to her, as though the colors of the times themselves had been stitched into the cloth" (66).

After Louisa has comforted an African American mother and her children, there is a particularly powerful gust of wind, and "Louisa folded up her sewing and tucked it into her portmanteau, got out her sketchbook and charcoal. The gritty sweep of pencil over paper was comforting, and the lines piled up faster on the blank page than the tiny stitches had filled the pillow top. That was comforting, too" (67). So sketching is like knitting, like sewing, and like writing.

In a perfectly postmodern scene, Louisa reads her ancestor's diary and imagines it to be Eliza Hilliard's final act, to sew her own name into the hem of the later-renowned baby gown, even though the art of the gown mainly belonged to Diana, the slave seamstress and possibly one of Mamie's ancestors.

And in Louisa's speculations about Eliza's final moments, the main themes of the novel—creative ability and racial injustice—come together.

Eliza Hilliard "sits in the chair near the window in her room, the gown across her lap, and studies its knots and vines for clues to Diana's whereabouts. Because 'property' cannot decide to remove itself from you, or else it is no longer property. And if it is not property, what is it? . . . Ungrateful, traitorous, disloyal wretch," she thinks. Then, "to quiet herself, she takes out needle and thread and begins to sew that series of careful stitches that form letters into words and words into claims: *Property of Eliza Hilliard. Done by her hand, June 1844.* Stitch by stitch, she feels herself grow calm, as though something that had been destroyed was being rebuilt and restored before her eyes. When it is done, it looks true" (209–10). Louisa imagines that her ancestor revenges herself on Diana, her lost "property," by laying claim to the baby gown as her own artwork. She feels justified in her fraudulent act because by being the better seamstress Diana has upset what Eliza Hilliard considered a divine order based on white supremacy in all areas of life and achievement.

The baby gown is the leitmotif of the novel, and it is a detailed symbol of the antebellum past *and* the racial situation of today:

> Sometimes, it was Eliza Hilliard's baby gown that Mamie ironed. Her mother [Louisa] was always giving talks about their seamstress ancestor [Eliza Hilliard], and before every talk, Mamie washed and starched the gown by hand. . . . [Louisa] could look at it every day and notice something new about it; it was as dense as a tapestry with needlework. One time, it would be the French knots that dotted the bodice and sprinkled down the skirt and hem that she noticed; the next time she saw it, the openwork around the hem would draw her eye; another time, it would be the vines or the leaves with their smooth tight edges. Or she would stand back and take it all in, the way the designs poured down the dress and swirled around the hem. (90–91)

When Louisa reads Eliza Hilliard's diary, the ghost of Diana begins to let her presence be felt. She has "come for her things" (91). She has come as an African American artist of the past to claim recognition in the present for her contribution to past achievement. Diana is like the wind set free to swirl and wash through the Hilliard House in old Charleston. Her rebellion, if known, would upset the tourist's version of the past, fed to the visitors to Charleston by, among others, Louisa's goddaughter, appropriately named Ann Simmons Culp, who is also guilty of editing her version of the past.

Pam Durban raises the question whether we are all tourists in a falsified past. In 1993, just one year after Louisa's death, Ann Simmons Culp guides tours through the Hilliard House. She is guilty of softening and blurring historical facts, for that is what tourists come to Charleston for, Ann thinks, and she shows replicas as if they were originals. And in spite of Louisa's and Evelyn Pope's

(Mamie's granddaughter) efforts to give Diana the credit she deserves for her art, Ann happily continues, in a parodied Charleston accent, with the traditional falsification of the past: "If you visit the Charleston Museum during your stay in our city, you will also see the handiwork of . . . Eliza Hilliard, Louisa's ancestor, who embroidered an exquisite baby gown that is part of the permanent textile collection there" (244–45). The card attached to the pedestal in the museum reads, "Baby Gown sewed by Eliza Hilliard, 1844. Linen, embroidery, and drawn-thread work" (230–31). It is this type of received and falsified history that becomes a part of our identity.

In an interview with me Pam Durban addressed the issue of falsifying the past:

> Maybe it is just a function of that Southern mythologizing, that denial, that attempt to make the past into something better than it was. . . . It's like the perfumed handkerchief held to your face as you walked the smelly streets of Charleston. . . . We falsify it [the past] by only allowing so little of it in. Of course it can't be changed; it can't be healed by apologies or anything else. The only thing that can happen now is that you can look at it and acknowledge that you see it more clearly. And the evidence is there, if you will look at it, the imbalance of it, and the evidence of the injustice of it. But we only see one side of the story as long as we only *have* that one side of it and don't want the reality of the other. We only tell the "white" side of it. . . . Part of my research for *So Far Back* was to go on every one of those house tours. How is it that they never once mention slaves? It was like those houses grew up out of the ground like flowers and only white people lived there. . . . Now I realize that all these things we claim as our own, all these walls in Charleston, the beautiful ironwork, the houses, the gates, the bricks of the streets, and all of that, which are symbols of *our* way of life once, do not belong to us at all. (Gretlund 2006, 113–14)

It would have been possible, of course, to see the gown as a glorious product of interracial collaboration in the past, as the gown is a result of buying the right quality cloth and thread, in the right colors, drawing up or buying the right pattern, cutting the cloth to exact measure, combined with the craftsmanship of the decorative embroidery. In other words the gown is the result of one very practical woman and a brilliantly artistic woman working toward the same goal. The same collaboration is behind much other antebellum achievement, for example, the architecture and the building of the famed nineteenth-century structures in Charleston and all over the Old South. But the contribution by black southerners is often ignored or hidden. Interestingly enough Pam Durban did see a gown on a pedestal in the Charleston Museum, but when she went back later, it was gone. She made an appointment with the textile archivist, who looked at all the garments they had, but was unable to locate the gown or explain its absence, which may, of course, have been due to accidental and perfectly mundane events (Gretlund 2006, 114).

In the novel Louisa had not wanted to hand the story on—unchanged, but it is almost impossible to set the record straight. She considers her options after she has deduced the truth from Eliza Hilliard's diary: "To tell another story might spoil the past, and if you spoiled the past, you'd spoil the present, too, because the past led to the present and made it true" (231). On the other hand, to knowingly falsify the past would therefore also be to falsify the present, as if it did not matter. The novel *is* the baby gown, just as the Hilliard christening gown is the past in the present. As if it were the gown, Pam Durban has washed, starched, and ironed the past, as if time were "a cloth and our lives flying in and out like needle and thread, leaving a design for others to trace and know" (186–87). Like the gown the story has been put aside and forgotten in the turmoil called "progress." But here it is in the Lowcountry Room of the Charleston Museum, all lit up on a pedestal, "one sleeve raised in a gesture of greeting or good-bye, the rest spread out behind, as if an invisible wearer were running or flying" (230). This truly Faulknerian image shows a past vibrantly alive, as if the gown, the artifact itself, were time fleeting. Time "yellowed and stained" to be sure, just as Eliza Hilliard's and Diana's, Elizabeth Marion's and Mamie Jones's, Louisa Marion's and Evelyn Pope's intertwined lives were not without "yellowed" passages and "stains" both in racial and gender relations. But like the gown, life is also "running with leaves, flowers, vines, an airy scribbling of thread." In this way Durban's "scribbling," in black on white paper, about the white and black lives makes it clear that even in the worst time for human relations in South Carolina, beauty was also created.

Life is like a gown, or life is like a narrative that winds around like curlicued decorative stitches—and writing is like sewing. The ideal for writing, sewing, and living is the same: every part should touch and influence every other part (259). There may be some delightful "featherstitches" and some "backstitches punctuated with French knots," all cascading down the length of the gown to the hem. But even when we get to the end of the novel, or to the end of life, or the bottom of the hem, art and beauty do not fail us, for the hem is held to the gown by "a fine web of openwork stitches and strewn with leaf shapes stiffened with precise and exquisite whip stitch" (230). The openwork is "bound into delicate sheaves, and another vine is worked around the hem in exceedingly delicate stem stitch" (169). These are Eliza Hilliard's words of August 1, 1837, used in her private musing, seventeen years after John Keats had published his immortal lines "'Beauty is truth, truth beauty,'—that is all / Ye know on earth, and all ye need to know" in his often discussed argument in "Ode on a Grecian Urn" (ll. 49–50). Is it enough today to observe the beauty of the gown? Will the beauty eventually reveal the truth about its history? And will we want to know the truth?

Miss Hilliard's general attitude had always been that "it was necessary—it was *essential*—that everyone keep to their rightful places in life, for on this fulcrum the entire weight of their civilization balanced" (201). Her problem is that she, and the upper-class society she belongs to, actually believes that her race, if tried, would prove the best at anything. She has absolutely no doubt about the God-given natural superiority of white people in all areas and at any time. She has to believe this if her everyday world in the Charleston refined society of the 1830s is to make any sense at all. This is why she sees herself in a competition with Diana in the art of sewing. But the beauty of Diana's craftsmanship makes her owner remove the gauze that usually veils the image of herself. By August 1837 Miss Hilliard is looking at Diana's craftsmanship in detail and actually comes to question her own ideas about her slaves and the whole system: "Where is it in the African that such a gift for beauty resides? . . . Now she has created this. How came this gift into the barbarous and unlettered soul? . . . In order for the flower to bloom, must not the seed already reside in the ground of the immortal soul?" The question troubles her rest (169–70).

It is Louisa's musings on past and present, in the year 1990, which lead to the positive racial moment in the novel—that is, when she tells Evelyn Pope that her "ancestor," Diana, did the fine sewing on the famous gown. They fail in their efforts to change the official story; the museum wants proof. But this is not of any significance compared to the fact that the two women overcome their racial prejudice and recognize each other as human beings. Evelyn, who has had strong feelings for years about the Hilliard-Marions' exploitation of her family, comes to realize that "it was easy to talk about *the white people this, the white people that* until one of them you'd known for a long time was crying on your shoulder and it was just the two of you sitting there on the piazza. It wasn't so easy or so simple then, to walk away when it was another human being, not an idea, that you'd turned your back on" (237). And she does attend Louisa's funeral.

Ann Culp, the tourist guide and spokesperson for the youngest generation, usually imagines Eliza Hilliard squatting in front of the hearth feeding her own fire, but she knows it did not happen: "The blacks did this work: slaves first, servants later. *Servants* is what they're [the guides] encouraged to call the Negroes of that time; it sounds less harsh than *slaves*. But lately . . . she can't reel off that story" of Miss Hilliard feeding her fire; "it sticks in her throat." Ann Culp admits to herself that "it's getting harder and harder to keep them apart, the black story and the white one; they pull toward each other, merge and tangle" (254).

In spite of its presentation of obvious injustice, past and present, *So Far Back* finally offers no ethical condemnation: "Whatever had been happening since time was not good and it wasn't evil; it simply was, and always had been" (7). Louisa's opinion at the beginning of the novel was also "that discrimination was wrong, but the past was the past. It was over, done and finished; you couldn't change it any more than you could change human nature, the habits of centuries, or the facts of native ability and intelligence" (22). "South Carolina had been South Carolina since time was," and Louisa titles her painting of a winter marsh at daybreak *Time Was* (41). What she learns from Diana's fate and Eliza Hilliard's diary is that time not only was, but time *is*. She realizes that injustice is not just something historic. There were the lynchings of her grandfather's time, August 1939, and it is ongoing: "Integration hadn't worked. The schools were a shambles and more segregated than ever: When black children arrived, the white children left. The housing projects were swamped with drugs. Given the choice, the races preferred to live separately" (22).

Ernest J. Gaines's question from the short story "Just Like a Tree," printed at the beginning of *So Far Back*, gave the novel its name and was perhaps what inspired Pam Durban to write it. Gaines's story quotes the spiritual "I Shall Not Be Moved" in its title, but the story consists of voices on Aunt Fe's removal to a distant cabin and her death there. In the section named for "Anne-Marie Duvall," the daughter of the plantation family who has moved Aunt Fe, the ancient nanny, to a cabin that is far back from the big house where she has spent her whole life, knows that. Aunt Fe has cooked for her father and nursed her when her mother died. Her brother will not go, so the girl drives and then walks alone through a bad rain storm to bring Aunt Fe a gift on her birthday. She does it because she knows that her father, her grandfather, and her great-grandfather would have done so. It is Anne-Marie Duvall who asks the question that takes on a symbolic meaning: "Why? God, why does she have to live so far back? . . . The answer to that is as hard for me as is the answer to everything else. It was ordained before I—before father—was born—that she should live back there. So why should I try to understand it now?" (Gaines 1968, 240). Durban's answer to Gaines's question—"why should I try to understand it now?"—is that the injustice is not merely far back, as if it were ordained, it is still with us and that is why we should still try to understand it.

Even in the present atmosphere of the giant private and public nursing home for history called Charleston, the record of past achievement may still be set straight and Diana's reputation can still be rescued, if only we can "bring what is distant close and make the invisible vivid" (187). And this is the power of words, according to Durban: "You ask what good were those words then? What good are they now? What do they change? Nothing, of course, but . . . we join words together to name what can be known, and for what cannot be known, we also find words and house things there until they come to sound like the truths we need in order to go on living the lives we've built around them" (188–89).

We cannot do anything to the past, as Eudora Welty pointed out in *The Optimist's Daughter*. The past is in a sense impervious to change, but *the memory* of it is in words and is subjective. A living memory is by definition unstable and inconclusive. It should not be forced to fit into an already selected pattern. There must be room for detachment. Louisa is able to be honest about the past and no longer allows the Hilliard past to devour her present. What she has learned through the diary is that the past can be revived, rediscovered, and repossessed. She stops her willful concentration on "ideal" moments from the past and admits other, certainly less ideal, circumstances of the past into her consciousness and thereby frees herself from the tyranny of the family past. What Louisa finally realizes is the subjectivity of her memory of the past, and in doing so, the subjectivity of her experience of the present. She gains a new sense of the continuity of self, for human experience is shaped by a confluence of *time was* with *time is*. So we can go back to the present and put the past of Eliza and Diana into words, "and it is enough for any life, is it not," asks Durban, "to keep promises to one another, to remember and to be remembered, to be remade in the stories of others, to live in their words?" (204–5).

In the Charleston Museum at the Lowcountry exhibit, Louisa Hilliard Marion says to Evelyn Pope, "I've come to the conclusion that Eliza Hilliard might have done everyday sewing on that dress, but most of the sewing, the fine sewing at least, was done by one of her slaves, a woman named Diana, who ran away and disappeared around 1842. Could she have been related to you?" (232). Louisa does not, after all, pronounce an open ethical judgment and a rejection of her ancestor, as it would be out of character, but for Evelyn what is offered is enough and an unexpected gift. Her joy of repossession is unmistakable. Evelyn knows Louisa did not have to tell her, "She didn't have to go to the trouble of taking me there and telling me that. . . . She could have kept it to herself all the rest of her born days. Her mother wouldn't have bothered, believe you me. Things do change, Son" (233).

Works Cited and Consulted

Durban, Pam. "A Southern Story." *American Studies in Scandinavia* 38 (2006): 95–103.
———. "Keep Talking." *Carolina Quarterly* 54, no. 3 (2002): 9–14.
———. "Rowing to Darien." *Five Points* 6, no. 3 (2002): 17–29.
———. *So Far Back*. New York: USA Picador, 2000.
———. *The Laughing Place*. New York: Charles Scribner's Sons, 1993.
———. *All Set About with Fever Trees and Other Stories*. Boston: David R. Godine, 1985.
Edgar, Walter. *South Carolina: A History*. Columbia: University of South Carolina Press, 1998.
Faulkner, William. *Absalom, Absalom!* 1936. Reprint, New York: Random House, 1964.
Gaines, Ernest J. "Just Like a Tree." *Bloodline*. New York: Dial Press, 1968. 221–49.
Gibbons, Kaye. *On the Occasion of My Last Afternoon*. New York: G. P. Putnam's Sons, 1998.
Gretlund, Jan Nordby. "Durban, Pam Rosa." *South Carolina Encyclopedia*. Ed. Walter Edgar. Columbia: University of South Carolina Press, 2006. 278.
———. "Lines Out across the Gap: An Interview with Pam Durban." *American Studies in Scandinavia* 38, no. 2 (2006): 104–9.
———. "Time *Is*: Pam Durban." *South Carolina Review* 39 (2006): 114–21.

———. "Fiction Is Like Fire: An Interview with Mary Hood." *American Studies in Scandinavia* 33, no. 2 (2001): 69–82.
Humphreys, Josephine. *Nowhere Else on Earth*. New York: Viking, 2000.
Kemble, Frances Anne. *Journal of a Residence on a Georgian Plantation in 1838–39*. 1863. Reprint, Athens: University of Georgia Press, 1984.
O'Connor, Flannery. *Mystery and Manners: Occasional Prose*. New York: Farrar, Straus and Giroux, 1969.
Percy, Walker. *The Moviegoer*. New York: Alfred A. Knopf, 1961.
Reid, Cheryl. "Making Fictions: An Interview with Pam Durban." *Carolina Quarterly* 52 (2000): 61–77.
Smith, Mark M., ed. *Stono: Documenting and Interpreting a Southern Slave Revolt*. Columbia: University of South Carolina Press, 2005.
Walker, Alice. "Everyday Use." *In Love and Trouble*. New York: Harcourt Brace Jovanovich, 1973. 47–59.
Welty, Eudora. *The Optimist's Daughter*. New York: Random House, 1972.

Percival Everett & *Erasure*

TARA POWELL

A Biographical Sketch

Percival Everett is among South Carolina's most acclaimed literary sons. The author of seventeen novels, three collections of short stories, two books of poetry, and a children's book, Everett is a writer whose style and interests continue to evolve in ways that resist categorization. Because he has made his adult life outside of the South and written rarely and indirectly about the region where he grew up, he is not always thought of as a South Carolina writer. Yet in his best-known novel, *Erasure* (2001), and many of his other works, his take on American life and individual identity, including issues of race, class, and region, his sense of humor, and his satirical approach to intellectual labor and politics, all point to a lively interaction with, if not adherence to, the imaginative landscape of the region where he spent his youth. Indeed, one of the central issues of *Erasure* is whether or not a person may choose his or her regional or racial identity or if such choices are finally "erased" by the expectations and prejudices of the world at large.

Everett was born in 1956 at Fort Gordon, Georgia, to Percival Leonard and Dorothy (Stinson) Everett. The Everett family moved later to Columbia, South Carolina, where Percival spent his childhood and graduated from A. C. Flora High School. His maternal grandfather was a farmer, but Everett grew up for the most part in a middle-class family of doctors and dentists that resembles the experience of the protagonist of *Erasure*. Though known as a private man who rarely talks about his family or provides reminiscences of Columbia, Everett says he has "pleasant memories of growing up in Columbia," riding his bicycle over to the river on the edge of the city as a boy, reading first the books of his father's that filled the Everett home, and, later, sneaking into the stacks of the state university library to explore and read for hours (Starr 2002, E1). These solitary habits followed Everett to adulthood, and he tells an interviewer, "My experience with the world is pretty much solitary. I'd much prefer to be with a horse than a pack of people. . . . It's how I understand the world" (Stewart 2007, 316–17).

Everett headed south to the University of Miami for college, where he studied philosophy and biochemistry, earning money by playing blues and jazz guitar in local clubs, and he received a bachelor's degree in philosophy in 1977. As part of his studies in philosophy, Everett became interested in the relationship between meaning and language, especially in the work of Ludwig Wittgenstein, whom he says "seduced me completely" (Newton 1999). It was also as part of his studies at Miami that Everett began the exercise of writing hypothetical dialogues between philosophers that arguably prefigured his interest in creative writing.

On a cross-country road trip in his early twenties, Everett fell in love with the people and open landscapes of the American West and has found ways to spend his life there almost ever since he left Florida to start graduate work in philosophy at the University of Oregon in 1978. He supported himself then and occasionally afterward by working on ranches. "Really I am a Westerner, and that's where I've wanted to be for a long time," he says (Starr 2002, E1). "I keep sliding to the West. Maybe next it's into the ocean" (Starr 1994, 1F). Everett's growing affection for the West, his interest in language, and the increasingly inadequate-seeming exercise of imagining dialogues came together to form a path toward a different way to explore his ideas about communication. Since the writing programs he decided to apply to required writing samples, Everett wrote his first short story to send in with his applications. After his graduation from Brown University in 1982 with a master's degree in fiction, his first novel, *Suder* (1983), was accepted for publication by Viking. The story of a baseball player for the Seattle Mariners from North Carolina whose slump leads him to pursue an entirely different life, *Suder* was published to good reviews, as was Everett's second novel, *Walk Me to the Distance* (1985), which inspired a movie for NBC called *Follow Your Heart* (1990).

These books launched a literary career that has varied widely in style and approach but has consistently drawn acclaim from reviewers for Everett's humor, finely drawn characters, unusual approaches to craft and wordplay, and, especially, his exploration of contemporary American identity through all the modes in which he writes. He received a literature award from the American Academy of Arts and Letters in 2003. His seventeen novels to date range from "westerns" such as *God's Country* (1994), *Watershed* (2003), and *Wounded* (2005), which won him the PEN USA 2006 Literary Award, to his science fiction novel *Zulus* (1990), which received the New American Writing Award, to his book-length academic satire called *Glyph* (1999), which is told from the point of view of a genius toddler. Everett has also retold Greek myths in *For Her Dark Skin* (1990) and *Frenzy* (1996) and written realistic contemporary fictions such as *Cutting Lisa* (1986) and *The Water Cure* (2007). And what to do with a novel such as *American Desert* (2004), which features a man with a severed head who unexpectedly comes back to life at his own funeral? *Erasure* does not contain any strategies that are that surreal, but is an essentially realistic satire on, among other things, American publishing, and it is told through a combination of traditional first-person narration and an unusual collection of various kinds of documents written, read, or imagined by the narrator. *Erasure* received the Hurston/Wright Legacy Award in 2002. The author also, uncharacteristically, agreed to do a book tour to help publicize the novel.

Since 1999 Everett has served as Distinguished Professor of English at the University of Southern California, where he teaches courses in literature, theory, and fiction writing. He currently makes his home in Los Angeles with his wife, writer Danzy Senna, and their two sons, Henry and Miles. In addition to teaching and writing, Everett's interests and accomplishments include training mules and horses, playing jazz guitar and piano, abstract oil painting, woodworking, insect collecting, bird watching, and fly fishing.

Everett has commented that he does not think of himself as a southern "expatriate" writer and that he "slid" westward rather than leaving the South for any particular reason (Starr 1994, 1F), but when he talks about his sense of home in his 2001 essay "Why I'm from Texas," he concludes that despite pleasant memories of growing up in the South, there are things about the Carolinas that keep him from feeling at home there. His fiction and other public commentary also suggest an ongoing sense of both investment in and displacement from the politics and culture of the region where he came of age. Earlier in his career Everett's name was at one time more recognizable in his home state for his embroilment in the longstanding controversy over the place of the Confederate battle flag in public life than for his fiction. Speaking at an awards ceremony held at the South Carolina state legislature in 1989, Everett objected to the presence of the flag in the room, setting off a firestorm of local controversy that has been credited by some as an important catalyst in the movement that eventually saw the flag's removal from the top of the state house in July 2000. One of Everett's best-known short stories, "The Appropriation of Cultures," dealing with the contested symbolism of the flag in the author's home state and across the South, appeared in 1996 in the midst of the ongoing controversy and was later collected in *Damned if I Do* (2004). Everett also collaborated on a satiric novel with James Kincaid called *A History of the African-American People (Proposed) by Strom Thurmond, as told to Percival Everett and James Kincaid* (2004), and a number of his "western" novels, throughout his career, have featured displaced protagonists for whom the South is a site of remembered trauma, including Craig Suder in *Suder* and Robert Hawks in *Watershed*. His most recent novel, *I Am Not Sidney Poitier* (2009), is set in the Deep South and features another such character.

Though the South is neither the primary site nor subject of Everett's fiction, it and its claim on him are topics to which he returns. Everett commented in an early interview, "There is a big chunk of me that won't let go. In a way, my life, my experiences in South Carolina, inform my vision, the way I think. I can't get away from that, and I don't want to reject it" (Starr 1988, 1A). On the other hand, twelve years and a big controversy later, he wrote that he refuses to "discuss South Carolina and the confederate flag anymore because [he's] sick of it" (62). William Ramsey and other close readers of Everett's fiction have argued that as a "contemporary black southerner who feels willfully free of and unbound to southern place and history" (128), his work foresees the future of the South, and that "his often stated love of the West is actually an outgrowth of a desire conditioned in the South for freedom from oppression" (131). Ramsey observes that one of the things that holds Everett's disparate body of work together is an evolving sense of limitations on the search for that freedom in America, even in the "open" western landscape.

Erasure

Everett told interviewer Ben Ehrenreich that *Erasure* was actually written by his pet crow Jim, who sat on his shoulder while he was working on the novel and subsequently flew away, never to return. In an essay called "Signing to the Blind," which appeared ten years before *Erasure*, Everett argued that black people "are at the economic mercy of a [literary] market which seeks to affirm its beliefs about African-Americans" (1991, 10), and that even when black writers seek to write in modes other than the essentially political, "it is a reaction to the position in which we and our works have been placed" (11). More recently, commenting on his decision to write about the black middle class, he stated, "I grew up where the Civil War started, in South Carolina, and I have never in my life heard someone say, 'Where fo' you be going?'" (49). Perhaps, then, although Everett's novels, stories, and poems are rarely set in the South, and even then more often a remembered South, and although they comment directly on race in America only intermittently, one might contend that old Jim Crow is always looking over this South Carolina native's shoulder as an author, even when he asserts that he is tired of talking about southernness and his tone is only half-joking when he writes, "I am from Texas. I live in California" (63).

Erasure begins with a dedication to the author's first wife, historian Francesca Rochberg, and an epigraph from Mark Twain's round-the-world travelogue *Following the Equator* (1897): "I could never tell a lie that anybody would doubt, nor a truth that anybody would believe." As a frame for the text that follows, these two introductions to the body of the novel suggest from the start a relationship to the author's literary, regional, and personal history and at the same time caution against taking that implied relationship too literally or too seriously. Readers quickly discover the need for caution, as the fictional protagonist Everett introduces in the pages that follow bears a remarkable physical, circumstantial, and intellectual resemblance to the author and yet is also not him. Both the protagonist and Everett are telling intertwined truths and fictions, and one of the novel's challenges is to distinguish the novel's point of view from the main character's. Everett is writing a novel about a novelist who is writing a journal, and that journal is the novel in front of the reader. Thelonious Ellison, "Monk" to his friends, tells the unknown future reader of his journal that he is an experimental novelist and university teacher who has put a lot of emotional distance, not to mention actual mileage, between his current career in California and his east coast upbringing in a middle-class family of literal-minded doctors. The trace of their influence is his suspicion of his intellectual version of labor: he would rather be known as a woodworker than a writer—and rather be out fly fishing by himself than at a writers' conference. Working with wood he is occasionally ashamed to find himself unable to keep from thinking of Michel Foucault's theories about language use and meaning. "To watch shavings fall away from a fine piece of ash wood and have such thoughts," he sighs. "I could feel my sister watching me" (133).

More interested professionally in Greek myths, philosophy, and protecting his private writing time than in the expectations of the mainstream publishing world or the cult of celebrity that surrounds it, Monk is having trouble selling his latest book despite an impressive curriculum vita. Reviewers have said that Monk's creative work is well written, but they devalue it because it does not have anything to do with what they think of as "the" black experience since, as he reveals, he went to Harvard, cannot dance, "did not grow up in any inner city or the rural South" (1), and does not want to write about things he did not experience and does not understand. Monk writes in his journal that a "book agent told me that I could sell many books if I'd forget about writing retellings of Euripides and French poststructuralists and settled down to write the true, gritty real stories of black life. I told him that I was living a *black* life, far blacker than he could ever know, that I had lived one, that I would be living one" (2). Monk's own literary agent reports back to him, "The line is, you're not black enough" (43), and his sister tells him, "I just wish you'd write something I could read" (7). The longtime family housekeeper Lorraine has barely spoken to him since she discovered he uses curse words in his books, and, to pour salt into the wound, everywhere Monk turns, people are reading and admiring Juanita Mae Jenkins's new bestseller, *We's Lives in da Ghetto*, a novel in dialect about violence and prostitution in the inner city inspired by the memories of its middle-class author's weekend trip to Harlem, when she was twelve. It is a novel that Monk believes is not only fraudulent in its use of stereotypes to depict black Americans, basically a latter-day minstrel show, but also, and a far worse sin to Monk's way of thinking, badly written.

The public judges Monk's writing by its adherence to a certain, very commercial version of "black life," and he has a problem both with that standard of literary merit and that version of blackness, which is one he has never experienced and to which he cannot relate. A review of Jenkins's novel gushes, "One can actually hear the voices of her people as they make their way through the experience which is and can only be Black America," but Monk is living evidence that "Black America" has other faces than the ones in *We's Lives in da*

Ghetto. The one time Monk got to meet his mother's blue collar family, he stood awkwardly among farmers and factory workers with his siblings "like frozen carrots" (152) until they were allowed to escape the visit. In the present time of *Erasure*, Monk's rejection of the literary stereotypes of blackness becomes obvious again in a painful exchange Monk has with one of his sister Lisa's patients. He inadvertently talks to the patient as if she were right out of Jenkins's novel, only to discover that she is intelligent and not at all what he expected, which embarrasses him but also bears out his sense that not only he but even people living the urban experience are victimized by the way the racist stereotypes in fiction like Jenkins's erases their individual identities, repackaging their lives into something more commercially viable. Even by the questionable artistic standard of authenticity the reviewer sets up, Jenkins, the publishing world, and Hollywood seem to be selling consumers extremely inadequate goods.

Monk, living inside visibly black skin, comes from a family of physicians that serve an urban, mostly black community. His name is a combination of two well-known late black artists, musician Thelonious Monk and writer Ralph Ellison, which suggests the reality of his indebtedness to black American history and culture. Yet Monk does not recognize the version of black life that Jenkins is selling and the reviewers and the reading public are fawning over. "The hard, *gritty* truth of the matter," he writes, "is that I hardly ever think about race" (2). Or at least he would not if it did not keep getting thrown in his face, often by well-meaning people who believe the stereotypes of *We's Lives in da Ghetto* but not the truths of Monk's own middle-class life as an intellectual—truths that are rendered invisible to most people under the duress of their own obfuscating expectations.

Fittingly, Monk was raised on a border, too, growing up in a middle-class black family in Washington, D.C., and Annapolis. Scattered through his journal are memories of failed social encounters in which he could not manage to be "black enough." He got beat up for talking about Hegel and was ostracized for saying "Egads!" on the basketball court. He fails again and again to fit in at school, to speak in dialect among friends, to impress women, to write commercially viable fiction, or even to be comfortable at home. He may be his father's golden boy, but the rest of the family just does not understand him or his interests. The memories Monk records in his journal demonstrate his longing to "fit in." Yet the intellectual life he has chosen and his beliefs about race keep him from being accepted by his family, as well as the larger world. He has reached a point were he does not want to think, write, or even see race at all. Of his one realistic novel, in which a young man of a mixed-race background responds to his family's experience of racism, Monk says, contemplating its relative success, "I hated writing the novel. I hated reading the novel. I hated thinking about the novel" (61).

In the midst of the growing popularity of *We's Lives in da Ghetto* and his mounting frustration with the difficulty of finding a publisher for his own writing, Monk heads east for a visit with his family that coincides with a professional meeting. He tweaks the noses of the other academics at the conference by making a presentation spoofing Roland Barthes's *S/Z* (1970), a lengthy work of literary criticism that lays out a variety of abstract strategies to explore closely the prose of a short story by Honoré de Balzac after beginning with the premise that the discovery of authorial intention is not a good strategy and that creative work exists apart from its author's identity and experiences. This essay appeared separately in *Callaloo* as a short story by Everett called "F/V: Placing the Experimental Novel," several years prior to the publication of *Erasure*, and was followed by an explanatory note. Everett asserted that what presenting the critical essay in the guise of fiction shows is that "the essential thing is that no matter how you tell it, it is a story, always a story, even if nothing happens, even if the action is somehow anti-actions, even if in the re-telling of it, all that is described is what the author doesn't do" (22). By calling into question the boundaries between modes of writing and suggesting that Barthes's famous critical project is less about Balzac's text than Barthes's own creative vision, Monk not only insults and alienates his colleagues at the conference, who do not appreciate the fun of the intellectual wordplay at what they see as being at their reluctant expense, but also lays the groundwork for his realization later in *Erasure:* that words and who hears them matter, that they matter more than who says them or any reason that he may have had for the saying of them, and that, because of this, documents can take on lives of their own, irrespective of any individual author's intentions.

Through Monk's journal, the reader encounters a protagonist who is isolated through a combination of circumstance and preference from all the communities of which he might seem on first examination to be a part: his family, colleagues, industry, race, and class. It is in that frame of mind that he faces the crisis of his sister's death and the subsequent disintegration of his family and career. On the heels of Lisa's murder, Monk discovers that his mother is succumbing to Alzheimer's, that elderly Lorraine has no savings and no place to go when her employer, his mother, dies, and that his older brother Bill in Arizona has recently revealed his homosexuality to his wife, is in the process of losing his children, savings, and medical practice, and will be of no financial or emotional help to Monk in taking care of their mother and Lorraine. Suddenly the impractical, outsider son, the dreamer who sees Foucault in wood shavings, is the only one left to hold it all together. Taking a leave of absence from his ivory tower job in California, Monk moves east to care for his mother and Lorraine and to settle Lisa's estate. He quickly runs out of money once he gets there, not to mention mental health reserves, having had to set aside his solitary pastimes of fishing and woodworking. In his journal he records conversations with his mother, brother, and agent, his version of encounters that contribute to his growing sense of losing everything he has except his art, memories of the fishing and woodworking he is no longer able to enjoy, and ideas for novels and stories that he does not ever seem to find the time or emotional energy to write.

In that frame of mind and still unable to sell his latest manuscript, Jenkins's novel and its success become the focus of Monk's rage, and in his journal even the story ideas and snippets of possible new creative projects become more and more about his struggle to protect the integrity of his art from the demands of an editorial establishment and as a readership that would willfully limit Monk's possibilities as an artist because of his race. Working this out for himself takes a number of forms in his journal, including meditations on the relationship between crafting wood and words, thinking about the importance of method and patience and even luck in the art of fishing, and, especially, imagined conversations about art and its value between a selection of early- to mid-twentieth-century modernist visual artists, especially European expressionists, a variety of other intellectuals, and several prominent Nazis. For example, in one exchange Monk imagines Ernst Kirchner, a German painter driven to suicide by the Nazi destruction of his life's work, telling Max Klinger, an older German painter who died in 1920, "I'm glad, no proud that those brown shirts are burning my paintings. . . . Imagine how I would feel if monsters like that tolerated my work" (60). What this montage of meditations has in common is that, in all of them, the artist, woodworker, or fisherman seeks answers to the problems before him in his craft itself, not in the outside world's expectations or approval.

After a particularly trying day that concludes with his discovering that Juanita Mae Jenkins's ubiquitous face is now plastered also on the cover of *Time Magazine*, Monk stares at her, and remembering passages of *Native Son*, *The Color Purple*, and *Amos 'n' Andy*, he has a vision: "My hands began to shake, the world opening around me, tree roots trembling on the ground outside, people in the street shouting *dint, ax, fo, screet* and *fahvre!* and I was screaming inside, complaining that I didn't sound like that, that my mother didn't sound like that, that my father didn't sound like that" (61–62). When he opens his mouth to speak in his vision, Monk finds himself saying, "Why fo you be axin?" Overwhelmed with the need to escape that version of himself, the one being imposed on him as an artist and black American by Jenkins and others, Monk seeks a way through art to exert control over a world that seems out of control. His solution is to write a satiric retelling of Richard Wright's *Native Son* that parodies Jenkins's narrative strategies, revealing the ridiculousness and offensiveness of her portrayal of black life in America, and of his life, as well as implying some of the limitations of Wright's version.

The resulting manuscript, which Monk first titles "My Pafology" and later retitles simply "Fuck," features a disaffected young black protagonist named Van Go Jenkins coming of age and turning inevitably to crime in the inner city. Drawing on every cliché about race and poverty that Monk can think of, the short novel in dialect that he produces is fast-paced, wholly predictable, and yet very funny in its efforts to go far enough to offend even Jenkins's most dedicated fans. Monk, in fact, includes the full text of the faux novel in his journal, and it makes up fifty of the most entertaining pages of *Erasure*. Van is a fatherless high school dropout who already has "fo' babies," whom he has named Aspireene, Tylenola, Dexetrina, and Rexall, by four women, and he dreams of having two dozen more so that he can name them alphabetically. He measures his manhood in sex and violence, and in the course of the short novel he avoids several ham-handed attempts by others to help him improve his lot before going on an apparently purposeless crime spree that includes robbery, rape, and murder. When it all catches up with him in the end, Van feels no remorse, but rather glee, as the cops close in and he notes, "Cameras is pointing at me. I on TV" (131).

Monk fires the completed novel off to his baffled agent, asking him to circulate it under the pseudonym Stagg R. Leigh. The name is recognizable as a version of Stagolee or Stagger Lee, both nicknames for Lee Shelton, a late-nineteenth-century carriage driver and pimp in St. Louis who was made famous by a series of popular songs about how he supposedly murdered a man in a quarrel over a Stetson hat. The stereotypical epitome of the "bad" black man, Stagg, as both legend and author, represents everything Monk is not, everything he has staked everything on resisting in his life and his art. His name on the manuscript is the first signal of its parodic nature as well as an indicator of why Monk feels he could "never" put his name on the project.

As Monk's familiar life unravels, however, Stagg emerges in the ruins to take his place, and everything Monk always wanted and never achieved as himself becomes possible. On one hand Monk still cannot sell his latest experimental novel or even get a decent short-term teaching position in D.C. Plus a newly discovered box of old letters from a lover casts doubt on how well he knew his late father, his brother Bill all but vanishes into his pursuit of his new life, Monk's mother continues her inexorable decline, and, when he tries to improve things with a nostalgic visit to their lake house, he loses the housekeeper to an old flame and sabotages a promising relationship of his own when he sees Jenkins's novel on his new girlfriend's nightstand. Yet, on the other hand, just as everything that makes Monk feel like Monk is disintegrating, Stagg is an overnight phenomenon. Despite the many ways Monk tries to make it clear that "My Pafology" is a satire, including the use of the name Stagg R. Leigh and giving his grotesque protagonist Juanita Mae's last name, it turns out to be impossible to exaggerate enough to make his point understood. Publishers and eventually a filmmaker take the manuscript completely seriously, and in a hysterical turn, the money Monk needs so badly starts rolling in. All he has to do to keep it coming is to bring Stagg to life and tolerate that his parody is being treated as the real thing: "The experience which is and can only be Black America." Monk rationalizes accepting this price, thinking that while "appearances" are most important in visual art, function is more important in objects such as, for example, chairs. "My Pafology," he reasons, "was more a chair than a painting, my having designed it not as a work of art, but as a functional device, its appearance a thing to behold, but more a thing to mark, a warning perhaps.... It was by this reasoning that I was able to look at my face in the mirror" (209).

First over the phone, then in meetings, and finally even on television, when he appears on a talk show (opposite a character through whom Everett clearly parodies Oprah Winfrey and her book club), Monk dresses and acts the part of Stagg, sliding surprisingly easily into his "bad man" role simply by being reticent to the point of rudeness and letting people draw what conclusions they will. He describes it as "conjur[ing]" Stagg, almost like a spirit or being possessed (247). As the conclusions people draw validate the criticisms of the publishing world that he was trying to make via the "device" of "My Pafology," Stagg increasingly becomes a public truth and Monk a private fiction, and he wonders, "Had I by annihilating my own presence actually asserted the individuality of Stagg Leigh? Or was it the book itself that had given him life?" (248). The novel's epigraph from Mark Twain has come true; Monk cannot tell a lie that anyone will doubt, nor a truth that anyone will believe.

With his siblings, girlfriend, and Lorraine gone, his mother increasingly rarely in her right mind, and his agent overjoyed at the unexpected commercial success of the fake novel, Monk spends more time with people who want to know him as Stagg and must confront the fact that it is Stagg the world wants him to be, not himself. He writes a new story in his journal about a game show on which a black man succeeds far beyond anyone's expectations by knowing every single answer, no matter how obscure, but is met by dead silence rather than applause from the white audience, who do not know what to do with his success. This suggests that success on Monk's own terms as an intellectual is impossible, because people will always want to see what they expect to see. So the story prefigures Monk's growing realization that, given the audience it has found and the eyes with which they are conditioned to read, "My Pafology" cannot shock people in the way he had hoped.

When Monk tries to reconcile his two identities, Stagg is always the stronger presence, the one to meet with the world's approval and trust. Even when Monk offers to give Lorraine a generous wedding gift out of his newfound wealth, her new son-in-law looks at him suspiciously, and he realizes that "Leon would have no problem with my having money... if I were that ballplayer. The problem was the one I had always had, that I was not a *regular* guy and I so much wanted to be. Can you spell *bourgeois*?" (195). When Monk goes in the guise of Stagg to meet the filmmaker Wiley Morgenstein, he tells the author that he is not at all like he imagined him to be, that he thought he would be "tougher or something. You know, more street. More." When Monk supplies the word "Black," Morgenstein replies, "Yeah, that's it. I'm glad you said it. I've seen the people you write about, the real people, the earthy, gutsy people. They can't teach you to write like that in no college" (217). Missing the irony of having just called the real-life Monk "unreal" and the fictional Stagg "real," Morgenstein is only one of the many people Monk encounters who are willing to pay or otherwise reward him for his bad-ass ex-con act. "The game was becoming fun," he writes. "And it was nice to get a check" (212). In his journal Monk imagines abstract artist Robert Rauschenberg commissioning a drawing from Willem de Kooning; after carefully erasing it, Rauschenberg sells the erased picture at a huge profit without crediting de Kooning, the original artist.

As his admirers turn out to be other writers and editors, though, Monk's sense of satisfaction with his joke and comfort with its ethical implications fade quickly. Once literary success starts to come his way, it is no longer a matter of taking the much-needed money and running with it. He begins to regard what he is going through as analogous to his mother's loss of her identity to disease and his brother's giving up one version of himself to find the other, which he had suppressed. None of them are any longer versions of themselves that they can recognize in a mirror. Like Rauschenberg's erasing, Monk's parody of Jenkins's novel and Stagg's parody of himself have lives of their own when taken seriously. As people react in belief and admiration to his satire, Monk wonders if, by playing along, it is himself and the real life he represents that are being effaced by his "device," rather than defended, as he had originally planned. Reconsidering his speech at the writer's conference from the beginning of the book, Monk sees the reception of his art mirroring his reader's expectations and erasing his own intentions. Apparently his colleagues also believe that "they can't teach you to write like that in no college," because Monk eventually finds himself, to his shock and dismay, in the running for the National Book Award—a committee on which he has ironically agreed to sit that same year. He decides to remain on the committee, certain that "Fuck" could never actually win the award and thus is maddeningly privy to the committee's fawning over the novel that he has begun to think of as belonging more to Stagg than to him and his Stagg disguise as a "house" in which he lives (251).

As the award ceremony approaches, Monk continues to dream of Nazi Germany and reluctantly admits that in inhabiting the body of Stagg, profiting by his success, and enjoying the acceptance he has always craved, he has compromised his art for the brown shirts. He decides that his self-respect hinges on not letting "the committee select *Fuck* as the winner of the most prestigious book award in the nation. I had to defeat myself to save my self, my own identity. I had to toss a spear through the mouth of my own creation, silence him forever . . . and have the whole world admit that he never existed" (259). Failing to sway the committee, which rebukes and then outvotes him, Monk is faced with the ethical dilemma of whether to reveal his "joke" at the awards ceremony or not—knowing that, whatever he chooses to do, his private world will implode.

Erasure concludes with the disappearance of Monk's family, of his hopes for his intellectual career, and of everything he has tried to stand for, as he steps on stage into the role of Stagg R. Leigh. In a sense he steps into what the world would call his "blackness." It does not matter whether he reveals his trick or whether he sells out and claims bad man Stagg for himself in earnest. Whatever he does after the last page, Monk has felt the racial veil drop down over his face forever, as the world accepts his lies for truths and his truths for fantasies. He compares being free of his "illusions" to being castrated, quoting the narrator of his namesake Ralph Ellison's *Invisible Man*, when he describes the feeling as "painful and empty" (265). Monk's life as an intellectual, his choices, and his reality are an elaborate farce, and his belief in art collapses under the weight of that realization. The impossibility of self-respect in a world that prefers "Stagg the bad man" to "Monk the real man" is what makes Monk's story a tragedy in a classic sense.

Just as Monk was haunted by the success of his "realistic novel" and seems poised on the brink of having the truths he has stood for in his life erased at the conclusion of his journal, Everett has been frustrated in some ways by the form the success of *Erasure* has taken, especially by readers who take the novel as Everett's having "acquiesced to the identity of black novelist" (Russett 2005, 366). Everett's five subsequent novels have continued to explore different shapes in terms of craft, and he has certainly not limited himself to issues of regional, class, or racial identity, though these topics continue to interest him. He reads from *Erasure* reluctantly when asked, wishes readers and reviewers would not focus so much on the "race stuff," and bemoans his choice of creating Monk as so superficially similar to himself. "I don't really want to be present," he says. "That's the only problem I have with the book—the character resembles me so much that it's harder for readers to divorce me from the work, and my mission has always been to disappear" (Ehrenreich 2002). Rather than disappearing into Monk and Stagg, Everett has found his characters disappearing into him, as readers are tempted to see them as his alter-egos, no matter how loudly he objects. The fact that readers keep looking to him for answers, rather than to the text, makes him less confident in the novel. He told Rone Shavers, "If anybody's thinking about me when they're reading my work, I've failed as a writer. The work is supposed to stand by itself" (48).

Some responses to the book, even the positive ones, have borne out Monk's criticisms of the publishing industry. When Doubleday offered to do the paperback of *Erasure* as the first in a new series of African American fiction called "Harlem Moon," Everett turned them down flat and went with one of the small presses that had supported his career in the past. He says of the incident, "Why not call it 'Stepin'fetchit,' and get it over with?" (Starr 2002, E1). He told another interviewer that "the easy road for American publishing has been to publish novels about black farmers, [the] inner city . . . and slaves. Because these are pictures that are easily commodified. But if it's the black middle class, and it's not so different from someone else, then what's exotic about that?" (Stewart 2007, 299). Additionally, more than one reader has found the "My

Pafology" section of the book to be not so much racist as it is raw and energetic. It is also possible, since Monk comes up against urban realities several times in the novel that he is not prepared to navigate, that there is more truth to the stereotypes he critiques than he wants to admit. Ana Sanchez-Arce observes, "It is left to the reader to decide whether writing the mock novel is Monk's literary downfall or an overdue recognition of his roots" (2007, 148).

Monk's dislocation from the black underclass, however, even after discovering his half-sister and paying her a share of his, to his mind, ill-gotten fortune, is not resolved with a neat click into place; the journal's closing phrase, "hypotheses non fingo" ("feign no hypotheses" in Latin, from Isaac Newton), gives the reader the reality of Monk's psychic pain without prescribing anything for its relief. The novel is, in the end, about Monk and his failed experiment more than it is about politics. His pain is more real than anything else at the close of the novel, as Monk faces the consequences of his ethical and emotional inability to save his family, communicate in terms other than money with his newfound sister, or to coexist in any acceptable way with Stagg. The primary reality Monk faces is that his life as he has lived and known it, the life he wants for himself as an artist, is not an option. "Egads," Monk says at the end, "I'm on television" (265).

Everett is too energetic a contemporary writer for anyone but him to predict the shape of the rest of his career, and that he will not do. "I want to train mules," Everett says. "I want to fish and I want to write novels" (Shavers 2004, 50). Although *Erasure* is in some ways a departure from his other work, dealing as it does directly with race, class, and, to some extent, regional difference, not to mention having so much of its author apparently present in the fiction, it is still a particularly good place to begin an appreciation of Everett's sizable body of work. The novel is realistic in its approach, since it narrates a fairly straightforward series of events in the form of a man's personal journal, interspersed with the flights of fancy one might expect from a working writer, and yet the varying types of writing Monk includes in his journal alongside his own reminiscences—book reviews, excerpts from *We's Lives in da Ghetto*, professional and personal letters, story ideas, an academic essay, a curriculum vita, the novel within a novel, and a short story—make it challenging and unusual prose that is exciting to read. *Erasure* is, in addition to being a moving tale about a man's search for himself in the mirrors the world holds up to him, a satire of the publishing industry that offers some insights into Everett's other novels and stories: why he writes, what and how he writes, and why he keeps publishing with small presses, despite his growing name recognition.

Works Cited and Consulted

Birnbaum, Robert. "Percival Everett: Author of *God's Country* Talks with Robert Birnbaum." *Identity Theory*. May 6, 2003. http://www.identitytheory.com/interviews/birnbaum105.php/.

Bolonik, Kera. "Mules, Men, and Barthes: Percival Everett Talks with *Bookforum*." 12, no. 3 (2005): 52–53.

Ehrenreich, Ben. "Invisible Man: Novelist Percival Everett on the Wrong Kind of Success and His Desire for Anonymity." *LA Weekly*. December 5, 2002. http://www.laweekly.com/2002-12-5/news/invisible-man/.

Everett, Percival. *I Am Not Sidney Poitier*. St. Paul: Graywolf, 2009.

———. *Abstraktion und Einfühlung*. New York: Akashic Books, 2008.

———. *The Water Cure*. St. Paul, Minn.: Graywolf, 2007.

———. *re: f (gesture)*. Granada Hills, Calif.: Red Hen Press, 2006.

———. *Wounded*. St. Paul, Minn.: Graywolf, 2005.

———. *American Desert*. New York: Hyperion, 2004.

———. *Damned If I Do*. St. Paul, Minn.: Graywolf, 2004.

———. "Why I'm from Texas." *Callaloo* 24, no. 1 (2004): 62–63.

———. *Erasure: A Novel*. New York: Hyperion, 2001.

———. *Grand Canyon, Inc.: A Novella*. San Francisco: Versus Press, 2001.

———. "F/V: Placing the Experimental Novel." *Callaloo* 22, no. 1 (1999): 18–23.

———. *Glyph: A Novel*. St. Paul, Minn.: Graywolf, 1999.

———. "The Appropriation of Cultures." *Callaloo* 19, no. 1 (1996): 24–30.

———. *Big Picture*. St. Paul, Minn.: Graywolf Press, 1996.

———. *Frenzy*. St. Paul, Minn.: Graywolf, 1996.

———. *Watershed*. St. Paul, Minn.: Graywolf Press, 1996.

———. *The Body of Martin Aguilera*. Seattle: Owl Creek Press, 1994.

———. *God's Country: A Novel*. Boston: Faber & Faber, 1994.

———. *The One that Got Away*. Illus. Dirk Zimmer. New York: Clarion, 1992.

———. "Signing to the Blind." *Callaloo* 14, no. 1 (1991): 9–11.

———. *For Her Dark Skin*. Seattle: Owl Creek Press, 1990.

———. *Zulus*. Sag Harbor, N.Y.: Permanent Press, 1990.

———. *The Weather and Women Treat Me Fair*. Little Rock, Ark.: August House, 1987.

———. *Cutting Lisa*. New York: Ticknor & Fields, 1986.

———. *Walk Me to the Distance*. New York: Ticknor & Fields, 1985.

———. *Suder*. New York: Viking Press, 1983.

Everett, Percival, and James Kincaid. *A History of the African-American People (Proposed) by Strom Thurmond, as Told to Percival Everett and James Kincaid*. New York: Akashic Books, 2004.

Hinshaw, Dawn. "Rebel Flag over State House Offends Artist." *State*, May 4, 1989, 1B.

Johnson, Michael K. "Looking at the Big Picture: Percival Everett's Western Fiction." *Western American Literature* 42, no. 1 (2007): 26–53.

Kincaid, Jim. "An Interview with Percival Everett." *Callaloo* 28, no. 2 (2005): 377–81.

Mack, Tom. "Percival L. Everett." *African-Americans and South Carolina: History, Politics, and Culture*. Ed. Carol Sears Bosch and Robert E. Bosch. 1998. http://www.usca.edu/aasc/everett.htm/.

Newton, Ed. "A Way with Words." *USC Trojan Family Magazine*. Spring 1999. http://www.usc.edu/dept/pubrel/trojan_family/spring99/whatsnew/wn_everett.html/.

Ramsey, William M. "Knowing Their Place: Three Black Writers and the Postmodern South." *Southern Literary Journal* 37, no. 2 (2005): 119–39.

Russett, Margaret. "Race under *Erasure:* For Percival Everett, a 'Piece of Fiction.'" *Callaloo* 28, no. 2 (2005): 358–68.

Sanchez-Arce, Ana Maria. "'Authenticism,' or the Authority of Authenticity." *Mosaic* 40, no. 3 (2007): 139–55.

Shauf, Michele S. "Percival L. Everett." *Contemporary Novelists.* 7th ed. Ed. Neil Schlager and Josh Lauer. Detroit: St. James Press, 2001. 300–301.

Shavers, Rone. "Percival Everett." *Bomb* 88 (2004): 46–51.

Starr, William. "I Get Bored Easily." *State* March 31, 2002, E1.

———. "Author Everett Prizes Privacy." *State*, May 29, 1994, 1F.

———. "Literary 'Expatriates' Come Home to South." *State*, September 9, 1988, 1A.

Stewart, Anthony. "Uncategorizable Is Still a Category: An Interview with Percival Everett." *Canadian Review of American Studies* 37, no. 3 (2007): 293–324.

Wickett, Dan. "Interview with Percival Everett." *Emerging Writers Forum.* March 15, 2003. http://www.breaktech.net/EmergingWritersForum/View_Interview.aspx?id=29/.

PART II *A Sense of Place*

Steve Yarbrough ～ *The Oxygen Man*

THOMAS E. DASHER

A Biographical Sketch

Steve Yarbrough was born in Indianola, Mississippi, on August 29, 1956, the son of John and Earlene Yarbrough. After receiving his bachelor's degree in 1979 and his master's degree in 1981, both in English from the University of Mississippi, he completed his master of fine arts in creative writing from the University of Arkansas in 1984. He then taught at Virginia Tech from 1984 to 1988 before he moved to California State University in Fresno, where he was the James and Coke Hallowell Professor of Creative Writing and directed the school's master of fine arts program in creative writing. He is currently a professor in the Department of Writing, Literature and Publishing at Emerson College in Boston. He lives with his wife in Stoneham, Massachusetts. During 1999–2000, he served as the Grisham writer-in-residence at the University of Mississippi, and he received the 2010 Richard Wright Award for Literary Excellence.

Influenced by Flannery O'Connor, William Faulkner, Larry McMurtry, William Trevor, James Salter, and Alice Munro, among others, Yarbrough published his first collection of short stories, *Family Men*, in 1990. "The earliest of the eleven stories had actually been written seven years earlier, in the summer of 1983; the latest, two years earlier, the summer of 1988," he noted in an interview. "So in a real sense the book was old to me by the time it appeared" ("Live E-Panel" 2005). Although it did not sell many copies, it was followed by two additional collections, *Mississippi History* in 1994 and *Veneer* in 1998. "My expectations [for *Family Men*], of course, were grossly unrealistic," Yarbrough said. "I knew no better than to think that my university press collection would set the world on fire. I was convinced that it would be featured prominently everywhere from the *New York Times Book Review* to *People Magazine*. In fact, the only major reviews it received came in the *San Francisco Chronicle* and the *Boston Globe*. It was blasted in the *Jackson Clarion-Ledger*, in a review titled 'Indianola Writer Goes One for Eleven.' It sold about nine hundred copies, as best I recall" ("Live E-Panel" 2005).

Yarbrough's first novel, *The Oxygen Man*, appeared in 1999 after having been "rejected 43 times over four years" ("Live E-Panel" 2005). It has been called "his finest novel to date and one of the best works of Southern fiction produced at the close of the twentieth century" (Guinn 2004, 584). In writing his first novel, Yarbrough commented that there "was a huge psychological hurdle when I tried to go from writing a short story to writing a novel.... You could be two or three years into it and realize, this isn't working at all and you've wasted three years of your life.... In a novel, you have to learn to pace yourself, keep a foot on the break. That was probably the hardest thing to learn" ("Interview" 2008).

Visible Spirits, Yarbrough's second novel, published in 2001, is loosely based on an actual incident that occurred in Indianola in 1902 and 1903. But, as he commented, "I'm not a historian, and sticking to what really happened would have rendered me incapable of writing about character the way I wanted to. So I felt perfectly free to alter and invent and have done so liberally" ("Conversation" 2008). *Visible Spirits* is set in Loring, Mississippi, Yarbrough's fictional community, which is also the setting for his two following novels. *Visible Spirits* concerns two brothers, Tandy and Leighton Payne, their intense antagonism, and the effects of racism upon them as individuals and in the community. Both brothers are finally destroyed by their own actions, one noble, one despicable, and the community remains deeply divided and torn. Yarbrough noted that he hoped the Paynes' struggles within Loring would force people to "spend a little time thinking about how difficult it sometimes has been, and indeed is even now, for some people in this very prosperous nation to go about the ordinary business of leading decent lives" ("Conversation" 2008).

Prisoners of War, Yarbrough's third novel, came out in 2004 and was a finalist for the 2005 PEN/Faulkner Award. *Prisoners* takes place during the 1940s. Dan Timms, the young protagonist, is waiting to be old enough to enlist in the Army and fight in World War II. But Dan is haunted by the memory of his father, whose inability to recover from his own experiences in World War I eventually contributed to his suicide. Marty Stark, another Loring youth who has recently returned from World War II, is deeply disturbed. He is assigned to guard the German prisoners of war imprisoned in a camp near Loring. A third Loring youth, L. C., faces his own challenges, because as an African American he is determined *not* to be sent into the war to fight for a country which refuses to recognize his identity as a man. *Visible Spirits* is a novel based on historical events, but it was not easy to write. "I had so many false starts trying to write this book that it just about killed me," Yarbrough said. "It turned out to be harder to write than anything I'd ever written" ("Interview" 2008).

Yarbrough's fourth novel, *The End of California*, appeared in 2006 and was a finalist for the Mississippi Institute of Arts and Letters Award for fiction. Pete Barrington, the novel's protagonist, grew up in Loring, where he was an outstanding student and athlete. He was also sexually involved with a classmate's mother. He leaves Loring to play football and eventually to study medicine, as far away from Mississippi as he can get, and he ends up in California with a successful medical practice. This lasts until he becomes sexually involved with one of his patients and the affair erupts into a public scandal. With his wife and daughter, Pete returns to Loring, seeking renewal and a new beginning. But much like other characters in Yarbrough's fiction, Pete finds that the past he had left behind remains there waiting for him and his family. As Yarbrough commented, "I guess what I'm really fascinated by—if I'm analyzing my own fiction, I think, usually the reason for the different temporal settings is that most of the characters are dogged by some sins from their past, some stain on their lives. And it's usually about twenty years back down the road, when it happened. I suppose I'm fascinated and horrified by the notion that there's a mistake you can make that you can't ever come back from" (Williams 2002, 118).

Safe from the Neighbors, Yarbrough's fifth novel, was published by Knopf in 2010. Interviewed while he was completing *The End of California*, he commented, "As for my own writing, I'm interested now in seeing ways I can develop the form; that is, I'm interested in different narrations, non-chronological order, getting into history" ("Interview" January 2008).

The Oxygen Man

The Oxygen Man opens with a brief prologue introducing Ned Rose's nightmare world—a world filled with water, words, and shadows. Ned is wandering the back roads near Indianola, Mississippi, looking for "*something solid* [that] *might surprise him*" (1). The solid present is, however, no match for the shadowy past. He discovers his dead father and his dead mother separately, both alive in the fog of his nightmare. His father tries to speak to him, but all Ned can hear is his father's assurance that he knows what Ned is trying to tell him. Unlike his father, Ned's mother never sees him. Instead he tries to speak to her, but he cannot make her hear his warning about the filthy water with which she is washing herself. Both parents disappear into Ned's vision with no words spoken between them, no recognition of what he needs to say and of what they cannot communicate. The nightmare features not only his parents, but also others from his past. He must face people whose stories are inextricably intertwined with his own. But what if there are no voices again, no communication, and no connection between his visions and reality, between his past and the present, between his actions and their terrible consequences? With its isolated fragments of life, Ned's divided self begins the novel with a terrible unfulfilled need.

The present time of the novel is 1996. Yarbrough brings his reader into the present in three sections, interspersed with two sections from the past; one takes place in 1972 and the other in 1973. But the two years from the past are not brought to life as flashbacks from 1996. These years, when both Ned and his sister Daisy are fifteen, are *not* remembered or filtered through the present of the narrative. Each section is a segment of the characters' lives in the present, how they live and interact, and how they act and respond. By 1996 Ned is the oxygen man. He is working for Mack Bell, a childhood friend. Ned's job is to make sure Mack's sixteen catfish ponds are aerated. Each night he travels among the ponds. Catfish is now the principal crop; it has replaced the cotton and soybeans on Mack's farm. Ned works alongside Larry, Q. C., and Booger, three black men who cultivate the catfish but who, along with other black workers in the community, are protesting their low wages. Ned is responsible for maintaining the proper oxygen level in the ponds, which, we discover, are sabotaged at night, and the fish suffocate. Mack believes the black men are responsible, and he orders Ned, his flunky, to stop the sabotage and to do whatever is necessary to end their protest. As an example to the other black workers, Ned consequently forces Q. C. and his family, whom he likes, to leave the farm.

Ned also lives in silent protest. While he has known Mack for much of his life, Ned clearly is not Mack's equal, nor does he share Mack's beliefs. Larry, one of the black workers, confronts Ned after he has evicted Q. C. and his family at the end of the first 1996 section: "You ain't nothing, man. You zero. You just a empty blank for Mack Bell to fill in" (45). Ned knows that Mack and the other farmers are exploiting the black workers in the catfish business. He works alongside the three black men every night; he knows them as individuals and knows their family histories. He bears them no animosity but understands that Mack expects him to restore order and rein in the men. Ned's silent objections are not only against Mack and the position in which he finds himself. He is also haunted by his own family; his father Billy, who was seldom at home, traveled from one paint job to another, and his mother Vonnie slept regularly with men from the community and the region. Both are dead by 1996, but their actions still reverberate in Ned's life.

Similar reverberations are also a constant reality for Ned's sister, Daisy or "Daze." She is estranged from Ned; although they share the same house, they seldom interact. Something terrible is between them, and Daze only listens as Ned, alone in his room, makes a sound "somewhere between a groan and a shriek" (7). Without expecting to ever leave Indianola, Daze works in Beer Smith's lounge, serving beer and ignoring the men who try to talk to her. Beer's daughter was killed in a random act of violence, and his wife died soon after. Beer takes Daze to dinner and begins a courtship. Like Ned, she had been all too aware of her parents' disastrous relationship, her mother's insatiable sexual needs, and her father's alcoholism. Throughout her childhood she waits for her mother, while her mother is having sex with one of her men, and Daze suffers regularly from the violent confrontations between her parents. But now, alone and bitter, unforgiving of her brother and uncertain of how to react to Beer's attention, she thinks, "Inside everybody's head was a funhouse mirror. Outside was something nobody could see, at least not as it really was, and she thought it possible that outside there really was nothing at all. At times she hoped this was so. If it was, then nothing mattered, and right now there were still too many things that mattered way too much" (133).

It is 1972, fourteen years earlier than the moment when Larry yells to Ned that he is only a "zero," an "empty blank for Mack Bell to fill in." Ned and Daze are both sophomores, attending the segregated private school where they have received scholarships to keep them out of the integrated school. Ned plays football with Mack Bell, Kyle Nessler, and Denny Gautreaux, the son of the town's banker, to whom almost everyone is in debt. Unlike Daze, Ned appears to fit into the school because he is a tough football player and impervious to physical pain. He is already isolated in his emotional turmoil, but it does not show. He is invited to his classmates' parties and offered beer. Mack and Kyle include him in their escapades; at one point they drive to Ole Miss to seduce a coed whom Mack had earlier met at a fraternity party. They desert the girl in an isolated area outside Oxford when she refuses to have sex with them. In fact, it is Ned who admits that they are only sophomores, not seniors, as Mack has told her. Ned is humiliated before his teammates and the whole school when his parents, who have brought Daze to see Ned play football, have a violent confrontation in the stands. His father, drunk and angry, verbally attacks their mother for her sexual behavior and ends up arrested for disorderly conduct. In the aftermath Mack and Kyle seek out Ned, while Denny Gautreaux surprisingly calls Daisy, who spurns his request for a date, believing that, like a mongrel dog, she is only worthy of being kicked.

This section of the novel ends in violence, not between Billy and Vonnie Rose but in an isolated country store where Ned, only fifteen, is trying to buy beer. Mack and Kyle watch from the car as he gathers the beer, places it on the counter, and starts to pay for it. The black man behind the counter, however, refuses to sell Ned the beer, knowing that he is under age. Through the store's window, Ned sees Mack and Kyle, back in the car; he is sure they are talking about his failure. Ned thinks, "For some folks, everything in between the beginning and the end was just a fight for breath, just one long struggle to suck in air or water or food, anything to fill the cavities that threatened to expand inside those folks until they themselves were walking raging nothings that couldn't do much but eat and drink, piss and shit, hurt and moan, that lived to writhe and tingle, kick ass and shoot off, that had a hole they could never fill because the hole was them and they were the hole, the sum of their natures null. His momma was that, and his daddy was, and he knew now that he would be too, that there was nothing he could do to avoid it" (104). And then Ned lifts a large glass Coke bottle and smashes it into the black man's head.

Again in 1996, fourteen years later, with Ned trying to stop the sabotage against the catfish ponds, Mack Bell is ready to act, planning another act of violence, this time against the black men who are destroying his fish. Ned's attempts to stop the sabotage have failed. When Mack tries to scare the workers by trapping Booger underwater in the seine in the catfish pond, Ned instinctively helps in order to rescue Booger. Every day, every night, Ned travels from pond to pond, monitors the oxygen levels, following Mack's orders, and constrains his own potentially violent response to the world around him. He shoots one of the cormorants, an endangered species, which is eating the catfish, and as its blood mingles with the dirty water, he watches it sink. Like a cormorant Mack Bell also feels no compunction about taking what he wants. He abuses his wife, mistreats his workers, and humiliates Ned.

Daze, meanwhile, becomes more involved with Beer Smith, even though he is fifteen years older. Beer loves her and tries to discover why she remains so bitter, so aware that young men, just like old men, can die unexpectedly. She is desperately alone and at first able to respond only tentatively to his kindness and concern. Yet she is willing to believe in Beer and his intentions in spite of a world where trust and hope seem no longer to exist. Ned too knows that a world where men like Mack are in control is one where rules and laws do not matter. He knows that he should call the sheriff to report that diesel fuel has been dumped in the ponds and that he should force Mack to act within the law. But Ned does not make the call, so Mack and the other catfish farm owners set out to stop the black workers in any way they can.

Ned is not arrested after striking the store owner with the Coke bottle. In the spring of 1973 he remains at home with his mother and sister, while his father remains largely on the road. Vonnie's sexual liaisons lead to their being evacuated from their home, which is surrounded by water due to heavy rain and a canal that has not been dredged. They end up in separate rooms at a local motel, and Daze begins an affair with Denny Gautreaux, who comes to her motel room, still seeking a relationship. Ned is at spring football practice, haunted by the events of the fall, such as his parents' violent public argument and his own violent response to the black man who would not sell him beer. Ned continues to hear "the dull thud of thick glass on bone" (182) even as his father returns, briefly, for some time at home. The boy is alone with his father and talks with him, but Ned realizes that his father is incapable of making the changes at home that would restore some harmony to the family and some balance in his father's own life. If there had ever been life in the family, it was dead. In this way Ned comes to believe that neither he nor the members of his family can escape the terrible darkness that swirls around them.

Ned is the one who has to tell Daze that their father is dead; he was killed in an accident on his way home from a job in Arkansas. Few people come to the funeral, and neither Vonnie nor Daze nor Ned can cry. His father's life, Ned thinks, was "not the sort of life you wept over" (199). Ned is lost. He is trapped in his relationship with Mack Bell, whose control over him grows after the Coke bottle bashed in the head of the storekeeper. Ned masturbates in terrible emotional agony but finds no relief or even momentary satisfaction. School ends, and he is working for Mack's father, digging the ponds that will soon be filled with catfish. Daze's affair with Denny Gautreaux, which has deepened and grown, is no longer a secret; Ned's animosity toward the world around him and especially toward Mack explodes in a moment when he almost chokes Mack to death. To make things worse, Mack and Rick Salter discover Daze having sex with Denny, parked on an isolated road, while Ned cowers in the backseat horrified and disgusted by what they have found.

It is during the summer of 1973 that violence again overwhelms Ned and the other characters. Mack and Ned are at the lake, again drinking beer, now with Mack's father in Mr. Bell's boat. Denny and his father approach in their boat, and the two fathers leave in Mr. Gautreaux's boat to discuss business. Denny, still infuriated over the incident on the isolated road, wants to be left alone, but Mack taunts him, as Ned, humiliated and angry about Daze and Denny, surrenders to an impulse that might cause a snake to strike, lunges at Denny and throws him from the boat. In the moments that follow Ned no longer sees Denny as a hated object but as a scared boy "who kept on moving forward, kept pulling himself onward because that was all he knew to do" (242). Mack suddenly pulls the boat around, bashing Denny in the head, crushing his skull, and 1973 ends with Denny's blood, like the cormorant's, blending with the dirty water of the lake.

The final section of the novel, again set in 1996, opens with Daze beside Beer in his bed, after a night together. At age forty Daze has connected with Beer, responding to his care and concern: "Now light was everywhere, it poured into the room through the slit in the curtains. It was daylight, nothing more, but this morning it possessed the qualities of a liquid. And she was scared the daylight would wash the nightlight away" (249). Unlike the dirty water into which Denny's blood had blended, this liquid Daze discovers is a kind of baptism into a life she had thought could no longer exist. She is with a man who deeply cares for her, no matter that he once drove the school bus that took her to school. She is ready to commit to a life with Beer, who knows that no such commitment can erase the void that has consumed her, unless she is able to reconnect with Ned. She must let go of the hatred; she must be able to forgive and to acknowledge that the image of Denny's death in her head, caused by Ned's determination to keep her from such a relationship, might not be the whole truth. Daze's realization leads to a moment of tentative reconciliation when Ned enters the bar, inquires about replacing her car, and hears her say, "I'm ready to let it go" (263).

But Ned has set upon a different course than one where he can live in future peace with his sister. He must do more to reconcile himself with the actions and people of his past, the community and responsibilities from which he has shrunk. He, like Daze in the bed beside Beer, must see the light:

> For most of his life he'd been looking at everything but the light. He'd seen that black man staring at the television set, even after the bottle hit him, as

> if he were still capable of making sense of what he saw. He'd seen his daddy's body going into the ground in the cheapest box his momma could find. He'd seen his momma's skin draw up and turn so green it began to smell of death, and he'd seen Denny Gautreaux lying limp in the water like a gut-shot bird.
>
> He didn't know if he'd seen the light or not. But one thing he did know: you only had to see the light once. (276)

The light that Ned sees is that he can no longer follow Mack's orders. He cannot just walk away, either. Instead he must act to put an end to the man and to the system that denigrates blacks, poor whites, and others without political and economic power.

Mack's abused wife; Larry, who drives a tractor into one of the catfish ponds; his father and mother, unable to escape their own destructive limitations; and his sister, who finally has a chance at some form of happiness with Beer Smith—all these individuals, both dead and alive, deserve better. Their destinies are not beyond their control. They all play a role in what happens to them and what they cause. But Mack Bell can no longer be allowed to set the rules and destroy lives. People like Mack exploit others, and nothing can heal a community trapped in exploitation and humiliation. Deeply flawed, suffering from almost unbearable guilt for what he has done and left undone, Ned acts. The vigilante group of men that Mack has assembled expects that Ned will be one of them and that he will join them as they force black workers to pay the price for dead catfish. Instead Ned turns his gun on Mack, who lunges toward him and kills him. This act ends Ned's own agony and, by implication, his life. All that is left is for Larry to inform Daze of what has happened. The revelation, which must come after the novel ends, is preceded by Daisy's response to meeting Larry: "I'm Daisy. . . . Ned's my brother" (280).

Daisy and Ned have reconciled at a great cost, and Mack Bell is no longer alive to bully the community. But significant issues are still in the world *The Oxygen Man* portrays. One man and his sister might find a kind of peace, but Indianola remains a divided community. Larry, one of the black protesters, brings the news to Daze of her brother's actions and death. But the deaths of Mack and Ned will not erase what Yarbrough has revealed in his novel. African Americans are largely still considered second-class citizens; they can agitate and protest and, in the process, threaten the economic status quo of the community. The economic threat is, of course, coupled with racism and the legacy of a system where white students, who do not object to studying beside blacks, receive scholarships just so they will not be a part of an integrated school system. Poor whites, then, are often co-opted to support a system that, while doomed, perpetuates the disparities within any community.

Because he is a good football player, Ned is "accepted" by his wealthier classmates, but Daze, whose very clothes mark her as lower class, is never an accepted part of the adolescent local culture. She is assumed to be her mother's daughter, outside the community's moral standards. Vonnie's sexual obsessions are never explained. In fact it is clear that Vonnie herself does not know what is driving her to have sex with so many men. Part of it must be tied to her own inadequacies, such as her inability to find an identity beyond that of a near prostitute. In this world she can work the late shift at a convenience store and slowly destroy her physical self. But she cannot escape her place, prescribed by the very conditions that define her. Her daughter expects nothing more of her own life. She can work in Beer Smith's lounge, repeating a deadly routine daily. She graduated from high school and was attractive to a doomed young man. But his wealth did not protect him from his own parents' behavior or his classmates' antagonism. Nevertheless Daze is perhaps promised a brighter future, married to Beer and lying next to a man who loves her, even though Ned is dead. We do not see the community's response to Ned's actions, but we know that his killing of Mack will not heal a broken community, where racial inequity, prescribed gender roles, and class distinctions still matter above all.

Yarbrough himself left Indianola and finally the South, but he has commented that, even though he lives in California, he chooses to write about Mississippi. "Mississippi has a storytelling culture. People talk endlessly about things that happened fifty years ago. I've lived in California for 17 years, but I find the culture to be shallow and everyone seems to live in the moment, or even more, in the future. I do it too when I'm here. In Mississippi, history is a part of the present . . . I think if you grew up in place like Mississippi, you wouldn't want to write about any place else" ("Interview" 2008). Yarbrough's fiction is filled with individuals who must return, for different reasons, to their communities. Their return is not to an edenic place that has been awaiting them. But they are drawn back. In many ways they have, of course, never left, for the community still remains the context for their lives.

In *The Oxygen Man* no one travels very far. Oxford and Greenville are about as far as a person will go. People may have dinner, they may try to seduce a sorority girl from Florida, but it is Indianola that defines them. Such definition may be suffocating, but it does not have to be. Neither Ned nor Daze is a victim of the community. Yarbrough's world is too complex to explain actions and consequences in terms only of what happens to individuals from the outside. It is, indeed, within the community that both Daze and Ned find a way out of their isolation. Denny Gautreaux is attracted to Daze because she is a different individual within the world he knows so well. She does not "fit" in, but she is "of" that world, representing and resisting the tenets of Indianola. Denny dreams of their escaping, traveling far away, and living in a world quite different from the one in which they have been reared. And we know that his dream is over when Mack's boat shatters his skull. But there is no reason to believe that what he dreamed was possible in reality. Could he have escaped his family and rescued Daze from the world that she believes she despises? What we do know is that Beer Smith does reach out to her. Fifteen years her senior, he once drove the school bus with her sitting on the seat behind him. The life he offers her is not one away from Indianola. They will surely stay in town, still run the lounge, and support one another. That support, however, will also come from the community out of which they have come. The consequences of Ned's actions, the black workers' struggle for fair wages, the seasonal flow of land, debt, and recovery will be the world in which they continue to live. We are not led to believe that this is some tragedy that overwhelms them. Instead we have every reason to believe that they will indeed manage to have a meaningful life together, in Indianola.

Yet we also know that the past is always there in the present. Yarbrough understands well the impact of history upon his native Mississippi and the South. Regional history and the personal past can be intertwined, but the structure of *The Oxygen Man* compels us to see, again, that even specific years in one's life continue to reap consequences in our daily interactions and goals. Both Ned and Daze were fifteen in 1972, just sophomores in high school, one playing football and one painfully aware of how she does not fit in. Their parents have a terrible relationship and have very little money. Ned and Daze recognize that their place in their peer group is precarious at best. But these realities for a teenager do not necessarily make one year more memorable than another. It comes down to the specific actions that the individual, whether fifteen or forty, commits that remain forever a part of the ongoing struggle for identity and place. Ned smashes a bottle into a black storekeeper's head; only months later Daze will commit to a sexual relationship with Denny Gautreaux, who, only weeks later, will die partially as a result of Ned's impulse, his rage, and his vulnerability. We measure the years by the changes that occur as we age, but in any given year, one act, one impulse, or one careless move can stay with us as specific turning points, after which we will never be the same. Daze allows herself to be swept up into Denny's dream of the future. Ned believes that he can make some sense of his parents' relationship and that being a successful athlete can at least momentarily erase the chaos into which they are continually thrust. But decisions are often not considered, consequences not anticipated, and actions not planned, and so both Ned and Daze are still haunted by particular years that remain not in the past, but, painfully still there, in the present.

Such reality is also true of the larger community. Indianola is the town in which Yarbrough was reared. The fictional Indianola is not very different from Loring, the town in which his next three novels take place. In Indianola, Denny Gautreaux's father is the town banker; Mack Bell's father is a major landowner; and Larry, Q. C., and Booger are the descendants of slaves. Beer Smith's daughter is killed in Memphis; Billy Rose dies in an accident in Arkansas. There was a major flood in 1973; there was another in 1927. Kyle Nessler, who played football with Ned and Mack in 1972, will kill his three-year-old daughter in 1996 and be sent to prison. In this way there is a continuum, a progression of events and people and histories that combine to create the whole of the community. Ned and Daze act individually, but their actions are a part of a much bigger whole. We know that the deaths of Denny Gautreaux, Billy and Vonnie Rose, and Milda and Judy Smith—Beer's wife and daughter—changed lives, thus changing the community. The deaths of Mack Bell and Ned Rose will reverberate throughout the community; years later there will still be speculation about what happened and contradictory reports about the events of that day in 1996. What could have led Ned Rose to pull the trigger? What did Larry tell Daze? How would these events of 1996 play out throughout the next twenty-four years, when Daze would be over sixty and Beer, if still alive, well into his seventies? These are questions Yarbrough does not answer, but we know that Indianola will never be exactly the same and never be truly different.

Ned and Daze, we know, grew up together, perhaps little more than nine months apart in age. Neither has known a life without the other. So their estrangement, following Denny's death, is especially painful, for it also mirrors the estrangement they both have from a fundamental side of themselves. They have struggled throughout their adult lives for a reconciliation with one another, but also, at even a greater cost, for a reconciliation within their very beings. Even as a teenager, Daze knows she is alive only because she continues to breathe: "She imagined a time when it would be all she ever heard, this sound that began as motion in her chest, this motion that emerged from her lips as a hiss, this hissing rising falling that kept her crawling, inch by inch, into tomorrow" (86). She despises what she believes she is fated to be—a woman driven by her sexuality, like her mother, rather than an individual who has more to offer others than her body. As a result she has closed herself off, refusing to believe that someone could love her, that her own brother had killed, with malice, her one chance at love.

Years later, driving home next to Beer, she tells him that her self-image is "as a historical figure. . . . Somebody that lived, if she lived at all, in the past" (153). She is frozen by Ned's action and her response. His violence has done violence to her, isolating her in an unrecorded historic period, a person who died, along with Denny, in the dirty water of that lake. As she and Denny had once agreed, there are elemental forces such as sex and fire and water that can turn "anything into something it never was before" (192). For her, "without water you couldn't be anything. Without water you'd be nothing at all" (193). Of course, it is water that drives Vonnie, Ned, and Daze out of their home and to the motel, where Daze starts the affair with Denny; it is water that lifts Daze out of the lake, as if rising after being baptized, when Denny teaches her to water ski; and it is water in which Denny dies. Thus, soon after she is resurrected by Denny's love, she is lost again, seemingly doomed to a lifeless existence, no better than a kind of death in life. Only when she is loved again, when Beer reaches out to her, only when she can let her anger and isolation go, can she, once again, come back to life. She is reconciled with herself.

For Ned such reconciliation comes only at the moment that Mack lunges at him and Ned pulls the trigger. Approaching that moment he realizes that for twenty years he and Mack have been headed to this moment, that, in fact, it is the moment toward which his entire life has driven him. The oxygen man has been lifeless, ironically aerating the catfish ponds, all the while knowing that only oxygen, not purpose or meaning, is keeping him breathing. Sitting with a group of men behind Mack's house, Ned shuts "his eyes to avoid seeing their eyes: four sets of eyes that burned rings in the night, seeking form if not substance in the absence that he was" (40). Even as a child he is haunted by what he is not, how alone he is. He talks in his sleep: "The names he called out were always those of relatives, as if in his sleep he sought evidence that he and other humans were connected" (81–82). Mack accuses him of not wanting to have sex with the Ole Miss coed, but Ned imagines burying his face between her breasts, hearing her words of passion, which might envelop him into another world. He kills the shopkeeper believing that he must prove his worth to Mack and Salter, waiting in the car. Working as the oxygen man for Mack, he feels "like he was living in a lake or a pond that was sustaining itself but getting smaller and smaller" (117).

As a teenager, sitting alone in the car with his father, he desperately wants to connect with his father and help him find his own connection with life. But he cannot manage this. "There were different kinds of dead—you could be dead while your heart was still beating. Dying didn't always happen at a specific moment in time. You could die over years or decades, and some people were dead long before they were born" (187). Ned and Daze, Billy and Vonnie are individuals whose connections are overwhelmed by the silences among them. They fail to see a way to live beyond the moments of each day, and they fail to understand how those moments, remaining unconnected, do not protect a person from patterns and relationships. As a child Ned had slipped into his parents' bedroom, where he rubbed his mother's nylon panties and stockings against his face: "He remembered the way this kind of material made you feel when you touched it, like you'd crossed some invisible line between what was fine and what wasn't, like you yourself were as naked as the skin the material was meant to hide, that everything which normally stayed inside you was outside you now, out in the open where everybody could see it, and you wanted them to, but there was no one nearby" (257).

Ned has lived a life isolated from others. He believes he is a void, seldom really visible to others, only the shadow of a man. For him, each year of his life has left him more alone and more aware of what he does not have. Ned concludes that everyone is on a kind of road, some literally, all of us at least figuratively. And the road, of course, has a destination. It ends in death: "Death on the road was no disgrace, though dying was always a failure of sorts" (274). Ned's journey has been one into himself, which he always has found to be empty.

What if, like Daze, he too can rise, resurrected out of the emptiness of his life? Beer Smith is there to help Daze, but Ned must take those final steps alone. He will not survive, and few will truly understand why he shot Mack Bell. But he knows. He has to shoot Mack because Mack has come to be the manifestation of all that Ned has failed to do. Mack did not make Ned do anything, but he had been the catalyst for the worst of his actions. Killing the storekeeper, pushing Denny out of the boat, and throwing Q. C. and his family out of their home, Ned had indeed been the zero filled in by Mack. But Ned must finally take full responsibility for being that zero. He cannot blame his parents, he cannot share his emptiness with Daze. And so he acts. In another moment, frozen in the narrative like the thud of the Coke bottle and the hull of the motorboat, he pulls the trigger and he finds himself.

The Oxygen Man is a powerful novel. Yarbrough returns to Mississippi to explore how the individual is both a product and a process. He is the product of his family and community, his teachers and coaches, classmates and fellow workers. But he remains always in process. His thoughts and his actions will propel him forward even as his past and his memories will tie him to a place and a time.

Indianola is a rich community, filled with a diversity of people, a fact that belies their small town identity. These people are, like others, trying to live lives of meaning. Much of what becomes meaningful will be the direct result of what they do and what they fail to do. But there are always aspects of every life that are beyond the individual's control. It is that mixture of responsibility and reconciliation that finally defines the individual, who, like Ned and Daze, finds a way to do more than only breathe.

Works Cited and Consulted

"A Conversation with . . . Steve Yarbrough." *Borzoi Reader . . . online*. http://www.randomhouse.com/knopf/authors/yarbrough/qna.html/.

Guinn, Matthew. "Writing in the South Now." *A Companion to The Literature and Culture of the American South*. Ed. Richard Gray and Owen Robinson. Malden, Mass.: Blackwell, 2004. 571–87.

"Interview with Steve Yarbrough." *Southern Literary Review*. http://www.southernlitreview.com/authors/steve_yarbrough_interview.html/.

"Live E-Panel: Mid-List Authors and the Publishing Industry." *Emerging Writers Network*. http://emergingwriters.typepad.com/emerging_writers_network/2005/10/live_epanel_mid.html/.

"Steve Yarbrough—Family Men." *Conversational Reading*. http://www.conversationalreading.com/2005/06/index.html/.

Williams, Tom. "'Dogged by Some Sins from Their Past': An Interview with Steve Yarbrough." *Arkansas Review: A Journal of Delta Studies* 33 (August 2002): 114–20.

Yarbrough, Steve. *Safe from the Neighbors*. New York: Alfred A. Knopf, 2010.

———. *End of California*. New York: Alfred A. Knopf, 2006.

———. *Prisoners of War.* New York: Alfred A. Knopf, 2004.
———. *Visible Spirits.* New York: Alfred A. Knopf, 2001.
———. *The Oxygen Man.* Denver: MacMurray & Beck, 1999.
———. *Veneer: Stories.* Columbia: University of Missouri Press, 1998.
———. *Family Men: Stories.* Baton Rouge: Louisiana University Press, 1990.

Larry Brown ⁓ *Fay*

JEAN W. CASH

A Biographical Sketch

Larry Brown (1951–2004) is arguably the most outstanding member of that group of contemporary southern writers for whom filmmaker Gary Hawkins coined the descriptive term "rough south." Among them, besides Brown, are Chris Offutt, Tim McLaurin, Dorothy Allison, and William Gay. Of this group, with the exception of William Gay, Larry Brown seems most authentic in his realistic treatment of poor whites, a class he knew well. The others came from working-class backgrounds similar to Brown's, but all of them had the benefit of at least some college training as they struggled to become writers. In contrast Larry Brown succeeded without the benefit of higher education. Through a combination of innate talent, considerable ability as a storyteller, which is a part of his family heritage, the encouragement of a book-reading mother and a steadfast wife, and—most important—sheer determination, he transformed himself from an Oxford, Mississippi, fireman into a writer of literary fiction of the first order.

Harry Crews, obviously a literary progenitor of Larry Brown, recognized his genius early, announcing in his review of *Facing the Music* that "talent has struck." Brown subsequently fulfilled that promise, publishing *Facing the Music* after spending most of the decade of the 1980s training to write. After that collection of short stories, he wrote five novels: *Dirty Work* (1989), *Joe* (1992), *Father and Son* (1996), *Fay* (2000), *The Rabbit Factory* (2003), a second collection of stories called *Big Bad Love* (1990), and two collections of nonfiction, *On Fire* (1993) and *Billy Ray's Farm* (2001). When he died on November 24, 2004, he was completing a sixth novel, published in 2007 as *A Miracle of Catfish*.

Writing in the tradition of Crews, one of the first southern writers to produce vivid portrayals of lower-class southerners, Brown produced a body of work that both portrays and humanizes such characters. Hard-packed, realistic, violent, and heavily fraught with emotion, Brown's work first drew readers from throughout the South and, later, from elsewhere in the country. Honors also followed. Brown received the Mississippi Institute of Arts and Letters Award in 1989 for *Dirty Work* and twice won the Southern Book Critics Award for Fiction (for *Joe* in 1992 and *Father and Son* in 1997). In 1998 he also received the Lila Wallace-Reader's Digest Fund Writers Award. In 2001 Brown became the second recipient of the Thomas Wolfe Award and was posthumously inducted into the Society of Southern Authors in 2005.

Born in Oxford, Mississippi, Larry Brown spent most of his life in Lafayette County. His father was a sharecropper in Potlockny. Between the ages of three and thirteen, Brown lived with his family in Memphis. The Browns returned to his mother's home area in Tula, where Brown became an aficionado of hunting, fishing, and dogs. He graduated from Lafayette County High School in 1969 with no intention of going to college; when his draft number came up, he joined the Marines. After two years serving at bases in North Carolina and Philadelphia, Brown returned to Mississippi, married Mary Annie Coleman, and became a paid fireman for the Oxford Fire Department; he was soon the father of three children. In 1980 he decided to become a writer, hoping to make enough money to save his children from the sort of hard work he had had to perform through the first ten years of his adult life. Ellen Douglas, then teaching at the University of Mississippi, allowed him to sit in on one of her creative writing classes, where he learned about the literary fiction that became the model for his subsequent work. He grew to love the work of William Faulkner, Flannery O'Connor, Harry Crews, and Cormac McCarthy. Barry Hannah, who had become writer-in-residence at the University of Mississippi in 1983, also encouraged Brown during this early period. When he was "discovered" by Shannon Ravenel, editor at Algonquin Press in 1986, Brown had written and discarded five novels and more than a hundred short stories. The publication of the short story "Facing the Music" in the *Mississippi Review* launched his career.

Fay

Fay (2000), Brown's fourth novel, expands on themes he explored in his earlier work: the glories of the Mississippi landscape, problems peculiar to members of the southern working class, family issues, Christian references, and the role of violence in the modern world. In the novel he also uses techniques familiar to his early readers: a highly intriguing plot, experimentation with narrative form, a strong emphasis on realistic diction, and use of a modern version of the Bildungsroman. *Fay* also enters the continuum of novels about women from the working class, establishing a connection to works such as *Moll Flanders*, *Sister Carrie*, and *Light in August*. Having published the novel *Joe*, in which the Jones family are central characters, Brown remained haunted by the older Jones daughter called Fay, who leaves her dirt-poor family behind midway through the novel. In an interview with *Publishers Weekly*, Brown described his continuing fascination with her: "Fay was a character in my second novel *Joe*. I always wondered what happened to her when she walked away from the house and left her family. I had it in the back of my head that I'd find out by writing about her. As soon as I finished *Father and Son*, I sat down to do it. That was four years ago" (44).

He told Dan O'Brient that all he knew about Fay when he began to tell her story was that "she had been raised in labor camps and she was naïve and didn't know much about the world. She just walked out and disappeared.... One day I just sat down and started writing about her walking down this dirt road that came out of this ridge over at Tula" (O'Brient 2000, L1). As he and O'Brient rode through the Mississippi countryside, Brown pointed out the actual road he had in mind: "Right here is where Fay walked out onto the highway.... I write about places I know so I won't have to do much research" (L6).

He also talked about his plans for structuring the novel on the basis of its three Mississippi settings: "up in the hills, around here [Oxford, Miss.], and down on the coast when Biloxi was just a little fishing village, in 1985" (Anon. 2000, 44). Brown did not consider *Fay* to be a sequel to *Joe* but a new story, a love story: "In my mind, it's supposed to be a love story, but a very dark and destructive love story" (Glendenning 1999). After completing *Fay*, Brown told several interviewers that he planned to write a third novel about the Jones family, one focused on Gary. His moving on to other interests, including nonfiction, longer, more comic novels, and film scripts distracted him from this idea, but his too-early death was the final reason that Gary's story remains unwritten.

Of all his novels *Fay* was the one Brown struggled with most in the writing. He began writing it shortly after he published *Father and Son*, a novel written primarily from the perspective of male characters. Over the next four years, he wrote hundreds of pages of manuscript, cutting and revising according to Shannon Ravenel's suggestions and retyping each new version. He did not begin to use a computer until *after* the publication of *Fay*. Through 1997 and 1998, while working steadily on his property at Tula, Brown continued work on the novel—he was then calling it "Wild Child." In the spring of 1998 he also taught in the master of fine arts program at Ole Miss, replacing Barry Hannah, who spent that semester at the University of Iowa. Teaching two classes at Ole Miss obviously kept Brown from completing the novel as quickly as he had hoped. He told Karin Glendenning that he had thought he would be able to work on the novel between classes, but he soon found that teaching consumed his time. Having completed his arduous semester at the university, Brown settled into continued work on the novel during the summer; he wrote to Jerry Leath Mills, a professor at the University of North Carolina, Chapel Hill, on July 12, "I'm still working on this long novel.... I've been on it about 27 months now and I'm trying to end it. I've got over 750 pages right now and hope to keep it under 900 pages. I figure to finish the first draft if everything goes right in five or six weeks" (Brown Papers, University of Mississippi).

By the time he left for Montana, where he taught the fall 1998 semester, he had completed and submitted the manuscript to Algonquin. His publisher scheduled *Fay* to be released on March 31, 2000. Katharine Walton, then publicist at Algonquin/Workman, handled prepublication promotion for the book. Her "tip sheet" for the novel describes the particular "handle" she planned to use for the novel: "Larry Brown, king of grit lit, turns his sights on a woman who's tougher than any man he's created so far. Think Helen of Troy, think Shakespeare's Cleopatra, think Dreiser's Sister Carrie, think Monica Lewinski. Meet Larry Brown's Fay Jones" (Walton [1999]).

Fay was, without doubt, the most widely reviewed of Brown's novels, with more than one hundred reviews appearing in newspapers, magazines, and on the Internet throughout the country. Most of the reviews were positive, asserting that the novel fulfilled the promise of his earlier work, proving that he was now able to write for a broader audience, that he was becoming less of a writers' writer. While some reviewers debated Brown's success in creating Fay as a believable female protagonist, most felt that he succeeded in his aim. Diann Blakely, for example, believes that "Brown's comprehension of women sets him apart from the crowd; weak portrayals of the opposite sex have been remarked upon in Southern male writers from Faulkner [forward]" (2000, n.p.). James Dickerson wrote, "Probably not since F. Scott Fitzgerald's incursions into the female sensibilities of the 1920s and 1930s has a writer been so successful crossing that literary minefield. . . . Fay is as complicated and beguiling as any real-life woman who ever walked the planet" (2000, F10).

Fay is full of cinematic action almost from the beginning. Significant events occur in all three of Brown's planned settings for the novel. The first events take place in the fairly remote Tula area. Quickly aware of Fay's lack of worldly experience, the reader waits to see what will befall her in a world of which she is primarily ignorant. Though the novel takes place in the 1980s, Fay and her family have virtually no contact with the media that we all take for granted. When she leaves their remote hovel, she is not even aware of exactly where Oxford is; she merely follows the first road she comes to. Brown uses the Oxford setting primarily to deal with the lives of Sam Harris and his wife, Amy. He incorporates some of his own experiences as a fireman in Oxford to depict events such as Sam's successful confrontation with Mozell Washington, a "thin black youth with no shirt and a baggy pair of camouflage pants that were unbuttoned and sagging below the waistband of his shorts . . . , brandishing a very big knife" (136–37). Events on the Gulf Coast are more worldly and more sensational but of great interest to any reader unaware of what the area was like before the modern era of casinos and the catastrophic aftermath of Katrina. Through a year in the lives of his main characters, Brown sets them up in a variety of situations, but Fay is always at the forefront—the young innocent who faces many dangers but manages to survive through luck and native wit. The novel appeals to a wide variety of readers. One of the novel's strongest fans is Lynn Hewlett, Brown's Lafayette County friend. "When I started that, everything else pretty much came to a standstill," he told his wife. "I read till I went to sleep that night and the next morning when I got up, I picked it up." Hewlett (2006, unpublished) says that *Fay* is the Brown novel he always gave to people.

In *Fay*, as in his other works, Brown wrote passages lauding the beauty of the area he called home. Larry Brown spent all of his adult life in northern Mississippi, building a home on land owned by his in-laws in the Yocona area, and ultimately he bought his much-cherished eight acres in Tula, the area where the Davises, his mother's family, had settled in the nineteenth century. Larry never seriously considered leaving this rural area, not even to move to Oxford about fifteen miles away. Whenever he was away from Mississippi, he lamented the distance, writing to his many friends of his desire to be at home in Lafayette County with his family and his land. Early in *Fay* he writes of the landscape in which Fay rests: "A creek ran over snapped pilings and faintly gleaming rocks below her. She was thirsty but she feared picking her way down the muddy bank and the snakes she could not see. She sat hugging her knees and watched the specks of stars in the sky above her. All of it so still and unmoving, the stars so bright" (9–10).

Sam and Amy Harris own a home on Sardis Lake, another beautiful area in Lafayette County. When Sam takes Fay out on one of his boats, Brown writes an appreciative description of the landscape: "They came out from behind the red dirt of the bluff and he turned the wheel to the left, and then growing out from the rough sand beach was the long looming shape of the distant levee and the spill of white rocks she had looked down on a few hours before. There were some stands of dead white trees off to the right where fishing boats were grouped and she could see people sitting in them. He eased off on the throttle just a bit and then he turned loose of it and steered the boat with one hand, casually, as if he were back on his highway again, and he watched everything around him just the way he did when he was driving the cruiser" (57).

Brown presents a totally different landscape when Fay reaches Biloxi and Pass Christian, areas that he knew from visits to the Gulf Coast. After the first night that Fay spends at Aaron's mother's house, she gets up early and watches the early morning scene: "Pink light in the bay rising up over the masts and people already beginning to stir down on the docks. She watched a few boats pull out, watched the care they took backing out of their berths. And then the water foaming behind them when they got turned and headed out, reading the names written back there in flowing script: *Bettye's Ride, Mama's Dinghy, Rosa Hartsell*. Far out in the bay a sail unfurled, tiny figures working at their tasks, and she watched how the boat took the wind under its sail and began to move out. Such a thing she'd never seen before, and for a few brief moments she was happy that she had come all this way" (251–52). But wherever his fiction takes him and his characters, Brown is always, like Fay, conscious of the beauties of the landscape and the people who inhabit it.

One main difference in technique in *Fay* is Brown's use of the female perspective. Earlier reviewers often emphasized the tough, masculinity of his male characters and implied that his readership was primarily male; Brown set out to undercut that stereotype by creating the seventeen-year-old Fay as center-of-consciousness in the novel. He told James Dickerson, "This is a real departure for me, to write a book from a woman's point of view. There were things I didn't know, things I had to ask people about women to find out. Their sensitivities are different and their concerns are different" (Dickerson 2000, F10). Don O'Brient reveals that Larry "frequently sought guidance from his wife, Mary Annie, about such feminine matters as morning sickness" because he wanted Fay's portrayal "to be genuine to women who read it" (O'Brient 2000, L1). When I saw Larry Brown in Oxford at the Faulkner Conference in 2000, he asked me whether I thought he had succeeded with Fay's portrayal; I told him, without reservation, that to me she seemed totally real—the kind of woman who, regardless of background, makes the best of what she has.

In *Fay* Brown created a clear example of female Bildungsroman. "This is a coming-of-age story of a femme fatale, "Marianne Gingher wrote. "The book's called Fay because, match after match, she's the one left standing" (2000, 4G). From the moment we encounter the seventeen-year-old protagonist setting off with only the clothes on her back, the few items in her purse, and a boundless desire to reach Biloxi, she captures us and we wonder: what will happen to this ignorant innocent, barely able to read? We need not worry, for Fay may not know the ways of the world, but she is more than ready to take on the dangers that lie ahead. On the verge of being raped in the isolated trailer by the rough boys, who ply her with drink and dope, Fay saves herself by vomiting on her attacker's genitals, escaping again to the road. As Rodney Welch (2001) writes, "For all her naiveté, Fay is never the victim; rather she's a youthful adventurer who is experiencing the real world with her own dumb courage, and she is at least the equal of the men in her life when it comes to exerting her own sexual power."

Having escaped both her father's unwanted advances and the rough boys who want to take physical advantage of her, Fay continues her trek toward the Gulf Coast, having no idea of how far it is from north Mississippi or the dangers that lie ahead. Rescued and taken in by Sam Harris and his wife, Amy, Fay becomes a temporary member of their family, long enough to become more literate and more knowledgeable about middle-class life. The Harrises unofficially adopt Fay, buying her clothes and eyeglasses, teaching her to read, and to drive an automobile. Though Sam and Amy do much to civilize the young girl, Fay ends up homeless again after Amy dies in an automobile accident, Fay and Sam become sexually involved, and she must deal with a romantic rival. During this pivotal year of her life, before Brown ends her picaresque odyssey, Fay loses her virginity and becomes pregnant, kills two people, is raped by a casual acquaintance, becomes the mistress of a strip club bouncer, and takes the stage as a New Orleans stripper herself. Whether Fay passes the Bildungsroman test and moves toward a more positive life is debatable, but she does survive with a smile on her face. In New Orleans "she mingled with the talking people on Royal and looked at old coins and Civil War muskets or mummies in shop windows and she smiled as she walked" (491).

Class and economic issues lie at the core of the novel as Fay struggles to leave her migrant worker background to achieve what she hopes will be a better life. Through vivid and sympathetic description, Brown reveals the hostile underclass background she desperately wants to escape. When she leaves her family, she carries everything she owns in her small purse: two dollars, a "mangled pack of cigarettes that her brother Gary had given her . . . tubes of cheap lipstick and plastic combs and hairbands, things she saved for years" (13). So out of touch with life outside the migrant existence of her family, she doesn't even recognize her first sanctuary as a church; she feasts off leavings from a church supper, thinking, "She wished she'd known of this place on those nights back in the woods when there was nothing to rock against her empty belly except for her knees, those times they'd waited for the old man to come in with something to eat and waited all night many nights and he never did" (12).

It is little wonder that Fay is eager to escape the only life that she has known; yet in her ignorance of how to survive outside of the woods, she falls into situations potentially even more dangerous than the one she has left. Three boys in a pickup truck, who have been fishing and drinking, take her to a trailer deep in the country where she finds another kind of marginal life. Fay avoids being victimized by the men, but even after Sam Harris rescues her, her life takes on a different uncertainty. Through Sam Harris, Brown shows that even middle-class life in North Mississippi is not without problems. Sam has the comfortable home on Sardis Lake and other trappings of his success as a state policeman, but the loss of his daughter and his subsequent infidelity ruin both his life and that of his wife, Amy. They cannot really offer Fay a permanent escape from the poverty and danger that have characterized her first seventeen years. Forced to escape once again, she enters an even seamier side of Mississippi life on the Gulf Coast—a life of drinking, drugs, strippers, pimps, prostitutes, and rapists—a milieu Brown described earlier in his short story "Golden Nuggets." Once there, like Carrie Meeber in Theodore Dreiser's *Sister Carrie*, Fay uses her most profitable asset, her physical beauty, to survive in a world that is generally indifferent to young girls from her level of society.

Fay, in fact, evolves as a contemporary representation of Lena Grove in *Light in August*, the late-nineteenth-century Carrie Meeber, and even Moll Flanders from Daniel Defoe's eighteenth-century narrative. Narratives written so many years apart might seem to offer little in the way of comparison, but *Moll Flanders*, *Sister Carrie*, *Light in August*, and *Fay* offer perspectives on how little roles have changed for women from the working class over the past two centuries. The four female protagonists exemplify how few economic opportunities women had in early modern England, in this country at the turn of the twentieth century, and continued to have in the United States at the onset of the twenty-first century. Women in all four works had to face the reality that without family support, sufficient education, and the bottom line—money—there was little they could do to better their lives in a manner acceptable to society. As Charlotte Perkins Gilman asserted in her book *Women and Economics:* until women achieve economic independence, they cannot fulfill themselves as viable human beings. As in his other stories of working-class people, his aim was to humanize his character to readers who often view the lower class as fodder for humor rather than people worthy of sympathy.

All four antiheroines emerge from family situations of little or no promise. Moll is born illegitimately to a mother who uses the excuse of pregnancy to avoid being executed for petty thievery. Almost immediately after Moll's birth, her mother goes off to ply her own unfortunate future in the Virginia colony. She bears other children, including the son whom Moll ultimately marries. There is no hint of incest in Dreiser's *Sister Carrie,* but she too is born into a working-class midwestern family with few economic prospects. When Carrie matures, her farm family is more than ready to have her leave for the city where she will seek the factory job that nearly ruins her health. The element of incest, however, is an unfortunate reality in many lower-class families, then and now. Of contemporary southern literature dealing sympathetically with characters who are victim to incest, the reader thinks immediately of Ruth Anne in Dorothy Allison's *Bastard Out of Carolina.* Incest is not an issue in Lena Grove's life, but her innocence about sexuality leads to her unwanted pregnancy. In *Fay* Brown does not directly make his title character the victim of incest, but it is her father's unwanted advances that prompt Fay to escape her blighted existence.

The central issues that make Moll, Carrie, Lena, and Fay seem so similar to each other is that all are women without real financial support; at the same time, they are also highly sexual beings, who use their physical appeal to insure financial security. Having left their first marriages with some money, Moll and Carrie do not find themselves in situations as desperate as that of Fay, but they blunder into relationships that undercut them financially and exploit them sexually. Carrie Meeber, seeking to improve her financial condition, leaves Drouet, the drummer for the bar manager Hurstwood, who at first seems to offer financial security. She soon finds, however, that she must become responsible for her own economic future, by using her sex appeal and incipient talent as an actress to achieve economic independence. Fay Jones's adventure is a good deal grimmer after she has committed murder and takes off again for the Gulf Coast. Reena Mize summarizes the economic situation of young women like Fay and herself: "Time off? What's that? You start having babies like I did when you're sixteen and you're fucked. You don't get no time off. Less you're lucky enough to find a rich husband. Or a good one. And you ain't gonna find no good one in a strip joint" (166).

Unlike Moll, who abandons her many children with little or no consideration, Fay has mixed feelings about the prospect of motherhood. As early as her adventure with the rough north Mississippi boys and the woman they live with, Fay shows more concern for that woman's child than its mother does. Arriving on the Gulf Coast, Fay voices concern about the child she is carrying, but at the same time she continues to drink and smoke. She loses the child, but if her miscarriage leaves her sterile, you could say that at least she will have less to worry about.

Fay's final economic situation is more like that of Carrie Meeber than that of Moll Flanders. There is only a qualified happy ending for Fay. In effect, at the age of eighteen she heads toward a life that will no doubt mirror those of Moll and Carrie. Economic necessity, then, impels all three of these women. Whatever they do, good or bad, results from their basic desire for survival. Moll, Carrie, Lena, and Fay know that without money, they are doomed to sordid lives that offer little in the way of fulfillment.

Fay Jones's connection with Lena Grove is slightly different from her relationship to Moll Flanders or Carrie Meeber. Clearly, though, Fay is a literary descendent of Lena. Like Moll Flanders, Carrie Meeber, and Fay Jones, Lena, too, evolves from the working class. Her early family situation is similar to that of the other women in that she must fend for herself from an early age. Without economic support, moral counsel, or any sort of genuine caring, Lena Grove, like Fay, makes a serious mistake when she falls victim to Lucas Burch. Pregnant and alone, she, like Fay in her search for the Gulf Coast, sets off to find the father of her child, believing that "a family ought to all be together when a chap comes" (18). Like Fay she gets help from people as she makes her on-foot odyssey across two states; Lena is also sexually appealing as evidenced by Byron Bunch's immediate fascination with her. Ultimately he becomes her surrogate husband. An adventurous spirit, womanly beauty and strength, and unwavering determination are what Lena and Fay share above all. Both women also share the admiration of the male authors who created them. Faulkner would approve, I believe, of Lena's twenty-first-century literary descendent.

The patriarchal confines of their respective eras limit the perspectives of all four heroines, but the strong qualities in their characters insure their survival. James Sutherland's description of Moll Flanders also applies to Carrie Meeber, Lena Grove, and Fay Jones: "Above all, Moll has the toughness, the resilience, the ability for mere survival that usually go with indomitable energy and great physical stamina" (vii). Sutherland also believed that Defoe created Moll "so sympathetically . . . that he may almost be said to have ended by becoming one of her many lovers" (v). Dreiser obviously approved of his Carrie Meeber, and Larry Brown developed a clear attachment to Fay Jones.

Aside from the Bildungsroman focus and his concern with the economic plight of a young woman on her own, Brown in *Fay* deals with thematic issues that he has pursued in his earlier work. As in *Joe* and *Father and Son*, family—usually presented as distorted in some way—figures significantly in *Fay*. The Jones clan seems a family in name only. Wade Jones, Fay's father, is arguably the most evil character Brown ever created; he is a human so vile that he will do anything for the next drink, including, as he does in *Joe*, prostituting his own young child for money and drink. Fay tells Sam Harris "about the two times her father had crept up on her in the dark, how he'd ripped her clothes and put his hand around her throat and tried to choke her down, and how she'd fought and kicked and scratched at his eyes until she was able to get away from him almost naked and run into the woods to hide, along with the night birds and the tree frogs calling and her heart hammering finally slower in her chest" (46).

Fay retains only negative memories of her even earlier existence. One of the worst, which bears some resemblance to similar episodes in the work of Erskine Caldwell, involves a migrant camp where she and her family lived temporarily. She remembers Barbara Lewis's sexual escapades with the older boys in the camp, who paid her in "food and candy." When Barbara's father discovers her prostitution, he beats her up so badly that she commits suicide by walking directly into the path of a truck.

The trailer "family" that Fay encounters is certainly a caricature of any normally connected group. The three boys share the single woman in the house; one of them is married to another woman not on the scene the night when Fay almost becomes their victim. Linda, the woman of the house, has borne a child but, unconcerned, lets it eat rocks. Sam and Amy Harris have lost their sense of family after the death of their daughter; they live together, but she has become an alcoholic and he has turned to another woman Alesandra Farris, whose own family background is also troubled. Her father visits Sam after her death, describing problems in his family: "I've got a new wife now. She's young. I traded in my old wife for her. That's what Alesandra said. They never did get along. Alesandra was already grown. She was already wild. She was wild when she was sixteen" (387). This father, feeling guilty, wants reassurance from Sam that his daughter, in spite of her wildness, was not a "bad girl. . . . She didn't hurt anybody that I know of" (387). Sam lies to protect Mr. Farris's memory of his daughter.

"Families" on the coast are equally perverse. Reena Mize, who first befriends Fay, subsists in "a trailer thing . . . more like a large RV" (164) than any kind of home. She lives with a man who is not the father of her two young children, whom Aaron, the strip-club bouncer, or his brother Cully, the club owner, have fathered. Nobody tends the children as Reena dances or prostitutes herself at the Love Cage. When Aaron takes Fay to his mother's home in Pass Christian, we learn the circumstances of *his* family. His mother Arlene had been a stripper herself and bore her two sons with different men. Now past middle age, she carries a patina of respectability but has no problem housing the various women Aaron brings home. It is sadly ironic that in spite of what Fay has experienced, both in her own family and in those that she encounters on the road, she continues to fantasize about a conventional family. But this longing is more dream than reality, for despite her losses, in the end Fay is an independent survivor with no family at all. By presenting so many families in disarray, Brown in this novel follows in the steps of Faulkner, who so ably prophesied the demise of the modern family.

The violence that permeates Brown's earlier work, particularly *Joe* and *Father and Son*, is also central to *Fay*. In using this violence Brown, as documentarian, simply reflects the violence of our modern world where rape and murder have become far too prevalent. Robert Beuka sees the road that Fay travels as the "central symbol of the novel," one that "embodies this aura of violence" (74). At the beginning of her odyssey, Fay barely escapes violent sexual attacks from the boys who pick her up; her last sight of them is a scene of violent sexual perversity: "the blond boy was on his back and the woman bent over him, her wet mouth stretched open and sliding up and down on him and the driver kneeling behind her, the skin of her big ass trembling and shaking as he slammed into her with his face turned toward the ceiling and his eyes pinched shut" (36).

Brown presents other violent scenes including those related to the automobile accidents Sam witnesses in the Oxford area. He was even one of the first officers on the scene of his own daughter's death. One scene, no doubt culled from Brown's own experience, involves a traffic accident near Holly Springs between a tanker and an automobile; the driver of the truck is pinned in his cab:

> He had a deep cut on his forehead that was leaking blood down into his pale blue eyes. The ear on the left side of his head was almost torn off, hung there by one little piece of meat where blood welled and seeped.
>
> "Please, mister," he said very clearly. "Just tell those boys to cut my foot off. I know they got an ax. I can live with one foot." (283)

Unable to free the trapped driver before a spark ignites a conflagration, Sam himself ends up seriously burnt in the fire.

Fay demonstrates her own penchant for violence when she kills Alesandra—arguably in self-defense but still with a certain vengeance: "She brought her knee up into Alesandra's nose and heard something give, and pulled the gun free. And she didn't even think about it, just pointed it down at her and squeezed the trigger" (149). On the Gulf Coast, Chris Dodd, the pilot who suspends advertisements in the sky above the beach, drugs Fay and rapes her, but she escapes after bashing him in the head with a tire iron. Aaron, both Fay's pseudo-protector and an absolute avatar of violence, shoots the pilot and his plane from the sky. The final scene between him and Sam encapsulates the violence in the novel:

> He saw the son of a bitch when he came in. He saw him outside at the screen door first. He eased the gun under his leg, hiding it beneath his knee. . . . The door opened, and he came on in. He had a revolver in his hand and he stood there looking down on him for a long time. . . .

> "Where's Fay?" he said, and Aaron pulled the gun from under his knee and raised it and squeezed the trigger. It kicked in his hand, and the shot was loud in the hall, and the guy with the revolver toppled backward into a table and knocked one of the antique lamps to the door, where it broke into curved shards of painted glass. (489)

Fay survives, but none of the other characters, with whom Brown has made us sympathize, do. In some respects, despite its appeal as a convincing story and its evocation of a viable female protagonist who prevails, *Fay* evolves as Brown's darkest work.

Though the novel is dark, Brown, as he usually does, offers certain references to Christianity in *Fay*. The work has fewer such allusions than his other novels partly because Fay Jones is so ignorant of Christianity that she cannot identify a church even when she wanders into one: "She walked past a building set well back from the road and saw a dark cross set into the wood high up near the gable. She stopped. There was a light somewhere inside, a yellow beam that shone through stained glass windows. She wondered if there might be a water tap in the yard or on the side of the house" (10).

Because of the paucity of her background, material, intellectual, and spiritual, Fay possesses no conscious moral values; thus she is unable to separate herself from depravity. Sam Harris, however, is another figure somewhat like the protagonist of "Samaritans"; he tries to bring order and responsibility to Fay's life as well as his own. Although his essential goodness is Christian, his all-too-human weaknesses impede his ability to function as a true Samaritan. Both Sam and his wife suffer unresolved psychological and spiritual damage from the loss of their teenage daughter, and so the new family they try to create with Fay fails. Sam's death at the conclusion of the novel seems to announce the end of any hope of Christian values for Fay.

The Gulf Coast world that Fay enters after she runs south is a virtual hell—with rape, prostitution, sexual perversion, drugs, and alcohol as its standard features. Fay is now in a world closely akin to that of Flannery O'Connor's cities in works such as "The Artificial Nigger" and *The Violent Bear It Away*. Good luck, native wit, and her own penchant for violence may save Fay Jones from urban horrors, but she may well become a Leora Watts, "so well-adjusted" to this brutal world that she will have no need to pursue spirituality (O'Connor 1989, 34).

Admittedly Larry Brown's *Fay* does not yet possess the classic stature of Faulkner's *Light in August*, O'Connor's *Wise Blood*, Defoe's *Moll Flanders*, or Dreiser's *Sister Carrie*, but the work does offer a significant evocation of what has happened or failed to happen in the lives of lower classed American women at the end of the twentieth century and into the twenty-first. Brown's creation of Fay Jones, an interesting generic name if one considers her as an emblematic character, offers readers a clear and sympathetic picture of what it is like to be a young woman from a class that many middle-class readers find offensive. Through her qualified triumph, Brown, as he had done in his earlier stories and novels, builds interest, understanding, and respect for a representative of a relatively unacknowledged class in the American South and elsewhere. In *Death of a Salesman*, Arthur Miller famously asserts, "Attention must be paid." Through Fay Jones and her social and economic trials, Larry Brown makes the same demand.

Works Cited and Consulted

Anonymous. "PW Talks with Larry Brown." *Publishers Weekly*, January 10, 2000, 44.

Beuka, Robert. "Hard Traveling: *Fay*'s Deep-South Landscape of Violence." *Larry Brown and the Blue-Collar South*. Ed. Jean W. Cash and Keith Perry. Jackson: University Press of Mississippi, 2008. 73–85.

Blakely, Diann. "Shades of Brown, Mississippi Writer's Latest Novel Affirms His Depth as a Storyteller." Review of *Fay*, by Larry Brown. *Nashville Scene Online*. August 14, 2000. http://www.weeklywire.com/ww/08-14-0/nash_8-books.html/.

Brown, Larry. *Dirty Work*. 1989. Reprint, Chapel Hill, N.C.: Algonquin/Workman, 2007.

———. *A Miracle of Catfish*. Chapel Hill, N.C.: Algonquin/Workman, 2007.

———. *The Rabbit Factory*. 2003. Reprint, New York: Simon and Schuster, 2004.

———. *Joe*. 1990. Reprint, Chapel Hill, N.C.: Algonquin/Workman, 2003.

———. *Billy Ray's Farm*. 2001. Reprint, New York: Touchstone, 2002.

———. *Fay*. New York: Scribner Paperback Fiction, Simon & Schuster, 2000.

———. *Father and Son*. 1996. New York: Owl Books, 1997.

———. *Facing the Music*. 1988. Reprint, Chapel Hill, N.C.: Algonquin/Workman, 1996.

———. *On Fire*. 1994. New York: Grand Central, 1995.

———. *Big Bad Love*. New York: Vintage, 1991.

Cash, Jean W., and Keith Perry, eds. *Larry Brown and the Blue-Collar South*. Jackson: University Press of Mississippi, 2008.

Defoe, Daniel. *Moll Flanders*. Ed. James Sutherland. Boston: Houghton Mifflin, Riverside Press, 1959.

Dickerson, James L. "America's 'Bad Boy Novelist' Enters Virgin Territory with *Fay*." Interview. *BookPage Online*. April 2000. http://www.bookpage.com/0004bp/larry-brown.html/.

Dreiser, Theodore. *Sister Carrie*. Ed. Donald Pizer. New York: Norton Critical Edition, 1970.

Faulkner, William. *Light in August*. New York: Vintage Paperback, 1972.

Gingher, Marianne. "Sweet and Innocent." Review of *Fay* by Larry Brown. *News and Observer*, April 9, 2000, 4G.

Glendenning, Karin. "Mississippi Writer Larry Brown Hard at Work on New Novel." *Chattanooga Times Daily*, February 7, 1999, n.p.

Gretlund, Jan Nordby. "The Man by the Jukebox: Larry Brown's Haunted Voices." *Frames of Southern Mind, Reflections on the Stoic, Bi-Racial and Existential South*. Odense: Odense University Press, 1996. 231–41.

Hewlett, Lynn. Unpublished interview with Larry Brown.
O'Brient, Dan. "Writer Larry Brown: In Faulkner's Footsteps." *Atlanta Journal and Constitution*, April 9, 2000, L1, L7.
O'Connor, Flannery. *Collected Works*. Boston: Library of America, 1989.
Sutherland, James. "Introduction." *Moll Flanders*. Ed. James Sutherland. Boston: Houghton Mifflin, Riverside Press, 1959. v–xvii.
Walton, Katharine. "Tip-Sheet for *Fay*." [1990] Algonquin Books of Chapel Hill, Records, 1982–2007. Collection Number 4736. Manuscripts Department, University Library of the University of North Carolina at Chapel Hill.
Welch, Rodney. "Larry Brown's Road Trip." Review of *Fay*, by Larry Brown. *Columbia Free Times*. February 14, 2001. http://www.free-times.com/reviews/fay.html/.

Chris Offutt ↬ *The Good Brother*

CARL WIECK

A Biographical Sketch

Much of what is known of Chris Offutt has Chris Offutt as its source, via memoirs, interviews, and biographical sketches. The following brief biographical information is indebted to much of that material. Offutt was born in Kentucky on August 24, 1958, and grew up in Haldeman, a small Rowan County town in Appalachia that had clay mining as its main source of jobs and income. His parents, Jodie and Andrew J. Offutt, had moved there from the larger city of Lexington. When the mine was closed down, the town also died, but Offutt's work is deeply rooted in the people and atmosphere of that town and region.

In order to free himself from what he experienced as Haldeman's claustrophobic environment, Offutt attempted to enlist in the military, but failing the physical, he turned to Morehead State University as his best alternative escape route. Art and theater were his main interests at Morehead, and there followed several Wanderjahre during which he lived in a number of different states, ranging from Massachusetts to Florida, from Montana to New Mexico. Along the way he found employment in more than fifty temporary jobs, including dishwashing, carnival work, carpentry, and house painting. About age thirty he married Rita, and with her encouragement, at a time when the young couple's backs were to the wall in Kentucky, he applied to and was accepted by the prestigious University of Iowa creative writing program, the Iowa Writers' Workshop. A book of short stories, *Kentucky Straight*, named for Kentucky straight bourbon, opened the door to major publishing as well as a Guggenheim grant and other important awards, including those from the American Academy of Arts and Letters and the National Endowment for the Arts. Since then Offutt has tried his hand at memoirs (*The Same River Twice*, 1993, and *No Heroes*, 2002), a novel (*The Good Brother*, 1997) and more short stories (*Out of the Woods*, 1999). More recently his efforts have extended to fantasy writing (in *McSweeney's Mammoth Treasury of Thrilling Tales*, 2003), comic book writing ("Another Man's Escape," 2005) and, currently, to television writing (*Tough Trade* and *True Blood*), editing (*Top Chef*), producing (*Tough Trade*), and coproducing (*Weeds*). He also played the role of "Charlie" in the film *The Slaughter Rule* (2002) and starred in the *Resist Evil* trilogy. From his credits it would appear that television work is now paying the bills for Offutt, much as Hollywood script writing once did for Dorothy Parker, F. Scott Fitzgerald, and William Faulkner.

Although Offutt paints Iowa as the place where he shaped his craft, it may have been with his father back in Appalachia where the bug first bit. Andrew Offutt wrote and published prolifically in the areas of science fiction and fantasy, as well as pornography, with his wife contributing to the effort by doing most of the manuscript typing. Chris Offutt does not credit his father with stimulating his interest in serious writing, although he praises the work of many other Appalachian and regional writers. But when his father gave up a profitable insurance business during Chris's youth in order to become a free-lance writer, the son was almost certainly aware just how precarious that decision might turn out to be. We thus find in Chris Offutt's father an immediate family precedent for the risky writing profession the son has chosen, if not a precedent for the son's choice of subject matter.

At this writing Offutt's own sons, Sam and James, are moving into adulthood; he himself is married to Melissa Ginsburg and is actively engaged in television work. He has promised two further novels, one to precede *The Good Brother* and one to follow it. At last sighting Offutt could be found in Los Angeles.

The Good Brother

Chris Offutt's *The Good Brother* is a lovingly written tale that seems beholden in many ways to Mark Twain's *Adventures of Huckleberry Finn*. We are given, for instance, a backcountry hero who is shown to be a naïf with native survival wit. Virgil Caudill exists in the tradition that gave birth to Huck, as a stubborn loner who manages to pivot away from difficult encounters while maintaining internal integrity. Facing up to his upbringing, and because the revenge tradition of his hills demands it of him, he feels obliged to kill Billy Rodale, the man who is assumed to have killed his wild brother Boyd. He commits this murder only after cleverly and carefully planning his escape under a newly created identity.

We may recall that Huckleberry Finn came to within a hair's breadth of killing his ne'er-do-well father and would have done so if necessary to preserve his own existence. For Huck this realization is at the root of a long and meticulously planned escape from captivity, which frees him from the need to kill Pap in order to survive. Thereafter Huck assumes a new identity at almost every fresh encounter with the world, and he finds living a lie not at all impossible. Like Huck, Virgil also soon becomes aware, following the murder of Rodale, that "lying was easier than he expected because people wanted to believe what they were told" (83). Neither Huck nor Virgil is thus averse to rebirth as someone else as a means of escaping a cycle of violence and retribution. And once the fresh identity is adopted, neither protagonist proves willing to deny it, even when faced with indisputable proof of its falsehood. Both discover that a slight variation in the cover story is usually all it takes to throw questioners sufficiently off the scent.

Both Huck and Virgil head west to a symbolic "territory" in seeking to begin again. For Huck it is unsettled land beyond the Mississippi. For Virgil, too, the Mississippi is a symbolic barrier he must cross as he wends his way west toward Montana. And when Montana does not pan out for him, we are given to believe that his last-stop outpost—the farthest west he can actually go in continental America—will be Alaska, which also, as we may recall, is a former "territory." This westering is traditional in American literature—in part thanks to Mark Twain himself—and both he and Offutt employ it by way of commenting on America and its potential. While Twain leaves that potential uncircumscribed, the problems he subsequently experienced with writing a sequel to *Huckleberry Finn* could well have had roots in what he knew of the negative features of that West, to which he himself had fled as a young man. With Offutt the potential contained by the West is limned as being much less promising than in Twain's novel, and he can be seen as calling into question the open-ended optimism with which Twain closed his narrative. It should be remembered in Twain's defense, however, that his was a book about a fourteen-year-old boy, while Offutt's concerns a full-fledged adult. Thus a portion of Twain's expected audience included the youthful element that had been so taken with *The Adventures of Tom Sawyer*; and seen from this perspective, *Huckleberry Finn*'s closing optimism is not unwarranted. Offutt's novel, on the other hand, does not pretend to reach beyond an adult readership.

A further likeness between the novels of Offutt and Twain is to be seen in the fact that each contains a major figure usually considered by the protagonist to be in some manner superior to himself, and more of a leader in adventurous undertakings: in *Huckleberry Finn* it is Tom Sawyer who "knowed how to do everything" (323); in *The Good Brother* it is Virgil's brother Boyd, who is portrayed as widely experienced and knowing things that Virgil had never dealt with, since Boyd was more venturesome and, at that stage of their lives, more effective than Virgil. While Boyd is encountered only as the dead shadow that hovers over so much of Virgil's own life, Virgil is nonetheless continually coming into contact with and learning more about the things that Boyd knew and the life he led. And Offutt has Boyd's echo heard by Virgil at almost every juncture of his post-Boyd life. Boyd Caudill and Tom Sawyer force upon the hero of their respective novels decisions that require that character to wrestle determinedly with concepts of good and evil, as well as with questions of morality of a more general nature. Virgil and Huck are driven to the wall by the actions of these figures, to which they somehow feel indebted, owing of respect, and subordinate. In this manner, both Offutt and Twain make full use of counterforces to extract from their protagonists as many of the juices of decency and humanity as can be squeezed from such virtual innocents without making them unbelievable goody-two-shoes types.

Another feature that links the two novels is that both Virgil and Huck are possessed of a natural sense of right and wrong that somehow overrides and informs their actions and decisions. When, for instance, Virgil needs to drug Rodale's dog in order to be able to get close enough to kill Rodale, he worries lest he has overdone it and perhaps put the dog to sleep for good. Throughout the rest of the novel, even on the final page, this worry never ceases to disturb his conscience. And when Orben Stargill, who has come from Kentucky to find Virgil in order to take revenge for Rodale's death and is someone who could put Virgil's mind at ease about the dog, is killed, Virgil realizes that the fate of Rodale's dog will almost certainly remain forever a mystery to him, continuing to trouble his conscience. From Virgil's point of view, killing Rodale was not an unmitigatedly positive act, but was the correct thing to do, according to the unwritten law of the hill country where he grew to maturity. Killing a dog that had not harmed him, on the other hand, would have been an unjustifiable wrong, causing him anguish at the thought that he might have unintentionally committed an act of which he would not be proud. By means of the seemingly minor note sounded by the recurrence in Virgil's memory of the dog incident, Offutt makes it clear that this unwilling murderer is not at heart inhumane, and can by no means be seen as the possessor of a granite-hard conscience.

Huck, too, has pangs of conscience that extend as far as to trouble him about the robbers he abandons to their fate on the sinking steamboat the "Walter Scott." The robbers are quite happy to leave their traitorous confederate tied up and unable to save himself from the rising waters, and no doubt would have treated Jim and Huck in like fashion had they caught them. Huck understands this but can nevertheless sympathize with the ruffians as fellow human beings who will suffer from the fact that he and Jim have stolen their escape skiff and thus doomed them to the fate they believed would belong only to their hog-tied former pal. Upon reflection Huck dismisses this burr under the saddle of his conscience with the offhand observation: "I felt a little bit heavy-hearted about the gang, but not much, for I reckoned if they could stand it, I could" (91). At first blush the statement would appear insensitive and even blasé, but upon closer examination, Huck's words actually seem meant to keep his soft side from getting more exposure than a still insecure and somewhat touchy fourteen-year-old would feel comfortable with. He is still young and unsure enough to need to create a protective carapace.

There are many other instances on the part of both protagonists that allow us to see the purity of spirit underlying exteriors sufficiently tough to handle the difficult situations and hard characters that they are forced to face head on. One of the major sources of tension in each work is the question of whether the hero's decent value system will survive the present onslaught from the outside world intact and uncompromised. Conscience, as both Twain and Offutt have realized, is not an easy thing to keep in even a moderately unsoiled state. Worth noting in this regard is that Mark Twain even went so far as to create a short story, just prior to beginning *Adventures of Huckleberry Finn*, in which the protagonist frees himself to embark upon a rampaging "carnival of crime" by physically murdering his conscience.

Another parallel between the texts of Offutt and Twain is found in the fact that both turn to the feud as a means of showing just how senseless, even in the contemporary world, an unexamined ancient tradition can be. Both Huck and Virgil find themselves caught up in the web of death at the heart of the blood-feud mentality, and each loses someone close to him: Virgil loses Boyd, Huck loses Buck. Offutt, moreover, goes Twain one better in showing us that even by moving west and away from one's native region the primitive tradition cannot be eluded. In *The Good Brother*, Offutt carries the problem as far west as Montana, where Virgil, now under his newly adopted name of Joe Tiller, finds Frank, the violent Minuteman type, and Frank's friends, feuding with the central government to the extent that they are ready to die for their cause. Frank displays all the chilly distance, mercilessness, arrogance, and rigidity of Twain's Colonel Grangerford; and with both characters a misbegotten, twisted sense of honor and justice leads to extensive destruction. The fact that only Frank and three other members of his group die in the final conflagration crisply underlines the hollow bluster of their claims to head an army of stalwarts, as well as the underlying foolishness of the feud concept.

An additional element that links Offutt's book to Twain's is water, found most often in the form of rivers. While for Twain it is the Ohio and the Mississippi that are the focus, Offutt supplements those two with the Wabash, the Missouri, and other western rivers, along with assorted creeks. For both authors a river is a central, defining force that carries a deeper comment on the frailty of mere human undertakings. Contact with a river, or simply the crossing of one, is almost always something on which the protagonist in each work needs to comment. Neither for Offutt nor Twain is an enormous ocean necessary to link their central characters to the symbolic power of water. When Virgil is abandoning his life as Virgil in order to become Joe, he is symbolically reborn as Joe via his ignorance of the fact that the Cincinnati airport is located on the Kentucky side of the Ohio River. For this reason he has to drive over that river twice and thus he undergoes a kind of dry "baptism" before managing to finally finish the successful adoption of his new identity. Out of his Kentucky hills and traversing such a large body of water for the first time, he is "amazed by its width" (95–96). When he subsequently drives away from Kentucky, we find him, on a single page of the novel, stopping near "the Wabash River," "astonished by the size of the Mississippi River," and, as night begins to fall, reaching "the Missouri River" (123).

When Lionel Trilling once cited Blaise Pascal as affirming that a river was "a road that moves" (Trilling 1948, xiv), he was speaking of the role of the river in *Adventures of Huckleberry Finn*; and Mark Twain had had long experience traveling such a "road" as a steamboat pilot. For Offutt his hero never crosses one of those "roads" without recognizing its importance to him, as well as its power—whether symbolical, physical, or in some manner spiritual. Virgil can even go so far as to sense, as he expresses it, "as if he'd moved from summer to autumn simply by crossing a creek" (102). For the new Joe one sign of his outsider status in the western state can be found in the following comment: "The most light was near the water, and the sound of Rock Creek carried easily over the snow. He rose and struggled through heavy brush to the water's edge. At a sharp curve in the creek's path he watched the water come out of a turn, race past him, and plunge into the next bend. It moved much faster than the Blackfoot or the Clark Fork River, and was at certain points wider than either one. He couldn't figure the difference between a creek and a river in Montana" (146). This confusion regarding the subtlety required in Montana to differentiate between these two kinds of flows leads him a few lines later to the conclusion that "this was not his world" (147). Water had been beneficial for him in the past by helping to link him to a new identity, but at this moment it is serving to keep him foreign to the world he is striving to join.

Mark Twain, who acquired his own new identity from a measurement used for fathoming the depth of water—in his case that of the Mississippi River—and who later moved into a society foreign to him when he married in the East, created Huck, a hero who also finds new identity linked with happenings on or along the river. But he can never fully manage to become an unquestioning part of the surrounding society, even when it is that of older "river rats" in the form of raftsmen. Huck, like Virgil/Joe, learns that the river has two faces. He habitually looks to the river for adventure, protection, and escape; and as long as it serves these functions it is his friend, despite the frequent negative experiences he undergoes while linked with its flow. But when he comes to understand at the end of the book that he must leave Tom Sawyer behind in order to take his first hesitant steps toward adulthood, it is with the realization that his future will need to be shaped in a less fluid and unstable environment. In the past the river has impressed Huck with its size and power, in particular during a frightening, dark night spent alone in a canoe when he was forced to comprehend that "it was a monstrous big river here" (102). But that unpredictable element must now be abandoned for dry land. Huck's new world, like Virgil/Joe's, will need to be found elsewhere.

Another feature of Offutt's novel that seems to parallel Twain's is the approach to racism. Virgil sees his first black person only when he leaves his backwoods home for the first time, and he knows nothing of "mud people." He hears that term used in Montana by the extremist element with which he has become entangled. Despite the pressures exerted on him by that right-wing group, Virgil/Joe at no point adopts their hate or hate-filled rhetoric. All of that is as foreign to him as is the world he encounters outside the Kentucky hills.

We find his open-minded attitude encapsulated in the observation "You can't fight prejudice with more prejudice" (259).

Huck, on the other hand, is not without contact with the color question since it was an integral part of the world into which he was born. But no more than Virgil/Joe can he adopt the hate that accompanies the rhetoric. Twain, however, does not blanch at putting much of that rhetoric into Huck's mouth, if only to contradict it through Huck's actions. Huck's gut, it seems, can never quite stomach the prejudices by which he is surrounded. It is his humane reaction to the man he shares so much time with that helps us, indeed forces us, to see Jim not as an unfeeling animal but as the kind decent equal of any other human being on the planet. Offutt's Virgil/Joe is also unable to find hate for "mud people," despite the pressure of the strange new social universe into which he has fallen.

In the novels of Twain and Offutt we find in addition to the similar treatment of "the darker brother" a similar treatment of the violent element of society. In *Huckleberry Finn* we see that demonstrated in connection with Pap and the black "p'fessor" that Pap pushes aside on the sidewalk. We also note it elsewhere: in connection, for example, with the actions of the King and the Duke, with their later rail riding, with the cruelty to dogs and pigs by the loafers at Bricksville, in the scenes with Colonel Sherburn, and in the treatment of Jim when he is caught near the end of the novel. Violence, it seems, is pervasive, and Mark Twain regularly underlines that prevalence in the world he presents us. Each case is informed not only by brutality, but also by a type of insanity that depends upon dismissing any sympathy for the victim.

Offutt's treatment of the violence threatened by Frank and his supporters is based on a similar viewpoint. The intensity of Frank's close-minded ideology leaves no space for sympathy for a common humanity. It is all black and white with no shadings. It is "with us or against us" extremism that brooks no tolerance of differing views. For both Offutt and Twain the element of insanity involved in such a blinkered perception of the world could not be clearer. Both authors take us up close to the violent characters' inhuman and unbending need to close off any personal softness in order to be able to carry out their actions with an untroubled conscience. Ironically enough it is conscience, but of a different stripe, that prepares Huck and Virgil/Joe for a wider tolerance and for their ultimate rejection of the violent actions of man.

Another feature in which we find the two novels in parallel is the "good versus bad" nature of the protagonists. The title of Offutt's novel points to Virgil/Joe being good in some way, despite the fact that he kills a man in cold blood to avenge his "bad" brother, who had never killed anyone. Twain's Huck is also considered by "good" society to be "bad," but Twain described him as having "a sound heart." In his "Notebook 35" Twain wrote that when a sound heart and a deformed conscience come into collision, conscience suffers defeat (34–36). The defeat is that suffered by Huck's original acceptance of slavery and its laws. With Virgil, who has, as we observe, a "sound heart" as well, the "deformed conscience" would seem to be concerned with his acceptance of the hill law regarding the need to take revenge on the killer of a relative. In accepting the precepts of that law, he takes a step backward in the society-approved human development. Virgil/Joe needs to move away from personal vengeance and to accept a more objective, socially acceptable punishment for murder. Virgil/Joe commits no evil, brutal, or cruel acts elsewhere in *The Good Brother*. Nowhere else does he show himself unworthy of the definition of him expressed by the title of the novel. As with Huck he ultimately and unequivocally rejects prevailing prejudices, even though such rejection promises to exclude him from the only society he is currently a part of. Virgil/Joe turns out, after all, to be "good" in a manner reminiscent of Huck.

A major theme of both *The Good Brother* and *Adventures of Huckleberry Finn* is freedom. In Offutt's novel it surfaces early in showing Virgil tightly chained by the unwritten law of the hills. In his frustrating quest to liberate himself he feels obligated to first obey that law through avenging his brother Boyd by killing Rodale. Having accomplished that task, he then manages to avoid prison and to free himself from his newly acquired criminal past by changing identity. Even that cannot keep him free, however. For in Montana he finds himself once again shackled, not only by his murder of Rodale and the ever-surfacing shadow of Boyd and Boyd's ways but also by his new environment with its own restrictive laws and duties where even his adopted identity comes into question. The alleged goal of the people he falls in with in Montana is also the attainment of freedom, but the freedom they seek requires them to reject the laws and responsibilities of the society in which they are living. To adhere to their philosophy would mean that, as Virgil/Joe sees it, the "only people who get to be free are the ones who think the same way as Frank" (291). And Frank has an extensive enemies list of people and institutions, which includes Jews, banks, "mud people," and the U.S. government.

Freedom is also central to *Huckleberry Finn:* the freedom Huck requires to live in peace with his surrounding world and the freedom of Jim from slavery, along with Jim's freedom to live free with his own free family. Huck's freedom, however, is regularly placed in jeopardy by his connections to other human beings, in particular by his idolization of Tom Sawyer. He nevertheless manages to shake free of all constraining ties in the end; but we would need to be blindly optimistic to believe that Huck's newfound freedom is more than temporary, for it is evident that he will never be able to live without contact to other people. It also happens, in a stroke of seeming serendipity, that at the same moment that Huck finds himself liberated from his fear of Pap and from his threatened adoption by Aunt Sally, Jim also finds that he is free. It is nonetheless clear that despite Jim's momentary rejoicing, his future will almost certainly be seriously circumscribed by the color of his skin. For neither Jim nor Huck does the future promise to be unfettered.

Virgil/Joe is, by the end of Offutt's novel, once again in the process, like Huck, of moving on, in order to escape the looming threats to his freedom. But his newfound love for and commitment to Botree and her children promises, at the very least, to limit his freedom of movement at precisely the moment when he considers heading for Alaska. Given impediments of this nature, it seems probable that neither the "territory" for Huck, nor Alaska for Virgil/Joe may, after all, provide that yearned for freedom each novel floats before the eyes of its protagonist like a shimmering holy grail.

As we watch each character go through experiences and participate in the events in their lives, we may note that a portion of their "goodness" comes from the fact that they remain somewhat distant from those experiences and events. It is as if they were consistently viewing everything from without, and being acted upon, much more than initiating action themselves. They are consistently in a reaction mode, rather than the reverse, and are weighing and judging far more often than simply going with the flow of events. Neither character allows himself to unhesitatingly follow the movement of the others. Both prefer avoidance to direct confrontation. When that confrontation nevertheless occurs, however much unwished for, each character shows spunk in some fashion and handles the problem with surprisingly effective panache. What is more, their seeming sideline stance makes the apparent brazenness of their reactions all the more surprising. Twain's Huck and Offutt's Virgil/Joe are thus cut from the same moral cloth, and, while seemingly passive and noncommittal in many situations, neither is a coward. Both are "good" in their own consistent way, and both are "bad" from the point of view of their contemporary society. Considered from within their own parameters, they are, however, survivors who deal with black and white extremes pragmatically, without allowing society's external judgment much play in the end.

The Good Brother and *Adventures of Huckleberry Finn* are also linked by a feature common to both but that in each case is based on a different reason. That feature is the absence of off-color language, explicit crudeness, or graphic sexual descriptions. This is not surprising regarding Mark Twain, who was writing a boy's book in the Victorian Age, when nothing could destroy a reputation quicker than "bad taste" writing. In *Huckleberry Finn* Twain is careful to tread feather lightly in presenting the bordello scene where Pap loses his life, and he is just as circumspect when it comes to muffling the full force of the crude scene on which the "Royal Nonesuch" was based (Twain 2003, 438–39, n. 195). Nor does any "vulgar" language appear in his novel.

Chris Offutt also eschews any sort of rough language, even substituting "I'll be go to hell" for the more common "I'll be damned" at one point (298). (Although it is possible that this is a phrase used in Appalachia with which I am not familiar, it seems to this non-Appalachian too stilted to be either common or comfortable in use.) Nor do we find described any but the mildest of love scenes between Botree and Virgil/Joe. This may seem somewhat odd when we come to realize that Offutt's father wrote pornographic novels for a living during Offutt's youth, and that the quality of Offutt's life during that period owed much to that genre. As he tells it, "Porn straightened my teeth. Porn supplied me with shoes, food, and clothing and the only football on the hill. Not all the boys had gloves, but porn kept my hands warm in winter. Porn paid the mortgage. Porn bought clothes and food and medicine. Porn provided Christmas and birthday presents. Porn would have financed my high school dates had not the widespread knowledge of Dad's occupation interfered with my ability to acquire dates" (Offutt 2006, 52).

Although Offutt in *The Good Brother* deals with raw themes and characters, he manages to do so without recourse to raw language or descriptions. It therefore seems evident that it is not his father that he has taken as his model in his writing. Nor should this astonish us since in the small town of Haldeman, Kentucky, with its few links to the outside world, there must have been some discord between a growing young man and a father who had to have his privacy to write porn. But the town is situated in hills and dense woods, to which the boy repaired when kept out of his home at such times (Offutt 2006, 50). His parents never went into those woods (Hamilton 2002). It is small wonder that Offutt in his own writing privileges those woods and the constricted surrounding society to which he was consigned by his father's need for quiet at home. Not only does Offutt have Virgil/Joe find refuge in nature, like Huck, but he also demonstrates by omission that one can write well without employing the register or appealing to the instincts exploited in his father's potboilers.

It might also be noted here that *The Good Brother* is not the first of Chris Offutt's works to show a clear debt to Mark Twain's *Huckleberry Finn*. In Offutt's short story "Blue Lick" (Offutt 1992, 115–27) we have as both narrator and protagonist—in the manner of Huck—a young man who lives with a violent ne'er-do-well father, who "borrows" things that do not belong to him, much as Huck's Pap thought nothing of "borrowing" chickens and justifying it with the line "take a chicken when you get a chance, because if you don't want him yourself you can easy find somebody that does, and a good deed ain't ever forgot" (Twain 2003, 79). The father figure in Offutt's short story calls his son a "river rat," perhaps this is Offutt paying homage to *Huck Finn*. The father in Offutt's work is, in the style of Pap, vengeful and destructive, not hesitating to burn the barn or steal and dismantle the car of someone who has gotten on the wrong side of him. We may also note that while the "river rat" in Offutt's story remains unnamed, the young man, like Virgil/Joe and Huck, is no stranger to lying under pressure; although, again like Huck, his skill in the art is as yet imperfect.

Offutt's story also includes a do-good female VISTA volunteer who is trying her best to "save" the boy in a manner akin to that of Aunt Polly and Mrs. Loftus. The naïve young narrator, like Huck, does not, however, feel comfortable with the idea of adopting society's ways, and physically fights against the efforts of the volunteer in order to keep some sort of grip on his own world, and to avoid being wrenched from it.

"Blue Lick" ends with the lines, "There was nothing but river, not a rat in sight. I sat there till a mile past dark" (126). For those familiar with Mark Twain's novel it should not be difficult to recall Huck's memorable description, as he floated down the river at night in his canoe, "Everything was dead quiet, and it looked late, and *smelt* late. You know what I mean—I don't know the words to put it in" (42). Twain, on the other hand, did know the words, and Huck's humility provides further evidence of his creator's art. Offutt's "river rat," in distinct contrast to Huck, is neither humble nor particular about his verbal expression, and he is still far too untamed and unschooled in the world's formalities to even conceive of an apology, as Offutt is fully aware. Huck, it should be pointed out, might seem to present-day readers tame in comparison, but it must be remembered that at the time the novel appeared, Huck was considered uncouth and objectionable enough to have the Concord Public Library, as well as a number of other institutions, ban his book. In today's society Offutt's work runs no such risk.

While Offutt's admirable short story comprises far more than what I have indicated, it nevertheless remains a contemporary reflection on proper and improper society in a style commensurate with Twain's *Huckleberry Finn*. And, given the resemblances pointed to above, it would not seem exaggerated to suggest that they owe more to *Huck Finn* than to happenstance.

Debts to previous writers do not necessarily a criminal or a plagiarist make, and we should recall that Twain himself was not averse to "borrowings." What is of key importance, of course, is that the writer create out of the materials he or she finds at hand, something new that lives, and that the writer infuse new life into the work and share it with the reader. This, I would maintain, Chris Offutt does, and in spades. For make no mistake, we are in the presence of no failed "borrower" but of a creative talent that does not hesitate to take risks. Daring to rework *Huckleberry Finn* themes and features allows Offutt to simultaneously bring those into a contemporary light and to give them new thrust. So well does he do this, and so subtly, that I doubt if it is noticeable to most readers.

One important aspect that separates Offutt's novel from Twain's is that in *Huckleberry Finn* we are told the story from a first-person point of view, while Virgil/Joe is presented to us through the eyes and ears of a third-person narrator. Neither of these narrators, to be sure, speaks or thinks for any of the secondary characters, which keeps those characters at a distinct distance from the reader; but with Offutt's novel that distance produces a much cooler effect than is the case with *Huckleberry Finn*. That is to be expected from the chosen method of narration, but that more objective distance prevents the novel from achieving the immediacy that would grab the reader at a more deeply emotional level. Offutt is an expert at creating surprises for us, but the warmth that emanates from *Huck Finn* is never approached. Offutt obviously understood this and chose the cooler approach for his own reasons. Twain had marked out a path that Offutt opted to ignore. His awareness of and ability to use the power of first-person narration is nevertheless displayed in his "Blue Lick" short story, where he employs it to excellent effect.

We also find evidence of Offutt's creative strengths in a number of other areas. We find it in Offutt's treatment of Kentucky roots. *The Good Brother* brings these roots and the hero's rootedness to the fore. Kentucky contains societal extremes that make for difficulty for many of its inhabitants, and Offutt does a serious service in clarifying for the outside world just how separate and cut off from much of the rest of America life is in the hills and mountains of Appalachia. The habits, traditions, and mores of those hill counties are not what most Americans have had any intercourse with, and the simple directness or lack of it in transmitting or expressing them on the part of the inhabitants can, for example, seem to outsiders like ignorance, naïveté, stupidity, or even dishonesty. Offutt begs to differ and shows that the Huck-like qualities he portrays are not of lesser value or importance. The savage traditions may be different, but no more savage than many of those found as far away as Montana, and no doubt Alaska, when the surface is but scratched a little. America houses many extremes, says Offutt, and Kentucky is neither an exception nor a unique and frightening model.

When Virgil leaves the hills to become Joe and to create a new world for himself, in a place where he believes his murder of Rodale cannot catch up with him, it turns out that he is headed toward a Huck-like "territory" that will prove just as violent, wild, and uncivilized as the area he is leaving. The dream of a pristine new "territory" to flee to, Offutt would appear to tell us, is just that: a dream. Huck, it would seem, never really has a chance, no more than Virgil does, of reaching such an Eden. In addition Offutt apparently wants us to realize that in order to maintain our personal integrity we may need to keep on the move—much as the rivers keep steadily flowing—in order to attain a modicum of satisfaction and to find an escape from ever imperfect and often violent surroundings within contemporary America.

Carrying Offutt's message is beautifully crafted prose; and many are the paragraphs honed into self-contained dramas. For example, when Virgil comes to kill Rodale and is holding a gun on the freshly awakened man, "Rodale's eyes opened. He stared without moving. He compressed his lips but didn't speak. He closed his eyes and opened them and they appeared to age as if a disease had attacked. His entire body seemed to retreat into itself, drawing in, as if to present a smaller target" (120).

An additional area in which Offutt shines in *The Good Brother* is in his effective use of humor, primarily in the Kentucky section of his novel. After Virgil/Joe reaches Montana, however, the good ol' boy camaraderie that framed so many felicitous exchanges during Virgil's life in the Kentucky hills diminishes drastically. The reason is a logical one: Virgil's old friends have been left behind in order for Virgil to begin to exist as Joe. Those friends and the joy Virgil had known with them must also be expunged from his new life and identity. One of the few moments—post-Kentucky—where Offutt's humor is allowed to emerge, if only for a short moment, but with the gentle charm that so often graces his writing, occurs when Joe, tongue in cheek, offers the no-neck young son of Botree a "neck" as a birthday gift. Taking Joe seriously, the child is overjoyed and Botree later tells Joe, "It's already his favorite present. His brother wants one now. A bigger one" (198).

In the earlier part of the book, prior to Virgil's murder of Rodale and subsequent flight, Offutt employs humor of a different and somewhat raucous kind that is not far from that found in Mark Twain. Offutt can permit himself more leeway than Twain for two reasons: he is writing for an adult audience and the propriety limits of the Victorian Age no longer enjoy currency. The following example shows Offutt creating a solid laugh with a minimally off-color exchange. Virgil says:

"I don't need no bullets hitting me. How about you, Dewey?"

"I done been shot once," Dewey said. "Bullet cut a crease in me big enough to lay a finger in."

"Where at?" Virgil said.

"In the ass," Taylor shouted. "Go ahead, Virgil. Lay your finger in it." (34)

For the most part Offutt's use of humor would no doubt have earned Twain's respect and laughter, given the range of humor Twain not only produced in *Huckleberry Finn* but also took pleasure in creating for more adult audiences. I believe, however, that one instance in particular in Offutt's novel would not have passed muster with Twain. That occurs when Offutt seeks to indicate Virgil's naïveté by telling us that as Virgil drives through Frankfort, Kentucky, he notes that the "governor's mansion was very big and Virgil figured he must have a good-sized family" (84). The Twainian humor evident here brings to mind the scene in *Huck Finn* where Jim, in discussing Solomon and his wives, figures "a harem's a bo'd'n house. I reck'n. Mos' likely day has rackety times in de nussery. En I reck'n de wives quarrels considable; en dat 'crease de racket. Yit dey say Sollermun de wises' man dat ever live" (Twain 2003, 94). While Twain's humor is sure, and Jim is justifiably presented as naïve, Offutt misses fire in this instance, for it does not ring true to have Virgil painted as quite so ingenuous when he displays unerring native smarts throughout the rest of the novel. Such Twainian humor works well with Huck and Jim because they are both painted as naïve and innocent throughout *Adventures of Huckleberry Finn*. Only once, in fact, do we ever hear of either of them laughing, and that occurs when Huck falls overboard and tells us, "It almost killed Jim a-laughing" (168). Virgil, however, though inexperienced, is not green enough about life to warrant his drawing his conclusion naïvely and with a straight face (as Jim does with the "bo'd'n house"). Nevertheless, and despite what I consider to have been a slip in this case, Chris Offutt's ability to produce a good belly laugh in the reader is one of the many strengths of his novel.

Another strength of Offutt's writing is his seemingly effortless use of metaphorical language. His talent in this area lends color and flavor to many moments, and his application of this tool allows for a story that often takes the reader to a greater depth than might be anticipated. In this manner Offutt creates a refreshing dimension that expands our imaginative journey. Reading Offutt's prose offers pleasure parallel to opening the petals of a flower, with each petal awakening quiet astonishment. So fascinating is that prose world that once having entered it the reader will find it truly difficult to soon step out again. A particular facet of that world is Offutt's respect for and perceptive treatment of nature. Here is an example of the author's deceptively subtle skill at forging unpretentious original poetic imagery: "Kentucky nights began on the ground, in the hollows and the woods, moving upwards to join the sky. Here, the darkness dropped from above" (124). Chris Offutt also does right by the English language as used in the Appalachian region of Kentucky. His ear is precise and the tone of the speech he reproduces is convincing, as the following dialogue selection illustrates:

> "Come on out, Mom."
> "Well, if you're wanting company."
> "Always yours."
> "I ain't a-caring, then."
> She stepped onto the porch and quickly pulled the door shut. She sat in her chair, picked up the fly swatter that lay beside it, and placed in her lap.
> "I shouldn't ort to have set," she said. "I don't know how I'll get up."
> "I'll start to get worried the day I find you sleeping there in the morning."
> "You remember the time Sara's first cat got up in the yard oak and she started crying."
> "We was all just kids," Virgil said.
> "Boyd, he told her to hush up, that cat would come down and he could prove it."
> "I don't remember that part."
> "Oh, yes. He said you could walk these hills a hundred years and there'd be one thing you'd never find—a cat skeleton in a tree." (47)

In *The Good Brother* Chris Offutt offers the reader a fresh and powerful depiction of a present-day Huckleberry Finn. As he traverses contemporary America, the naïve but inwardly strong Virgil follows his own unflagging angels in his struggles with the devils he meets on his journey through the thickets hindering his progress. That Huck-like journey, however, could not have had a better model than Mark Twain's *Adventures of Huckleberry Finn*, and it is to Offutt's credit that he can bring his hero so effectively into the modern world while linking him with issues with which Twain wrestled and which continue to trouble America.

As inspiration for his own writing Chris Offutt gives credit to many Appalachian and other Kentucky writers, including Bobbie Ann Mason, James Still, Robert Penn Warren, Wendell Berry, and Breece Pancake (Offutt 2000). Elsewhere he mentions Flannery O'Connor as a formative influence (Grant n.d.). It seems a curious oversight, however, to allow any possible debt to Mark Twain to go unmentioned in Offutt's credit lists, given the many similarities noted above. Could it be that Twain's ubiquitous influence on American writers is simply taken for granted in today's writing, including that of Offutt? Is being beholden to Twain now considered a given that no longer need to be acknowledged? Whatever the reason for passing over Twain, it would seem that the force of Twain's work has nevertheless left deep grooves in Chris Offutt's treatment of the rain gullies of the eastern Kentucky hills he has done so much to make his own and to share with his readers.

It should also now be clear that *The Good Brother* goes well beyond a mere rewriting of Mark Twain's *Adventures of Huckleberry Finn*. With his novel Chris Offutt has given us an adult protagonist who is strong and alive. I see this novel as a strong and important one that pulls its weight and will retain its influence. It is sincerely to be hoped that Chris Offutt will not let this be his only venture into the field of the novel. He has much to share and we can only be grateful if he chooses to do so.

Works Cited and Consulted

Grant, Gavin J. "Chris Offutt: Looking Back, Looking In." Telephone interview with Chris Offutt. BookSense.com. N.d. http://www.indiebound.org-interviews/ offuttchris/.

Hamilton, William L. "At Home with Chris Offutt; Learning Not to Trespass on the Gently Rolling Past." *New York Times*, April 18, 2002. www.nytimes.com/ .../at-home-with-chris-offutt-learning-not-to-trespass-on-the-gently-rolling -past.html.

Offutt, Chris. "Porn Bought My Football." *River Teeth* 8, no. 1 (2006): 44–53.

———. *No Heroes: A Memoir of Coming Home*. New York: Simon and Schuster, 2002.

———. "Getting It Straight." *Ace Weekly*. November 16, 2000. http://www.aceweekly .com/backissues_ACE.Weekly/001116/cover_story001116.html/.

———. *Out of the Woods*. New York: Simon and Schuster, 1999.

———. *The Good Brother*. New York: Simon and Schuster, 1997.

———. *The Same River Twice*. New York: Simon and Schuster, 1993.

———. "Blue Lick." *Kentucky Straight*. New York: Random House, 1992. 115–72.

Trilling, Lionel, "Introduction." *Adventures of Huckleberry Finn*. By Mark Twain. New York: Rinehart, 1948. xvi.

Twain, Mark. *Adventures of Huckleberry Finn*. Ed. Victor Fischer, Lin Salamo, and Walter Blair. Berkeley and Los Angeles: University of California Press, 2003.

———. "The Facts Concerning the Recent Carnival of Crime in Connecticut." *Collected Tales, Sketches, Speeches, and Essays, 1852–1890*. New York: Library of America, 1992. 644–60.

———. "Notebook 35." Typescript, 34–36. Mark Twain Papers. Bancroft Library, University of California, Berkeley. As quoted in *Adventures of Huckleberry Finn*. Vol. 8 of *The Works of Mark Twain*. Berkeley and Los Angeles: University of California Press, 2003. 619.

Barry Hannah ⚡ *Yonder Stands Your Orphan*

OWEN W. GILMAN JR.

A Biographical Sketch

Since the early 1970s Barry Hannah has been widely recognized as one of the liveliest and most provocative of writers active on the southern scene. From his first novel, *Geronimo Rex* (1972), to his most recent, *Yonder Stands Your Orphan* (2001), Hannah's edgy, staccato style has been distinctive. His narratives take sharp turns at a turbo-charged pace, often many on a page, and it takes a reader with tenacious spirit to hang on for the whole ride.

It has seemed from the very beginning that Hannah relishes most of all the shock of a turn of phrase, the darting introduction of some piece of background information out of the blue, the jarring surprise of sex or violence, or violent sex—anything that goes like a lightening bolt through the reader's filters and straight to the cerebral cortex. Information comes as *shock, shock, shock*. Hannah has lived his life in the same way, hard and fast, pushing the limits, decade by decade, relationship by relationship, and book by book.

For Barry Hannah Mississippi is always the central gathering place, although characters in his fiction can and do go east to Alabama and west to Louisiana—or up north to Arkansas or Missouri. But his home is the same at every outing: the South. Given the gravitational pull of Mississippi throughout Hannah's life, there are no surprises here regarding the locales featured in his fiction.

Barry Hannah's life began soon after America's entrance into World War II, with a birth date of April 23, 1942. The son of Elizabeth King Hannah and William Hannah, who made his living selling insurance, Barry Hannah grew up in Clinton, Mississippi. He eventually matriculated at Mississippi College, which is located in Clinton, and received a degree in a premed program in 1964. That detail has loomed large in quite a few of Hannah's stories over a writing career of forty-plus years, as doctors often emerge for a role of some note, most recently in the figure of Dr. Harvard in *Yonder Stands Your Orphan*, and it is worth mentioning right away that although Dr. Harvard has had a great many travails and numerous setbacks in his lifetime, he survives into old age, and at the end of the novel, he is married to the woman of his geriatric dreams, Melanie Wooten.

The words "They clung" (*Yonder Stands Your Orphan*, 336), describing Harvard and his bride Melanie after their marriage on a pleasure barge, serve to finish the story. These words are in an epilogue, and they clearly are meant to echo the closing words of another defining text of Mississippi and the South, William Faulkner's *The Sound and the Fury*, which finally settles into quiet with the last two words of the "Appendix": "They endured." While Faulkner's words speak to the particular condition of Dilsey and her family, African Americans subordinate to whites but remarkably durable, Hannah's "They clung" addresses more broadly the tenuous surviving condition of Mississippians as a whole, perhaps even southerners in general. That would include Barry Hannah himself, still clinging after a hard life.

Hannah headed off to Arkansas following his undergraduate program and forthrightly collected a master's degree in English and a master of fine arts degree at the University of Arkansas. He married Meridith Johnson, and they soon had three children. By the late 1960s Hannah had commenced the pattern he would follow to the present time: writing books and serving as writer-in-residence at schools around the country, but mostly in the South. He started at Clemson University (1967–73); then there were stops at Middlebury College (way up north, for three years), the University of Alabama in Tuscaloosa (a five-year stint), the University of Iowa (1981; you know you've really arrived when you get to work at the grandfather of superlative creative-writing workshop programs), the University of Mississippi (1981), and again to the north at the University of Montana–Missoula (1982–83). A significant detour from this pattern happened in 1980, when Hannah wound up in Hollywood, California, for treatment of alcoholism and a stab at the movie business, which are other Faulkner parallels.

By the mid-1980s Hannah was ensconced in writer-in-residence status back home at the University of Mississippi, where he still occupied a public stage of distinguished reputation and considerable consequence for aspiring writers who sought his guidance. He was, for example, able to provide a helpful guiding hand of friendship and encouragement to Larry Brown, whose career trajectory from firefighter to widely acclaimed author was thoroughly remarkable. Brown took over for Hannah for a semester as writer-in-residence at Ole Miss, and Brown's academic posts also included the University of Montana–Missoula.

Besides teaching, drinking, and going through traumas of emotional angst, he wrote—also during his divorce from Meridith and the short but intense marriage to Patricia Busch. When he died on March 1, 2010, Hannah had for years been in a settled and durable relationship, his marriage to Susan Varas. As he noted in an interview in 1982, his creative work has always tracks close to his own life experiences. Through nine novels and three short-story collections between 1972 and 2001, the correlative points between Hannah's living experience and the world of his fiction are numerous and consistent. There is always the frenetic push and pull of testosterone in high gear and lots of sex;

there is a great deal of hard drinking, with largely predictable results; there is music, food, and fishing—all fine features of the Mississippi landscape. And there is Mississippi, Mississippi, Mississippi—the South.

Yonder Stands Your Orphan

Before we look in detail at *Yonder Stands Your Orphan*, it is worth considering the political situation of the American South from the time Hannah emerged as one of its more provocative writers. By the time of Hannah's first novel, Richard Nixon had already twice employed his "southern strategy," that is, he appealed to the patriotism, lingering racism, and general southern conservatism in order to pull many of them away from the Democratic Party so he could be elected president. Following closely in Nixon's footsteps, there were three Republican presidents, Ronald Reagan, George H. W. Bush, and George W. Bush, who won only because the South backed them.

Since Nixon's first victory, three presidents have come from the Democrats. The first two were bona fide southerners: Jimmy Carter from Georgia and Bill Clinton from Arkansas. In general terms up until the cataclysmic presidential election of 2008 it would be reasonable to claim that with regard to political influence, the South belatedly won the Civil War by taking full and consistent control of American destiny through the last three decades of the twentieth century and the first decade of the twenty-first. The outcome in 2008, with the election of America's first African American man to the presidency, completes a different circle, looping back to dot the "i" and cross the "t" in Father Abraham's vision of "victory" in 1865. To put it briefly, throughout the years of Barry Hannah's career, which includes *Yonder Stands Your Orphan* published early in the twenty-first century, the South was in an ascendant pattern and even dominant on the national scene. With this sort of backdrop one might expect to see grand and glorious things in Hannah's Mississippi, the adopted home of Jefferson Davis, who was president of the Confederate States of America.

This is not the case, however, when we scrutinize the body of Hannah's fiction. In *Yonder Stands Your Orphan*, we see Mississippi as a virtual orphan: rootless, cut from its origins, adrift rather haplessly on diverse waters, groping almost blindly, gambling along, and barely dodging disaster after disaster after disaster. The state is a pathetic diminution of itself, if there ever was one. The doom that was the past, inescapable and intractable, proved far too much for the wanna-be escapist Quentin Compson in *Absalom, Absalom!*—Faulkner's greatest novel—and Hannah's fiction fills itself with the same downward spirit. Mississippi is a great swamp, and it seems to be slowly sinking into itself in Hannah's fiction. The word "swamp" may be the key.

In 1989 Louis D. Rubin Jr., perhaps the preeminent scholar of southern literature and culture in the last half of the twentieth century, published a book called *The Edge of the Swamp: A Study in the Literature and Society of the Old*

South. Rubin sought to explain the failure of antebellum southern writers to reach the heights of achievement represented in the work of the American Renaissance: Hawthorne, Melville, Thoreau, Emerson, and Whitman. Rubin pointed out that something contaminated life in the Old South, something that would ensnare all, including writers, from the region. The name of that something was chattel slavery. And it contaminated so much that even the wondrous world of nature became essentially a swamp, as Rubin notes in quoting a line from William Gilmore Simms's poem, "The Edge of the Swamp": "A rank growth, Spreads venomously round, with power to taint" (Rubin 1989, 52).

We see much of the swamp in *Yonder Stands Your Orphan*. It has mysterious qualities, including very strange hydraulics, as sometimes water leaks out of a swamp hole, yielding up from beneath the dark waters of the backwoods important secrets lost earlier, such as bodies in the trunk of a 1948 red Chevrolet—the first car in a series of makes and models evoking the evolution of America from domestic-car producer to foreign-car consumer; think Lexus. But this Mississippi swamp's strangeness is not entirely or exactly the one that, according to Rubin, captivated Simms and company and detoured them from greatness. Race is now not nearly so obvious a "swamp" factor. Race issues do shimmer and shudder a bit in the many twisted story lines of *Yonder Stands Your Orphan*, but they do not prove to be decisive for the outcome, as they were in the great works of Faulkner just a generation before Hannah.

The swamp is still an ominous place, however, almost immediately in the first chapter surrounding a "church, a little white steepled one in a glen set among live oaks and three acres of clover. The jungle swamps encroached on and squared the glen, deep green to black" (9). Then again, much later, "Lightning loved the swamp. The willows thrashed now where all the souls of dead bad poets roamed day and night" (177). The forces metaphorically represented by the swamp are several and they have everything to do with a different set of assumptions about the ideal good life as subscribed to by another group of southern writers, the ones whose essays are gathered in the collection from 1930 called *I'll Take My Stand*. In that collaborative work many of Faulkner's contemporaries addressed the key virtues of the South: it was an agrarian economy, with a steady and restoring closeness to the land, with lively social communities bonded by the love of story telling, food, talk, and music, and with a disposition to hold on to the past in order to keep a distance to the slippery slope of "progress," so foolishly and pervasively operating in other parts of America.

Closeness to the land, even the swamps, tight and almost incestuous social communities, a love of history, savory food, music in the folk tradition: these attributes would keep the South above the disasters that would settle elsewhere, so were the claims, among some others, that swirled through the "agrarian manifesto" of 1930. Some seventy years later, in *Yonder Stands Your Orphan*, Hannah finds diverse ways to invoke these alleged attributes of the good life, southern style, but to make the postmodern swamp complete, and perhaps to provide a sad coda to *I'll Take My Stand* with a dose of very hard truth, Hannah's latest novel tacitly acknowledges the economic realities of Mississippi at the millennial turn.

By almost all of the economic indices, Mississippi is a very poor state. According to the "Interactive Poverty Map," which shows the geography of American poverty based on U.S. Census Bureau statistics (http://www.usccb.org/cchd/povertyusa/map.htm/), Mississippi has the highest poverty rate in the nation, with 21.1 percent of the population being below the poverty line. Poor states have a hard time raising the revenue to provide necessary public services, and so it was not surprising that Mississippi turned aggressively to the casino industry in the 1990s as a source of revenue. Within a decade the state had the third largest gaming market in the country; this lasted until Katrina knocked out the Gulf Coast casinos. Vicksburg is one of the key locations for casino activity in Mississippi, with the Ameristar, Rainbow, and Resort casinos all operating in Vicksburg along the river.

Hence an important and timely foreground element in Barry Hannah's Mississippi environment in *Yonder Stands Your Orphan* is a casino in Vicksburg. One of the central characters, a demon of anger and violence and relentless evil (almost a Thomas Sutpen in the eyes of Miss Rosa Coldfield redux) is a figure named Man Mortimer. His various sordid businesses, such as prostitution, corruptions of minors, and traffic in stolen cars, all spawn out from the Vicksburg casino territory. As a name "Man" succinctly and symbolically represents the general condition of everyone. Man's influence is spread through all the grotesque action in the novel. Even as his life winds down toward a pitiful finish, the devastating effect of his presence contaminates nearly everyone. Poverty gives rise to casinos; casinos provide a base of support for Man Mortimer and his ilk; violence and mayhem in various forms precipitate out from the turbulence of Man Mortimer's path through life; and the reach of poverty is extended and its consequences aggravated. As a result the spreading reach of real poverty is now a recognized central feature of swamp Mississippi.

Nevertheless, as noted earlier, Hannah loves to spring surprises on readers, and his prose keeps us on our toes. So it goes with the poverty point. Even as the signs of poverty manifest themselves in falling-apart incidents in the novel, including the need for an orphanage, Hannah brings us up short with a counterpunch: "Mississippians were good folks. They gave more in charity than any in the nation" (69). If we ever doubted the durable folk wisdom that poor people are often the most generous, Hannah is ready to make us subscribers again. A quick check of the "Catalogue for Philanthropy" (2005) shows indeed Mississippi as the top state in philanthropy. It should be mentioned that there have been challenges to the formula used to arrive at such a ranking, which usually puts the most prosperous states in the lower tiers of national generosity.

Generosity notwithstanding, the postmodern Mississippi of *Yonder Stands Your Orphan* is a very rough place. What else would we expect from a novel with

"Orphan" in the title. Being an orphan is not on anyone's wish list, and from Charles Dickens to John Irving (see *The Cider House Rules*) the plight of the orphan has been given sympathetic treatment in fiction. There are orphans in Hannah's story, but the sympathy is missing. This is Barry Hannah land, and he does not do soft and gentle. Every turn of events in *Yonder Stands* is hard, also hard to anticipate—we have already seen how Hannah loves to pop his readers with surprises—and hard to accept, unless your emotions have become casehardened steel. You would not look for likeable, loveable people among the grotesques of Flannery O'Connor's fiction, and there are none here either. Hannah's book represents O'Connor in hyperdrive, a closed-circuit fun house, derivative in part from John Barth's narratives, which anticipate the chaos and character collisions (libidinous mayhem in the main) that we find throughout *Yonder Stands Your Orphan*. If you want to believe that the perversion and twistedness of all things in the South are far beyond the redemption of either intelligence or faith, then this is your book.

Yonder Stands Your Orphan is the story of a place in descent. Carl Bob Feeney is one of the background characters Hannah uses as a kind of chorus to try to put the dominant figures into meaningful perspective. Feeney addresses himself directly to problems of the contemporary South not long before he disappears: "'Hail fellow well met' is not a description down south, it is the *vocation* of most of the South. It has ruined it. We have lost something precious, Ulrich, and you must, must acknowledge this. We just don't give a shit. Machines started it, but we finished the job" (159).

If the bonded, compassionate community of the old South becomes lost, a fate feared most by the writers of *I'll Take My Stand*, is there not still a unifying sense of place? Not according to an authorial observation made when Sheriff Facetto takes his new lover Melanie (not to be confused with the long-suffering, impossibly sweet, forgiving, and dying Melanie of *Gone With the Wind*) to a football game, which is surely a secure place in the landscape of the South, where Bear Bryant was God back in Hannah's youth: "You just couldn't tell even who was where anymore" (133). In the absence of a guiding spirit of kinship and lacking a sense of place, Hannah's characters drift . . . and collide.

Along the way Hannah provides a minute inventory of the detritus of what was once a human race, now just a mass of babbling and stabbing eccentrics, unmoored and unhinged. The fact that there are survivors at all, albeit aged ones whose hot days are all in the past—people to warrant "They clung"—is nothing short of miraculous. In the main, the characters of Hannah's latest novel are not "people to have a beer with," which is our foolish gold standard for selecting presidents these days, that is unless you want to wind up badly cut on the face or near the seat of life betwixt the legs.

Hannah crams his pages with people. *Yonder Stands Your Orphan* swells with the relentless comings and goings, goings and comings of a diverse cast of characters. His model of fiction is an antithesis to the spare efficiency evident in

Nathaniel Hawthorne's *The Scarlet Letter*, always the American standard for a tightly focused symbolic narrative. Because the relentless activity of Hannah's characters defies reduction into a simple plot line, we really need to think in terms of motifs or themes that will allow us to track this orphan from beginning to end. Here's the list of topics that should cover his preoccupations: sex, religion, bait shop community, music, and violence.

Sex has to be first, as it has always represented ferocious energy in Hannah's fictional world. In an earlier overview of Hannah's work as a writer, I suggested that the reader might expect to encounter some kind of sex act about every four pages. Now, as Hannah heads toward the finish of his career, the interval might be closer to every three pages, and the variety is increasing apace. Consider, for example, a sexual act noted in the "Prologue," barely three pages into the story as the community-gathering function of a roadhouse is described. The roadhouse provides drink, some pool shooting, and a place for yarns to be swapped, all in the vicinity of Eagle Lake, where the fish are to be caught all through the story and where the orphanage is to be located. This is across from the Farté bait shop, which evolves into the place where everything rises and converges (in the spirit of Flannery O'Connor's title): "One man had a giant catfish fellate him there. He was not ashamed to return" (3).

Normally you fillet the catfish you catch, and the fish does not return the favor. I would be willing to bet at least one Confederate dollar that you have not encountered that particular sex act in any other text. It is tough to be inventive with sex, since it has been around for such a long time, but Hannah loves the challenge, and his male readers may be struggling with this catfish-sucking-penis image for a long time.

Another new development in sexual activity concerns the variable of age. Hannah has aged; so have his lovers. As the story unfolds Melanie Wooten has lost her husband in several ways. Dr. Wooten was a college president, and in aging, his interest in her waned: "Theirs was a kind of marriage without much fever, and in his sixties Wootie began falling in love with boy students and writing them letters. He was fired" (23). Eventually Wootie left for good, he died and left behind a seventy-one-year-old widow, who promptly starts watching men of all kinds. She fancies John Roman, who zips around on a motorcycle and loves fishing. But she mostly fornicates with the Sheriff Facetto. It starts with an energetic night at her lakeside vacation house: "He had brought *Fantasia*.... She had planned to talk an age, but what did she know.... He chuckled and then he was all over her. It was a long hour with several engagements. She could not believe it when he took her from the rear. She felt spasms and loved him backwards as if trained to this work because she was not only older, *she was old*, and she couldn't have it that she seemed naïve. That would be obscene" (113).

This particular sexual scene is one of the longest in *Yonder Stands Your Orphan*. There are no five-page treatments of a single sex/orgasm experience as portrayed in the contemporary romance genre. Hannah simply tosses in lots of quick references to various options: rough heterosexual sex, whores servicing men in diverse strange circumstances, oral sex between a witch and young boys, boys and men are fascinated by a woman's naked body, audiences of various kinds watch others in acts of sex. But Hannah does seem to have invested rather deeply in Melanie Wooten's enthusiasm for what she and the sheriff can do. And they do plenty before she eventually settles for Dr. Harvard, a much older admirer. Before we leave Melanie and the sheriff after their first set of sex acts, we learn what it was like for the sheriff: "It felt good, that good, like sin. If it hadn't, I guess it would have just been ugly" (114). And we have to remember that Sheriff Facetto is just thirty-six, half the age of Melanie. It is almost a coffin-robbing sin, but that twist is just the sort of hearty spice that is packaged in any Barry Hannah fiction.

Not surprisingly Man Mortimer is all testosterone, and he is all over the story. He has to dominate all the males in the neighborhood, and by the end of the story he has mated with innumerable women. In the present he fixates on Dee Allison, whose sexual favors are distributed widely. She eventually marries Harold Laird, a stalwart mechanic, and maybe even settles down, although that is hard to believe given her profligate behavior earlier. Along the way Mortimer very seriously cuts up Frank Booth because Dee took Frank to her bed. Mortimer is a complete psycho on the loose. He is the nexus of a youth driven by seriously unresolved parent-child conflicts and an adult life of relentless sex begetting violence. Mortimer's parents remember "how selfish a child he had been" and recall "he was vicious, calculating and secretive" (309). If you want to get a wild story going and keep it going, all you will need is *one* Man Mortimer. He does the job for Hannah.

In Man Mortimer's deep past he mated with a woman who later confronted him with a love child, whom he promptly denied. The woman then killed herself and the child. Mortimer is mortified (an easy Hannahesque linguistic gambit), but to keep himself out of public culpability, he arranges to have an old American car, vintage 1948, with their bodies in the trunk dispatched to the waters of swamp Mississippi. However, as part of the novel's interrogation of traditional Christian religious beliefs, this unholy mother and child are resurrected when the water mysteriously is sucked away. The bones of the deceased are then, all in keeping with the tradition of presenting the relics of saints to inspire the faithful, put on display in various poses by Dee Allison's sons with the good Old Testament names Isaac and Jacob. They are sons from her first marriage, which was to a decent Canadian gentleman named Cato, a name with a southern echo of the classical world. But the old bones on exhibit just drive Man Mortimer to distraction and further acts of revenge upon everyone who gives him offense, which would be just about everyone.

For more than a hundred years now, the South has been indelibly linked to religion and religious practices of the über-conservative, fundamentalist sort.

Hannah liberally salts his story with religious cant. At one point or another practically every character tosses out something with a religious flavor. There is even a pastor, Byron Egan, who holds forth in sermons at the church, although he sometimes seems just as comfortable in Peden's St. Aloysius Junkyard, where Dee is married to Harold Laird. Peden graciously yields the pulpit to Egan: "The Lord has given me this junken place, freed me of drink and drug, and sent a friend, Byron Egan, all the priest a Christian American ever needed. And best, He has given us His Book, which every man and every woman can read" (260). Along the way Egan has noted, at least to himself, "*You are postwar, postmodern, posthuman*" (201). With the resurrection variation; with Isaac and Jacob; with pastors both drunk and sober assuming pulpits in white-steepled churches encroached by the swamp and in junkyards, where Mortimer's stolen cars are sometimes readied for remarketing; with Maxwell Raymond the moody saxophonist (Hannah almost always has a main character who is an accomplished musician—and he favors the saxophone) trying to seduce his wife Mimi with a poem that ranges freely from ancestral prayers about getting a headshot on Grant or Sherman or some other Yankee intruder to "I always loved You Jesus and didn't understand much else. . . . I would like the straight Aramaic right from His lips" (243), Hannah's story is awash in religious references and inferences.

The words spew out, fervor abounds, and confusion reigns. In the midst of such cacophony one could only hope that some voice might rise above the din and speak the everlasting truth. A fool, such as in Shakespeare's *King Lear*, might do the trick; fools abound here, but they all appear to be on par, with none a cut above the norm, none capable of taking us to profundity, or even to insight, which is the key to Lear's story. Ironically one of the most calming moments comes not from a religious person or location, but from a snatch of poetry recalled by Melanie as she gazes into the face of a greyhound dog left by Facetto as a comfort to her until his return for more sex. The lines are from T. S. Eliot's "The Preludes": "some infinitely gentle, / infinitely suffering thing" (209).

If the conventional church and religion in a tradition do not calm all the troubled waters in swamp Mississippi, perhaps some other form of community solidarity might do the trick. Hannah centers much of his action on a bait store out by the lake, an establishment run by Pepper Farté until his beheading by Man Mortimer—who else?—just for a perceived slight in a look of disgust. Since then the store has been run by his son, Sidney Farté, who manages to hold off cancer with aggressive chemotherapy treatment. If we were looking for something scatological or obscene, it could readily be found in the neighborhood of the Farté family. Hannah had broached this dimension of experience even more directly earlier when Dee Allison ripped a t-shirt off one of her sons in order to address the hostility and obscenity joined in its message, which she thought perhaps belonged better on a bumper sticker: "If I Had Wanted to Hear an Asshole, I Would Have Farted" (88). Hence Farté, another nimble linguistic Hannah surprise.

Just about all of the characters wind up at the bait store at some point in order to get bait, to talk about where the fish are biting and what they are eating, to find out what is going on, whether in an official capacity in the form of interrogation of possible suspects in the murder of Pepper Farté or in a more informal swapping of gossip, such as who was going down on Sheriff Facetto, and to embark upon the lake for exploration over on the orphanage side of life then return to the bosom of the community. The bait store is a specific variation on the country store gathering place or the family dinner table.

To witness the marvels of community solidarity in full operational mode, despite significant fractious impulses, any reader might want to migrate over to Clyde Edgerton's novels. Mattie Rigsbee's table in *Walking Across Egypt* can accommodate and embrace squabbling siblings, outlaws, and the law, as long as the biscuits, fried chicken, and sweet tea servings are in steady supply. The dinner table also serves to help bridge the fundamentalist religion/secular humanist chasm as it appears in Edgerton's *Raney*. Similarly Fannie Flagg described this particular feature of the South very well in *Fried Green Tomatoes at the Whistle Stop Café*, where Idgie and Ruth serve everyone fair and well, regardless of race or sexual identity. Hannah's bait store is a potent gathering place, as just about every character in the narrative is there at one time or another, but it generates no particular sense of solidarity, and no spirit of the common good. It does not soothe or ameliorate the human condition; in fact, a horrible murder, the beheading of Pepper Farté, is the most notable single event linked to the place.

Still the bait store provides a commonsense focal point, providing food on the go, technical know-how on ways to land the lake's prize fish, an opportunity to swap gossip, and a vantage point to watch the lake traffic. To get over to the orphans, you depart from the bait store. When the orphans come over, they arrive at the bait store. Convergence of a certain kind takes place at the bait store, but it is a far cry from the Whistle Stop Café or the ballroom over at Twelve Oaks.

At public houses and community social events, music is often the medium of unity, and Hannah's novel is certainly packed with music. Max Raymond is a failed doctor but a good saxophonist; he can play in "certain needy and vicious ways... like a tomcat dragging away from a long fight down an alley." He is married to Mimi Suarez, a singer performing as "The Coyote" who practices her craft "singing to the edges of the swamp" (171). When the narrative swoops into close focus on them, music and the South become one—a full range of soulful feeling—earthy and tawdry, plaintive cry and bluesy emotion, all wrapped inseparably close together.

Plenty of famous musicians get mentioned along the way as well. The mentioning is better integrated than all the music referenced, for example, in

Bobbie Ann Mason's *In Country*, in which the songs noted serve mostly to place the narrative precisely in the early 1980s. In Hannah's novel the music evokes the essence of the South. This is also true even when the artist is not actually from the South, as in the reference to Bob Dylan. The music and musicians are summoned to reflect the mood and temper of the region. By the way, the title of Hannah's novel, *Yonder Stands Your Orphan*, is a line in Dylan's "It's All Over Now, Baby Blue," a song from 1965.

Conway Twitty is the recording artist most frequently mentioned in the novel, which should not be a surprise since he is actually a native of Hannah's Mississippi. Twitty's original name, Harold Lloyd Jenkins, was selected by a great uncle as a tribute to the silent comic actor Harold Lloyd. In the novel it is probably no coincidence that Harold Laird gets to marry Dee Allison sometime after a character named Lloyd has also been involved in a sexual escapade with Dee. Hannah loves that kind of entanglement of names and relationships. Conway Twitty becomes almost ubiquitous in the story. Frank Booth heals slowly after being cut savagely in the face by Man Mortimer, and as the healing proceeds, Booth comes increasingly to resemble Conway Twitty. Soon everyone is seeing him as Conway Twitty, and as such, he in essence becomes the face of "Mississippi Man," a man good with music and with moves on the ladies. Man Mortimer himself even has a dream in which his mirror image says that "he was an impostor in the body of Conway Twitty" (255).

Other music references in the novel include the work of Patsy Cline, Roy Orbison (one of the background characters, named Ulrich, wants to sing like Orbison), Johnny Cash, the Oak Ridge Boys in concert at Branson, Missouri, Conway Twitty, and Chet Baker. Music matters here. Music is a touchstone of culture, a way of being and a means of knowing. If there is anything remotely like a soul in Hannah's world, it has much to do with music.

Violence is also a major motif in *Yonder Stands Your Orphan*. Man Mortimer cuts a swath of blood and death in his path through life. He is just one man, but he sure leaves his mark with a ferocious onslaught of cutting and carving, and there is plenty of death and pain in his wake. He is finally put away in Parchman Prison at the end of the book. Early on, there is a woman and her child, neither well known to the reader but terribly important to Man, whose cold rejection of them leaves them both dead by the woman's hand and, as we have seen, then resurrected from the swamp. Frank Booth is stabbed in the liver and then later sliced in the face at a football game, of all places. Dee Allison is cut in the thigh when a four-way orgy at the Casino does not go well. A parking lot attendant is cut on the arm. A workman at Mortimer's house is cut in the face for a look of disgust. Penny Ten Hoor, the woman of the couple who establish the orphanage as a way to deal with the loss of their son in an accident, has her head nearly cut off by Mortimer in his assault on the orphanage near the conclusion of the story. And then there is Pepper Farté, an admittedly ugly and unappealing old man full of prejudice and bile, whose head is cut off and replaced with a football stuffed down his neck. Here we have another vivid image to reverberate long in the mind, and the symbolism might be sardonic, even cutting: The South becomes a region where a football can be put in place of a head. The old man crossed Man Mortimer with a look of displeasure, of rebuke. Pepper paid for his judgment with his life.

Not all of the violence is the work of Man Mortimer, of course. Some of it is visited on him, as when he chases a football into a nest of cottonmouth snakes at the edge of the lake. Nature seems ready to strike back at this murderous monster. The violence is also aimed at Mortimer when he is stabbed in a testicle by Frank Booth during their first altercation over the rights to Dee Allison's vagina. Nor is it Mortimer's fault when Sidney Farté, soon after a chemotherapy session, vomits uncontrollably on Sponce, one of Dee's children, and then is promptly decked by Sponce with a fist to the face. Guns, knives, and fists—the full arsenal is on display in *Yonder Stands Your Orphan*, and almost constantly we see the victims fall. This sort of mayhem, with dark and feral forces on the loose, would logically produce orphans, and indeed the orphanage fills almost instantly.

Barry Hannah reportedly has been working on a new novel for the past several years, potentially to be called *Long, Last, Happy*. However, the style and mood of the "Epilogue" for *Yonder Stands Your Orphan* come close to hitting the notes sounded by Prospero in his farewell at the end of Shakespeare's *The Tempest*. A good many details are tidied up in the "Epilogue" of the novel. In Hannah's sign-off Sheriff Facetto gets an election victory, but when Melanie tells him "he was childish and she did not want a child in the house anymore," Facetto's sadness soon causes him to move far away. Deputy Bernard arrests Man Mortimer in Peden's junkyard while Mortimer is "looking for something among the wrecked cars"—presumably the skeletons once locked away in the trunk of that '48 in the swamp (335). Sent to the penitentiary, Man Mortimer starts to talk, and talk, and talk, dumping the details of his sorry life on all who will listen. Nobody seems interested. John Roman and Max Raymond heal their rift, and rather miraculously Roman "loved God cautiously" although he "did not know how long this love would last" (336).

Finally there is the marriage of the aging ones, Harvard and Melanie, a match that is "that of pals after a fight and long silence." What realm of time is this? In the closing words of the narrative, "It had become too late in time for fights, and often even memories. They clung" (336). Gone is the wind and the violence. Sex seems not to be on the horizon here. A man and a woman, with lives of wandering and wild experience between them, and most certainly behind them, are together at last in relative quiet and remarkable peace. Another tempest is at last finished. There may well be more from Hannah in coming years, but the ending of *Yonder Stands Your Orphan* does sound much like a rehearsal for the last chapter of a career.

Works Cited and Consulted

Bone, Martyn. *Perspectives on Barry Hannah*. Jackson: University Press of Mississippi, 2006.

"Catalogue for Philanthropy." *National Generosity Index 2005*. http://www.catalogueforphilanthropy,org/cfp/db/generosity.php?year=2005/.

Edgerton, Clyde. *Walking Across Egypt*. New York: Ballantine Books, 1987.

———. *Raney*. New York: Ballantine Books, 1985.

Eliot, T. S. "Preludes." *Collected Poems, 1909–1962*. New York: Harcourt, Brace & World, 1963.

Faulkner, William. *Absalom, Absalom!* New York: Vintage Books, 1987.

———. *The Sound and the Fury*. Ed. David Minter. New York: W. W. Norton, 1987.

Flagg, Fannie. *Fried Green Tomatoes at the Whistlestop Café*. New York: Ballantine Books, 2000.

Gilman, Owen, Jr. "Barry Hannah." *Contemporary Fiction Writers of the South*. Ed. Joseph M. Flora and Robert Bain. Westport, Conn.: Greenwood Press, 1993.

Gretlund, Jan Nordby. "Interview with Barry Hannah." *Contemporary Authors*. Ed. Hal May. Detroit: Gale Research, 1984. 110:233–39.

Hannah, Barry. *Long, Last, Happy: New and Selected Stories*. New York: Grove, 2010.

———. *Yonder Stands Your Orphan*. New York: Grove Press, 2001.

———. *High Lonesome*. New York: Grove Press, 1997.

———. *Bats Out of Hell*. New York: Grove Press, 1994.

———. *Never Die*. Boston: Houghton Mifflin/Seymour Lawrence, 1991.

———. *Boomerang*. Boston: Houghton Mifflin/Seymour Lawrence, 1989.

———. *Hey Jack!* New York: E. P. Dutton/Seymour Lawrence, 1987.

———. *Captain Maximus*. New York: Knopf, 1985.

———. *The Tennis Handsome*. New York: Knopf, 1983.

———. *Ray*. New York: Knopf, 1980.

———. *Airships*. New York: Knopf, 1978.

———. *Nightwatchmen*. New York: Viking, 1973.

———. *Geronimo Rex*. New York: Viking, 1972.

Hawthorne, Nathaniel. *The Scarlet Letter*. New York: Signet Classic, 1999.

I'll Take My Stand: The South and the Agrarian Tradition. Baton Rouge: Louisiana State University Press, 1977.

"Interactive Poverty Map." U.S. Census Bureau. http://www/usccb.org/cchd/povertyusa/map.htm/.

Irving, John. *The Cider House Rules: A Novel*. New York: William Morrow, 1985.

Rubin, Louis D., Jr. *The Edge of the Swamp: A Study in the Literature and Society of the Old South*. Baton Rouge: Louisiana State University Press, 1989.

Shakespeare, William. *King Lear*. New York: Signet Classic, 1998.

———. *The Tempest*. New York: Signet Classic, 1998.

Weston, Ruth. *Barry Hannah: Postmodern Romantic*. Baton Rouge: Louisiana State University Press, 1998.

James Lee Burke ↭ *Crusader's Cross*

HANS H. SKEI

A Biographical Sketch

James Lee Burke is probably the best of all American crime writers on the contemporary scene, and since so many of his best books challenge the borders and limits of the genre, he is also among the best fiction writers in the United States today. Born in 1936 in Houston, Texas, he now lives in New Iberia, Louisiana, and Missoula, Montana. He published his first book, *Half of Paradise*, in 1965. For a long period he divided his time between university teaching and writing, and his production was accordingly sparse and occasional until the mid-1980s. Then, in 1987, in *The Neon Rain*, he introduced his Cajun New Orleans and New Iberia detective Dave Robicheaux and created, it turned out, a serial figure in a rich and colorful environment with enough crime to last any writer a lifetime. Ten years later Burke introduced former cop and Texas Ranger Billy Bob Holland as a new hero in the novel *Cimarron Rose*, and in later books moved Holland and his law practice to Missoula, Montana.

Two of Burke's novels have been made into motion pictures, and he has received two Edgar Awards for the best crime book of the year. He has even written an "ordinary" novel set during the Civil War, *White Doves at Morning* (2002), and he seems to have become more and more prolific. He has reached complete mastery of his preferred genre, crime fiction, which in his hands has become a hybrid form of the police novel in which not only a central character but also a number of cops often play significant roles.

His novels can, almost inevitably, be read as serious comments on negative developments in the state of Louisiana, particularly in New Orleans and the Gulf Coast area. Hurricane Katrina and its aftermath gave new fuel to the outrage Dave Robicheaux and his creator seem to share, an outrage directed against local as well as federal politicians for their corruption, neglect, and failure in all areas. This aspect of Burke's novels may not be the most prominent and may be overlooked by readers whose fascination is with crime and investigation. The implied criticism of a corrupt and crime-ridden society is well integrated in his fiction, and it is an aspect that contributes significantly to the excellence of his novels. Burke's writing is at times even lyrical, in the sense that he describes the natural beauty of the landscape, the changing seasons, the wonderful joy of good fishing, the wonder of watching two pelicans flying out over the bay, and the hope that lies in the fact that the pelicans have returned after years of absence. He seems to say that maybe the world can be set right after all; maybe everything large and small can still be savored and enjoyed.

James Lee Burke's Robicheaux novels are placed in richly evoked southern landscapes with the smells and sounds and colors of palm trees, live oaks, impenetrable shrubs of pine, and stretches of desolate or abandoned land (the exception is *Swan Peak* [2008], which is set in Montana). More than a crime scene or even a landscape, southern Louisiana in Burke's novels becomes a place in fiction in a real sense, a place with a long tradition of the men and women who lived and died there, of hopes and aspirations and love and despair. It becomes a microcosm in which an author can bring to life believable characters, who act in accordance with a shared set of rules and values, and who must pay if these—even if they only are social conventions—are broken.

James Lee Burke's detective cum hero shares the doubts and misgivings, frustrations, and difficulties of the antihero, a familiar and lonely figure in an indifferent world also in serious fiction. Yet this figure achieves redemption through acts of bravery or stupidity because he is decent and honorable. The reader never doubts his honesty and integrity; our sympathy is always on his side and against stupid or corrupt colleagues, as well as criminals of all sorts.

Dave Robicheaux fought in Vietnam and has later been down and out with a severe alcohol problem that threatened to destroy him. He has had constant conflicts with his colleagues and superiors when he worked at the New Orleans Police Department. He sobered up and worked with the New Iberia Police Force as a homicide investigator, and he ran a small business. For a long period he was a proud and happy family man, with his wife, Bootsie, and their adopted daughter, Alafair. In *Crusader's Cross* this has all changed, as we shall see.

Dave Robicheaux never simply solves the crimes; his involvement is often personal and moral, and he more often than not fights to maintain his honor and decency. In two of the most successful books in the Robicheaux series, Dave's deadly fight involves a discovery of the father he never had time or opportunity to get to know in *Burning Angel*, and it becomes even more dangerous and painful when he tries to ascertain the legacy his mother left him in *Purple Cane Road*. Who was she, who killed her, and did she ever think of the son she left behind when he was just a boy?

James Lee Burke writes crime fiction in the noir or hard-boiled tradition, but he does it with such force and with a language so vibrantly alive, so tuned to every change in mood and atmosphere, so poetic even in descriptions of violence and death, that it puts him in the first rank among American novelists today. His Cajun detective never only finds the facts behind a case and solves it, but is forced to take a moral stance toward events that in Burke's best books become personal if not existential. Money and sex are always at stake, and hookers, pimps, junkies, and former prisoners prowl the streets or drive the highways and gravel roads where Robicheaux must follow in his pickup truck or police cruiser. In her *James Lee Burke and the Soul of Dave Robicheaux*, Barbara Bogue presents Robicheaux's troubled existence based on all the novels up to and including *Crusader's Cross*.

Maybe Robicheaux is an anti-antihero. When he walks down the mean streets he is often on the brink of falling into the kind of inhumanity and cruelty that he sees all around him. Being a cop among cops, who walk in dirt all day, is a dangerous business if you want to keep your humanity, your self-respect, and your integrity—because in Dave's world one of the most critical problems is corruption among policemen or the silent agreement that cops cover for each other. James Lee Burke has inherited some of Dashiell Hammett's bleak pessimism, almost to the point where he sees violence and corruption as a part of the human condition. But if we look more closely at the "hookers, pimps, house creeps, stalls, dips, strong-arm robbers, fences, money washers, carjackers, petty boosters and addicts and crack dealers" (*Purple Cane Road*, 85), crime is shown above all to be a result of American capitalism and greed.

Crusader's Cross

James Lee Burke's fourteenth novel with Dave Robicheaux as narrator, central character, and hero, *Crusader's Cross*, was published in 2005. It is a complex and compelling story about violent crime, investigation, and final solutions to all the mysteries in the book. Everything is interdependent, related, or interlocked in the combined search for a serial killer and for Ida Durbin, a girl from Dave and his half-brother's youth. One could say that Dave is on a personal crusade, or that he has a heavy cross to carry, but the cross of the historical Crusades is also a part of the coat of arms of the Chalons family. The members of this family are in all sorts of ways at the center of the novel and serve to link past and present events; even to the point where deeds of the past offer the final solution to the present investigations.

Although the pace of the novel is rapid, with its numerous killings, confrontations, fights, threats, and violent encounters, there is also space and time for quiet moments, solitude, and reflections on life in general and on the development in New Orleans and Louisiana at large. Since everything is told and seen from Dave's perspective, his private struggles with the demons from his past and with the forces that threaten to destroy him in the present investigation are at the core of the novel. The tormented soul of Dave Robicheaux mirrors and doubles a society on the verge of being destroyed by the rich and powerful and by organized crime. The streets are mean and violent and dirty, but down these streets our hero must go to solve crimes, even if the system may remain unchanged, in order to survive as a moral human being, and because someone must report from the margins of a dark world in which man's injustice and cruelty to man have absolutely no limits. Let us turn to a superbly handled crime story with a strong undercurrent that indicates that this is also a crusade against the social injustice that lives on and thrives in "the new South," perhaps in new disguises.

The novel opens with a description of "the last decade of American innocence," the 1950s. It describes the end of an era, in terms of images and sounds, of being young and having few cares. It is perhaps the nostalgia of an older man that recreates the summer of 1958 and makes it into something special, because it is lost and with it, everything he then hoped for and believed in: "The season seemed eternal, not subject to the laws of mutability. At best, it was improbable that the spring of our graduation year would ever be stained by the tannic smell of winter. If we experienced visions of mortality, we needed only to look into one another's faces to reassure ourselves that none of us would ever die, that rumors of distant wars had nothing to do with our own lives" (1–2).

Dave Robicheaux looks back on this summer of his youth when he and his half brother Jimmie worked ten days on and five days off on a seismograph crew that laid out cable along the Louisiana and Texas coastline. He tells little of the work, but more about the days when they were on land at Galveston Island, having a good time. The narrative then singles out one peculiar event on the Fourth of July that year, because Jimmie and Dave were stranded on the third sandbar from the shore when the tide came in with great force and sharks began to circle in the water around them. The narrator many years later almost laconically states that "it was going to be a long haul to the beach" (5). Then a voice calls, and a young girl appears on tubes roped together and with a wood paddle to navigate. They climb aboard the makeshift raft and are safely carried to the beach. The girl's name is Ida Durbin, and she had discovered the brothers through binoculars and had already heard that sharks had attacked elsewhere. Her comment is simple: "There's always some folks who need looking after, at least those who haven't figured out sharks live in deep water" (6).

But as we soon learn, Ida also needs to be looked after, or it may already be too late to save her from other predators and other threats. In the 1946 canary-yellow Ford convertible that the brothers own, they take Ida to a beer garden and celebrate Fourth of July in each other's company. Before the next ten days at work, they are also on a picnic together. When they return Jimmie finds Ida in a music store where she plays the mandolin and sings, and she sounds like Kitty Wells (who in 1952, with her "It Wasn't God Who Made Honky Tonk Angels," was the first woman to sell a million records). But the music store is actually a pawn shop and the owner advices the boys not to come back because the girl has enough trouble in her life. But Jimmie obviously is in love and does not take advice. He buys the mandolin to give it to Ida as a present, but he soon learns that she lives and works as a whore on Post Office Street—that is in a "hot pillow joint." Jimmie still thinks he can save Ida and does not go back to work.

He even meets Lou Kale, her pimp, and pays what Kale claims is Ida's debt to him. Jimmie is planning to run away with Ida. As readers we all fear that Jimmie's plan of escaping to Mexico with Ida will not work out. We are, of course, right: Ida is not at the bus depot where she was supposed to be picked up by Jimmie, and she is gone from the brothel when the police check. "The years passed and I tried not to think about Ida Durbin and her fate" (31), but sometimes Dave hears a voice on the jukebox that reminds him of Kitty Wells and comes to think of Ida.

Dave states that he would "almost forget about Ida Durbin" (33), so why does he devote two lengthy chapters to the memories of her and the summer of 1958 as the opening of a narrative that deals with a Baton Rouge serial killer—murders, investigation, and detection—many decades later? What could the disappearance of Ida back in 1958 possibly mean to an investigation so much later? The truth is that it has nothing to do with the serial killings but in devious and mysterious ways a lot to do with the killer himself. The reason for reminiscing about the summer of 1958 and the missing Ida is also a phone call that Dave receives from the wife of a notorious bully called Troy Bordelon, who had gone to the same college as Dave. For reasons unknown Troy always had called up Dave for a cup of coffee or such when passing through New Iberia. The wife simply says that Troy, now that he is seriously wounded and in the hospital, wants to see Dave. Troy can barely whisper but apparently wants to apologize for the abuse of everyone minor or weaker than himself, trying to get Dave to support the idea that they had a good time back then. But the confession Troy has to make is about Ida, and it is the reason why Dave's story begins on Galveston Island in 1958: "'Years ago, you knew a girl who was a whore,' he said. 'They snatched her up'" (39).

One of the men who took Ida away was Troy's uncle who was a cop in Galveston. He tells that they busted her mandolin and that cops and a pimp took her away. He does not know whether they killed Ida; he remembers that he saw blood on a chair, but he was just a kid back then. The search for Ida Durbin, who may or may not have made a record, who may or may not have been dead all these years, could have stopped here, and probably would have, were it not for two police officers who try to question Dave about his visit to Troy and want to know what he had said, when he unburdened his sins. Dave refuses to answer, but he knows that the policemen, Billy Joel Pitts and J. W. Shockley, are there on behalf of someone. Later he learns that 'the someone' is the Chalons family in St. Mary Parish. Troy cannot reveal any more secrets, for when Dave tries to see him the next day, Troy has died during the night. Dave tries not to think of the possible connections between Ida's disappearance and the rich and powerful Chalons family, led by Raphael Chalons, with their mafia connections and their control of everything and everybody in the parish. So the narrative breaks off in order to let our hero introduce himself and describe the situation he now finds himself in, as a widower, living alone now that his adopted daughter is away to college. Most of this brief and personal account deals with loss, with what has been: "For years I had been a detective with the Iberia Parish Sheriff's Department and also the owner of a bait shop and boat rental business outside of town" (42). He does not mention it at this point, but Dave has been married three times, and on a number of occasions his mind wanders off to thoughts of his second wife, Annie, and more frequently to Bootsie, his third wife, whose grave he visits more than once. There are times when he wishes to be with Bootsie, but he also remembers her belief that the pelicans one day would return to the Bayou Teche, which to her would be proof that "the world was still a grand place in which to live" (229).

Dave is also a dry drunk, an alcoholic who goes regularly to Alcoholics Anonymous meetings and even belongs to an AA bunch known as the Insanity Group. He tries desperately to cope with his addiction. Alcoholism and the struggle against it are classic elements in the formula for creating a detective in hard-boiled fiction. To be successful James Lee Burke must give his detective personal problems in his private life and as it is traditional in the genre, alcoholism is one problem and another is everyday life with a woman. Although the struggle to stay sober calls more attention to itself in this novel than we expect, it is still the crime investigation and the elimination of the perpetrator that matter in the end. Ironically Robicheaux states that "introspection and solitude are the perfect combination for a dry drunk" (43), yet if he decides to investigate the disappearance of Ida Durbin and the possible crimes committed, his ability to think, reflect, and deduct are necessary. Moreover he needs to return to police work, and not the least because Pitts and Shockley visit him again, trying to scare him off whatever investigation they fear he is undertaking. He is also attacked at night and hit by a two-by-four and kicked across his mouth by someone with a nylon stocking over his face. Robicheaux needs to get his shield back, to reopen the old case of Ida Durbin's disappearance, and to find his attacker.

In the totality of the narrative that makes up *Crusader's Cross*, it is extremely important that the Baton Rouge serial killer is introduced at this point, almost a little awkwardly, as if the narrator did not really know how to begin this aspect of his story, although it will be so closely linked to everything else in the end. Dave simply reads the lead story in the newspaper about a murder of a young black woman who had been abducted while visiting her brother's grave. The murder bears similarities to other homicides in Baton Rouge, although this is the first body found so close to New Iberia. A little later we are told that the DNA of the killer has been found on five prior victims. As the killer moves farther away from Baton Rouge and into the area of the Iberia Parish sheriff's office, there is every reason to let Dave Robicheaux work as a homicide investigator, and he gets his shield back from Helen Soileau, the first woman sheriff of the parish. The relationship between Dave and Helen is one of many ups and downs; she has to give him desk work to keep him off the street and to halt what at times appear to be personal vendettas. She is very much aware of his investigative talent, no matter what shortcuts he and his friend, the private investigator Clete Purcel, may take. Purcel has been Dave's closest friend since they fought together in Vietnam, and even though he brings a lot of trouble to Dave as well as to himself, his help is invaluable in the sense that the story and the plotting simply need a character like this. Clete refers to himself and Dave as "the Bobbsey twins from homicide." Clete can do things that Dave may not have wanted him to do, but in the end they prove to raise dust, provoke action. Ultimately the chaos and disturbance he creates, often at the risk of his own life, is instrumental in the solution of crimes. Clete plays a central role also in the long-winding investigation into Ida Durbin's disappearance back in 1958, and helps out when there is a contract on Dave's head, although he brings a hit man so close to Dave that only a quick reaction and an exact shot save his life.

Dave escapes the threats from those who tried to find out what Troy told him about Ida, but he knows that other people stand behind them. The chief suspect is Val Chalons, the son of Raphael Chalons, who owns a television company and is capable of using his media power to destroy anyone's reputation. For a long time it is difficult to see that Dave has other reasons for hating Val Chalons than a general suspicion of the rich and mighty. But there is also the problem with his sister, Honoria Chalons, who seems slightly disturbed as she lives in a world of her own dreams and hopes, out of touch with the realities of her life and the family she belongs to. For some reason—maybe just that Dave is friendly and polite to her when he sees her—she looks him up and spends the night at his house after having handcuffed him. No sex is involved, and he tells her to go home in the morning. Unfortunately, or perhaps just as well, three other persons show up to see Honoria leave his house. These are characters of the utmost importance in the further development of the story of crime, investigation, and detection, which we, at this point, understand will bring together the two different strands: the Ida Durbin disappearance case and the serial killer's murders. The narrative is focused more and more closely on the Chalons family and its legacy of wealth, riches, and active participation in organized crime.

The visitors are Molly Boyle, a former Catholic nun who now runs a kind of community center for the poor, including a folk craft workshop where they make birdhouses for sale. Her company is Andre Bergeron and his son, Tee Bleu. Andre helps Molly with various chores at her place, but is otherwise handyman on the Chalons estate, living in quarters at the back of the enormous house from the 1850s. He is a craftsman and builds the birdhouses that his son peddles at thirty-five dollars a piece. Dave later buys one when his old one falls down in one of the many storms that visit the area. In the world of serious crime fiction, where deduction and reason must be accompanied by intuition, we should not be surprised that even an innocent bird house will be a clue and play a role in the ongoing investigation. But this comes much later.

In the meantime we follow the development of a double investigation—into the whereabouts of Ida Durbin, who seems to be alive somewhere in the Miami district, and into the murders by the serial killer, who strikes closer to our investigator than they ever expected. More than anything else we follow Dave Robicheaux as his narrative retraces the ups and downs of the investigation, with serious threats to his own life and with the ever-present danger of his taking an easy escape from the hardships and troubles by allowing himself a drink. He is the narrator, he is the central character, he is the one who acts and against whom acts are planned, realized, or prevented. Whatever he does, he creates some sort of new development or he creates chaos and havoc. He knows strange and dangerous people who can be helpful, and he has strong support in his work from Helen, his boss, and, at times, from Clete, his friend. He gets better acquainted with Molly, and when she discovers that he buys an alcoholic beverage, she acts immediately and on impulse to prevent him from drinking. Instead they end up in bed, and Dave's loneliness seems to be broken. Molly is definitely "his kind of girl"—she even has qualities that he previously attributed only to Bootsie.

With accusations from Val Chalons of having had sex with Honoria and with the threats from the slugs who try to stop him from looking into the Ida Durbin affair, Dave most certainly does not need the scandal that soon follows when police bring a search warrant to his house, followed by a TV team, who are at the house almost before he and Molly can get out of bed. Val Chalons is furious and willing to do everything in his power to destroy Dave, in particular after Honoria has been brutally murdered. Dave knows that the accusations are outrageous, but he also knows that he has broken all his vows and been on a serious "bender" and has had a total blackout for a period of twenty four hours. The surveillance camera at the house shows that he could have been there, as person number two, and he knows that he has in his possession a CD with a blood smear and a song, written much later than 1958, but apparently sung by Ida Durbin. So what is the connection between Ida in 1958 and the Chalons, then and now?

More and more information reveals that Raphael Chalons had an interest in prostitution and ran some of the brothels on Post Office Street, where we know that Ida worked before she disappeared into thin air. A call from the Keys also makes Dave think that Ida is alive, and a letter from Honoria, found after her death, shows that she also knew about Ida and her connection to the Chalons family. Fortunately it is Clete who travels to Miami to check out Jimmie's lead on Lou Kale, who might be running an escort service there, although Dave claims it was a mistake by Clete to do so. A whole chapter (chapter 19) of Dave's narrative is thus his telling of what Clete must have told him about his experiences and narrow escape from hard hitting and rough guys in Miami. A tale within a tale, and a number of small tales that are meant to function as illustrations, parallels, or parables, are ubiquitous in the text. They may refer to bravery and comradeship in Vietnam, or gallant valor on the battlefields of the Civil War, or how a colored baby was saved out of the jaws of an alligator by a white man. The longest story, which is attributed to someone other than Dave, is the story about what happened when Ida did not show up at the Bus Depot (chapter 22). It becomes a part of Dave's narrative, but he freely admits that this is what Jimmie told him, which is, of course, in fact Jimmie's version of what Ida told *him*.

It vouches for verisimilitude and accuracy, and it is proof of the author's masterful control in the distribution of sympathy and antipathy that we accept Dave's values, attitudes, shortcomings, uncontrolled rage, and childish behavior because it all seems part of a complex and difficult personality whose best judge and psychoanalyst perhaps is Dave himself, as witnessed through the story he narrates. And it does not matter if we think he acts foolishly or should have known better, since he acts within character and in accordance with the almost formulaic tradition of the hard-boiled school of crime fiction. We know that he will be exposed to serious danger at the hands of hired killers or dangerous psychopaths, whether they are called Bad Texas Bob, B. J. Pitts, Jericho Johnny Wineburger, or names even more telling of their profession and capacity. We expect bar room brawls and fistfights that leave one or both fighters in a hospital ward or in jail, and so even Clete's outrageous acts (as when he has smoked some imported Mexican weed, but also when his mind is clear) are accepted, if not condoned.

We are in the wonderful and terrible world of crime fiction at its best, where realist details, social criticism, and sociological explanations of how a criminal could become so depraved are little more than attempts to create a setting, an environment, and a milieu in which the actions can take place with some logic and reason. Thus what really matters in a book such as *Crusader's Cross* is the story of numerous crimes of the most hideous nature, the investigation into them, and the final solution and attribution of guilt and responsibility, not the more or less digressive material that is needed to create a believable setting for the events. This being said, and somewhat in opposition to the tradition, Burke's novel also laments and mourns the loss of innocence, the golden days of youth, the old beauty of a Louisiana coastal area untainted by industry and pollution, and Dave time and again turns to thoughts about the past and the future, trying somehow to place himself and the present in some sort of perspective that makes it possible to endure and get one's work done.

It is not sufficient to see the surface developments of the more and more aggressive and dangerous conflict between Val Chalons and Dave, and accept that Val is trying to tear Dave and his life to pieces because he suspects that Dave has had sex with his sister. Dave knows that this is an excuse for something deeper and more important—Val must have other reasons for his vendetta, and it is more than likely a question of money—that is, the Chalons property and who stands to inherit Raphael, the old and frail man. This is one link in a long chain of minor indices, all of which are related to questions of parenthood. Whose son is Val really? Are there other illegitimate children who stand to inherit? Must we return to 1958 and Ida Durbin to answer some of these questions, and must we interpret Andre Bergeron's tale about the baby and the alligator so that Andre is the baby and ask why Raphael Chalons risked his life for what, in his world of power and abuse, should matter very little?

It becomes more and more obvious that the two plots are interrelated and that the crimes of the past as well as of the present can only be solved if the secrets of the Chalons family are revealed. Far into the book and the narrative about Dave's investigation, it is difficult to see how the Baton Rouge serial killer could possibly fit into all this. It would clearly be acceptable and reasonable if the serial killings were committed by someone far removed from New Iberia, the Chalons family, and Dave Robicheaux. But Burke in this particular novel manages to connect what would in the hands of most writers be separate plots and would work satisfactorily as such.

Parallel investigations are carried out in real life and in police novels all the time, even if one investigation often may prove to be helpful in the solution of other crimes. In *Crusader's Cross* we see a slow development toward a solution where everything is connected and where only a few and insignificant elements in the story are left unaccounted for. When things begin to converge, we see how well prepared they have been in the very plotting of the story and in the details of Dave's narrative. When a young prostitute is killed a short time after Dave and Clete have spoken with her in New Orleans and the evidence shows that she is yet another victim of the serial killer, Dave knows that the monster killer may be much closer to his home turf, and that he may in fact be sending a signal to Dave and his colleagues to keep their hands off the case.

Crusader's Cross is a crime novel with a homicide detective as its central figure, and numerous investigators from a sheriff's office contribute to the combined effort to nail a serial killer. It is clearly within the hard-boiled school of crime fiction, yet it retains so many elements and aspects of the classical detective story that we must pay attention to minute details. Nothing is without significance; everything matters. Advanced and modern methods such as DNA identification are put to good use, but the marks left by boots in a flowerbed may be as important. When Dave has casts made of the prints outside his window, we may be sure that these will sooner or later match other prints from a crime scene and put Dave in even greater jeopardy and the serial killer closer to his area. All this combined with new information about Ida Durbin, alive and working with Lou Kale in their escort service, place the serial killer closer to the Chalons family and their secrets as the text moves toward its conclusion in the "Epilogue."

Ida has given birth to a child nine months after she was taken away from Galveston—by Raphael Chalons. So Dave has yet another problem where his powers of ratiocination will be tested if the methods and means applied in a modern whodunit will not provide other clues of a more factual character. Who is the father of this child, who obviously must be Val Chalons? When Dave learns that Raphael has had a kidney transplant and is told that the old man had to get a kidney from his daughter, Honoria, he can easily deduce that Val is not Raphael's son and that his father most likely is Lou Kale. Dave's suspicion that Val must have other reasons than his sister's "honor" for going after him proves to be correct, and it all comes down to a question of who stands to inherit the Chalons property and money. When the body of Honoria is in the morgue, Dave can simply ask if there is a scar on her body that indicates that a kidney has been removed. No such scar can be found—and so we know that Raphael must have received a kidney from an unknown illegitimate child.

If we read the text closely, paying attention to anecdotes, rumors, gossip, dreams, and brief stories that seem to be illustrations rather than integrated in the main story line, we will come to suspect one person and this person alone. So far he has been on the margin of the story and all its dramatic events, but we also know that with the detective at the center of a story of investigation and detection, it is almost a prerequisite that the killer is one of the least likely of all possible suspects. The fact that we as readers may find and name the killer, although we only have our suspicions and no ultimate proof, before Dave suddenly discovers a tiny but decisive link between the builder of the birdhouses and the serial killer, is in many ways typical for this kind of crime fiction. It relies on some of the basic traits of the formula for the classical detective story, but it cannot solve the crimes only on the basis of intuition and rational thought.

We are far removed from the situation in which all possible suspects and everyone closely linked to a murder case are summoned and placed in front of the detective, who through ingenious interrogation and by means of elimination either points to the guilty person or tricks that person into admitting his guilt. In the old puzzle mysteries the outside world did not matter much, and while investigation and detection work went on, nothing outside seemed to matter at all. In the buzzing and teeming world of New Orleans and New Iberia, with Dave involved in the scandalous affair with a former nun, pestered by a television team, and all the media trying to tear him to pieces, things are different. In addition to this, we have real threats from hired guns and the fact that vital information must be secured by using force and violence and may finally be obtained only at gun point. This is true for the absolutely crucial clue about the kidney transplant. Dave plays some form of Russian roulette with Lou Kale and in the end he has his suspicion confirmed, Val is not Raphael's son. Only then, a few pages before the narrative ends, is the kidney transplant introduced, as if this were necessary in order to prove, beyond all possible doubt, not who the serial killer is, but to establish him as an heir to the Chalons estate, relegated to a shed in the back of the antebellum building on the Chalons property, with all the burdens of misogyny, racism, inequality, denial, and neglect.

If the text did not ask the obvious and all-too-modern question about the sociological factors that produced the monstrous serial killer in order to indicate that a white father's treatment of an illegitimate black son is a critical factor in creating this monster, we could have had an almost Faulknerian understanding of the complexities of sin and guilt, neglect, abuse, revolt, and revenge. In other words, we could have left the world of crime fiction and entered a literary world where questions of guilt, expiation, and punishment remain open and linger on when the book is closed. In modern crime fiction we get some sort of assurance that crimes will be solved and the guilty will be punished, although we are also convinced that new crimes will be committed and that many of them are never solved.

The serial killer cannot be explained, accounted for, although many attempts are made in the course of *Crusader's Cross*. We are told about other and famous serial killers, we get sociological and psychological explanations of why and how, but in the end Dave Robicheaux, who has been through so much and almost seen it all, seems to accept the existence of some inborn human evil that cannot be understood or explained. When he finally takes down Andre Bergeron with his .45 auto, he does not care about the forces that produced him, nor about the limitlessness of evil and stupidity in people's lives. His only concern is for Molly, whom he barely saves from the killer and his machete, which he may have borrowed from her.

The climax is quick, decisive, and violent—a fitting finale to an investigation that has gone in many directions but always converged on or around the Chalon family. The events leading up to and staging this final countdown with the serial killer include Andre's killing of the hit man, who had been hired to have Andre removed. Dave knows for sure that Val must have hired the very professional hit man, Jericho Johnny Wineburger, whom he knows well. Dave seems to suspect that Andre actually was prepared for the attack, which must mean that he had some secret knowledge, or simply that he is not only a hired hand living at the estate. The final clue comes as a sudden revelation when Dave realizes that the bird house he bought from Bergeron's son has a chain similar to or identical with the one used to strangle the last of the serial killer's victims.

The story of the little black boy, the alligator, and the kind white man from the big house now makes sense. Everything makes sense, finally. Even the hasty marriage between Dave and Molly makes sense. They married in the midst of the scandal and the hardships, when Val and numerous people he had paid to pester Dave were after him, because it tells us a lot about our detective hero and his incessant fight to keep the demons of his past at bay. Loneliness or living alone with a cat and a three legged raccoon is unbearable for Dave and his tormented soul, and thus the comfort of female company, good sex, and someone strong enough to believe in you and support you is what he seeks. With his friend Clete he has male company of the best and worst kind, but they most certainly share some good fishing and some exciting investigation. As his superior at the sheriff's department, he is more than fortunate to have Helen Soileau. The small skirmishes they have are inevitable and also a standard element in hard-boiled crime fiction. It could, in relation to the genre and its tradition, have been much worse.

The investigation of the serial killings, with its dramatic final encounter and a solution where everything is accounted for, is very closely related to the minor investigation into the fate of the young girl with the mandolin back in 1958. Yet in a sense this is to turn the story upside down. Everything that makes up the many-layered yet fairly simple narrative of *Crusader's Cross* begins with the confessions of Troy Bordelon on his deathbed. The possibility that Ida Durbin, who has never been quite forgotten by either of the Robicheaux brothers, may still be alive is the reason for and the beginning of an investigation that ingeniously but convincingly parallels and then becomes identical with the investigation into the bestial killings of innocent and random females by the Baton Rouge serial killer. The memories of youth's sweet and untroubled days on Galveston Island are rendered in some of the most moving prose of the whole book, and Jimmie's story, as told to Dave who narrates it for us to read, is more troubling and tragic than moving, but absolutely satisfactory. The story of Ida runs through the narrative to link the past with the present and to show how events early in life can shape one's destiny, even when they appear to have been relegated to oblivion and are of no concern. We are convinced that "it wasn't God who made honky-tonk angels," because the text so often reminds us of this and because Ida's story is very much within the realms of the blues.

A case could have been made for this novel—as for all Dave Robicheaux mysteries—that social criticism is an important aspect of the text. It shows Louisiana at its most corrupt; it demonstrates through the array of strange characters what poverty, inequality, prostitution, and crack cocaine lead to in a society where money and power rule almost as if rules, laws, regulation, and control by the authorities do not function or do not matter. This comes almost as a part of the territory that a modern crime novel covers, and much of the text that describes modern-day developments in Louisiana may well be understood as lamentations of a better past, which may well be misunderstood by the narrator as his own longing for a youth that cannot be recovered or relived. This being said, there is a sadness and a pain reflected in the very language, of what the world of his beloved region of Louisiana is coming to. Stupidity, neglect, incompetence, and greed lead to loss and deterioration and finally to a less humane environment to live in. Dave is mad at the world, at the authorities who should at least have done their job, at the dope dealers, pimps, abusers, and murderers, all of whom seem unaware of the consequences of their actions and do what they do for private reasons, without any consideration of suffering and pain inflicted upon others.

Dave laments the loss of Bootsie and seeks comfort by her grave; at times he even wants to join her beyond the grave. He finds new comfort in a female companion, and although the truly exceptional era of his youth is described time and again as the best ever, he also knows that these days must be relegated to memory and that you cannot recreate your past. Dave has the experience "that age brings few gifts, but one of them is the acceptance that the past is the past" (482–83). Yet the memories of the past are "forever inviolate, never to be shared or explained, and, like images on a Grecian urn, never subject to time and decay" (483). Not everything is all right with the world of Bayou Teche, New Iberia, New Orleans, or even southern Louisiana along the Gulf Coast. It will become worse after Katrina hits. But now, at the end of Burke's best Dave Robicheaux novel, the pelicans Bootsie was sure would return are back, and the world is at peace.

In the "Epilogue" a brief story is told of Val Chalons's undoing through his own stupidity, and some of Dave's more extended philosophies about human beings and their actions are outlined, with a reference to George Orwell, whose experience seems to have been the same. There is little reason for such generalities in a book that has told a story that speaks for itself. "Our moral failure lies in the frailty of our vision and not in our hearts" (477), meaning perhaps that most people are better than we think, but that they are easily fooled by those who wish to use us. This is nothing new or sensational at the end of this story, but before it reaches its conclusion, even Val has died with a song playing over and over again on the stereo. The song is "It Wasn't God Who Made Honky Tonk Angels."

Dave Robicheaux will have new challenges and new mysteries to solve in the future. But at the end of *Crusader's Cross* everything is quiet and calm and peaceful: "I attend meetings at the Insanity Group and still have not learned how to sleep through the night. Every Sunday, Clete picks me up in his Caddie and we fish for speckled trout out on West Cote Blanche Bay. Molly, Snuggs, Tripod, and I live on Bayou Teche and in the early morning hours often see two pelicans sailing low over the water, their extended wings touched by the sunrise. For me, these are gifts enough" (483).

Works Cited and Consulted

Bogue, Barbara. *James Lee Burke and the Soul of Dave Robichaux*. Jefferson, N.C.: McFarland, 2006.
Burke, James Lee. *Crusader's Cross*. New York: Simon & Schuster, 2005.

Dave Robicheaux Novels

Swan Peak. New York: Simon & Schuster, 2008.
The Tin Roof Blowdown. New York: Simon & Schuster, 2007.
Pegasus Descending. New York: Simon & Schuster, 2006.
Crusader's Cross. New York: Simon & Schuster, 2005.
Last Car to Elysian Fields. New York: Simon & Schuster, 2003.

Jolie Blon's Bounce. New York: Simon & Schuster, 2002.
Purple Cane Road. New York: Random House, 2000.
Sunset Limited. New York: Doubleday, 1998.
Cadillac Jukebox. New York: Hyperion, 1996.
Burning Angel. New York: Hyperion, 1995.
Dixie City Jam. New York: Hyperion, 1994.
In the Electric Mist with Confederate Dead. New York: Hyperion, 1993.
A Stained White Radiance. New York: Hyperion, 1992.
A Morning for Flamingos. New York: Little, Brown, 1990.
Black Cherry Blues. New York: Little, Brown, 1989.
Heaven's Prisoners. New York: Henry Holt, 1988.
The Neon Rain. New York: Henry Holt, 1987.

Billy Bob Holland Novels

In the Moon of Red Ponies. New York: Simon & Schuster, 2004.
Bitteroot. New York: Simon & Schuster, 2001.
Heartwood. New York: Doubleday, 1999.
Cimarron Rose. New York: Hyperion, 1997.

Miscellaneous Novels

White Doves at Morning. New York: Simon & Schuster, 2002.
The Lost Get-Back Boogie. Baton Rouge: Louisiana State University Press, 1986.
Two for Texas. New York: Pocket Books, 1982.
Lay Down My Sword and Shield. New York: Crowell, 1971.
To the Bright and Shining Sun. New York: Scribner's, 1970.
Half of Paradise. New York: Houghton Mifflin, 1965.

PART III *A Sense of Humor*

George Singleton ~ *Work Shirts for Madmen*

CHARLES ISRAEL

A Biographical Sketch

George Singleton was born in 1958 in Anaheim, California. When he was seven, his family moved to Greenwood, South Carolina, where he grew up. He attended schools in Greenwood, which serve as setting for many of his short stories and his novel, called *Novel*. In 1980 Singleton received his undergraduate degree from Furman University in Greenville, South Carolina, with a major in philosophy. He began writing seriously while he was a student at Furman, a time during which he was, as he says, "trying to find my voice—or a real voice" for his fiction. At that time he was writing novels and short stories, sending away manuscripts and learning from many of the rejection replies he received.

He had plans to enter law school after his days at Furman. He wanted to be a public defender, an advocate for the forgotten, downtrodden, and dispossessed. As his interest in a writing career increased, his interest in law cooled. But his stories and novels contain multiple instances of his concern and sympathy for the characters who are the pushed-aside, mostly marginal, people whose lives are a consistent source of comedy and drama. In an interview with a Harcourt editor, Singleton makes it clear that he has respect for the simple backwoods characters and they populate his fiction: "First off, I try not to make fun of them. I want the reader to recognize that these characters are endeavoring to play a game of chess even though they are missing some important pieces. But at least they are trying" (Singleton, 2005). Their "trying" against the odds stacked against them helps create the comic tension in Singleton's work.

After graduating from Furman University, Singleton held a variety of jobs and then enrolled in the graduate program at the University of North Carolina at Greensboro, from which he received a master of fine arts degree in creative writing. During these apprenticeship years, he was writing stories and novels. According to Singleton he realized that the novels were false starts, so he began concentrating on short stories. In an interview published at harcourtbooks.com, he said, "As for writing both genres, writing a novel is a walk across a bridge, while a short story is a walk across a tightrope. . . . I doubt that it's possible to write a perfect novel, but there's always the hope of writing the perfect short story" (Singleton 2005). His early short stories were published in *Playboy*, *Apalachee Quarterly*, *New Southern Harmonies*, *Georgia Review*, and *Southern Review*. He had early stories published in the 1994, 1998, and 1999 editions of *New Stories from the South*. His first collection of stories, *These People Are Us*, was published in 2001.

Singleton has taught creative writing and literature at Francis Marion University in Florence, South Carolina, and at the Fine Arts Center of Greenville, South Carolina. He has been visiting professor of writing at the University of South Carolina and at University of North Carolina at Wilmington. He presently teaches creative writing at the South Carolina Governor's School for the Arts and Humanities in Greenville.

George Singleton's 2007 novel, *Work Shirts for Madmen*, tells the story of Harp Spillman, eccentric sculptor in metals and South Carolina native who is sobering up after years of hard drinking. It was preceded by his novel titled *Novel* and four collections of short stories. More than one hundred of his short stories have been published in national magazines and journals, giving him the reputation as one of the nation's most popular comic writers.

Singleton lives in rural Dacusville, South Carolina, a farming community in Pickens County in the Blue Ridge foothills. He lives with Glenda Guion, the clay artist. He was recently awarded a Guggenheim Fellowship.

Work Shirts for Madmen

In a recent collection of essays titled *The Enduring Legacy of Old Southwest Humor*, editor Ed Piacentino, in his introductory essay to the volume, suggests that contemporary southern literary humor converges on "intersecting paths" with southern humor of the nineteenth century, specifically with the humor characterized by the umbrella term "humor of the Old Southwest." Piacentino's idea is not of direct literary influence. His suggestion is that contemporary southern humor has a comic foundation shared by the older humor writings. That foundation is comprised, among other things, by the long tradition of southern story telling, by the use of eccentric and recognizable southern characters as models, by the continuous use of the tall tale as a narrative device, and by the employment of southern speech patterns.

In many ways *Work Shirts for Madmen* follows the paths of earlier southern humor. Singleton's narrative language, for instance, is that of hyperbole and pervasive exaggeration. In several episodes in the novel, he employs the old tradition of the southern tall tale. Both of Harp's parents make appearances in the present of the novel. Harp is raised by his mother, a gin-swilling misfit who generally stifles her son's sense of self. Harp's father deserted his son and his wife for a woman from the Irish Travelers, a group of gypsy families who lived nearby. Twenty-five years later the father turns up at Harp's home on Ember Glow and in a revealing tall tale tells his son of his current career. It is a job founded on an idea he claims to have "patented" and "copyrighted," a kind of scam supposedly approved by local police departments: "So I thought about how state departments of highway could put a double yellow stripe down secondary roads that had long straightaways. Then someone like me could intentionally drive back and forth on those roads way under the speed limit. There'd be a cop hidden at either end, waiting to see if people would pass on the double yellow. You know how much it costs here in South Carolina if you get caught doing that? It's a bunch, especially if you ain't from the same county as the arresting patrolman" (152–53).

Singleton also shares the tradition of dialect writing with the earlier southern humorists. The typical dialect of Harp's Alcoholics Anonymous helpers and colleagues is the Appalachian dialect of the Carolina Piedmont, the talk heard from small farmers, textile workers, and carpenters. In one instance Singleton recreates the curious speech of an African poet named Kumi, who is a recent immigrant to the United States. Kumi is speaking about his addiction to alcohol: "'I'm Kumi!' he yelled out. 'It means *forceful* in my native Ghana. I came to America in order to catch the education! But instead of go to college, I drank! Kumi means *forceful*! I am Taurus! You will not drink again with me.'" Here Harp informs Raylou, "That guy isn't from around here" (105).

Readers of Singleton's fiction will be reminded frequently that he is a student of western philosophy. Sprinkled throughout his work one finds references to and discussion of Jean-Paul Sartre, Friedrich Nietzsche, G. W. Hegel, Immanuel Kant, and William James. As you read Singleton's fiction, you may be bouncing along in a fast-paced story about the antics of various rednecks and rubes, and suddenly you come across a backwoods character who is puzzling over a book by Martin Heidegger or over Aristotle's ruminations on ethics in *Ethica Nicomachea*, for instance. The tension created by the two disparate streams of thought and action form one of Singleton's creative strengths.

Work Shirts for Madmen is introduced by a statement from Jean-Paul Sartre's *Being and Nothingness*: "Shame reveals to me that I *am* this being, not in the mode of 'was' or 'having to be.' But *in-itself*." The statement serves as frame and motif for the novel. One of the overarching concerns of the novel is the difficulty that Harp Spillman has in understanding himself, his motivations, and the consequences of his actions. Harp also has difficulty in understanding others, in an existential sense, just as they have in understanding themselves. That is, self-knowledge is illusive for the novel's characters, and their attempts to communicate with each other are mostly misdirected and therefore thwarted. Blocking and misdirection create much of the comedy in the novel, as when Harp discovers the identity scrambles that give the novel its title. At Harp's first Alcoholics Anonymous meeting, he learns that many of the clients have bought work shirts at thrift stores or garage sales, so that the shirts embroidered with names do not correctly identify the wearer: "And all of them wore work shirts once owned by someone else. I checked. When, say, one of the Wills said he was an alcoholic, I looked down to read FRANKLIN on his shirt, right across from VARNADORE'S LAWN CARE. And although they might be dancing with one another on Saturday nights, they didn't seem to be shirt swapping. There was no Franklin there, is what I'm saying" (43–44). The problem of identity and self-identity is a constant in Singleton's fiction. One of his short-story collections is titled *These People Are Us*. The title is an answer to the often heard elitist question, usually aimed at social underlings: Who are these people anyway? The one big category of characters, including narrators, in Singleton's fiction is not the *Lumpenproletariat* but that large group of people trying to do the best they can against difficult odds. They make up a kind of failing but yet-striving democracy.

One of Harp's friends in the novel is Bayward, a companion in AA meetings and Harp's employee. When they first meet Harp sees that Bayward is wearing a work shirt with his name over one pocket and a welding company's name beside it. So Harp concludes that Bayward is a welder and can therefore assist him with his project of welding twelve angels using hex nuts. Harp later discovers that Bayward is a *roofer*, not a welder.

One of Harp's neighbors, a Mr. Poole, cares for a retarded sister named Arthette, "a DNA disaster," as Harp says. Harp describes her as wearing pajama bottoms and a light blue work shirt bought at a Flea Market. The work shirt has CAROLINA WASTE stitched over one pocket and PAYTON on the other. Mr. Poole describes her outfit: "It's cheaper to buy her dollar shirts . . . and throw them away than to wash them. I've had a bunch, mostly from this joint Carolina Waste. Yesterday she went by Jason, I believe. Day before that, Jaycee, one word. Day before that, J. C., like initials I used to keep track. I got no idea what Carolina Waste does, but they got themselves a mess of employees" (198).

Arthette's mental retardation has taken all identity from her. She has an animal consciousness but she lacks human identity. In such an identity vacuum any name or no name will do. The "Madmen" of the title applies to most of the characters as they struggle to find themselves and as they struggle to make meaningful human contact with others. The central Madman is Harp himself. He remembers his alcoholic past as a disjointed series of blackouts and alcohol-induced misunderstandings.

Harp's mother appears in the novel after she gets a call from Raylou, Harp's wife, to help with his rehabilitation. His mother has taken her retirement money to pay for a correspondence course in documentary film making offered by the Southern California Junior Film College. She intends to make a documentary film about Harp's alcoholism being caused by his father's desertion. The film will be a cause-and-effect effort to make sense of what the novel declares to be nonsensical.

Raylou is the one character who is able to bind together the loose ends created by the multiple identity crises. She is persistent in her quest to recover Harp from his alcoholism. She is constant in her vision of a meaningful world. Harp's parents want to help, Harp's friends want to help, but Raylou is his salvation. After he has been sober for a year, he is able to complete welding the twelve angels, ordered by the City of Birmingham, and he regains his reputation as artist. At this point Raylou says to him, "'We're going to have people from the media calling here. I wouldn't be surprised if they came to the door, Harp. I'll take care of it. You just take a book or two and stow away in the bedroom for a few days.' She reached for the bookshelf and pulled out her copy of *Being and Nothingness*" (309).

Work Shirts for Madmen, like most of Singleton's fiction, is set in rural South Carolina, specifically in the foothills of the Blue Ridge Mountains and in the Savannah River Valley. Ben Robertson, an earlier South Carolina writer, eulogized the yeoman farmers of this area, suggesting a noble savagery for them in his romantic memoir *Red Hills and Cotton: An Upcountry Memory* (1942). But Singleton's upstate South Carolina is not the territory of the Lost Cause or the Wordsworthian yeoman. Instead Singleton writes about the people and landside of the South Carolina upcountry at the end of the twentieth century and the beginning of the twenty-first. In his work the small farms have mostly vanished, and the cotton mills that so dominated the countryside and the working lives of citizens have been razed or converted into upscale condominiums. Interstate highways now crisscross the land, and the descendants of former millhands now work in automobile manufacturing plants.

The people who inhabit the pages of *Work Shirts for Madmen* are the ordinary people of what Singleton calls the "New New South," the land of the shopping mall and the gentrified five-block village of the Carolina foothills. Harp Spillman, the narrator and driving force of the novel, is a part of this new South. It is a land, as he says, that he "hates and loves" at the same time. As a metal sculptor Harp is set apart from his neighbors, but he does not count himself superior to them. At the beginning of the novel, when Harp is struggling to free himself from alcoholism, his wife, Raylou, sets in motion his entry into rehabilitation, and the story of that journey to recovery serves as one on the overarching themes of the book. Early in the novel Harp describes his lost career as a notable sculptor: "As Raylou's reputation as a traditional potter grew nationwide, my reputation as an avant-garde welder diminished. It took fifty hate letters detailing everything I said and did in a drunken stupor at a particular unveiling before I said fuck it all and threw my acetylene torch down one of the man-made mini-caves on Ember Glow" (10).

In a humorous shift in occupations, Harp goes to work for Ico-Thermal, a company that commissions ice sculptures for special events such as wedding receptions. His first big work is a commission from the South Carolina Republican Party for an ice sculpture depicting the southern politicians Strom Thurmond, Lester Maddox, Trent Lott, Jesse Helms, and Newt Gingrich, those men who "meant so much to the national Republican Party . . . when the region I lived in and loved turned radically red," Harp says. As the massive ice sculpture begins to melt under the hot television lights and because of the "heat of

Republicans," Harp's joke is revealed. He has craftily fitted smaller busts under the large ones of the southern patriarchs, so that Jesse Helms melts down to the bust of a Grand Wizard of the Klan, Strom Thurmond becomes Mussolini, and the two Bushes and Ronald Reagan melt down to become the Three Stooges. The others become various demons and villains.

As the fund-raiser goes on and as the ice melts, Republican women at the event begin fainting and the Republican men roar with anger. Their threats and indignation set in motion a leap in Harp's alcohol-induced paranoia. The conflict spreads into a major motif when Raylou gets involved in a conscientious and complicated attempt to save Harp from the ravages of excessive drink. The running joke begins when Raylou—a serious animal lover—rescues a group of snapping turtles from a Clemson University biologist who was using them as test animals for environmental toxins. She brings the hijacked turtles to her home on Ember Glow, the large granite mountain in the Blue Ridge foothills, where they are housed in a large pit carved out of the granite. She puts them there to serve as guards against the threat of Republican attacks.

The Ico-Thermal Company has provided Harp with health insurance, so Raylou uses the insurance to begin Harp's rehabilitation from alcoholism. Harp checks himself in at the Carolina Behavior Center as an outpatient. There he meets a gaggle of mercenary and incompetent therapists, drug addicts, and alcoholics. These characters form a comic chorus for his own recovery woes. The group includes a trio of misfits who offer to be Harp's sponsors in his rehabilitation program. The three have traveled to a hospital in Costa Rica to have metal rods inserted into their arms so they can not put a bottle or glass to their lips. They are given the name the "Elbow Brethren." Here is Harp's response to the Brethren: "Well, automatically I thought about how they could use straws. I thought about how they could hold each other's cups and bottles and pour good guzzles. They could pour booze in a pan and lean down. Certainly they drank water, right? Kumi said, 'I hear what you think—but we will not use those crazy straws. We will not drink from a pan, like a dog'" (107).

As Harp is recovering from his drinking habit, he resumes his career as a metal sculptor, making gigantic abstract figures by welding hex nuts together. He is sober for a year, though he craves strong drink throughout the novel. Sober he repairs the rifts in his marriage. Sober he completes eight giant angels welded from hex nuts for a commission in Birmingham, Alabama. As the novel ends, Harp and Raylou plan to move away from Ember Glow to the small South Carolina town of Gruel, a fictional town that appears many times in Singleton's fiction.

At its core *Work Shirts for Madmen* is a satiric novel. Some of the satire is topical. South Carolina's neoconservatives in this novel serve as a very big target as they thrive on racism and assorted intolerances, at least in the fiction. Harp's paranoia arising from attacks on him by the Republican Party urges the plot forward and serves to keep him alert to his enemies. At the end of the novel, he imagines that the Republicans have launched a scud missile at the truck they think is carrying his welded angels to Birmingham. And Harp's dark look at the alcohol and drug rehabilitation industry is Swiftian in its intensity.

In a scene early in the novel Singleton introduces Vince Vance, director of the Carolina Behavior Center. Vance is an officious oaf who has made a career out of misleading addicts. Singleton writes that Vance's office was decorated in a modern Alcoholics Anonymous motif: "There must've been two dozen of those sappy crossstiched framed dictums on the wall—LET GO AND LET GOD!, ONE DAY AT A TIME!, STAY SOBER!, IT'S BAFFLING AND CUNNING!, YOU CAN'T TURN A PICKLE BACK INTO A CUCUMBER!, and so on. When Vince Vance returned, I said, 'Do y'all have some kind of arts-and-crafts classes that are part of everyone's recovery process?'" (22)

At one point in the novel Singleton gives one of his characters the name of a local book reviewer who has given one of his novels a negative review. The character is ridiculed by giving him unsavory occupations and foolish ambitions. The character is painted as a failed novelist who has fallen into the grief of drunkenness. Other objects of satire are the numerous festivals, such as the Chitlin' Strut Festival, held in South Carolina towns, and the pomposity and pretense of professors of religion.

The novel's satire is most bitter when it is directed at national and universal failures, such as endemic American racism and universal greed. But Singleton does not strive for satiric allegory in this novel. Harp Spillman's story is one of a man's struggle against his own weakness—and about his victory over himself. The novel is also the story of a marriage, one beset by conflict and frustration and one finally sustained, so Harp hopes, by devotion and mutual respect. However, at the novel's end an uneasy breakdown of identity is registered. When Raylou sends Harp into bedroom isolation for two days, she gives him the Jean-Paul Sartre book to read. If he does read and understand it, he may feel that he is looking into a mirror of alienation. At the end of the novel, Raylou serves as a gatekeeper for Harp, the artist, protecting him from imagined fame, but her role is actually to separate and isolate him from what she perceives to be a dangerous world.

Finally Harp comes to terms with his alcoholism, cures himself, at least for one year, without the help of what he considers to be the bogus twelve-step programs. He speaks for George Singleton as he contemplates his new life: "I started to say how this was a new Harp Spillman, that I would be my wife's keeper and perhaps turn really effeminate and redecorate our house. Right away I knew that my best defense when confronted with life-changing situations occurred in the arena of humor, of self-deprecation, of the absurd" (81).

One notable device that Singleton uses in this novel is the tall tale. The tall tale is a mainstay of southern literature, in particular in the humor of the Old Southwest, where it establishes, among other things, the spirit of a society that is new and thriving in its newness. The tall tale, then, is optimistic at its core, showing the infinite possibilities of imagination in a country of infinite possibilities. *Work Shirts for Madmen* can be seen as a fabric composed of related tall tales. Near the beginning of the novel, Harp sets the comic tall tale tone by telling of his and Raylou's home atop the granite mountain named Ember Glow. He is speaking of the mountain's previous occupants, the Coomer family: "The previous four or five generations of owners, a family... of questionable genes, moral standards, and rational capacities—spent their time believing that they'd find a vein of gold somewhere on Ember Glow. I wished that they had dug three-foot-deep holes instead of the narrow bores that were twenty feet deep and wide enough only to be a danger for misstepping stargazers, drunks, blind people, and awkward stray dogs. They didn't find gold, of course, and over the years they got buried... standing straight up in the graves they had unknowingly dug in their youth. Then Jinks Coomer moved to Nevada because... he could get a civilian job with the government seeing as he had firsthand knowledge of missile silos and barren landscapes" (4–5).

The critical response to *Work Shirts for Madmen* is found mostly in book reviews, literary websites, and blogs. And most of the response is enthusiastically positive. Kathryn Joyce's review in *Newsweek Web* is typical in its enthusiasm for the humor of the novel and its appreciation for its hero. She sees Harp's comic trials as a "fun read on a normally bleak subject. And perhaps that's what's intended: recovery, in the best of all possible worlds, as an adventure to be undertaken, rather than a trial to be withstood."

As narrator Harp follows a familiar pattern found in the traditional humor of the Southwest sketches. He is well educated, sophisticated, and introspective. Many of his helpers are just country bumpkins and rubes; they provide the comic backdrop for Harp's journey into sobriety, but without them there would not have been any recovery for Harp. His narration constructs a frame for the comic antics of the backwoodsmen of Pickens County, South Carolina. It is comedy with a long tradition of southern comic writing behind it. In Singleton's fiction there is the echo of the backwoods and frontier antics, human frailty, and physical humor that illuminate the pages of George Washington Harris and Mark Twain. George Singleton updates the picaresque tradition of earlier southern humor by placing his heroes' human frailty in dark episodes that reveal life's underlying strikingly comic frenzy.

Works Cited and Consulted

Heidegger, Martin. *Being and Time*. Trans. John Macquarrie and Edward Robinson. 1927. Reprint, New York: HarperOne, 1962.

Joyce, Kathryn. "The Madcap Side of Sobering Up." *Newsweek Web*. October 23, 2007.

Kant, Immanuel. *Critique of Pure Reason*. Trans. Norman Kemp Smith. 1781. Reprint, London: Palgrave/Macmillan, 2003.

Robertson, Ben. *Red Hills and Cotton: An Upcountry Memory*. Ed. Lacy K. Ford. 1942. Reprint, Columbia: University of South Carolina Press, 1983.

Piacentino, Ed. "Introduction." *The Enduring Legacy of Old Southwest Humor*. Baton Rouge: Louisiana State University Press, 2006.

Sartre, Jean-Paul. *Being and Nothingness*. 1943. Reprint, New York: Pocket Books, 1979.

Singleton, George. *Pep Talks, Warnings, and Screeds*. New York: Writers Digest Books, 2008.

———. Interview. Http://www.harcourtbooks.com/drowningingruel/interview.asp 2005.

———. *Work Shirts for Madmen*. Orlando, Fla.: Harcourt, 2007.

———. *Drowning in Gruel*. Orlando, Fla.: Harcourt, 2006.

———. *Novel*. Orlando, Fla.: Harcourt, 2005.

———. *Why Dogs Chase Cars*. Chapel Hill, N.C.: Algonquin, 2004.

———. *The Half-Mammals of Dixie*. Chapel Hill, N.C.: Algonquin, 2002.

———. *These People Are Us*. Montgomery, Ala.: River City Press, 2001.

Clyde Edgerton ∞ *The Bible Salesman*

JOHN GRAMMER

A Biographical Sketch

On May 14, 1978, Clyde Edgerton, a thirty-four-year-old professor of education at a Baptist college in North Carolina, wrote in his journal, "Tomorrow . . . I would like to start being a writer" (Hennis 1993, 116). He had been moved to this resolution by seeing Eudora Welty read one of her stories on public television. In view of the novels Edgerton has written while making good on that resolution, the inspiration makes sense. Tony Earley, his fellow Tar Heel, has noted that southern writers are a divided population, half of which "gathers after church in Miss Welty's yard and listens to the other half cursing and breaking bottles in the neighborhood Cormac McCarthy lived in before he moved west." Most of Edgerton's work treats, with gentle humor, kindly small town Baptists who might surreptitiously drink a beer but would be more likely to recycle the bottle than break it. Some of them, it is true, would worry about picking up the wrong fork at Miss Welty's table, but they would find the company there much less alarming than at the brawl going on down at the McCarthy place.

They are more or less the people Edgerton grew up with in Bethesda, North Carolina, a rural community outside Durham, where he was born in 1944. They are town people, but not far removed from the tobacco and cotton farms from which Edgerton's own parents had come. Like the author's Southern Baptist parents, who hoped he might become a missionary, they are religious—or at least pretend to be. Like Edgerton, who grew up "in the company of 23 aunts and uncles and many cousins," they are rich in family. They are economically comfortable but not rich (Hennis 1993, 113). After a conventional southern boyhood punctuated by baseball, hunting, and fishing, he attended the state university in Chapel Hill, where he joined the Air Force ROTC and learned to fly—an activity that figures in a couple of his books. After five years of service as a fighter pilot in Southeast Asia, he returned to Chapel Hill to earn his Ph.D. in "English Education," which led him to his position in the Education Department at Campbell University in Buies Creek, North Carolina.

It was there that he began to make good on that resolution to "start being a writer." The first result, appearing seven years later, was *Raney*, a gentle novel about the first two years in a modern southern marriage. The title character is Raney Bell, a lovably naïve small-town Baptist girl who must come to terms with the more worldly habits of her new Episcopalian husband; he's from Atlanta, drinks, talks about sex, and has a black friend. The novel enjoyed a considerable success critically and commercially, but it provoked a remarkable controversy at Campbell. Edgerton had been a star of the faculty before his novel appeared, a gifted teacher whose Baptist upbringing and military experience made him seem ideal for the conservative Christian college (Hovis 2001, 63–64). But now the novelist found his contract for the forthcoming academic year withheld while the dean and president determined whether *Raney* "caricatured the Body of Christ"—that is, the church—and thus interfered with the purpose of the university (Hovis 2001, 66). What followed was a nightmare for Edgerton, who was forced to watch helplessly for months while his bosses performed a ham-handed exegesis on his novel, trying to make it divulge a meaning that was either pro- or anti-Baptist. This ugly little episode in the history of academic freedom ended with Edgerton being offered a contract at last, but he resigned in disgust.

The episode captured, in capsule form, what Edgerton later saw as the essential shape of his young life: his college education and military experiences, he explained, created conflicts "between what I'd been taught at home and what I came to see and believe" (Ketchin 1994, 363). This is of course the same conflict that Raney experiences, and the same one that besets many characters in the novels Edgerton has produced steadily in the twenty-three years since he left Campbell, including the protagonist of the most recent one, *The Bible Salesman*. Most of those characters come from tiny, secure Listre, North Carolina, Edgerton's Yoknapatawpha County, but are brought, by comic or painful circumstances, into contact with the mores of a wider modern world. The result is that they must contemplate the limits of the moral traditions in which they have been raised.

There are now nine novels: *Raney, Walking Across Egypt, The Floatplane Notebooks, Killer Diller, In Memory of Junior, Redeye, Where Trouble Sleeps, Lunch at the Picadilly,* and *The Bible Salesman*. Besides these Edgerton has also written a memoir about his career as a pilot, *Solo: My Adventures in the Air*. He has continued to work as a college teacher during most of that writing career, at St. Andrew's Presbyterian College in North Carolina, at Millsaps College in Mississippi, where, gratifyingly, he held the Eudora Welty Chair in Southern Studies, and most recently at the University of North Carolina at Wilmington.

The Bible Salesman

The Bible Salesman, Clyde Edgerton's most recent novel, was published in the fall of 2008. It takes place, like most of his other novels, in North Carolina and concerns the same kindly and provincial small-town southerners who have populated his most characteristic work. But *The Bible Salesman* does not take place in "Listre," the fictional village where so many of Edgerton's books are set, and indeed the darker and more serious tone of the new novel would seem jarringly out of place on the sunny streets traveled by Raney Bell, Mattie Rigsbee, Wesley Benfield, and the other characters we know from the previous works. The Listre novels have generally focused on those "smiling aspects of life" that William Dean Howells thought most suitable for American writers. They were driven mainly by Edgerton's affectionate interest in character and place and his penchant for comic incident; ideas were kept firmly subordinate. Though the familiar elements are present in *The Bible Salesman*, the total effect is quite different. One of the major characters is a criminal with a knack for casual, remorseless violence; the other one, initially his accomplice, is engaged for most of the book in a quest for religious truth. If it isn't quite Dostoevsky (the writer Howells warned Americans against emulating), it sometimes approaches Flannery O'Connor in its dark pondering of hard issues. In his acknowledgments Edgerton commends to us three learned studies of the Bible that he found "helpful and inspirational" while writing the novel, serving notice of his book's fundamentally serious concerns (241). It is not just about the salesman but about the Bible as well, and more broadly about the situation of someone, like this novel's protagonist and its author, caught between the certainties of childhood and the more ambiguous lessons of worldly experience.

That protagonist is Henry Dampier, a twenty-year-old man who, as the book opens, is traveling the American Southeast plying the trade named in the book's title. Henry, we learn before long, was raised in tiny Simmons, North Carolina, by a pious aunt and kindly uncle because his father died and his mother found herself unable to manage single parenthood. Besides Aunt Dorie and Uncle Jack, the important figures in his background are a sister, Caroline, a pair of grandparents, and a vast network of cousins, uncles, and aunts. His aunt having "raised him to be a Christian gentleman," he is happy to be serving God by distributing His Word to sinners, but also unapologetic in his desire to profit from the transactions (3). This last quality has led Henry, for instance, to his method for procuring inventory: he writes to northern Bible societies, claiming to be a preacher, and asks them to donate Bibles for him to give to southern sinners. Henry then razors out the pages that indicate their provenance and sells the Bibles at full price, his belief that he is doing God's work apparently none the worse for wear.

This convergence of shrewdness and moral confusion largely defines his character. It is also what commends him to the attention of the book's other major character, Preston Clearwater, who picks the boy up hitchhiking on a mountain road in North Carolina because he needs an assistant and perceives "something smart and businesslike in the boy's stance . . . and he also sensed some gullibility and innocence" (4). The former quality will be important because Clearwater is a member of a crime organization, presently engaged in car theft, and he needs someone to deliver stolen vehicles. The latter will come in handy because Clearwater does not plan to reveal his true enterprise to the new man, preferring to feed him a wildly improbable cover story. He is an FBI agent, he explains to Henry, indeed an intimate of J. Edgar Hoover himself: "J. Edgar and me are pretty good buddies. I've shot pool with him." Clearwater is supposedly engaged in *infiltrating* a car-theft ring (24). Would Henry like to be a federal agent, too, at a hundred dollars a week? The job is just driving and need not interfere with the selling of Bibles. Henry loses no time agreeing to this unlikely proposition, the fact that "it sounded like a comic book adventure, or something from the movies" in no way casting doubt on its veracity (26). Though Clearwater is in fact as transparent as his name implies, and though Henry is his constant companion for the remainder of the book, his true identity remains opaque to the hero until the final chapter. The suspense of waiting for that discovery is what propels the loose and episodic plot of *The Bible Salesman*.

The story of a young man, credited with high intelligence but somehow helplessly enthralled to a foolish delusion, traveling in the company of the mentor who convinced him of it: that is the plot of *The Bible Salesman*, but also that of one of the books that seems to have inspired it, a classic text, which begins in this way: "Once upon a time in Westphalia, in the castle of Monsieur the Baron von Thunder-ten-tronckh, there lived a young boy on whom nature had bestowed the gentlest of dispositions. His countenance expressed his soul. He combined solid judgment with complete openness of mind; which is the reason, I believe, that he was called Candide" (Voltaire 2005, 3).

The parallels are strong enough to be suggestive: Voltaire's protagonist has been persuaded by his tutor Pangloss of the philosophy of "Optimism," the belief that all events, however destructive, are necessary parts of a cosmic chain of cause and effect leading to "the best of all possible worlds" (Voltaire 2005, 4). Though Candide wanders all over the world and witnesses imperial warfare, religious persecution, cannibalism, and the devastating earthquake that struck Lisbon in 1755, he remains unshakable for much of the book in his belief that he indeed lives in that best possible world. So it is with Henry Dampier (does his name also announce his character—"damp-behind-the-ears"?), who will travel the American southeast, stumbling regularly over the clues that he has in fact joined a criminal enterprise, but always accepting the far-fetched explanations of his own Pangloss. And like *Candide* this will finally be a story of education, tending toward the moment when the blinders come off and the protagonist emerges from darkness into light.

Also like Voltaire's great satire, *The Bible Salesman* is ultimately a book of ideas, though dressed in picaresque narrative and slapstick comedy. The issue will be young Henry's emergence from the simple creed learned in childhood from "the Bible and Sunday school and Antioch Baptist Church and Preacher Gibson and Aunt Dorie" and his discovery of one that can sustain him as an adult (107). The Clearwater plot functions as a narrative symbol of that quest: he will come to doubt Preacher Gibson's Bible and Clearwater's toy badge at essentially the same moment. And once he conceives these doubts, like Candide after he loses faith in Optimism, Henry will be looking for an alternative. Though not lacking in the broad humor and shaggy-dog episodes Edgerton's fans expect of him, this story resolves itself ultimately into a spiritual quest.

The novel itself is organized like a Bible—or rather, like the foreshortened, selectively read Bible that Henry and many Christians experienced in youth. The book alternates between sections headed "Genesis," all of which concern Henry's childhood years between 1930 and 1944, and the ones headed "Exodus," which focus on his experiences with Clearwater in 1950 and 1951. A coda, naturally called "Revelation," comes at the end. The organization implies Henry's passage from innocence through experience and on, finally, to understanding. The best way to make sense of the novel will be to try to follow that progress, one stage at a time.

The "Genesis" sections describe, as might be expected, young Henry's life in, and eventual ejection from, a kind of paradise. In part it is simply the paradise of innocence commonly associated with childhood: young Henry grows up in a seemingly enchanted world of the imagination in which nursery rhymes, Bible stories, and the tall tales made up by his Uncle Jack mingle together into a single, delightful myth (did the king—the one who failed to reassemble Humpty-Dumpty—know Moses?). Down the road lives Mrs. Albright, whose dozens of cats, all named from the Bible, can talk (with the help of Mrs. Albright's ventriloquism). In part as well, Henry's youthful paradise is the agrarian one that so much American and particularly southern thought has taken as the natural home of moral innocence. Henry's large extended family—more aunts, uncles, and cousins than a reader can easily keep track of—mostly live near "the homeplace," a tobacco farm operated by his grandparents, and return there every Sunday for dinner. Henry's life there is full of the standard rural pleasures of hunting, fishing, and swimming in the pond.

But more than anything else Henry's young life is informed by the religion propounded at the local Baptist church and embodied in his unfailingly generous, loving Aunt Dorie. She patiently answers his religious questions—such as "Why was it okay for Jesus to cuss?"—but more than that offers him a picture of what God's love must be like (52). Dorie was the only Dampier who was kind to Henry's mother, and she directs a steady stream of charity toward the Albrights down the road. The biblical text Henry associates with Aunt Dorie is the Twenty-third Psalm, whose "still waters" seem like the pond at the homeplace and whose promise of comfort simply means "being in bed with Aunt Dorie and her soft pillow and her reading from *The Children's Book of Bible Stories*" (54). "He memorized the Twenty-third Psalm for his Sunday School class," we are told, "and drew a picture of the road that went on forever, on past the end of this life and into his life in heaven" (54).

And yet young Henry's world, like the original Garden of Eden, proves less secure than it appears. He has arrived at the home of Aunt Dorie only because of two catastrophes that befell him while still an infant. In the year of his birth his father Danny died in a freak accident, being struck by a piece of lumber protruding from the back of a truck. His mother Libby, after one particularly intolerable day of single motherhood, shoots her misbehaving dog, changes Henry's diaper, leaves him in a box on her in-laws' dinner table, and leaves forever. And even once he is taken in by Uncle Jack and Aunt Dorie, he sees (without recognizing it) evidence of a world in which the "goodness and mercy" promised by the psalmist are not to be taken for granted. At the neighboring house live not only Mrs. Albright and her talking cats but also her grown son Yancy, a retarded man afflicted with a large goiter on his neck who never seems to emerge from his blue flannel pajamas and who dies when Henry is eleven. At family reunions he encounters kindly Uncle Samuel and his wife Linda, who is dying of cancer.

Even good-humored Uncle Jack, the surrogate father who teaches Henry how to fish, turns out to have a drinking problem and an ominous instinct for trouble. In one significant episode, for instance, he decides to show his family a good time quite beyond their means by taking them to the Electra, a beachside resort on Swan Island near the city of McNeil. These settings are based on the Lumina, a once-famous entertainment pavilion that operated for several decades on Wrightsville Beach near Wilmington, North Carolina. There's a grand hotel, a ballroom with an orchestra, a crowd of beautifully dressed tourists, and even a movie screen set on posts amid the breakers, showing films projected from the beach. Dressed so as to impersonate a waiter, Jack drags Henry, Caroline, and the very unwilling Dorie into this precinct of privilege, assuring her that "we're as good as any of these people" (74). Jack's ruse works long enough for the family to enjoy a splendid meal, watch the movie, and admire the big full moon throwing out "beams of love that go into your heart" (78). But this idyll comes to an abrupt end when the subterfuge is discovered and the family humiliatingly ejected, Jack mumbling furiously about a class system that "just chaps my ass" (79).

This ejection from Paradise prefigures a later and much more serious catastrophe in Henry's young life: Jack's resentments and his innate recklessness eventually lead him into minor crime, and when Henry is twelve Jack abandons his family, leaving town one step ahead of the law, never to return. Henry has lost a second father, and his seemingly secure home is never the same again.

His true father, Henry knows, is God, but in some ways He seems as mysterious as the biological father who died when he was a baby. Henry knows, for instance, that after creating the world in six days, God rested on the seventh. But why, he asks his Sunday school teacher, would God need to rest? Wasn't he perfect? Poor Mr. Harris, who has just exhausted his theological reserves by explaining that man's dominion over the beasts is what permits us to "go to

Africa and shoot lions and tigers," is stumped (47). "Well, Henry," he ventures, "that seems like a good question . . . at first." But "we have to be very careful about what we ask questions about. Because we can commit blasphemy, and blasphemy is a sin." Trying to manage a smile, he concludes, "We don't want to get into any blasphemy, because Jesus will be unhappy with that, now won't he?" (49). Later Aunt Dorie reassures him that if he couldn't understand something, that was okay. All he had to do was believe in Jesus, God, and the Bible (51).

At age nine Henry certainly does believe, but his questions do not completely subside. Eventually they mingle with others, the ones he ponders in the company of his cousin Carson in their shared bedroom after lights-out, such as what condoms are for, and how one unhooks a brassiere, and why, if the Song of Solomon can speak so frankly about sex, Christians are expected to avoid it so carefully. By this time Henry is fourteen and still a believer, but he is poised on the brink of a world that will make him question all those assumptions.

An episode from Henry's babyhood sums up a great deal of what happens in "Genesis." One Sunday at the home place, Henry is taken into the pond by Caroline, slips from the float where she has placed him, and nearly drowns in its still waters. He is quickly rescued, but as he lies in his crib, being examined for any lingering ill effects, his Uncle Jack notices something new about the boy and delightedly observes, "Look. He's got a woody" (67). Aunt Dorie silences him, but his sister has overheard the comment and is troubled. "Caroline wondered if a woody was something caused by Henry almost drowning. . . . She saw a small piece of wood stuck to his side somehow. She thought about the big plank that killed her daddy, and the man who drove the truck" (67). Henry's dip in the pond prefigures his inevitable fall into a world whose deceptively clear waters conceal dangerous possibilities: sex, death, and tragedy. It is the valley of the shadow after all; whose rod and staff can one count on for comfort?

In the "Exodus" sections of the novel the adult Henry tries to arrive at an answer, even as he plies his new trade as a traveling Bible salesman. This vocation seems to offer a secure bridge from childhood to adulthood, letting him serve God while also exercising his adult prerogatives of travel, adventure, and the accumulation of profit. He shows some proficiency at it. In one extended episode, for instance, the kind of comic set-piece we have come to expect in Edgerton's work, Henry approaches the home of Mrs. Kelly, who proves to be a distraught middle-aged lady. Her cat "Bunny" has just died; though she can just make out her inert body under the porch, she has not yet faced the task of burying her. Sensing a chance to get his foot in the door, Henry offers not only to bury the fallen feline but to offer a prayer at her grave (13–14). Mrs. Kelly thinks that would be lovely. To his horror Henry finds that Bunny has not succumbed quietly to a heart attack as her mistress assumes but met a more violent end: one of her fangs is still impaled on the head of the copperhead snake that killed her, and Bunny's own head is swollen from the venom to nearly human size. Worried about the effect the grisly spectacle will have on his potential customer, Henry digs a grave as quickly as he can, deposits the conjoined cat and snake therein, and covers them up. Then Mrs. Kelly realizes that she must view Bunny one more time; would Henry mind disinterring her briefly? Thinking fast, Henry extricates the cat, detaches and disposes of the snake, and folds his handkerchief around Bunny's distended cranium to conceal it from her mistress. It is called a "burial tuck," he improvises. "It's the way they bury all the cats in England nowadays. . . . Catching on here" (19). By this time Henry has become so solicitous of poor Mrs. Kelly that he simply gives her two Bibles before taking his leave.

The episode reveals, I suppose, Edgerton's reluctance to take his subject or his protagonist too seriously; it also reveals Henry's essential benevolence, one piece of his moral inheritance from Aunt Dorie that he will retain no matter what. But this encounter with a poisonous snake, so soon after his departure from the Eden of his childhood and immediately after his first meeting with the dangerous tempter Preston Clearwater, should set off some interpretive alarms as well. In the end, as in the Bible and *Paradise Lost*—and *Candide*, which also begins with the hero being "expelled from the earthly paradise" of the Baron's estate—Henry's brush with temptation and fall from innocence will turn out to be morally fortunate (Voltaire 2005, 5).

By this time Henry has found that the unanswered questions from childhood, the ones that defeated Aunt Dorie and Mr. Harris, refuse to subside, so he has begun looking in the place where all answers may be found. It seems that his Baptist upbringing has left him surprisingly innocent of the contents of the Bible: Henry has really only "dip-read" the book and knows little of it. He is still partial to the Twenty-third Psalm and adverts frequently to Second Timothy 3:16: "All scripture is given by the inspiration of God." But what does scripture actually say? The answers to this question, which Henry discovers night after night in the cheap motel rooms where he spends his nights, are disturbing, revealing to him a completely different book than the one he remembers from his comfortable childhood. Did God create human beings first, then the animals, or was it the other way around? Genesis, it turns out, says *both*. So Henry reads on, intrigued but deeply puzzled.

He needs a guide and believes he has found him in Preston Clearwater. One realizes almost as soon as they meet that Clearwater is offering Henry more than just excitement and a hundred dollars a week. The older man seems like the father Henry has never managed to find. And what American boy would not wish for a father like Clearwater: confident, well-dressed, driving a new Chrysler and looking "a little bit like Clark Gable, but without a mustache" (4)? Eventually Clearwater will actually bring Henry back to the "Electra" on Swan Island, the scene of Uncle Jack's humiliation, as a paying customer with money in his pockets, seeming to prove Clearwater's superiority to that predecessor. Henry is smitten even before Clearwater flashes his fake badge and identifies himself as a G-man; once he does, what chance has the boy got? If Clark Gable asks you to help him and J. Edgar Hoover catch criminals, *and* get rich, without ceasing to distribute Bibles in your off-duty hours, what is a Christian gentleman to do? As a federal agent Henry will be "serving God in a different way," he reasons (26).

No wonder Henry does not question Clearwater's offer too closely. Henry is being offered precisely what he has been seeking: an adult life still sustained by the pieties of youth. Happily there is no need to choose between them: you can work for J. Edgar Hoover and Jesus all at once, and Clearwater's assured authority seems to derive from both sources. Or it does until Henry tries to involve Clearwater in his religious quest, with disappointing results:

> "Did you know there were two different stories about the beginning of the world in Genesis?"
> "No."
> "I don't see how they can both be wrote by the same God."
> Clearwater turned onto his back, came up onto his elbows, pulled back the covers, and swung his feet to the floor. "I guess I'll have me a little drink. You want one?" (90)

Refusing to be discouraged, Henry contents himself with making Clearwater his guide in purely secular matters. With mounting exasperation the veteran criminal will endure Henry's efforts to get him to go fishing, to come meet his girlfriend, to teach him to "light a match in a thirty-knot wind" (152). But if Clearwater is an unwilling father figure, he nonetheless ends up leading Henry toward some important revelations. His name might be a place to begin pondering his thematic significance. He is, as I have mentioned, perfectly transparent to the reader and to most characters other than Henry, and his transparency is a measure of Henry's naïveté. His name may also associate him with those "still waters" in Henry's favorite psalm, and with the pond that deceptively reminded him of those waters but nearly took his life. The name points to the role Clearwater will eventually and inadvertently have in Henry's life, that of *clarifying* matters heretofore troublingly opaque.

It is also, of course, a name Flannery O'Connor might have thought of—indeed, she almost did when she named Francis Marion Tarwater protagonist of *The Violent Bear It Away*. This is no coincidence; the influence of O'Connor's work on *The Bible Salesman* is considerable, as one could probably infer without getting past Edgerton's title. Who could read it without immediately thinking of Manley Pointer, the vicious Bible salesman in "Good Country People" who manages to teach Joy-Hulga Hopewell that she is not as smart as she thinks? But in case we miss it, Edgerton offers a pretty broad hint when Henry, apropos of nothing, tells another character that he suffers from a "heart condition" (97). What made him think of that? It was not his idea originally; another Bible salesman he has met, "with yellow socks—up at Calhoun Crossing, in the mountains—kept talking about his heart condition. He'd had a Bible with a cutout place for a whiskey flask, and he had all these stories" (97). That would be, of course, Manley Pointer himself, "not a bad-looking young man," as O'Connor described him, "though he had on a bright blue suit and yellow socks that were not pulled up far enough" (277).

In fact several characters in *The Bible Salesman* seem to have their originals in O'Connor. Uncle Jack, a determined religious skeptic, is a bit like Rayber in *The Violent Bear It Away*, and Yancy Albright, Henry's retarded neighbor, resembles Rayber's retarded son Bishop. Clearwater himself, who violates Henry's innocence but also violently enlightens him, might remind us of the driver who picks up Tarwater near the end of that novel. Throughout the book we hear rumors about a serial killer, "The Night Shooter," who is at large in the area and who cannot help reminding us of "the Misfit" from O'Connor's "A Good Man is Hard to Find." These borrowed details add up to a kind of generalized allusion to O'Connor's work; they serve as notice that Edgerton's novel is taking place in O'Connor territory, geographically and morally.

What goes on in that territory? The story "Good Country People" seems like the best place to begin. The main character in that story is Joy Hopewell, a thirty-two-year-old woman with a prosthetic leg—she was injured in a hunting accident as a child—a weak heart, and a Ph.D. in philosophy. Owing to her afflictions, she has to live with her mother on a family farm, where she spends her days seething with contempt for Mrs. Hopewell's shallow mind and empty life. As a symbol of this contempt, Joy has rejected the name her mother gave her and taken the ugliest one she could imagine: Hulga (274). She derives pleasure only from philosophical nihilism and the license it affords her to feel superior to those around her. "I don't have illusions," she boasts. "I'm one of those people who see *through*, to nothing" (287).

Her claim of sophistication, however, is quickly undercut when she decides to seduce Manley Pointer, the Bible salesman who has appeared at her door. She imagines the experience will be deeply enlightening for Pointer, and since "true genius can get an idea across even to an inferior mind," she will have no trouble turning his inevitable remorse "into something useful," presumably it will be a version of her own nihilism (284). But when the proposed assignation takes place, all the instruction runs the other way. The earnest young Bible salesman seduces Hulga to the deepest intimacy she can achieve: she removes her artificial leg and her glasses for him, which makes her helpless. She is incredulous when he opens his hollowed-out Bible and produces a whiskey flask, condoms, and a deck of pornographic playing cards. "Aren't you just good country people?" she asks. "I may sell Bibles," he explains, "but I know which end is up and I wasn't born yesterday and I know where I'm going!" (290). Where he is going immediately is far from the Hopewell farm, carrying Hulga's leg and glasses with him, but leaving her with, in fact, just the information she needs. "You ain't so smart," he calls back to her. "I been believing in nothing ever since I was born!" (291).

The Bible salesman functions precisely as a "pointer" to Hulga; by depriving her of the intellectual vanity that has been her armor against experience and forcing her to confront her actual blindness and weakness, he makes her vulnerable to some access of greater wisdom. In other stories O'Connor makes it plain what form this wisdom might take. In "The Artificial Nigger," for instance, a disastrous trip to the city with his nephew forces Mr. Head to surrender his vanity and confront his enormous moral shortcomings: he "saw now that his true depravity had been hidden from him lest it cause him despair. He realized that he was forgiven for sins from the beginning of time, when he had conceived in his own heart the sin of Adam, until the present" (270). Over and over in O'Connor's fiction, harsh and humiliating experience, introduced by characters who mean nothing but harm, serves as the beginning of Christian wisdom, a recognition of one's depravity and need for grace.

I think Edgerton is alluding precisely to this pattern when he names his novel, its villain, and several of its characters and incidents out of O'Connor's fictional lexicon. His question, ultimately, is hers: what must one do to be saved? Though Henry is the Bible salesman, Clearwater is the "pointer" of the novel. Like Manley Pointer, for instance, Clearwater has been "believing in nothing" for a long time, living in "a world that was no more than a place for things to happen" (88). His assault on Henry's innocence, though devoid of moral purpose, will prove just the treatment the young man requires.

Essentially three things happen to Henry during his travels with Clearwater. The first is the one we anticipate from the beginning, that is, his inevitable penetration of Clearwater's disguise. In the middle of one of their robberies, this one of a doctor who supposedly launders money for the "crime ring," Henry suddenly pieces together several clues and realizes that his mentor must have committed a recent murder attributed to the "Night Shooter." He cannot be an FBI agent and the operation is simply a crime, as were all their previous ones. Henry runs from the scene, Clearwater pursues, and the resulting chase ends with his killing Clearwater in self-defense. But even before that epiphany and liberation, Henry had begun to notice previously invisible weaknesses and uncertainties in the man he had admired. His ability to doubt Clearwater, to penetrate his disguise, and finally to kill him, obviously indicate Henry's growing maturity and independence. They are symptoms of a larger ability Henry is developing, which is that of questioning received authority. Clearwater "seemed different," Henry reflects. "He'd always seemed bigger than life. Now he seemed not quite so big" (210).

The other authority he has relied upon, for an even longer time, also looks different: "He'd been reading a Bible lately that was different from the Bible he'd been reading growing up. And the one he was now reading was the real one. He'd only dip-read the first one. That dip-reading had something to do with the big problem he had now, he was thinking. The big bright cloud that was his belief, delivered by the Bible and Sunday school and Antioch Baptist

Church and Preacher Gibson and Aunt Dorie, seemed smaller and less white than it once was" (107).

Where Clearwater seems smaller, the Bible now seems *larger* than before: large enough to contain more contradictions than Henry can sort out. It clearly condemns adultery, for instance, but neglects to blame Abraham for "going in unto" Hagar, his wife's handmaid, which is biblical code for a "sex relation," as Henry realizes (28). But confusing sexual ethics are just the beginning: the Bible said that Adam would return to dust. Why wouldn't he go to heaven or hell? That's where everybody went, wasn't it? Nobody just returned to dust, did they? Was there not a heaven when Adam was alive? Wait, in Genesis 1:1 God created heaven and earth; so there *was* a heaven when he told Adam he was going back to dust, but God hadn't created hell. Did he create hell? It didn't *say* so. Did he just think about it down the line? That didn't sound like somebody "all-knowing" (108–9). And there was more, much more, of the same. Eventually the perplexed Henry finds that he cannot get past "Dear God" in his prayers. So he prays to Jesus, asking for "some kind of understanding about what's wrote down in the Bible," a prayer that is eventually answered (109). "Everything is in there," he decides at last—and therefore it is not very useful as the source of an ethical system (233).

But there is still "The Lord is my shepherd, I shall not want. He maketh me to lie down in green pastures." "*This*," Henry reflects, "seemed almost like it was about a different kind of God. The Lord. The Lord seemed kind of like a *mama* might be" (109). In the disenchanted, post-Baptist reality Henry has survived into, *where* would one locate those green pastures and the love they represent? Henry finds the answer in the third significant occurrence of his adult career. Approaching a roadside fruit stand hoping to sell some Bibles, he notices the young girl who works there. She was "a kind of big-boned, blond, curly-headed girl with a dress so thin it seemed to show her skin beneath. The curls dropped around her face. As he stepped under the tent, thunder sounded far off. A chilled breeze came up" (93). The moment is as portentous as it seems: when Marleen Green invites him to sit down, Henry immediately thinks, "And the evening and the morning were the first day" (95). Lest we miss the point, the two then fall to discussing gardens, Henry recalling the one his Aunt and Uncle maintained back in Simmons. His wanderings have indeed led him to a new Eden. Its curly-headed Eve begins by offering him eight cents worth of peaches for a nickel—far from being forbidden, the fruit here is marked down— and will, a few visits later, relieve him of his virginity. This sexual initiation, enacted outdoors on an army blanket, in "a grassy area about the size of a room," brings Henry precisely to those "green pastures" where he can find a new morality based on love (202). Her very name is Green. The love he experiences with Marleen is simultaneously sentimental (she writes a very bad poem for him at one point), sexual, yet also somehow "kind of like a *mama*" might offer: the buxom Marleen begins her seduction of Henry by inviting him to bite her nipple. The combination proves irresistible. No wonder Henry, within a few moments of meeting her, has decided that "this is it. . . . She's the one" (98).

The relationship Henry achieves with Marleen clarifies a good deal about Edgerton's purposes in the novel. In O'Connor's fiction the temptations that a Marleen can offer are important because they expose the inadequacies and weaknesses of damaged people and reveal that romantic certainty, such as Henry's, is probably a delusion. In fact romantic love is barely present in O'Connor's work, because in her world everybody—not just Manley Pointer and Joy Hopewell—suffers from a "heart condition," the one inherited from Adam. When he first meets Marleen, Henry borrows a line from Pointer by telling her that he too has such a condition. But after their first tryst, Henry confesses the lie: "I don't know why I told you that about my heart. My heart's fine." Marleen isn't surprised. "You look too healthy to have heart problems," she observes (206). Indeed he is, and too healthy as well to feel any lingering Baptist guilt over this adventure, or any of his others. This is essentially what Henry has learned about himself in the course of this Bildungsroman. He comes to recognize not his moral weakness but his essential health, not his need for grace but his entire self-sufficiency. This, after all, is the man who took such care with the burial of "Bunny" simply to shield Mrs. Kelly from knowledge of her violent demise, who spent his childhood carrying blankets to Mrs. Albright and Yancy. Heart condition? Henry has a heart of gold.

This means that the erotic love he enjoys with Marleen can *be* the new religious vision he has been seeking. At one point his prayers to Jesus elide unconsciously into the chant "Marleen, Marleen. Marleen Green." He finds that "the shape of Marleen's face, the texture of her voice, the laugh, her loveliness, all made themselves into a new form that Henry could almost feel with his hands, as real to him as the Jesus he'd once followed down the aisle at church" (109, 128). Here is the redemption he has been seeking: on his honeymoon with Marleen, for instance, he will revisit Swan Island, the scene of previous disappointments; now he will be able to reclaim that lost Paradise as his own. This religion even comes with its own thoroughly secular vision of the afterlife: on the honeymoon, as they hold hands and watch their shadows lengthen across the beach at sunset, Marleen reflects that those shadows will continue being cast across infinite space for millions of years, almost forever. And I will "dwell in the house of the Lord forever," Henry thinks, having finally glimpsed the true likeness of the promise he tried to illustrate back in Sunday school (54). He then produces an unlikely piece of honeymoon equipment, a copy of Edgar J. Goodspeed's *The Bible: An American Translation*—a skeptic's Bible once in vogue among liberal Protestants in the United States—and Henry reads again his favorite psalm, which now concludes, "And I shall dwell in the house of the Lord to old age." "That last sentence has got some meat on it," he announces (237).

After discovering the truth about Clearwater, we are told, Henry "was on his own now. Certainty had birthed an uncertainty" (222). But by then Henry is fully up to the task of acting alone in an uncertain world. If there are wrongs to be righted or sins to be redeemed, he will do it himself. When he finally confronts Clearwater during that final robbery, the doctor's motherless son—a retarded boy in blue pajamas, the double of Henry's long-dead neighbor Yancy—attaches himself to the hero and refuses to let go. When the ensuing melee is over, with the doctor dead, he finds himself responsible for Randy, suddenly orphaned as Henry once was. He promptly drives the boy to Mrs. Albright's house in Simmons, where the still-grieving mother instantly recognizes Randy as Yancy's miraculous replacement. Eventually Henry will arrange for her to adopt the boy. His remarkably economical gesture restores Randy's mother and Mrs. Albright's son, and symbolically undoes the primal trauma of his own childhood. With equal aplomb Henry gives the authorities the information they need to destroy the car-theft ring, becoming in effect the G-man Clearwater never could have made him. In the end Henry is his own savior, the author of miracles, righter of wrongs, and redeemer of his own damaged soul. He is "on his own" and happily so.

The novel leaves us to imagine what happens next, when he and Marleen leave Swan Island to begin their life together. The world will be all before them, as it was before another couple departing Paradise, but unlike Milton's Adam and Eve, Henry and Marleen will neither have nor need Providence as a guide. Their case, Edgerton implies, will be more like that of another exile, who found that salvation is in one's own hands and is available to anyone willing to work in the garden.

Works Cited and Consulted

Earley, Tony. "Mephisto Tennessee Waltz." Review of *The Long Home*, by William Gay. *New York Times Book Review*, November 21, 1999, 12.

Edgerton, Clyde. *The Bible Salesman: A Novel*. New York: Little, Brown, 2008.

———. *Solo: My Adventures in the Air*. Chapel Hill, N.C.: Algonquin, 2005.

———. *Lunch at the Picadilly: A Novel*. Chapel Hill, N.C.: Algonquin, 2003.

———. *Where Trouble Sleeps: A Novel*. Chapel Hill, N.C.: Algonquin, 1997.

———. *Redeye: A Western*. Chapel Hill, N.C.: Algonquin, 1995.

———. *In Memory of Junior: A Novel*. Chapel Hill, N.C.: Algonquin, 1992.

———. *Killer Diller: A Novel*. Chapel Hill, N.C.: Algonquin, 1991.

———. *The Floatplane Notebooks: A Novel*. Chapel Hill, N.C.: Algonquin, 1988.

———. *Walking through Egypt: A Novel*. Chapel Hill, N.C.: Algonquin, 1987.

———. *Raney: A Novel*. Chapel Hill, N.C.: Algonquin, 1985.

Grimshaw, James A., Jr. "Clyde Edgerton: Death and Dying." *Southern Writers at Century's End*. Ed. Jeffrey J. Folks and James A. Perkins. Lexington: University Press of Kentucky, 1997. 238–46.

Hennis, R. Sterling. "Clyde Edgerton." *Contemporary Fiction Writers of the South*. Ed. Joseph Flora and Robert Bain. Westport, Conn.: Greenwood Press, 1993.

Hovis, George. "The *Raney* Controversy: Clyde Edgerton's Fight for Creative Freedom." *Southern Cultures* 7 (2001): 60–83.

Howells, William Dean. "Dostoyevsky and the More Smiling Aspects of Life." *Harper's* 73 (1886): 641–42.

Ketchin, Susan. *The Christ-Haunted Landscape: Faith and Doubt in Southern Fiction.* Jackson: University Press of Mississippi, 1994.

O'Connor, Flannery. "Good Country People." *The Complete Stories of Flannery O'Connor.* New York: Farrar, Straus and Giroux, 1979. 271–91.

Voltaire [Francois-Marie Arouet]. *Candide.* Trans. Theo Cuffe. New York: Penguin, 2005.

James Wilcox ~ *Heavenly Days*

SCOTT ROMINE

A Biographical Sketch

With the 2003 publication of *Heavenly Days*, James Wilcox returned South from a three-novel hiatus in New York City. The move followed Wilcox's own migration southward from New York City, where he had lived for nearly three decades, to teach creative writing at Mississippi State University and, later, Louisiana State University. In returning South, Wilcox also returned to one of the richest literary territories in recent southern letters. The fifth of his novels to be set in Tula Springs, Louisiana, *Heavenly Days* constitutes a homecoming in more ways than one. Not only does it mark a literal return to Wilcox's home ground; it also continues a theme—the search for home in a world of exiles—prominent in his work since his first novel, *Modern Baptists*, appeared in 1983.

Modern Baptists is the story of Bobby Pickens, amateur theologian and assistant manager of the Sonny Boy Bargain Store. The novel's title comes from the church for modern Baptists Mr. Pickens imagines opening after he receives his "preaching diploma." Devoid of "old-fashioned ranting and raving" and committed to "reason and logic," the church of modern Baptists will appeal to Baptists "sick to death of hell and sin being stuffed down their gullets every Sunday" (145). Like all of Wilcox's novels, *Modern Baptists* resists easy summary; multiple and sometimes perplexing plot lines reflect the bewildered state in which characters typically find themselves. Attempting, as Mr. Pickens does, to formulate moral, aesthetic, and political codes that will impose order on anarchy, Wilcox's characters remain mostly mired in anarchy, both literally and figuratively, the church for modern Baptists never opens its door. But however comical, ineffective, fraudulent, or even mean-spirited such efforts might appear, they are never fully contemptible. Nor are the characters who generate them. Even Mr. Pickens, whose entrapment in "bitterness and defeat" causes him to fail his brother in crucial ways, is able, finally, to recognize in his brother's "eyes black with pain, a story that was somehow like his own" (239).

Wilcox followed *Modern Baptists* in 1985 with *North Gladiola*, the story of Ethyl Mae Coco and her quixotic efforts to bring culture to Tula Springs with her classical quartet. Unable to orchestrate either musicians or her family, Mrs.

Coco finds that her efforts to articulate a self within a social world flounder—not least, she finally recognizes, because of her own inflexible and self-serving moral codes. With *Miss Undine's Living Room* (1987), Wilcox's narrative style deviated further from traditional plot structures. Called "maddeningly digressive" by Marianne Gingher and "Dickensian in its wealth of eccentric characters" by Michiko Kakutani, *Miss Undine's Living Room* follows Olive Mackey through the labyrinthine corridors of Tula Springs politics, both municipal and sexual. *Sort of Rich* (1989) tells the more economical story of Gretchen Peabody, a Manhattan émigré who finds herself, through a chance marriage to a Tula Springs native, living in a town she finds to be not as "Faulknerian" as she had hoped. Frustrated in her attempt to find "real values in this remote hamlet where everyone wasn't caught up in all the hype that had made her life in New York such a burden" (23), and to fit within a household whose logic escapes her, Gretchen remains in Tula Springs after her husband's death and ultimately finds her place within it.

With his next novel, *Polite Sex* (1991), Wilcox turned to New York City for his setting, albeit using several characters who hail from Tula Springs. New York would also serve as the setting for *Guest of a Sinner* (1993) and *Plain and Normal* (1998). The change in locale occasioned certain changes in Wilcox's work—not surprisingly for a self-described "novelist of manners" with a gift for capturing the nuances of distinctive social milieus. The blue-state ethos of New York stands in sharp contrast to the red-state environment of Tula Springs, where even modern Baptists attend Bible study. New themes emerged, including the subject of homosexuality in *Plain and Normal*. Even so there is a strong continuity in Wilcox's work. The humor remains, although it has tended to acquire a more melancholy edge as his career has progressed. Like Flannery O'Connor, his most important precursor, Wilcox writes from a perspective informed by a Catholic worldview, although one decidedly less severe and judgmental than that of his predecessor. O'Connor famously described her fiction as charting the "action of grace in a territory inhabited largely by the Devil," and the description could apply, with modification, to Wilcox as well (1969, 118). His notion of grace, scaled to a more human level, lacks the sublime dimension of violent revelation that marks so much of O'Connor's work, while his Devil is less a principality—an incarnation of evil—than a Screwtape-style master of banality who distracts individuals from recognizing their capacity for grace. Here I allude to C. S. Lewis's *Screwtape Letters*, in which a "senior demon" writes to his nephew, named Wormwood, offering advice for compromising the faith of a recently converted Christian. Suggesting that the "safest road to Hell is the gradual one," Screwtape cautions against temptations toward "evil" as it is usually understood (2001, 61, 60). Wilcox identifies Lewis as an important influence on his thinking, a point suggested by the epigraph to *Heavenly Days* from C. S. Lewis's *Great Divorce*, which I discuss below. I should hasten to add that while Wilcox claims that his Christian perspective is fundamental to his conception of character, his work by no means can be considered didactic or doctrinaire.

Heavenly Days

With his fictional return to Tula Springs, Wilcox invites, as does any southern writer who uses the same fictional locale in multiple works, comparisons with Faulkner and his "postage stamp of native soil" in Yoknapatawpha County. Just as Faulkner reintroduced characters from novel to novel, minor characters becoming major characters and vice versa, so Wilcox inserts Bobby Pickens and his erstwhile admirer Burma LaSteele as bit players in *Heavenly Days*. Wilcox's most recent novel, *Hunk City* (2007), returns to the story of Mr. Pickens and Burma following the latter's inheritance of her husband's lottery-fueled estate, as described in *Heavenly Days*.

Sites and scenes in and around Tula Springs are also, as in Faulkner's work, revisited from novel to novel. The shopping mall just across the Mississippi state border where, as we learn in *North Gladiola*, "everyone in Tula Springs did their serious shopping," is also visited in *Heavenly Days*. Lou Jones, the protagonist of the later novel, works across the street from the Sonny Boy Bargain Store, which serves as a central location in *Modern Baptists* and, to a lesser degree, in *Miss Undine's Living Room*. The store itself, however, has changed. Having been bought out by a chain, its distinctive candy counter is replaced by "a display of generic bleach." "Painted turtles, gerbils, and roasted cashews once gave Sonny Boy its "own peculiar musk, both enticing and repulsive," but the store now emits an "antiseptic aura" (68). Like Yoknapatawpha, Tula Springs is a dynamic locale whose economy changes over time: in *Heavenly Days* there is an air of material prosperity markedly absent in the shabby backwater of Wilcox's early fiction.

Ultimately, however, comparisons with Faulkner are less striking than the contrasts. Gretchen Dambar is right: Tula Springs is not very Faulknerian. Where Yoknapatawpha County is organized around the Confederate Memorial that stands, literally and symbolically, in the center of the town square, Tula Springs emerges as a disorganized fictional domain. Where Yoknapatawpha County is arranged as a set of margins surrounding a center, Tula Springs sprawls incoherently. It is not that the center does not hold, but that there is no center in the first place. Where Yoknapatawpha is populated mainly by poor whites, the planter class, and African Americans, Tula Springs bears the ethnic traces of a globalized world: Koreans, Germans, Filipinos, Brits, and Kenyans are as likely to appear as are members of the South's traditional demographic groups. Yoknapatawpha maps against the central themes and grand narratives of southern history: the dispossession of native populations by white settlers, the traumas of Civil War and Reconstruction, the replacement of the old aristocracy by the tribe of Snopes, the eternal conflict of race relations, and the shift from bound labor to free labor. The historical dimension of Tula Springs is, by contrast, an altogether more haphazard affair. Originally settled by Tories from Virginia and the Carolinas, the area had briefly, during the early nineteenth century, "pledged allegiance to no one, not to the U.S. or Spain or even England." The town itself emerges around the turn of the twentieth century, when the Illinois Central Railroad, drawn by an emergent timber industry, "began colonizing these parishes with northerners, the shiftless kind that didn't have sense enough to stay where they belonged" (*Modern Baptists*, 8, 9).

Most significantly, however, Faulkner's geography constitutes a kind of fate: in Yoknapatawpha County to be born into a race, a family, a gender, and a social class is to acquire a place—a position—from which deterministic pressures and coercive codes are inevitably confronted. In Faulkner, *what* you are tells you *who* you are. In Tula Springs the problem confronting the individual is fundamentally different. Tula Springs is a mushy world. Lacking solidity, it confronts the individual as a hall of mirrors frustrating efforts to reflect, verify, or validate a self. An almost infinite array of social networks and consumer options make building a stable identity like climbing a wall of sand. Put another way, as characters try to press outward into a social domain where they might find themselves at home, they find themselves instead frustrated and lost, subject to a kind of vertigo deriving from both their own limitations and the nature of a world comprised of surfaces and simulacra.

For Lou Jones, the main character of *Heavenly Days*, home proves inaccessible in a number of ways. The novel begins with Lou in a toolshed writing a monthly column for the North American Bassoon Society newsletter; both the activity and the location are significant. Like many of Lou's activities, the column acts as a kind of identitarian hobbyhorse, a way of expressing herself for the edification of others who, in turn, persistently fail to appreciate her efforts. Despite having spent a "small fortune on Federal Express" to mail the column, she remains unremunerated: "Needless to say, the Society never reimbursed her—not one red cent" (2). The key words here are "needless to say," which bring to bear Lou's own perspective on the matter: she is used to being unappreciated; it becomes a matter of pride. Meanwhile, her own seventeen-thousand-dollar bassoon, a gift from her husband, Don, sits unplayed. As for the toolshed, the local tax assessor has declared it a guest house, despite Don's removal of the refrigerator and the daybed. The remaining amenities—air conditioner, sink, toilet—are necessary for reasons unrelated to residence, even guest residence.

In a curious way, Lou carries her guest status with her wherever she goes. She is never at home, least of all in her own house, a $295,000 faux-Cajun cabin located in the gated community of Brougham Gardens. Similar developments appear throughout Wilcox's fiction, most notably in *North Gladiola*, where the Beáu Art Estates is surrounded not by a gate but by an electric fence. The symbolic significance of the "gated community" is perhaps self-evident, as it marks the paradoxical effort—pervasive in Wilcox's fiction—toward "community" (that is, wholeness, integration, and connection) and withdrawal (that is, insularity, isolation, and separation). Lou's house is similarly perplexing. "Like a SoHo loft," the first floor of the cabin is open, leaving Lou unable to shake the feeling "that she's in some sort of public space, perhaps the lobby of an arts-and-crafts museum" (89). For Lou real homes are, categorically speaking, located elsewhere. The house of her husband Don's parents, for example, where he currently resides, "is real," the result of slow landscaping that makes her own development seem "like a project in comparison" (85). Similarly the patina acquired by Grady Morgen's house, which dates back to 1880, throws into stark relief her own dwelling's conspicuous lack of aura. Lou's mistake, however, is to confuse real estate with the existential condition of homelessness and alienation. One of her characteristic and most telling gestures is to push away from spaces she regards as empty or artificial. Tula Springs offers ample opportunities for such movement. But precisely because such spaces are weightless, she does not get very far. Accompanying Don to a job interview, she passes Mawmaw's Country Store, which Lou has always viewed with "a certain grain of salt":

> A real country store wouldn't call itself a country store. And the logs look a little too trim and neat.
> Don flicks on the turn signal, saying that he wants to stop for gas. But Lou urges him on. She will not get gas at Mawmaw's. Whether it's authentic redneck or a tourist trap, it will be too pricey. Anyway, Lou feels that they should wait for a Texaco, because of the opera. Not that she approves of advertising—even underwriting is suspect. But how else would people ever get a chance to hear the more difficult masterpieces? (76)

Disappointed that a recent Houston Opera performance of Schoenberg's *Moses und Aron* had not staged Moses as an "an illegal alien wandering in from Mexico," Lou notices a water tower proclaiming "FREE HBO & VIDE-O! POKER" "to the weary" (77). When Don zooms past a police car, Lou realizes that the driver is a "discontinued mannequin, something that no decent store would be caught dead with today" (78). Finally arriving at the St. Jude Yacht club, the site of Don's interview, Lou registers her disapproval of what she regards as a refuge for "old farts and yuppies who'd fled" from New Orleans and "gentrified the entire North Shore, raising property values in a ripple effect as far north as Tula Springs." "If Lou had the power," the narrative continues, "she'd deport them all back to the city, where they could learn to get along with their fellow citizens" (79). At literally every turn Lou finds a space that allows her to articulate her identity themes. She is not the sort of person to be taken in by simulation or cultural commodification. Mawmaw's will not suffice; its suspiciously neat logs give it away, and Lou is not buying. Even Texaco's underwriting of opera—the one cultural form of which she approves—proves suspect, immediately to be improved by a scenario more in harmony with Lou's political liberalism: a Mexican Moses in exodus to Houston. For Lou, the problem is that her journey ends where it begins, in a white flight enclave not dissimilar from Brougham Gardens. As she moves from her disorienting house to the stability of the St. Jude Yacht Club, she finds that she can disapprove of others in ways that do not *hit home:* these, not she, are the real yuppies fleeing from their fellow citizens.

But while travel as disavowal keeps Lou on the road, her journey obtains a certain magnitude as a quest for the real thing, a search for home. Earlier, during a shopping expedition to a mall, we learn that "Lou doesn't believe in malls. Whenever she can, she makes a point of not shopping in one" (30): "The mall's stale, recycled air, the tepid tea in a flimsy cup, the cramped seat, all make Lou feel the weariness of a transatlantic passenger on a chartered flight. Yet at the same time she's dogged by a tourist's faith that she's going somewhere important, that over these dark, fathomless time zones lie celebrated, ageless ruins. The real thing. No chintzy Vegas pyramids or antiseptic canals" (36).

No VIDE-O! POKER or Vegas simulacra for this weary traveler, but the real thing. Against the farcical nature of the quest—here exacerbated by Lou's alignment of authenticity with primitivism, since she would give her "eyeteeth" to live in mall-less Mombasa (30)—is counterpoised a poignant lack. If home is where Lou is not, her project is to get there; her quest is for what Jonathan Matthew Schwartz defends, in his book *In Defense of Homesickness*, as the "urge to feel at home, to recognize one's surroundings and belong there" (Schwartz 1989, 32).

In an essay titled "From Pilgrim to Tourist," Zygmunt Bauman observes that "for pilgrims through time, the truth is elsewhere; the true place is always some distance, some time away." According to Bauman, the ascendancy of tourism as a model of postmodern identity results historically from the success of pilgrims in making "the world solid by making it pliable, so that identity could be *built at will*, but built *systematically*, floor by floor and brick by brick" (1996, 23, 24). For Bauman modern pilgrims built "a kind of world in which one can tell life as a 'sense-making' story, such a story as makes each event the effect of the event before and the cause of the event after, each age a station on the road pointing toward fulfilment." But their expertise as "identity-*builders*" proved excessive: as the technologies of identity building expanded, the plasticity of the world so constructed made identities grounded in them harder to preserve. In a "world inhospitable to pilgrims," Bauman argues, the pilgrim-cum-tourist finds it increasingly difficult to "distinguish a forward march from going in circles" (25). With some precision Bauman's analysis describes Lou's plight. Continually striving to locate spaces and scenarios that will reflect back to her an idealized self-image, she finds herself disoriented, frustrated, and exhausted.

Bauman's suggestion that the deterioration of pilgrim-style "progress" makes time "no longer a river, but a collection of ponds and pools" registers stylistically in the narrative's use of present-tense narration (1996, 25). The use of the present tense signals a time-locked perspective in which events resist organization into causal pattern. *Heavenly Days* is the first of Wilcox's novels to use a significant amount of present-tense narration. But his experimentation with disrupted temporal patterns is not new. His most typical technique—most prominent, perhaps, in *North Gladiola*—is a kind of retroactive narration wherein events themselves are bypassed to be narrated from the perspective of a character who seeks, usually without success, to impose order on what has happened.

Lou finds herself, as it were, caught in a series of inscrutable subplots leading, as she might put it, God knows where. To conceive of a subplot per se is, however, to assume the presence of a main plot line in a way that *Heavenly Days* subtly complicates. On the one hand, as I hope to show, the text does ultimately generate a kind of sorting mechanism whereby distraction is differentiated from plot. The unusually helpful plot description on the novel's flyleaf, which describes the various subplots as "distractions . . . from Lou's true, if unacknowledged, aim: to find the grace of heaven in the days of her own life through the bonds of love." On the other hand this differentiation occurs late in the novel, with the effect of structurally aligning the reader's experience of the narrative with Lou's own sense of bafflement and perplexity as she strives to extract legibility and order from the events surrounding her. Although even a brief consideration of the various plot threads is well beyond the scope of this essay, it bears noting that none of them exists in isolation from the others. Spatially and socially there is a deep interconnectedness in the terrain Lou attempts to navigate, a point that can be illustrated through a brief examination of one of the novel's central nodes: WaistWatch, the fundamentalist weight-loss clinic where Lou works. Through her contact with Maigrite Pickens, her boss, Lou becomes embroiled in her troubled marriage with Bobby Pickens, who may or may not be involved with Burma Van Buren, who had supplied tenants for Don's parents' house, a situation terminating with an ambiguous fight between Don and a lesbian librarian whom he apparently mistakes for a man. In an effort to help Maigrite, Lou repaints a handicapped parking space, which gets her in trouble with Mrs. Melvin Tudie, the wife of the man who had fathered Lou's aborted child. Seeking to rescue Lou from the clutches of WaistWatch fundamentalism, Grady, a WaistWatch client, schemes behind the scenes to get Lou a job teaching music at St. Jude state, which in turn involves Lou in the intrigues of small college politics. Grady also wants to rescue Lou from the clutches of Brother Moodie, with whom she imagines Lou is having an affair, which is galling since Brother Moodie had resisted her own overtures. As a critical matter untangling these various plot strands is less important than recognizing their deep entanglement and chaotic resistance to Lou's efforts to impose order.

Just as WaistWatch situates the unsettlement of Lou's relationship to events, so it also locates the novel's complex approach to characterization. Brother Moodie, for example, looks every bit to be the "sleazy Vegas sex machine" Grady describes (54). But despite some rather severe shortcomings—he raps for Jesus on a CD titled *Rappin' Sons of Thunder* and enjoins "Couples in Crisis" to exorcise their "mutual hatred with kickboxing" (52); he also knows Susan Sontag and, more important, assures Lou, "We all love you something awful" (54). In Wilcox's *North Gladiola* a Samoan priest named Father Fua provides a similar combination of absurdity and wisdom. Misperceiving a parishioner's spiritual crisis as the effect of menopause, Father Fua nevertheless articulates the novel's moral center in his exhortation to "fight to love, fight every day, every minute. Use all your muscles, both fits, cause most people are against it" (60). Brother Moodie's staff is integrated; he knows what Lou does not: the real name of her black housekeeper. Most significant, he comforts Lou without taking advantage of her when, during a period of depression, she makes a play for him: "Gently, graciously, without actually saying it, he refused" (54). Similarly Mrs. Melvin Tudie, who as the owner of AAA SecureCare and as tax assessor haunts Lou as the specter of private and public authority, also visits her in the hospital and tries, graciously, to arrange a liposuction for her while she's there (162). Taken cumulatively—and indeed there is little differentiation in this respect—the citizens of Tula Springs come before the reader as fundamentally flawed, subject to peculiar strains of original sin, but also capable of redemption through grace. In this precise sense, they are complex in ways that they themselves—and Lou in particular—fail to recognize. To borrow E. M. Forster's classic terms, characters see each other as flat and predictable, whereas the novel imagines them as round and complex. According to Grady, for example, Lou presents Maigrite as "some Madonna in a wheelchair," an image we recognize from Lou's own thoughts about Maigrite, not the "little hussy, Miss Priss," who actually "struts" into Grady's home, which is an image we recognize from Maigrite's actions elsewhere (46). Of Wilcox's novels Hugh Ruppersburg writes that "characters and landscape are presented without much authorial commentary, as commonplace fact, with no ironic context to inform us that something about them is askew" (1997, 36). To the kind of normal abnormality Ruppersburg identifies, I would add that no character is beyond redemption; indeed, part of Wilcox's brilliance as a writer is that he replicates in his reader the patterns of revulsion and empathy toward characters that they themselves experience toward each other.

If Lou is charitable toward Maigrite and her WaistWatch cohort, toward others she displays the crudest sort of characterization in an effort to eliminate the ambiguities that plague her. Rather than submitting to bewilderment, she strives to organize characters and events into an allegory starring herself as moral heroine. She and Don do not have children, she explains to Mrs. Ompala, because they "decided long ago to help compensate for everyone who's straining the earth's resources" (36). Like several characters in Wilcox's fiction, Lou casts herself as the savior of the racially oppressed. Although her mother-in-law had left her house and retirement fund to Alpha, her African American maid, Lou withholds moral credit from a woman who "said *colored* all the time" and once owned a "Jackie Kennedy pillbox made out of a Confederate flag." Although Lou is not, Grady suggests, "sounding very Christian," she refuses to budge from her position that "That woman was a racist, plain and simple" (87). Lou, by contrast, displays rigorously enlightened racial views: Alpha is her "domestic engineer," not her maid. Even so, Lou notifies her domestic engineer by letter that "her services will no longer be required in Brougham Gardens" (63)—owing, no doubt, to her belief that "Alpha deserved a job with more dignity" (6). In *Modern Baptists* Donna Lee Keely displays a similar condescending regard for her mother's maid, who in turn rejects Donna Lee's conversational overtures. Just as "Moab's silence hurt Donna Lee and made her wonder about herself" (140), Alpha's rejection of Lou's patronizing solicitude leaves her confused and resentful. As she later complains, "I've tried so hard to get Alpha to be my friend. . . . If she just said one kind word to me, gave me a smile, a pat on the back, I could die happy" (143–44).

Lou seeks a moral universe in which intention translates into action without loss of energy—a world, in short, of almost allegorical purity. As a result she becomes something of a moral pedagogue. As Grady, who knows her better than anyone else, puts it at one point, "Come on, Lou. Don't try to teach me any lessons now." Although localized in its application—Lou is chiding Grady for her "rash and inappropriate generosity" (84)—Grady's comment highlights the problem with Lou's moral exactitude: in addition to being quixotic, it is often uncharitable and controlling. While Lou can't even get Alpha to have a cup of coffee with her, she is galled that Alpha has had lunch with Grady, though Grady's father, a judge, "had blocked the voter registration drive that Lou's mother had initiated in the Sixties" (60). While "Lou's mother had conducted the band in the black high school, and now it's *Grady* who's invited to lunch" (60). Lou's emplotment here of her mother, the saint, and Judge Morgen, the sinner, displays the same fetishistic desire for moral clarity that plagues her own life. In order to install Judge Morgen in the role of stock segregationist, Lou must suppress momentarily the moral complexity of the man, who also, precisely because he was firmly embedded in Tula Spring's old-boy network, was able to protect her own father, a refugee from the Nazis, by planting morphine in the glove compartment of an overzealous INS agent. As Lou herself has conceded moments earlier, Judge Morgen "may have been racist, but he wasn't a pig. No one who loved my father could be a real pig" (59).

Throughout *Heavenly Days* Lou struggles to cram those around her into the kind of morally legible plots—the sense-making stories—that she desires as a means of grounding her own identity. As a result she finds herself inhabiting a ghostly domain tilting against windmills and finding reality maddeningly elusive. Nowhere is her effort so pronounced, and ultimately so baffling, as with her attempts to make sense of Mrs. Ompala. Initially Lou believes her to be Alpha's mother, a recently widowed woman, who "had booked passage on a freighter from Mombasa to visit her daughter" (7). Surprised to find that Mrs. Ompala is not black, Lou "badly . . . wants to know her story, how Mrs. Ompala had had the courage to marry an African, a black man," an act that "makes her a heroine in Lou's eyes" (36). As Lou gathers further bits and pieces of information, however, the story falls apart. She did not live in Mombasa for twenty-five years; she resided in Houston, Mississippi. To Lou this seems impossible: "Such style, such elegance, cannot possibly have come from Elvis Country" (39). Even so the story can be repaired, and Lou repairs it, marveling at the story the woman must have: "Mrs. Ompala had stuck by her husband when he decided to leave Mombasa. Going with him to Mississippi, of all places. The only white woman in a black household. And in a virtual police state" (45). Except that Mrs. Ompala had married not a black man, but a Boer—"some of the worst racists on earth," in Lou's estimation—located for her after she becomes pregnant by the grandson of a Rhodesian tribal queen studying at Oxford. His family, not just hers, opposes the marriage. Lou's response is telling: "To think that she and Don have been harboring the widow of a Boer, a Mississippi Boer at that." Lou's disappointment is "fierce," and it is exacerbated when it becomes clear that Alpha is not Mrs. Ompala's daughter. Lou can no longer repair the integrity of Mrs. Ompala's narrative: "All the revisions this entails—the entire story in ruins now" (64–65).

The ruins, however, are not merely of Mrs. Ompala's story but also of Lou's. This is because, based on the moral heroism and transcendent elegance Lou attributes to her, Mrs. Ompala stands positioned to reflect back to Lou an idealized image of herself. With her Ph.D. in music theory from Florida State University, Lou cannot help but parade her academic credentials to a woman she perceives as uniquely qualified to appreciate them. Although prior to their second meeting Lou is delighted "to have another chance" after an embarrassingly crude mention of "her Ph.D., the way she dissected the Lydian mode in *Verklärte Nacht*" (7), she finds herself again holding forth, embarrassingly, on the Lydian mode and the merits of Florida State's music program relative to Yale, Princeton, and Harvard (18). Deeply gratified when Mrs. Ompala addresses her as "Dr. Jones," she is equally pleased that the older woman, as Grady reports, thinks Lou has got "the most something marriage she's ever seen. 'Seemly'—or was it 'suitable'?" (59). Although this evaluation is made on the basis that "only someone a little dotty could put up with a man like J. Donald Jones," Lou insists to Don that "Mrs. Ompala is the sanest person I know. She's the only one who sees what a great marriage we have, Don" (66). And yet despite Lou's desire to be recognized and sanctioned by Mrs. Ompala, who makes her feel as if she has "stepped back in time—into late [Henry] James" (58), the deterioration of the older woman's story allows new meanings to emerge. Midway through the novel, Lou again tries to install Mrs. Ompala as some sort of saint in touch with "other dimensions" (109), only to have her interlocutor cast new doubts on the integrity of Mrs. Ompala's story. A "lot of what she's read has gotten mixed up" with her own life, Carla suggests, adding, "I've really begun to wonder if she's not confusing herself with something she's read. Like Dinesen" (110). The theme of a character modeling him- or herself on an earlier literary character recurs, as I have discussed elsewhere, throughout Wilcox's fiction, often indicating a grandiose and artificial sense of self.

Although we might expect Lou's response to be defensive or disappointed, she instead recognizes a connection: her life, she realizes, "would sound just as suspicious, as if I were making it up as I went along . . ." (110; Wilcox's ellipsis). This insight, narratively embedded in a "darkness, more soothing than her usual Gibsons," seems to be "what Lou has always longed for—without quite knowing it" (110). The language here suggests the complex transition that Lou must undergo. In order to recuperate her life as a sense-making story—in order to experience a kind of homecoming—she must transcend the narrow conception of "sense" that has generated her story of exile.

The novel's epigraph, from C. S. Lewis's *The Great Divorce*, offers a clue as to what this might mean: "Heaven, once attained, will work backward and turn even that agony into a glory." In his dream vision Lewis describes inhabitants ("ghosts") of a "grey town" (hell) who board a bus for an excursion into the foothills of heaven, where most reject their opportunity to engage "reality" and prefer to return to hell, which they do not recognize as such. The epigraph, however, indicates that inhabitants of the town can choose to remain in heaven, in which case their agonies and sorrows will be transformed as the goodness of heaven works retroactively. Several details in *Heavenly Days* connect it with *The Great Divorce* (whose working title, interestingly, was "Who Goes Home?"). Among them there is the similarity between Maigrite's appearance in the final scene and the shining figures from heaven encountered by the tourists from hell.

The retroactive work of grace finds complex articulation in Wilcox's novel, most notably in relation to a dense scene occurring in the novel's penultimate chapter where many plot lines converge. Presented as a flashback during her stay at the hospital—she may have suffered a stroke—this chapter describes a visit Lou had made to Burdin, Mississippi, to offer a seminar on wind instruments for children with attention deficit disorder. Needing to use the restroom, she refuses to enter a Baptist church displaying a Confederate flag and a sign that reads "KEEP THE CAPITAL IN PUNISHMENT" (190). Becoming lost, she tries to turn around only to find that her car's wheels are balanced precariously over a gully. When a man approaches through the blinding sun, she mistakes him for a rapist and becomes frantic with terror. Don has insisted she bring along his pistol, and she makes a decision: if the man is white, "one of those awful rednecks, men who glory in a flag celebrating the savage enslavement of innocent souls," she will shoot him; if he is African American, she will shoot herself. Brandishing the pistol, she believes she has driven him away, but her "sense of relief begins to founder" as he turns—threateningly, Lou thinks—toward a lady in a nearby field. When the woman "takes his paw, holds it to her cheek,"

Lou realizes that the man had been helping her remove her car from the gully. "Wracked with shame," Lou fails to apologize because she fears another automotive mishap and so "heads off into the night, carrying inside her this terrible need to thank him" (192–94). There are several instances of what might be labeled Lou's moral hesitation, moments in which her good intentions are not acted upon but rather deferred until a more convenient time. She fails, for example, to return the sunglasses of Grady's butler, Bill, so that Don can wear them at his job interview. More important she fails, prior to Bill's departure, to say, *"I'll miss you"* because "her mouth is too dry" (188).

Although the visit to Burdin has been referenced several times previously, its detailed articulation here follows an accumulation of knowledge that allows Lou to recognize the scene for the first time, to understand that "the alien ground she walked upon was actually her own soil," and to "see how lovely Burdin was" (185). For one thing the Baptist church, as Grady informs her at the hospital, was once presided over by Lou's own grandfather. Lou, whose mother, unbeknown to Lou, had converted to Judaism because she was not allowed to attend the funeral of a Jewish friend, is highly invested in having been a Jew—"the very core of who she is" (171)—although she has become an Episcopalian in the meantime. At any rate Lou can experience her being "really" a Southern Baptist only as an assault on her identity. More important, however, Lou can, in retrospect, recognize the man and the woman as Mr. and Mrs. Ompala, a point made explicit in the next and final chapter when Lou, in a delirious state, believes she is speaking to Mrs. Ompala: *"Yes, I know. I should have thanked your husband long ago. I've been hoping for a chance to apologize, to thank him for getting me out of that rut. Isn't it funny, dear, it turns out I've known you all along, even before we met"* (197–98). The rut referenced here is a capacious one, entailing all of Lou's pernicious strategies of identity maintenance: her easy denunciation of the moral depravity of Boers, boors, and Baptists and her self-serving canonization of Mrs. Ompala. In a way the Boer *has* helped her out of her rut by complicating the typology of characters that has become a distracting mental habit. In this profound moment of recognition—literally re-cognition—Lou's bond with Mrs. Ompala is transformed. Rather than conspiring with her as the co-embodiments of superiority and class, Lou recognizes her as a fellow sufferer as Lou's pain over her abortion merges with Mrs. Ompala's confused search for her lost child: *"I'll help you find your child, dear woman. I know how hard it must be to wander all over creation, searching for an end to that pain, that guilt"* (197).

The final chapter is altogether subtle, infused with Lou's own idiom, and yet at the same time marks a profound transfiguration of her relationship with others. In this moment of extremity the physical nature of the world seems altered; like the ghosts of C. S. Lewis's allegory who find the smallest objects in heaven unbearably heavy, Lou can hardly pick up the telephone: *"Do all hospital phones weigh a ton?"* (197). But when she does, she speaks to Don in a way that illuminates her love for him minus the habit of badgering that, at its worst, configures her husband as puppet. Protective of her "darling boy," Lou looks forward to her coming home to their new house: "Soon I'll be with you on the porch. No, please don't carve my name on the rocker, Donnie. What will people think? You're just too crazy, little man. Too crazy for me. Yes, yes . . . Soon. It won't be long" (197). In a similar way, Lou encounters Maigrite as an illuminated version of her earlier self: "What Lou remembers of Maigrite in the office is only a fitful parody of the reality here before her now" (198). Recalling Lou's earlier perception at the mall that she is traveling toward the "real thing," Maigrite appears in a purified form; the alteration is not in her but in Lou. Another detail suggesting Lou's approach to reality is the genuine ermine cape Maigrite is wearing, a replacement for her Belgian hare collar that Lou earlier mistook for ermine. As Roy Blount Jr. writes, "Wilcox's novels are so subtle, deep down, that I need to read them twice, and so funny that I want to" (*Heavenly Days*, back cover).

As with Don, Lou's appreciation of Maigrite extends what has always shown itself as a deep concern—even love—for those around her, but without the encumbrances and qualifications that have typically clogged her relationships. Even the agony of Lou's relationship with Alpha is subtly transformed into a kind of glory as the novel draws to a close. Near death, Lou imagines speaking to Alpha: "*Let's sit down for a few minutes. Have a little chat. You don't need to vacuum any more. I'll do the rest if . . . Please, just one cup, that's all. O heavenly days, I know you're busy, but . . .*" (199). Reworking Lou's earlier complaint that she could "die happy" if Alpha would just say "one kind word," Lou here offers, despite her protestations to the contrary, what she has not offered before: an actual invitation. Rather than advertising the unfairness of it all in a display of her exquisite (and unappreciated) racial sensibilities, Lou instead *opens* herself to Alpha: "Come, sweet Alpha. Come."

And so ends *Heavenly Days* not with an actual homecoming but with the promise of a heavenly one. In a novel rich in irony, the title ultimately signifies on a somewhat literal level. Although used on several occasions during the novel as an expression of exasperation, the phrase comes to reference the concrete workings of regenerative grace. To be sure the moment is a melancholic one, since Lou apparently dies, leaving behind many who love her and will grieve her loss. The possibility of death is clearly indicated by the text, both in the presentation of the scene and the multiple hints of Lou's medical condition that appear throughout the text. Even so, the final scene does not specifically show Lou's death.

But at this moment Lou shows a capacity for grace that has heretofore been thwarted by habits of mind and spirit that have consigned her to a world not unlike the "grey town" of C. S. Lewis's dream vision. The achievement of *Heavenly Days* lies, finally, not only in its acute register of that gray world but in offering a map of how to escape it. Like E. M. Forster, who famously organized his novel *Howards End* around the injunction "only connect," Wilcox offers a grammar of connection and homecoming as an antidote to a contemporary world of alienation and exile.

Works Cited and Consulted

Bauman, Zygmunt. "From Pilgrim to Tourist—or a Short History of Identity." *Questions of Cultural Identity*. Ed. Stuart Hall and Paul du Gay. London: Sage, 1996. 18–36.

Gingher, Marianne. "A Comedy of Bad Manners." Review of *Miss Undine's Living Room*. *Washington Post*, August 16, 1987. http://www.highbeam.com/doc/1P2-1338298.html/.

Kakutani, Michiko. Review of *Miss Undine's Living Room*. *New York Times*, August 12, 1987. http://www.nytimes.com/1987/08/12/books-of-the-times-016487.html/.

Lewis, C. S. *The Great Divorce*. 1945. Reprint, New York: HarperOne, 2009.

———. *The Screwtape Letters*. 1942. New York: HarperOne, 2001.

O'Connor, Flannery. *Mystery and Manners: Occasional Prose*. New York: Farrar, Straus and Giroux, 1969.

Romine, Scott. *The Real South: Southern Narrative in the Age of Cultural Reproduction*. Baton Rouge: Louisiana State University Press, 2008.

Ruppersburg, Hugh. "James Wilcox: The Normality of Madness." *Southern Writers at Century's End*. Ed. Jeffrey J. Folks and James A. Perkins. Lexington: University Press of Kentucky, 1997. 32–43.

Schwartz, Jonathan Matthew. *In Defense of Homesickness: Nine Essays on Identity and Locality*. Copenhagen: Akademisk Forlag, 1989.

Wilcox, James. *Hunk City*. New York: Viking, 2007.

———. *Heavenly Days*. New York: Viking, 2003.

———. *North Gladiola*. 1985. Reprint, Baton Rouge: Louisiana State University Press, 2000.

———. *Modern Baptists*. 1983. Reprint, Boston: Little, Brown, 1999.

———. *Plain and Normal*. New York: Little Brown, 1998.

———. *Guest of a Sinner*. New York: HarperCollins, 1993.

———. *Polite Sex*. New York: HarperCollins, 1991.

———. *Sort of Rich*. 1989. Reprint, New York: Perennial Library, 1990.

———. *Miss Undine's Living Room*. New York: Harper, 1987.

Donald Harington ~ *Enduring*

EDWIN T. ARNOLD

A Biographical Sketch

For more than forty years Arkansas writer Donald Harington has been searching in his fiction for a state of perpetuity. Born in Little Rock in 1935, Harington spent summers with his mother's parents in the small town of Drakes Creek, near Fayetteville, where they owned a country store. At the age of twelve he contracted meningococcal meningitis and lost most of his hearing. While recuperating he began reading "serious literature," such writers as William Faulkner, Feodor Dostoyevsky, and Joseph Conrad, which led to other authors as varied as Erskine Caldwell, Mickey Spillane, Walt Kelly, who was the creator of the comic strip *Pogo*, and Al Capp, the creator of *Li'l Abner*. After earning a master of fine arts degree in studio art from the University of Arkansas and a master's degree in art history from Boston University, Harington began a doctoral degree in art history at Harvard in 1959 but dropped out the following year and took a position teaching the subject at Bennett College in New York. It was also in 1960 that Harington read William Styron's second novel, *Set This House on Fire*, which he recalled as the "greatest single reading experience I had ever had" (Arnold 1995, 83). After reading negative reviews of the book, Harington contacted Styron, who invited him to visit and soon became a friend and mentor (Arnold 2002). Harington quit his job at Bennett in 1962 and concentrated on becoming a writer, living for a summer in Styron's guest house in Roxbury, Connecticut. The novel is Harington's chosen narrative form, the one best suited to his expansive storytelling. With Styron's help Harington's first novel, *The Cherry Pit*, was published by Random House in 1965. By that time Harington had begun teaching at Windham College in Putney, Vermont, where he would work until the college closed in 1978. While there Harington would come to know the young John Irving, whom he considered his "protégé" in much the same way that he had worked under the influence of William Styron.

The Cherry Pit received respectful reviews; Harington recalls that it came in second for the PEN/Faulkner Award for best first novel, losing to Cormac McCarthy's *Orchard Keeper* (Arnold 1995, 84). It was in his second published book, *Lightning Bug* (1970), that Harington laid claim to the world he has developed through twelve subsequent works centered on the fanciful hamlet of Stay More, located in the mountains of the Arkansas Ozarks. Although not all of the books that followed are set primarily in Stay More, its presence is always felt as an almost mythical place that beckons his characters as much as it dissuades intrusion by outsiders. It is tempting to compare this creation with Faulkner's Yoknapatawpha, and Harington has encouraged such a connection by drawing his own map of the town (population 179, give or take) and surroundings, modeled on Faulkner's sketching of his fictional county. The map, roughly drafted and marked, serves as the portal to Harington's official web site, donaldharington.com. As such it gives both entrance and direction to a rich, sprawling work of comic imagination.

Another, perhaps more surprising influence on Harington, however, was Vladimir Nabokov, whose literary playfulness and experimentation with narrative would become a hallmark of Harington's fiction. Traces of *Lolita* and *Pale Fire*, to name only two, can be found throughout his work, and his 1993 novel *Ekaterina* is in part paying homage to Nabokov both in its story—the heroine is attracted to prepubescent boys—and with its bag of literary tricks. Later in his career Harington became good friends with the novelist Jack Butler and, more recently, the poet-author Fred Chappell, who has famously described Harington's work as an "undiscovered continent" awaiting wider recognition.

Harington published his fourth novel, *The Architecture of the Arkansas Ozarks*, in 1975. It is the centerpiece of his fiction, a postmodern testament that provides the foundation for the novels that come after and before. This book covers more than 140 years of Stay More history, from its founding by the town's patriarch Jacob Ingledew and his brother Noah to the present of the book's publication and beyond. Harington had great hopes for its success, but the book sold poorly, and it would be eleven years before he published another work. After Windham College closed, Harington, whose first marriage had ended, began drinking heavily and moved from job to job before returning to Arkansas. He was hired to teach art history at the University of Arkansas in Fayetteville in 1986, and he retired from there as distinguished professor in 2007. A second marriage brought stability to his life and a rebirth of his writing, which has continued unabated to the present time (Razer 2006).

Enduring

While each of Harington's books can be read as a separate work, together they form an epic narrative detailing the founding of a world and the development of a race, a celebration of heroes and the wonderments of a golden age, but also the inevitable tragedies caused by human foibles and the slow decline into an obscurity leavened only by memory and legend. Much of this is told as broad hillbilly comedy, but what gives the books an unusual affect is an unabashed eroticism. At times this includes disconcerting sexual practices, for incest is not uncommon in Stay More families, nor is adolescent sex, which sometimes veers toward pedophilia. They are often highly sophisticated portrayals of country bumptiousness. "I do feel that I might be misunderstood as just writing about country yokels," Harington has said. "I've written about a mythical place, Stay More, that exists only in the mind of the reader. That place may seem to be populated by hillbillies, but those hillbillies are actually the parts of oneself that one recognizes in the process of encountering them and laughs at them, learns from them, and has through them some kind of interaction with one's own self" (Walter 2007, 238).

However, Harington is not constrained by the limits of chronological time or by the traditional conventions of fictional narrative. One of the characters in *The Cherry Pit* says, "If there were any word to describe the opposite of history, to mean for the future what history means for the past, then that would be my favorite word, my favorite subject." She comes up with the word "futurity" and exclaims, "I want to be lost in futurity" (334). This character might well speak for Harington himself, who habitually concludes his books by anticipating the continuation of the narrative beyond the apparent "end" of the work. His traditional narrative past tense slowly shades into the present and then projects into future or future perfect, so that events that have not yet occurred in the narrative confines of the story at hand "will have" occurred at some point after the last page is read. It is Harington's method of keeping the story going past the tangible limits of the book itself. As he has commented, "I *hate* endings [and] . . . the future tense shift is specifically designed to help prevent the book from ending, because anything in the future tense does not end. . . . My books are 'propped open' to a subsequent book and the reader can be assured that none of my books will end at that particular place, but that it will always be propped open to some future book" (Arnold 1995, 85).

It is from Harington's perspective on time that we must approach the novel here discussed. When I wrote this essay there was simply a massive typescript titled "Enduring," but now the novel is in print and fortunately in a version very close to the manuscript I examined. It seemed to me then, and it still does, that a fitting way to discuss Harington's work is to consider that in some future perfect time *Enduring* "will have existed" as an expansive summation of the thirteen other books in the Stay More saga that make up the corpus of Harington's fiction. *Enduring* is the life story of Latha Bourne, Harington's most prominent character, and as such it recounts past events, as would be expected. Nevertheless it also projects into the future, into a world existing presently only in Harington's imagination.

Harington has often identified Latha Bourne as the "goddess of Stay More," and he means this in a literal sense. Harington introduced Latha in *Lightning Bug* (1970), which is the proper beginning of his Stay More series. He has acknowledged that when he began to write *Lightning Bug*, he thought at the time that it would be his "swan song to the Ozarks": "I thought once I'd gotten the

Ozarks out of my system, or exorcised, by writing *Lightning Bug*, that would liberate me to write about the rest of the world. I discovered after writing *Lightning Bug* that I was hooked on the Ozarks" (Arnold 1995, 85). He had planned to write more conventional novels, less regional novels, but had to accept that there was no way he could escape the Ozarks. So ever since he has devoted his writing to Stay More. Since she was first introduced in *Lightning Bug*, the character Latha, the postmistress of Stay More, has appeared as a major or minor figure in every novel Harington has written.

Lightning Bug, which is dedicated to William Styron, reflects a postmodern sensibility in terms of structure and narration. It is divided into three primary sections, identified as "Beginning," "Middling," and "Ending." The lengthy "Middling" section makes up the central narrative of Latha Bourne's story, told in traditional third-person, past-tense style, which covers "Morning," "Noon," "Afternoon," "Evening," and "Night" of one full day in July 1939, when Every Dill, a former suitor of Latha, returns to Stay More as an evangelist. Subsections, which then further separate the narrative, relay the history of Latha and Every's relationship, but they are spoken in first person by a controlling authorial voice that often addresses Latha directly. From the interplay of these contrasting sections, the reader learns of Every's courtship but eventual rape of Latha; his running away to war; the birth of their child, Sonora; Latha's psychic breakdown and placement in an asylum; and Every's eventual rescue of Latha.

Enduring is a simpler narrative, divided into fifty chapters. When the story begins, Latha is 106 years old; by the time it concludes, but does not end, she is well into her twelfth decade, conferred immortality by the writer of her story. But by which writer? The ostensible author of the book is Sharon Ingledew, Latha's granddaughter, and for much of the narrative the conventions of storytelling are realistically observed. The conventional set-up for the narrative is that after the death of their father, Hank Ingledew, widower of Latha's daughter Sonora, Sharon is encouraged by her sisters to preserve her conversations with their grandmother Latha. "You know, just for the record, you ought to write down anything she tells you about her life," one of the sisters says. "It would make a book." Another adds, "I'll bet there are all sorts of things that have happened to her in those hundred and six years that nobody knows about" (8). In the second chapter Sharon takes up that challenge. She asks Latha about her first memory, Latha responds with a story, and soon Sharon's presence is erased as the book follows Latha from childhood through her early sexual experimentation and romance with Every Dill, into the story told in *Lightning Bug* of his rape and impregnation of Latha, the loss of her daughter Sonora to her sister, her confinement in the state hospital, Every's eventual rescue of her, another lengthy separation, and her eventual return to Stay More. At this point, the beginning of chapter 30, when Latha is about to see her daughter Sorona for the first time in many years, Sharon suddenly reappears, exclaiming, "That's my mother! I don't mean to intrude in this story I've been telling with such objectivity that there is no room for myself, but I can't help remarking on the fact that this house where I live, this porch where I often sit, these steps which I daily climb, was the setting for the first meeting of Gran with her daughter, my mother, or at least the first since Mom as a baby had been stolen away from Gran" (287).

From that point on, Sharon's presence is an essential part of the narrative, and in the latter sections of the book she occasionally becomes a character in the story she is relating, although Sharon as narrator for the most part maintains a separation from Sharon as actor. As an example we are told that "Latha's favorite of the granddaughters, Sharon, or Little Sis as everyone called her, including her father, came to Latha privately seeking advice on whether or not she should elope with her boyfriend, Junior Stapleton, since there was no chance she would get permission from Hank, who thought that Junior was an all-around scamp. (I must be forgiven for talking about myself as if I'm just a character in a book, but after all, that's what I am.)" (425). Thus as long as Sharon relates the story of her grandmother, whether from Latha's own recollections or from Sharon's experiences with her, a more or less traditional narrative form is maintained.

The difficulty arises in the latter sections of the story when Harington shifts into the present and then the future-perfect tenses. Although Latha grows older, we have been told that she will never die. "She grants that she is slow. Her stride is no longer broad, and it takes her a while to bend over. But what's the hurry? Time is something she has plenty of, and will always have in abundance" (465). But although Latha is a goddess and immortal, Sharon is not, and the last lines of the penultimate chapter address the fact that Sharon, eventually, will die: "Which will leave an enormous problem . . .: if Sharon will have been telling this story, what will happen to this story after Sharon will have died?" (486). Clearly this is no longer Sharon's voice speaking:

> Latha will be so consumed with grief over the death of her favorite granddaughter that she will not even notice that Sharon's narrative will have come to an end, although the life it will have sought to chronicle will not have. . . . In time, as the funeral hymn "Farther Along" sung at all these funerals will have promised, Latha will come to realize that only the survivor will understand the depth of the loss, while only the lost will understand that they are not lost at all, but found. And she will remember what she herself had realized years before, that the secret of enduring is not to harden oneself against loss but to soften oneself in acceptance. (487–88)

There is some solace in knowing that Sharon's story, parts of which Harington has related in earlier Stay More novels such as *The Cockroaches of Stay More* (1989) and *Ekaterina* (1993), will be explored in greater detail in a novel called *Rose of Sharon* that is yet to be written. Harington has occasionally alerted readers to future Stay More stories that he intends to write, and some of these have later become published books. Nevertheless this knowledge does not obviate the narrative dilemma Harington has created for himself in this book: if the narrator dies before the story is concluded, what happens to the rest of the story?

The answer is both simple and integral to Harington's concept of fiction. At this point the reader must take over: "Latha herself will get credit for voicing the answer: that we have all of us become so familiar with Sharon's narrative techniques throughout this enduring chronicle that we can each of us go on doing the telling ourselves. We can hear Sharon's voice still speaking and telling. And since, as we already know or have guessed, this chronicle has no conclusion, the perpetual rights of storytelling may be allowed to devolve upon whoever may endure thus far through a reading of the book" (488).

Starting with *Lightning Bug*, Harington has debated the solipsistic nature of fiction. BUG (Harington identifies his books by capitalized acronymic or shortened versions of the title; *The Architecture of the Arkansas Ozarks* becomes TAOTAO, for example) carries René Descartes's "Cogito, Ergo Sum" as an epigraph, and *Enduring* uses a longer quote from chapter 4, the second paragraph of Descartes's *Discourse on Method*, to express the same idea: "I thence concluded that I was a substance whose whole essence or nature consists only in thinking, and which, that it may exist, has need of no place, nor is dependent on any material thing; so that 'I,' that is to say, the mind by which I am what I am, is wholly distinct from the body, and is even more easily known than the latter, and is such, that although the latter were not, it would still continue to be all that it is."

In extending this concept to reading, Harington describes the activity as a vitally solipsistic process:

> You live and breathe and hold a book in your lap. The book does not live and breathe, but you are going to pretend very quickly that it is populated with living, breathing characters like yourself. Something in the back of your mind always reminds you that they are not really alive, that only you exist, that all of those people are simply being pretended into existence by yourself (with the help of the author), but for the duration of your enjoyment of the book, you "willingly suspend disbelief" and convince yourself you are moving among real people. . . . The imagination is a very powerful thing" (Arnold 1994, 442).

Thus to move *Enduring* into the future, past the death of its narrator Sharon, to a time when Latha is 121 and counting, the reader's active engagement in the creation of the story is essential. There is no way for Sharon to know what will happen to her grandmother after Sharon has died, so, in essence, the readers' guess is as good as hers.

But to complicate his narrative further, Harington does acknowledge that Sharon, and Latha, are imaginary creations of someone else, the author Donald

Harington, whose name is on the title page. But most of Harington's novels include a fictional version of himself as prime creator of Stay More. In *Enduring* we find the character of "Dawny" (Donnie), who is introduced as a boy visiting his aunt and uncle in Stay More, just as Harington himself spent summers in Drakes Creek. Dawny first appeared in *Lightning Bug*, and he is a major character in *When Angels Rest* (WAR, 1998), which is set during World War II. In both of these books, Dawny is a child, but because *Enduring* covers such a long period of time, over a century of Latha's life, Dawny grows from child to adult and to old man. He first appears helping out in a canning factory. He is a small boy, not yet five years old, "but he pretty well came and went as he pleased, and as long as he kept putting the cans into the chute nobody ever paid him any mind. He spent all of his free time, Saturdays and Sundays, at Latha's store." His role as observer is emphasized. "Latha sometimes felt disconcerted because of the way Dawny stared at her, but then she noticed he stared at everyone else in the same way, as if he were trying to memorize what they looked like.... He wasn't shy at all, but he'd much rather listen than talk, and when he wasn't staring he was listening. And sometimes both" (303). Dawny is ubiquitous, always watching and remembering. He and his dog Gumper roam throughout Stay More, collecting the stories he will later tell.

Although Dawny is a small boy in these first episodes, Harington emphasizes his youthful sexual curiosity. He comes across Latha's daughter Sonora having sex with a Stay More swain in the woods and watches "entranced but secretly" (306). Later Sonora, playfully, grabs the boy in his crotch and says, "My, Dawny, for such a little feller I bet you've got a big one!" Latha tells her daughter not to "tease the boy" (307), but Latha is also a figure of preadolescent sexual desire for Dawny. He spends many hours on her porch, listening to her stories. On one occasion he asks to spend the night, to sleep with Latha in her bed, and the story takes a disturbing turn. Latha sleeps naked, she tells him, and Dawny asks if he can also sleep in the nude with her. Latha has already wondered if Dawny "knew the facts of life, and, if not, [whether] to begin his education" (319), but she realizes that this forwardness would go beyond the conventions even of the often libidinous Stay Morons. "If you ever told anybody, your Aunt Rosie or anybody, that me and you slept together, let alone without our clothes, do you know that they would cover me with hot tar and feathers and ride me out of town on a rail?" she warns the boy. "Aw, Latha! Do you honestly think I would ever tell anybody? I aint never gon tell *any*body *any*thing about me'n you," Dawny reassures her (324). The next morning she awakes before the boy: "In the heat of the night he had kicked off the sheet and was naked and cute, his tiny dinger cutest of all. She was tempted to give it a kiss, but instead kissed him on the brow, at the same time reproaching herself for having allowed him to spend the night with her" (325).

What do we make of such scenes? No matter how open-minded a reader might be, how willing to acknowledge that small children are sexual beings and that ranges of adult affection for children involve complicated emotional and physical responses, these are nonetheless moments that make us pause, especially since they occur throughout Harington's work, most notably in *Ekaterina* and *With* (2003). Like Nabokov and Caldwell, Harington, almost nonchalantly, tells us what we probably know: that sex, no matter how taboo, is rarely absent from any relationship. Latha does recognize how inappropriate her emotions are, at least in the context of her community. We could argue that her temptation to kiss Dawny's penis is innocent of sexual desires, that Harington in Stay More is creating a prelapsarian world in which such acts are natural and carry no harm. But that seems too easy an answer. In *With*, for example, Sog Allen has every intention of sexually molesting Robin Kerr, the young girl he kidnaps, no matter how much he explains the desire to himself in terms of love and protection. There are consequences in Harington's fiction. Today's readers of *Lightning Bug* have to struggle with the description of Every Dill's rape of Latha Bourne, which is both an attack and a seduction. Latha loves Every, in part, because of the rape. But the rape results in her pregnancy, and it is after her sister takes away the baby, the daughter Sonora, that Latha loses her ability to talk and to communicate. She is placed for years in the state asylum.

In *Lightning Bug, When Angels Rest,* and *Enduring,* Dawny serves as a surrogate for Harington, but he is one of a number of fictionalized versions of the author Harington has used. "To the extent that characters appearing in my books are based on me or offer allusions to me, they are presented as objectively as possible, as if I were writing from a psychic distance about a character not myself," Harington has said (Arnold 1994, 440). But Dawny, like Harington, is rendered deaf as a child. He attends Harvard and later teaches at the University of Pittsburgh, as Harington did. As an adult he publishes a book titled *The Cockroaches of Stay More*, which he sends to Latha. Harington's book with that title was published in 1989. Latha thinks that "the book is very funny but she is uneasy that the author has concocted it out of the happenings of this actual place and the doings of these actual people and insects and animals, living and dead. Is there no clear line between observation and imagination? Is good humor an excuse for defamation? She knows what Dawny's answer to that question might be: you can't be defamed if you aren't famous" (427). Dawny writes other books about Stay More, such as *Some Other Place, The Right Place* (Harington's novel of that title was published in 1972), *The Architecture of the Arkansas Ozarks,* and *Ekaterina*. Latha reads them all, and from the character Ekaterina she learns why Dawny, as a grown man, has never come back to see her in Stay More: "He loves Latha so much, and always has, and always will, that it gives him physical pain to be in her presence." "Of course I've read all the novels he's written about you," Ekaterina says to Latha, "so I can easily imagine why he'd feel that way. But you mustn't let it lead you to believe that he holds any ill will whatsoever against you. Quite the contrary. He worships you, and always will" (*Enduring*, 479–80).

When Latha turns one hundred, Dawny sends her a copy of Garcia Marquez's *One Hundred Years of Solitude*, a primary inspiration for Harington's *Architecture of the Arkansas Ozarks*. In the book she discovers the character of Pilar Ternera, who lives to be 142. "Latha chuckles with the realization that she will easily surpass that" (480). By the last pages of *Enduring*, after the narrative has shifted from traditional past tense and we, the readers, have recognized our involvement in continuing this story focused on a hero who is immortal, "we" "realize that we have employed the future tense over twenty times already in this chapter, as if eager to get to that tense in which nothing ever comes to an end, so we will decide that we might as well make the tense shift official as of now. We will be forgiven, first Sharon whose handiwork this narrative is, and eventually Dawny, who will seem to be desperately tugging at the future tense to save us all" (483).

Dawny's "desperately tugging at the future tense to save us all" is a good way to describe Harington's intentions. But as the novel enters its last chapter, Dawny is himself old. Latha recalls when she last saw him: "He was white-haired and stooped and slow, but I could tell he was still the same tender sentimentalist he'd always been" (489–90). She is being interviewed in this future time by an English professor named Brian Walter (an actual person who has written on Harington and is now in the process of making a documentary on him, *The Architect of Stay More*). The character Walter asks Latha:

> "What is your favorite story about Dawny that has never made it into his books?" This last question she will be loath to answer, declaring that she will only answer it after Dawny is dead.
> "But what if he survives you?" the professor will protest.
> "He won't," she declares.
> "Do you think the only reason you're still alive at the age of one hundred and twenty-one is that Dawny has granted you immortality?"
> Latha will not be able to prevent a scoff escaping her lips. "Didn't you ever ask *him* that?" she will want to know.
> "Several times," Brian Walter will answer. "The best answer I ever recorded was, 'I may have created her, but I am not in charge of her.'" (490)

Here Harington acknowledges that his creation will, must outlive him. Dawny, we are told or tell ourselves, will "breathe his last at the age of eighty-six. That last breath will be with difficulty owing to pneumonia, which will have plagued him periodically for years and which took away his mentor, William Styron, in 2006. He will use that last breath to whisper into the ear of his beloved wife Kim his parting sentiments and also a reminder that Latha . . . will have already determined that the remainder of the *Enduring* book can be readily composed by the reader" (493).

Are such literary devices merely cleverness on Harington's part? Some of his critics have argued that Harington overplays his own ingenuity. "In my effort to make the reader a participant in the creation of the imaginary world of 'reality,' I choose narrative techniques which require the reader not only to figure out the stories but also to investigate, usually with the benefit of a second or third reading, the multiple levels of 'existence,' meaning allusion, 'reality.' . . . And as long as I am in control of your perception while you're reading one of my books, I am going to use every trick I know to take you into realities where you've never been," he has admitted (Arnold 1994, 442). This "trickiness" can be disconcerting to readers who expect their authors to abide by conventional rules of storytelling or who do not share his investment in the world he has created. And it must be said that the self-referencing nature of his work, his constant insertion of a Harington persona into his stories, and his insistence on concluding his books in the present and future tense have now become conventions in themselves, no matter how brilliantly he employs the techniques.

With *Enduring* a larger issue must be addressed. Since this is the "full-length story" of Latha's life, as Harington has described *Enduring*, and since Latha is the constant figure in the Stay More saga, the book necessarily retells events previously explored in earlier works. Harington has acknowledged that his editor asked for changes in the first submitted version of the novel, "particularly in those passages which are self-plagiarized from my other books." His rationale was that good stories often bear retelling. "I was not trying to deceive but to demonstrate that good parts of other books could be repeated, as we listen to good music repeatedly or watch a movie more than once," Harington explained (e-mail to author, August 13, 2008). Just as Faulkner would revisit stories, retell them with variations so that they became organic, growing, and changing with each version, so Harington incorporates scenes from many of his previous books in *Enduring*, imposing a chronology on them that would not be found by reading the works in order of publication. In the retelling, he sometimes switches perspective as he narrates the story. For example, in *With*, Robin Kerr, who was kidnapped as a child by Sog Allen, makes her way years later to Stay More, where she talks with an old lady who is revealed to be Latha. In *Enduring* we follow this scene from Latha's point of view, and for those who have read *With*, the pleasure comes from identifying the strange girl who appears in Latha's yard. Many other characters, including the insects from *The Cockroaches of Stay More*, make cameo appearances throughout *Enduring*. The balance Harington looks for in these "recognized repetitions" is to provide the satisfaction of retelling a familiar story without "giving away the plots of my other novels" (e-mail to author, September 29, 2008). For those books in which Latha plays a main role, such as *Lightning Bug*, this may be difficult to avoid, but even here Harington expands his account to such a degree that the reader may find enjoyment in experiencing the events anew. "We argued and dickered a lot," Harington says of the editorial process, "but most of the self-plagiarized passages remain," although he cut about four thousand words from his first draft.

It is therefore tempting to read *Enduring* as a backward look and a summing up for Harington, much as some read William Faulkner's last book, *The Reivers* (1962), as a preparation to wrap up his chronicle of Yoknapatawpha. After all the shortened title Harington has given *Enduring* is END. But according to Harington this would be a mistake. "Just because we call it END doesn't mean that it's the end of my oeuvre. I never thought of it as a swan song to Stay More and I hope I have several more Stay More novels haunting my sleep. . . . I've always been in love with Latha, and I intended it simply as a full-length story of her life" (e-mail to author, August 14, 2008). It does seem likely that Harington, in bringing together so much material from his previous books, has found yet more story lines to develop. Using Sharon Ingledew as his primary narrator has taken him back to her story, and it is reasonable to assume that her book, already given the title *Rose of Sharon*, is among those "haunting" Harington's sleep. But he says that his next novel will be the life story of Every Dill, Latha's great love, intended "to match (or bookend) *Enduring*." "There's a lot of novelistic material in his years at David Lipscomb College [a seminary] and on the road as a circuit rider," Harington notes. At this time he intends to title the book *And God Saw Every* (after discarding *Every Inch a King*), although he would not begin the writing until the spring of 2009 (e-mail to author, September 29, 2008).

Nevertheless *Enduring* is an essential novel in Harington's oeuvre and, I argue, a work destined for honor in the new century. In 2006 the *Oxford American* magazine presented its first Oxford American Lifetime Award for Contributions to Southern Literature to Donald Harington. The editors wrote, "We swoon over Mr. Harington's taut plots, lyrical prose, and endearing oddball characters, and wonder how he manages to be so weird, funny, disturbing, sexy, and deeply moving all at once." Harington's response was to protest good-naturedly, "But really, to call an award 'Lifetime' makes it sound as if they've already pulled the green quilt over me. And all of those wonderful tributes from my fellow writers are in the nature of a memorial service" (*Oxford American* 2006). *Enduring*, then, does serve two purposes: to look backward, to "memorialize" the work Harington has accomplished over a forty-plus-year career, but also to look forward, into the "futurity" that is always leading to the next book. In the last pages of *Lightning Bug*, we are told that the story "WILL END WITH THIS MOOD" (239), "WILL END WITH THESE PEOPLE" (241), "WILL END WITH THIS SOUND" (the last of which is the sound of a swing door opening and closing, "*which, more than any other sound . . . evokes the heart of summer, of summer evenings, of summer evenings* there *in that place*") (*Lightning Bug*, 239, 241, 243). *Enduring* begs to differ. Of this book we are told, "It will not end with the sound of the spring on a screen door stretching and twanging. . . . It will not end with a goodbye, or a farewell or a godspeed or a catch you later. It will not end with any sort of valedictory." Instead, quite simply, "it will not end" (495).

In accepting the *Oxford American* award, Harington acknowledged that he remains unknown to the large body of readers even after so many years and such a production of books. Over the some fifteen years I have known Don Harington, the two things that have most impressed me are his unflagging creativity and his essential optimism. With each book he expects that his "undiscovered continent" will finally be found by a wider audience, and when it is not, he shrugs his shoulders and writes another book. His own *endurance* keeps him going. As he remarked to the *Oxford American* audience, "Much more important to me than the award, however, is the possibility that it might increase the population of Stay More, that mythical, magical little town that is the setting for all my work. You can't physically go there; it isn't on any map, except the map of your own mind, which you are allowed to redraw as you like. There's truth in the idea that Stay More is hard to find but even harder to leave . . . which is the real meaning of its name. If somehow I can get you there, you won't ever want to leave" (*Oxford American* 2006, 8). Which is a pretty good example of eternity.

Works Cited and Consulted

Arnold, Edwin T. "The William Styron–Donald Harington Letters." *Southern Quarterly* 40 (2002): 99–141. Donald Harington issue. Ed. Edwin T. Arnold.

———. "Donald Harington." *Dictionary of Literary Biography: American Novelists since World War II*. Vol. 152. Ed. James and Wanda Giles. Detroit: Gale, 1995. 82–91.

———. "Interview with Donald Harington." *Appalachian Journal* 21 (1994): 432–35.

Chicago Review 38, no. 4 (1993). With a special Donald Harington section.

Descartes, René. "Discourse on the Method of Rightly Conducting the Reason, and Seeking the Truth in the Sciences," 1637. Online Literature Library. http://www.literature.org/authors/descartes-rene/reason-discourse/chapter-04.html/.

Harington, Donald. *Enduring*. New Milford, Conn.: Toby Press, 2009.

———. *Farther Along*. New Milford, Conn.: Toby Press, 2008.

———. *The Pitcher Shower*. New Milford, Conn.: Toby Press, 2005.

———. *With*. New Milford, Conn.: Toby Press, 2004.

———. *Thirteen Albatrosses (or, Falling off the Mountain)*. New York: Henry Holt, 2002.

———. *When Angels Rest*. Washington, D.C.: Counterpoint, 1998.

———. *Butterfly Weed*. San Diego: Harcourt Brace, 1996.

———. *Ekaterina*. San Diego: Harcourt Brace, 1993.

———. *The Choiring of the Trees*. San Diego: Harcourt Brace Jovanovich, 1991.

———. *The Cockroaches of Stay More*. San Diego: Harcourt Brace Jovanovich, 1989.

———. *Let Us Build Us a City: Eleven Lost Towns*. San Diego: Harcourt Brace Jovanovich, 1986.

———. *The Architecture of the Arkansas Ozarks*. Boston: Little, Brown, 1975.

———. *Some Other Place. The Right Place*. Boston: Little, Brown, 1972.

———. *Lightning Bug*. New York: Harcourt Brace Jovanovich, 1970.

———. *The Cherry Pit*. New York: Random House, 1965.
Oxford American. October 2006, 1–10. Issue celebrating Harington. http://www.oxfordamericanmag.com/content.cfm?ArticleID=142&entry=Extras/.
Razer, Bob. *Donald Harington and His Stay More Novels: A Celebration of 35 Years*. Publication of the Special Collections, University of Arkansas Libraries. 2006. http://libinfo.uark.edu/SpecialCollections/events/Harington.pdf/.
Walter, Brian. "America's 'Undiscovered Continent.'" *Ozarks Magazine*. 2007. http://www.ozarksmagazine.com/index.html?p=238/.

Lewis Nordan ~ *Lightning Song*

MARCEL ARBEIT

A Biographical Sketch

Lewis Nordan, born in 1939, spent his childhood years in the small Mississippi town of Itta Bena, only a few miles from Money, the town that entered history as the place where Emmett Till, a fourteen-year-old African American who wolf whistled at a white woman, was brutally killed. Many years later Nordan dared to grasp this event from a comic viewpoint in *Wolf Whistle* (1993). Reviewers across the ethnic spectrum appreciated his unusual approach to the painful issue of racial violence and the novel won the Southern Book Critics Circle Award.

Nordan's father died suddenly when his son was just eighteen months old. The boy grew up with his stepfather, Wilbur, who later served as a prototype for Gilbert Mecklin, the painter and decorator wavering between pragmatism and romance, in a short-story cycle set in the imaginary town of Arrow Catcher in the Mississippi Delta. The town bears its name after a game in which one member of a two-player team shoots arrows at his colleague, who catches them in the air. The town is introduced for the first time in the title story of Nordan's first collection, *Welcome to the Arrow Catcher Fair* (1983).

Five of the nine stories from Nordan's second collection, *The All-Girl Football Team* (1986), are also set in Arrow Catcher. It is a typical southern town where men drink their share of whiskey and enjoy taking their sons on hunting trips while women suffer from depression, hoping that their children's destinies will be more favorable than those of the fathers. Death, which is always described as grotesque, never marks the end of the story, as the deceased gain immortality in narratives that the whole community shares, cherishes, and arbitrarily adjusts. The main character of the Arrow Catcher stories is Sugar Mecklin, a developing boy whose emotions toward his father constantly oscillate between love and hate. The stories became the core of a new collection, *Sugar among the Freaks* (1996). Sugar is also the protagonist of the episodic novel *Music of the Swamp* (1991), which is a sequence of stories in the manner of Sherwood Anderson's *Winesburg, Ohio* or William Faulkner's *The Unvanquished*.

Early in his writing career, Nordan developed a unique style: his prose is playful and extremely musical, with a strong sense of rhythm. He can change moods several times within a single compound sentence, use the most hackneyed metaphors and clichés in a highly original way, and move to the verge of sentimentality without falling into its traps. Starting with *Music of the Swamp*, all his fiction is comical, no matter how serious his topics are and how much tragedy flows into the stories. His coat of arms has always borne fantasy and imagination. He does not waste time adhering to a proper chronology of events in his books. Sometimes he describes the same incidents several times, but never in the same way. The best narrators for him seem to have a bad memory, and in the lives of his protagonists, invented events often play a much more important role than the actual ones. He is the master of blending the mundane with the magical. Like magical realists he often uses fantastic elements in such a way that readers and his characters both experience them as ordinary and everyday.

After *Wolf Whistle* Nordan took a good look at the violent grotesque in the South. In *The Sharpshooter Blues* (1995) he revives several characters from his previous books and describes the tragedy that is the inevitable result of any encounter between innocence and cruelty or perversity. At the same time Nordan returns in this novel to another lifelong theme of his, lies that can become the truth. In this novel citizens of Arrow Catcher believe any invented story, no matter how tall, while real deeds are shrugged off as mere fantasies.

In *Lightning Song* (1997) Nordan changed the setting and subordinated his unrestrained imagination to the compactness of the story line. Although it is also a Bildungsroman, the focus is primarily on family stresses and traumas, and more than ever Nordan emphasizes the sad fact that a single event, be it the death of a relative or a dream come true, can irreparably ruin a person's life. This darker vein comes to the forefront again in his fictional autobiography *Boy with Loaded Gun* (2000), where for the first time he openly faces the most traumatic event of his life, the death of one of his sons by suicide.

If we were to compare Nordan with another contemporary southern writer, Fred Chappell would immediately come to mind, as he can equally turn swiftly from the serious to the comic. The influence of Faulkner on Nordan is even more obvious, but it is not the Faulkner of *The Sound and the Fury* but of *The Reivers*. Nordan's fiction also owes much to popular culture, especially comic books, jazz and blues music, and TV shows of the 1950s.

Lightning Song

Southern literature abounds with growing-up stories, both real and fictional, but not many southern writers wrote a work of fiction in which all of the major characters, children and adults alike, live through an extremely traumatizing event. Yet when Lewis Nordan presents such a story, reading it is a joyful experience and not traumatizing at all. This is definitely true of *Lightning Song*, his most compact novel so far. It is the story of a boy's early initiation into manhood. The third-person narrator uses the main protagonist, Leroy Dearman, as a focalizer, giving us his thoughts of the time when the described events happened as well as his later memories of them. These recollections are, to a certain extent, adjusted as a result of the imperfections of both the focalizer's and the narrator's memories, but they also owe much to the narratives of others, who witnessed some of the events or, more likely, only heard of them. The stories, in spite of their incompleteness and often speculative character, became a part of the local storytelling tradition. The novel takes place in the summer of 1978 in a red-clay hill area in Mississippi on a llama farm, near a fictitious town with the symbolical name of Fateville.

Twelve-year-old Leroy lives an ordinary farm life with his parents, Swami Don and Elsie, and his two younger sisters, eight-year-old Laurie and three-year-old Molly. Their daily routines are shattered when Uncle Harris, Swami Don's brother, comes one day to pay a short visit, which turns out to be close to permanent. Harris brings with him his urban habits, but also old grudges. Many years ago Harris stole Swami Don's beloved girlfriend and married her, but they separated and she is now asking for a divorce. Another intrusion of the big and dangerous external world into the local community is the arrival of the New People. They are a couple who bought an old dilapidated cottage in the neighborhood and have come to live there in order to forget the loss of their fourteen-year-old son, the victim of an unmotivated murder.

Besides being the history of a young boy's maturation, the story is also a rich catalogue of traumas and their necessary consequences. All of the boy's mind-shattering encounters concern death and sex, often in close relationship. While the boy often feels in his confused mind "all alone in the world," which is one of Nordan's favorite phrases (Bjerre 2007, 746), the description of his joys and sorrows spontaneously investigates the possibility of trauma not as a plague but as a basis upon which similarly affected people can come to understand each other. Leroy's acquaintance with death, as well as with sex, comes in several steps, and in both cases the direction is from the mediated to the immediate, experienced personally.

The boy's first encounter with death is through Old Pappy, the immobile father of Swami Don, who spent over a year confined to a bed in an attic room on his son's farm. When Swami Don was a child, Old Pappy, due to his negligence and malice, marked him for life when he irreparably injured his arm with a gunshot and later cynically laughed at the memory of how the hand that was struck slapped the boy's face in a reflex. Old Pappy's psychotic behavior culminated in his old age in self-destruction. In "the halfway house" (*Lightning Song*, 17), as the institution where old people are brought to die is euphemistically called, he drank a poison that left him in a coma. Leroy, quenching his curiosity through his regular snooping, is in the attic just at the moment when the comatose old man stops breathing. The boy's reactions are, chronologically:

confusion, a feeling of responsibility, resignation, and, finally, action. After initial hesitation about what to do with Old Pappy, the boy's interest shifts to his own guilt and he asks himself whether he might have caused the old man's death. Then there is a moment of helplessness accompanied by a sudden outburst of love for the man: "He thought he might cry, or he might just lie down in the bed with the old man for a minute, pull up the covers and stay there. He did lie down. He stretched out. He turned on his side then and cuddled up to the old man, as he had cuddled up to his parents in their bed when he was a little boy" (19). After the brief moments of stasis, Leroy tries resuscitation and his attempts at artificial respiration to revive Old Pappy are successful—the old man resumes breathing and Leroy leaves the attic to join the rest of the family at the dinner table. Leroy is well aware that his victory over death is short lived and the man probably died right after he left, but he manages to persuade himself that what he did was "the best he could do" (21). A few minutes later his mother announces the death of the old man, and Leroy says apologetically, "I didn't kill Old Pappy" (23).

In his groundbreaking book *The Denial of Death*, Ernest Becker states that the "gradual realization of the inevitability of death can take up until the ninth or tenth year" (13), and he explains the conflict between those who claim that the "fear of death is not a natural thing for man" (13) but is acquired and those according to whom the fear of death is inborn, "present in everyone" (15). Leroy's approach to death and dying corresponds with the former opinion—he does not feel fear of death until others, not necessarily possessing the fear themselves, introduce him to the notion.

When Old Pappy is still alive, Leroy faces his state of prolonged dying, with a catheter implanted and bowel movements artificially controlled, as an ordinary fact, without any emotional agitation. Correspondingly, after Old Pappy's death he can feel totally at ease during Uncle Harris's favorite pastime, the reciting of newspaper obituaries in front of any family member who is willing to listen. While Leroy and his sisters enthusiastically consent to be exposed to "the tales of the dead" (72), adults prefer to leave in haste, but their early departures do not plant fear in the children, as the reasons for it seem to be primarily plain disgust and boredom.

The next step to Leroy's initiation into the realm of death is active participation in other people's mourning. The scene, one of the most powerful in this novel, takes place in the muddy front yard of the New People's cottage. Leroy, who is just passing by, is invited by the New Man to join the couple in a ride in backward circles in their massive but rusted car. This ride serves them as "grief therapy" (101), the aim of which is to annul the violent death of the couple's son and to transport the surviving parents into a pre-grief state, to rewind their lives (107). Although Leroy is warned beforehand, when the New Guy insists that the front seat, where he sits unbelted, should be called "the suicide seat" rather than "the shotgun seat," he feels that "he had found a safe place, with people like himself" (102) and does not experience even a little bit of fear when the car, sounding "like a hurricane" (105), starts to destroy everything in sight, covering the interior as well as the passengers in mud.

The New People do not pass the fear of death on to Leroy, but they pass on remorse. At first they still regret that, instead of caring for their son's whereabouts, they watched a pornographic movie, while Leroy finds himself reviving his feeling of guilt for Old Pappy's death. But then it becomes obvious that the drastic "grief therapy" works; the guilt evaporates and soon Leroy imagines that he can see the old man "standing on the porch smiling at him" (104) and even considers waving to him, although he immediately decides against it, as the friendly gesture could scare the specter off. Later, when Leroy looks at his depressed mother, he remembers the positive effect of the therapy and wonders "if his mama didn't need a good fast backwards drive through the mud in an oversized car to calm her down some" (114).

The breakthrough comes during target practice that Swami Don planned for his children. Early on that day they discover a dead baby llama, obviously slain by a pack of wild dogs. What makes Leroy uneasy is not the death of the animal but the cold-blooded behavior of his sister in facing death. While he ponders "whether the dead llama could be revived" (138), Laurie gives the cadaver "a solid kick in the side" (136). Leroy feels wonder and admiration for his sister, but for the first time he also becomes a little scared of death (138). The anxiety deepens several minutes later, when the eight-year-old Laurie fires at one of the wild dogs and kills it. Leroy and his father helplessly listen to the echo of Laurie's shot and they "seemed to diminish in size, as if into the distance. They became a distant rumble, a memory, a prayer" (146). During that trip Leroy also develops another fear different from the one of death: the fear of women, which escalates as he is gradually transformed into a sexual being.

The first sign of Leroy's sexual maturation is his interest in Uncle Harris's *Playboy* and *Penthouse* magazines. When, in the very first chapter of the novel, he sneaks into his attic room, the periodicals, although not buried deep like a real treasure, become hard-won sacred objects, "their colors shown like a cache of gold in a fairy tale" (6). The scene wonderfully sets the novel's comic mood, which the author constantly challenges, but never completely overthrows, by the gradual additions of uneven doses of tragic ingredients. The constant intrusion of the tragic into the prevalently comic plot of *Lightning Song* invites an examination of the author's clever use of the grotesque and the absurd (Arbeit 2007, 635–60).

The description of Leroy's first acquaintance with nude pictures reads as hilarious comedy. The innocent boy views the cover of one of the magazines on which there is a girl wearing a cowboy hat and a ten-sizes-too-small vest with no buttons and pities the poor woman for having been photographed in her little sister's outfit or, if the dress is really hers, for being cheated by the shop assistant. A few moments later he is even more confused by another picture of the same young woman in which she is wearing only the cowboy hat and cowboy boots and is aiming two silvery six-shooters at the reader. On one hand she could be making "a citizen's arrest of the person with the camera," on the other hand, clothed like that, she obviously "suffered from mental illness, was retarded possibly, deranged, completely out of touch with reality" (10).

Leroy approaches the magazines like the forbidden fruit from the tree of knowledge; he alternately wants and does not want to see them, and he perceives his secret visit to Uncle Harris's room as morally dubious. He does not understand why a young woman should display her scarcely clad or even totally naked body. He blames some practical jokers or malicious pranksters for taking snapshots of her while dressing, and like a proper Cavalier he wants to save her "each day from some new danger, fire, wild beasts, evil men" (13). But at the same time Leroy cannot help being sexually aroused so that there is "no oxygen getting to his brain" (9), and later he masturbates over a composite mind image of a beautiful whore and an ugly saint. Autoeroticism is here, in agreement with Sigmund Freud's opinion, seen as a stage in a child's sexual development, "the training ground for heterosexuality" (Laqueur 2004, 392).

Thomas Ærvold Bjerre, elucidating the roles of sex and death in the initiation of young male protagonists in Nordan's fiction, points out that "Leroy comes to realize that the naked women in Harris's magazines and his mother are somehow connected, that his mother is a sexual being" (Bjerre 2007, 743). On the night of the day when Leroy searched for his uncle's treasures, his mother comes into his room to say good night, and he can "feel the warmth of her rear end against his leg. An electrical spark seemed to flash between their two bodies" (14). This scene opens the Oedipal theme Bjerre recognized in Nordan's other books as well (Bjerre 2007, 737–38, 743–45), the theme gaining prominence every time Elsie and Uncle Harris kiss. Upon Uncle Harris's arrival, Leroy is so taken by surprise by his mother's spontaneous response to his uncle's kisses that he wants "to fall in love with somebody like his mother" (49). Later, when he stumbles across Elsie and Uncle Harris exchanging a long kiss in the kitchen, he realizes the feminine beauty of his mother, and after that, when he imagines she had slept with his uncle, he thinks of her "in a western vest" like the one the *Playboy* girl wore.

After this first stage of his sexual awakening, Leroy perceives all women as attractive. Even the Evil Queen, the best friend of his mother, whom he always considered a nuisance, "reminded him of the woman in the magazine, though they looked nothing alike" (12). But at the same time he views women as dangerous and therefore scary beings that the men in the Dearman family are too weak to match. The feminization of the Dearman males starts with Swami Don, practically one-armed after receiving a load of number-six shots from Old Pappy. Swami Don's nickname—his real name is Donald—sounds odd in the southern context. He once said that "he was named for a man down in the Delta who ran a salvage business" (51), but in fact nobody really "seemed to remember why he was called that" (20), which is extremely strange in a place where people know everything about each other. There are other things about Swami Don that are unusual for a Mississippi farmer: he met his wife at a college where he studied literature, he never drinks alcohol, and the llamas he breeds are exotic animals that are more at home in Latin America than in Mississippi (Broncano 2007, 667). He also ignores his wife's crush on Uncle Harris, a very unusual reaction in the South with its well-established code of honor that would call for a violent retaliation on both the seducer and the seduced.

Swami Don's brother, Uncle Harris, looks like a worldly globe-trotter, but this is just a mask, and at the core he is another example of a feminized southerner. He might drive an open-top sports car with a wooden steering wheel, but in the sportster's extravagant horn melody we can hear "a few notes of 'Dixie'" (44). He might have seduced and married Swami Don's former girlfriend, but now she has kicked him out and given his "clothes to the Salvation Army and changed all the locks on the door" (58). He might seem to Leroy like a character from a Hollywood film, a Broadway drama, or a cartoon, but he is an ordinary lazy guy not willing to pay the rent. He might have carried his outfit in a single carpetbag, the symbol of strangers who directly after the Civil War came to the defeated South to become rich and influential, but he was born in the Mississippi Delta and is deeply rooted in its storytelling tradition. He might look like an immoral destroyer of Swami Don's family, but when Leroy's mother comes, drunk and naked, to him in his attic room, he not only refuses to have sex with her but also promptly turns the event into a funny story he tells everybody, including her husband.

Nordan emphasizes the similarity between the two brothers when he lets them perform with hand puppets an improvised play of a sea captain and a red-haired woman that impersonate Harris's foster parents, with whom Swami Don had also lived for one year. In this funny reenactment of their sorry adolescence, Swami Don surprisingly matches his brother in exhilaration, joy, and wit (77). The play as a reenactment is an established method for the cure of psychological stress and trauma. For the proper terminology concerning trauma I turn to Lenore Terr's *Too Scared to Cry*, a comprehensive study of childhood traumas, their consequences, and their influence on adults. The difference between stress and trauma lies not only in the intensity but in the direction from whence they come; while stress comes from inside, psychic trauma "occurs when a sudden unexpected, overwhelmingly intense emotional blow or a series of blows assaults the person *from outside*" (Terr 1990, 8; emphasis added). Besides its external nature, another sign of trauma is the victim's feeling of total helplessness.

The trauma that connects Swami Don and Uncle Harris starts with the unanticipated shot that made Swami Don's right arm "just a withered limp little wet rag" (20). Although Harris suffers no physical injury, he shares with his brother a psychological one: when their father is declared unfit to take care of his sons, they both end up in the care of a foster family. But while Harris can repudiate his psychological problems by means of his storytelling skills, Swami Don's lifelong reactions to his trauma are passive; he is ashamed to display his vulnerability, which surfaces whenever anybody wants to shake his hand.

According to Terr a trauma can be contagious; even those exposed to it indirectly, often through previous generations, can develop a few symptoms that "may indicate changes in . . . developing psychologies." On the other hand it is not necessary to overestimate such secondhand traumas for these "traumatic exposures occur as part of almost any developing child's experience" (Terr 1990, 318).

From the very beginning of his life Leroy is exposed to his father's trauma, which makes him more sensitive but also more imaginative and creative. The post-traumatic game that expands his "creative experience" (Terr 1990, 246) is his never-ending quest for family secrets. After days of creeping about the house, searching his mother's purse and his daddy's pockets, not "looking for anything especially . . . just looking," and finding only a few condoms, he disappointedly has to conclude that "his mama and daddy didn't seem to have any secrets" (*Lightning Song*, 78). Traumatized children often do not recognize the real source of their traumas, especially the secondhand ones, but Leroy gradually does, which is confirmed at the end of the novel when he listens to his parents' lovemaking and, embarrassed, tries "not to think of the ways a one-armed man makes love" (270).

Leroy is not the only child in the family who is traumatized through exposure to other people's traumas, even though his two sisters developed different symptoms: Laurie, too wise and intelligent for her age, is getting increasingly meaner and bossier, and Molly, as is common with traumatized three year olds, is constantly wetting her pants (Terr 1990, 270).

Unlike their parents' traumas, the traumas of other people prove not to be infectious for the children but serve more as an education for them. When Leroy and Laurie sneak into the yard of the New People, they witness a weird performance. In his shabby kitchen the New Guy is sitting on a table, wailing, rolling on the floor, and bouncing off appliances in the room "like a pinball in a dream" (37). While for Leroy it is just an unsettling comedy, Laurie understands what the man is doing, possibly informed by the mental state of Old Pappy, which had led to the suicide attempt that left him paralyzed: "He's collecting his thoughts. He's thinking of the bleak future, he's wondering if life's worth living, whether its dim hopes aren't really self-deluding dreams and not worth all the pain of going on, he's coming to the bitter realization that we're all alone in the world" (38).

For the New People the ride in reverse is a mixture of a post-traumatic play and a post-traumatic reenactment, the boundary between which is extremely thin (Terr 1990, 265). Acting and pretending is connected here with an attempt at a flight into invisibility or a return to the pre-traumatic past. As a compensatory fantasy each of the New People creates an alter ego, "a fake person" (Terr 1990, 202). During their "grief therapy" the New Man becomes an Indian on the warpath, wearing a bonnet with chicken feathers, and the New Lady an angel, equipped with a pair of large wings, outfits they choose from a variety of costumes they own (*Lightning Song*, 232). In Leroy's unreliable memory, which Nordan describes as too "dreamlike," with an inclination to exaggerated details and full of contradictions (44), Uncle Harris wears costumes, too. He arrives alternately as a tanned dandy in a flowered shirt and with mousse in his hair; an early-twentieth-century motorist in a long driving coat, a jaunty cap, and goggles; a Superman who vaults from his car seat as if ejected by a supernatural force; or a rich man with a white straw Panama hat and a red handkerchief sticking out from his suit-jacket pocket (43–46, 54).

Traumatized men generally look for strong women as partners or role models. The reason why Leroy prefers his mother to his father has less to do with his Oedipal desires than with her imagination. When the boy scans through nude magazines in his uncle's attic room, he is inventing stories of the models and expects interactivity. He wants to know the seminude woman in the picture better, to solve the enigma of why "this perfectly nice lady" in such an embarrassing pose is smiling, instead of being angry, and he is genuinely bothered by the possibility that she suffers from a mental disease, because nobody "could wear this getup and blend in with any group of normal people" (8–9). He is learning from his mother to see romance even in the most mundane, hence his urge to listen over and over to Elsie's description of a date with his father-to-be, in the course of which, after watching running llamas, she fell in love with him, overwhelmed by the beauty of the scenery: "Their hooves were flying. . . . They were running for the fun of it" (15). To run "for the fun of it" can also serve as a piece of good advice for traumatized people who, according to Terr, often cannot see their future and "renounce perspective, context, or a broader view" (337).

Elsie, at least until her sexual advances are rejected by Uncle Harris, seems to be the only member of the Dearman family free of any real trauma and keeping her level of stress at an acceptable level. She has a regular social contact in her friend, the Evil Queen, who comes to show her baby, and she even takes a steady interest in world events, which traumatized people regularly lose (Terr 1990, 337). The event that captures both her mind and heart for almost two months is the kidnapping of sixty-one-year-old Aldo Moro, the president of the Italian Christian Democrats, by Red Brigades terrorists in Rome on March 16, 1978, an event closely followed by journalists all over the world. Elsie does not care much for the political aspect of the act, the goal of which is the release of thirteen Red Brigades members, at that time on trial; she is more interested in the romantic background story. But Elsie goes even further, betraying that even she is not free of trauma, living with a man with a funny arm. She not only cuts out articles on Moro from periodicals and glues them into a scrapbook but also whispers the European politician's name, imagining that she is his wife, Noretta: "She wrote his name a hundred times on a sheet of lined paper. She wrote her own name, then, as if she shared his name, Elsie Moro—Elsie didn't quite fit, didn't sound quite right, unless you whispered it in Elsie's own silent fantastic version of the Italian language, an accent of sorts, with a faint echo of *mamma mia* somewhere in the background" (115).

She imagines Aldo "in horrible captivity" (115), and the world of imagination even prevails over the everyday one when she greets her husband with touching lines from Aldo Moro's farewell letter to his wife. Elsie is able to make the foreign her own, which is another recognized antitraumatic strategy, and she passes this skill on to her son. It is from his mother that Leroy learns to replace a real trauma with a fake one, created by his imagination as a harmless substitute.

But his mother, endowed with the precious gift of imagination, is not the only role model for Leroy. He also adores his younger sister Laurie, who suppresses her secondhand traumatic symptoms by means of cynicism. Even though she is four years younger than Leroy, she confirms the truth of the generally accepted opinion of psychologists that "with respect to vision, hearing, speech, writing, manual and physical control—all the senses and physical capacities through which people *learn*—boys are disadvantaged" (Sexton 1970, 10).

It looks as if the thoughts of physical deformity, death, violence, and cruelty were not bothering Laurie at all. She is the only one who behaves as if her father's crumpled arm was "a normal, real extension of his father's life" (123), and she is willing to walk with him hand in hand. When she embarrasses both her father and Leroy by hurling a dead baby llama into a ravine and shooting one of the wild dogs that killed it, her brother admires her as a true little Amazon: "She looked beautiful and strange holding this gleaming, rich-wooded, sweet-smelling rifle. She looked dangerous, and Leroy loved this about her" (145). Laurie makes a successful attempt at domesticating her fears and traumas, knowing that if she can make the weird, the abnormal, and the scary look ordinary, their power over her will vanish.

This strategy works fine with secondhand traumas, but turns out to be ineffective when a traumatizing event hits her directly. It happens when Laurie stands up to her father to win the right to taste alcohol, provoking him into a fit of anger and brutality, which is, paradoxically, his first real action in the story. An unexpectedly cruel beating that Laurie gets from Swami Don becomes a firsthand trauma for her and stops her progress toward maturity immediately. Elsie offers her a drink of wine as compensation, and Laurie behaves as the child that she is, when after the first gulp she accepts the offer of more, even though she does not like the taste. The personality shift, which is a standard post-traumatic reaction, also turns Laurie's interest to activities more proper for a girl of eight, such as baton twirling. Now it is not a rifle but a baton that is for her "some sacred thing, Excalibur or the Holy Grail, a relic from the True

Cross" (169). Although her cheekiness has not vanished completely, Laurie becomes friendlier to Leroy and even allows him to touch her baton. Leroy does not relate the change in her behavior to Swami Don's cruel punishment of her but to the magical instrument: "Leroy was unaccustomed to seeing his sister so vulnerable, so nakedly in love and purely affected and unable to hide the fullness of her feeling" (169). At that time he cannot know that Laurie will become even more sensitive as a result of her secondhand exposure to the two powerful traumas waiting in store for *him:* his unexpected early sexual experience and his almost fatal electrocution by a lightning bolt.

Among the Native Americans of the Southwest, "the old men take the boy away at the age of twelve and bring him *down* into the all-male area of the kiva [a subterranean ceremonial chamber]. He stays *down* there for six weeks" (Bly 1992, 14–15). Conversely Leroy at the same age is sent to an all-girl summer holiday camp, where girls "aged three through ten" are supposed to learn baton twirling (166. His ultimate sexual initiation comes from a high school student, the beautiful instructor Ruby Rae, a distant echo of William Faulkner's Eula Varner, characterized as having "just too much of what she was for any just one female package to contain and hold" (5).

Ruby Rae is described alternately as an archetype of a sexual goddess, "otherworldly... the most beautiful vision ever to have been visited upon human eyes" (174); a dirigible, "Graf von Zeppelin" or "Hindenburg" (212), able to transport a man to another world; and a natural force who waves her arms to make children quiet "like a tree swaying in the wind" (197) and whose huge breasts seem to have "their own weather" (223).

Leroy, the only boy among female children, suffers through his first lesson of twirling without a baton, and the absence of the phallic instrument deprives him of his masculinity. It is Ruby Rae who explicitly confirms the obvious symbolism of baton as penis in her introductory speech about the history of twirling. Without a baton Leroy is "impotent, spiritually bereft, helpless" (199); still, he does the exercise using an imaginary prop. The "lost sanity induced by a rush of pure testosterone to the brain" (206) brings him, as on the afternoon with Uncle Harris's magazines, to masturbation, and Ruby Rae awards his activities by telling his father that he "had showed exceptional promise as a twirler" and praising him for "his willingness to take risks." To prove "that with an actual baton in his hand Leroy could have made even greater strides," she offers to lend him one of her own batons—an obvious lascivious hint, which Leroy seems to understand (212).

The boy starts dreaming of sex with Ruby Rae the very moment he lays eyes on her, and at the same time he seems to see a catastrophe coming. But as the story is narrated from the distance of time and from Leroy's perspective, we cannot be sure whether the warning signs Leroy detects were not added after the fact—after severe traumas, kids "will retroactively put things that followed a traumatic event into places that precede it," the phenomenon that Terr calls "time-skew." To hide their vulnerability and defenselessness, traumatized people often create tales with fake omens in which "the uncontrollable might have been controlled" (Terr 1990, 158–60), preferring guilt to shame, just as Leroy did when Old Pappy died. Realization of this may shed a new light on what looks at first sight to be the struggle between Leroy's mind and his body.

The narrator tells readers that at the age of twelve Leroy "understood that love is a hopeless dream, that it is seldom what it seems but only evil done in a holy name" and was aware that the possibility of reciprocated physical desire at that age "would signal pathology, not hope" (194–95). Leroy is nevertheless attracted to Ruby Rae because she is not only a pretty woman but also a fellow sufferer whose post-traumatic play he joins. No matter what exactly did happen to Ruby Rae in childhood, she is severely traumatized and has the multiple symptoms of an abused child. One of her "mental disturbances" is compulsive fabulation, a symptom that Leroy, richly endowed with imagination, can appreciate. It is no problem for Ruby Rae to invent a history of baton twirling that makes every ethnic group happy and, just in case, even gets extraterrestrials involved. For the likes of her, Terr coined the term "hail fellows well met"; they are young people who make friends easily, are attractive and seductive, but have "a fundamental problem with human relationships," show "little discrimination between people," and lack empathy, one important feeling that Leroy has in abundance (Terr 1990, 85–86). Another of Ruby Rae's symptoms is "her excessive emphasis upon control and all of beauty's perfections," which in turn, as even Leroy notices, "constituted darkness visible beneath purple leotards" (212). As the image of her hands, with the "well-manicured nails of a young athlete" but "bony fingers, the fingers of a hag-witch" suggests, the personality of Ruby Rae is split into two parts, one visible and one invisible, but both real. She is "the terrified little girl in the body of a woman" with one self "that aches alone" and another self "that every man admires and becomes changed by" (216).

When Ruby Rae says about Leroy that he is an "extra-special little grown-up" who will "make his choice" at her home, it is with a mixture of sinister cynicism and straightforward honesty. Her sex with the underaged Leroy is no rape. The directions Leroy can give her (218) are not just about traffic; he is not only "her slave" but also "her master" (198). After the sexual act, both participants behave normally and part like friends, only with a "Don't tell, okay?" on her part and a dry giggle, "almost laughter, almost wail" on his (225). This, again, corresponds to what Terr found about the behavior of children during traumatic events: "Nobody was hysterical. Nobody shook. Nobody was crazy. Nobody was crying" (Terr 1990, 19). As an adult Leroy "does not in his memory romanticize that day, or minimize its consequences, does not pretend to have escaped suffering gravely the effects of what happened" (221). The trauma will stay with him the rest of his life and will influence all spheres of his life, both private and social; it will bring on specific motions, behavior, and ways of thinking, and at least a portion of it will be passed on to people who get too close.

But there are also emotions connected with a psychological trauma that might appear very soon after the event, among them, besides denial and numbing, terror and rage. Leroy suffers from both and unintentionally copies the behavior of the traumatized New People. His destructive rage is reminiscent of the New People's "grief therapy" in that he is "tearing the curtains down from the window," turning over a table, and throwing a kitchen knife across the room Laurie has just entered. When he visits the New People again, he wears costumes they keep for him, including "full drag, with lipstick and makeup and a wig" (233). Before the seduction by Ruby Rae, when he touches a baton for the first time in his life, he wants "to renounce himself, his whole identity, and to be a girl," and he does not "mind the humiliation . . . of chasing a girl's dream" (171–72), which is to become a champion twirler. But after his sexual initiation he almost instantly comes to the understanding that the baton represents the masculine, not the feminine, being "the living bone" of men, too precious to be left to women to play with.

Leroy's trauma becomes contagious, especially to the female members of the family; it makes Elsie stronger and less tolerant toward her husband's weaknesses and makes Laurie, by contrast, more submissive. Elsie gets drunk and, after having tried unsuccessfully to seduce Uncle Harris, runs naked in a storm toward the house of the New People, from where Leroy can see her. Laurie, having witnessed the aggressiveness of her brother, even develops a fear of death through him; she thinks that her knife-throwing brother wants to kill her. Later, when Leroy is almost killed by lightning, she fears for his life, "sticking close" to him. Now it is she who at the New People's cottage wears the angel's wings, turning into a "bird girl" (255–56), and she also reevaluates her courageous shot at the wild dog as a transgression that must be confessed to her mother.

Leroy himself is brought by his wet dream come true even further, to the close proximity of death. At first he only wrestles with a huge armadillo and hopes that the animal will pull him underground and he will be buried alive, but then, during a storm, he runs with a rusty baton in his hand—the rust symbolizing the unhealthiness of his masculinity—into the rain and is struck by lightning.

The lightning that struck Leroy is the climax and, at the same time, the dénouement of all the conflicts within the Dearman family, overt as well as covert. As the title of the novel suggests, it is also, together with the accompanying thunder, its central metaphor, a kind of natural litmus paper. When characters hear thunder or a sound similar to it without seeing lightning, it is a possibility of a change in their lives, which if it happens does not necessarily have to be for the better. Years ago Elsie listened to the beautiful running llamas that sounded "like thunder in the hills" (15) and fell for Swami Don, but their marriage did not turn to be as happy as she expected. When Swami Don takes his girlfriend, a Native American factory worker from Oklahoma, to a motel, there is a thunder in the hills, "probably above his own house" (181), but no lightning, and he decides against cheating on his wife, his extramarital relationship never outgrowing a nonsexual romantic friendship.

Lightning provides a powerful warning sign. Before Leroy discovers his mother's secret kisses with Uncle Harris, he can see "a bright ball of fire" drifting "down the sky along a curious course, down, down, slowly, slowly, toward the earth" (80). Elsie is marked, after her active response to Harris's wooing, by static electricity, her hair floating "behind her like Superman's cape" (84). The bolts do not hit the innocent; that is why a ball of fire that falls through the chimney onto the hearth and is moving through the rooms does not hurt Leroy, even though it bounces right across his legs (86). When Laurie fires her father's rifle for the very first time in the presence of Swami Don and Leroy, an echo "as crisp as a thunderclap smacked the three of them square in the face" (145–46), but only later, when she actually kills one of the wild dogs, a courageous but also frightening act, can they see "the halo of lightning as it strikes a pine tree" (147). When Ruby Rae, the deranged majorette, undresses in front of Leroy, her huge breasts make a sound "like thunder." The boy accepts the challenge, but his imaginings of "lightning crashing around them and striking his house" (223) show that he understands the danger. After the traumatizing sex with Ruby Rae, Leroy visits the New People, and from their cottage he listens to thunder that "cracked like the heavy couplings of metal boxcars in a train yard" (236) and watches fireballs. This is the night the behavior of Leroy's mother threatens to completely disjoin the whole family, which is announced through the lightning that repeatedly strikes the house and even unseals all the dill pickles (240). After his mother's Lady Godiva–like naked run in the rain, Leroy starts into the storm, "filled with rage and confusion" from feeling shame for her as well as for himself. When the lightning strikes the baton he is carrying, Leroy lights up "like a bulb," is surrounded by "a blue halo," and seems to walk "on a column of flame" (246–47).

The event is presented both as a beautiful and magical performance and a moment of understanding—literally, light dawned on Leroy. It can also be seen as redemption: Leroy's survival borders on a miracle, and although his sexual trauma is not erased completely, as is obvious from his memories, it helps glue the family back together. The Dearmans decide not to ignore their traumas but to look them straight in the face—they tell the truth to each other even when it is painful and turn from mere talking into communication. The storm season is over and even the domestic storm has its end; the children's parents get appeased, Swami Don converts from the "slow and clumsy beast" (250) into the agile man able to shoot the rest of the dog pack to protect his livestock, and even little Molly stops wetting her pants. It looks as if even in the worst trauma something positive can sometimes be detected. As Swami Don says, "Two thousand people in the United States last year were struck by lightning" and Leroy "was lucky enough to be one of them"; he was chosen "by the universe, he is special, he hit the meteorological lottery!" Nordan does not extend his metaphor to the history or social climate of the South, which makes his growing-up novel even more universal. If lightning "is the source of life on our planet" (267–68), as Swami Don claims, knowledge and recognition of our traumas make us unique, albeit suffering, individuals.

Works Cited and Consulted

Arbeit, Marcel. "Desperate and Happy in the Disharmonious World: Lewis Nordan and the Absurd." *Mississippi Quarterly* 60, no. 4 (2007): 635–60.
Arbeit, Marcel, and Thomas Ærvold Bjerre, eds. "Special Issue: Lewis Nordan." *Mississippi Quarterly* 60, no. 4 (2007): 621–758.
Becker, Ernest. *The Denial of Death*. 1973. Reprint, New York: Free Press, 1997.
Bjerre, Thomas Ærvold. "Shocked into Maturity: Sex and Death as Initiation in the Fiction of Lewis Nordan." *Mississippi Quarterly* 60, no. 4 (2007): 735–47.
Bly, Robert. *Iron John: A Book about Men*. 1990. Reprint, New York: Vintage, 1992.
Broncano, Manuel. "Writing the Caribbean with a Mississippian Accent." *Mississippi Quarterly* 60, no. 4 (2007): 661–76.
Dupuy, Edward J., ed. "Special Feature: Lewis Nordan." *Southern Quarterly* 41, no. 3 (2003): 5–108.
Faulkner, William. *The Town*. *Novels, 1957–1962*. Ed. Joseph Blotner and Noel Polk. New York: Library of America, 1999. 1–326.
Laqueur, Thomas W. *Solitary Sex: A Cultural History of Masturbation*. New York: Zone Books, 2004.
Nordan, Lewis. *Boy with Loaded Gun*. Chapel Hill, N.C.: Algonquin, 2000.
———. *Lightning Song*. Chapel Hill, N.C.: Algonquin, 1997.
———. "The Making of a Book." *Oxford American*, March–April 1995, 75–81.
———. *The Sharpshooter Blues*. Chapel Hill, N.C.: Algonquin, 1995.
———. *Wolf Whistle*. Chapel Hill, N.C.: Algonquin, 1993.
———. *Music of the Swamp*. Chapel Hill, N.C.: Algonquin, 1991.
———. *All-Girl Football Team*. Baton Rouge: Louisiana University Press, 1986.
Sexton, Patricia Cayo. *The Feminized Male: Classrooms, White Collars and the Decline of Manliness*. 1969. Reprint, New York: Vintage, 1970.
Terr, Lenore. *Too Scared to Cry: Psychic Trauma in Childhood*. New York: Basic Books, 1990.

PART IV *A Sense of Malaise*

Ron Rash ~ *One Foot in Eden*

THOMAS ÆRVOLD BJERRE

A Biographical Sketch

    South Carolina poet, short-story writer, and novelist Ron Rash (born 1953) is one of the new southern writers whose work is firmly situated in the southern tradition. Rash's rural Appalachia characters represent a marginal South in the twenty-first century, and their deep attachment to the land suggests a feeling of belonging that is lost in the New South. Rash hails from the southern Appalachian Mountains, where his family settled in the mid-1700s. Born in Chester, South Carolina, and raised in Boiling Springs, North Carolina, Rash published his first book in 1994. It is a collection of linked short stories titled *The Night the New Jesus Fell to Earth* in which he established his own voice while tapping into the solid tradition of southern literature. *Eureka Mill*, his 1998 poetry collection, gives a poignant and unflinching portrait of North Carolina's cotton mill workers in the early 1900s. Two publications appeared in the year 2000: the short-story collection *Casualties* and *Among the Believers*, a book of poems.

    In 2002 Rash published his third poetry collection, *Raising the Dead*, which deals with loss and displacement as a result of the flooding of Jocassee Valley, South Carolina. That same year Rash made his debut as a novelist with *One Foot in Eden*, a novel that fleshes out the characters and themes of the poems in *Raising the Dead*. Disguised as a murder mystery and imbued with Rash's poetic language, the novel is a powerful tale of a community displaced. *One Foot in Eden* was awarded *ForeWord* magazine's Gold Medal in Literary Fiction and named Appalachian Book of the Year. In 2004 Rash published his second novel, *Saints at the River*, about a South Carolina community torn over the issue of environmentalism. The novel was named Fiction Book of the Year by both the Southern Book Critics Circle and the Southeastern Booksellers Association, and it was awarded the Weatherford Award for Best Novel of 2004. In 2005 Rash's short story "Speckled Trout" received the O. Henry Award, and that story formed the first chapter of his third novel, *The World Made Straight*, published in 2006. It is both a coming-of-age story set in the 1970s Appalachia and a meditation on the role of the past in the present in the shape of a Civil War massacre that has divided Madison County, North Carolina, ever since. In 2007 Rash published the collection *Chemistry and Other Stories*, with thirteen stories, eight previously published in *Casualties*. The new collection was a finalist for the 2008 PEN/Faulkner Award for Fiction. Rash's latest novel, *Serena* (2008), takes place in the North Carolina mountains in the 1930s and is an Appalachian retelling of Shakespeare's *Macbeth*. As a sociopolitical backdrop the novel has the ruthless lumber industry that destroyed a large part of the wilderness. *Serena* was a finalist for the 2009 PEN/Faulkner Award.

One Foot in Eden

Most of Ron Rash's characters display a deep attachment to the land that suggests a feeling of belonging that is lost in the New South. In both poetry, short fiction, and in his novels, Rash has been determined to tell *their* story. *One Foot in Eden* began as a poem about a "farmer standing in a field of dying crops," but Rash realized, as he has said, that "what I wanted to write, *what that farmer wanted me to write*, could not be contained in a poem . . . I knew that if I were to give him and his story their due I would have to write a novel. . . . All I knew was that I had to try, because for some inexplicable reason I owed it to that man in the field" (Rash, "The Story behind the Book," n.d. [2002]). Thus Rash presents himself as the voice of the forgotten farmer, whose culture has all but vanished in today's technological society.

One Foot in Eden is a powerful story with Old Testament allusions, echoes of Shakespearean tragedy, and crime novel aspirations, all written in a wonderful language that is both poetic and dead-on colloquial and that manages to make the uniquely southern landscape come alive in front of the reader's eyes. The story is set in the small Appalachian community of Seneca, South Carolina, from the 1950s to the early 1970s. Through five narrators we follow the community in the years before it is destroyed by state-controlled flooding—the actual flooding of Jocassee Valley, which is now Jocassee Lake. A murder is committed, and while we know who the murderer is, neither the sheriff nor the reader knows where the body is hidden. Rash focuses on the psychological effect of knowing that one's community will be erased from the map. The novel is both poetic and nostalgic longing for an agrarian era. But it is also a complex murder mystery. Rash expands the normally tight and fast-paced structure of the crime novel by allowing several voices to tell the story, including the sheriff, the poor struggling farmer, and his pregnant wife. Each voice tells its own story of a time and a place, but what they have in common is a sense of loss, brought on by rural communities being trampled under by encroaching technologies. Beneath the crime story a series of sociological clashes unfold: there is the class battle between farmers and townspeople in the small Appalachian communities. The split is further symbolized by the recurring family conflicts: children versus parents, sibling versus sibling, and husband versus wife. In other words *One Foot in Eden* is a novel of dissent, a dissent grounded in issues as diverse as industrialization, class, history, and family.

By focusing on conflicts between town and country, the past and the future, Rash places himself in a long tradition in southern literature. It is obvious that Rash writes out of the strong tradition of America as an agrarian paradise, pointed out in Henry Nash Smith's seminal *Virgin Land*. But he is also painfully aware of the "machine in the garden," as Leo Marx has termed the clash between technology and pastoral ideal. In his focus on the farming community, Rash evokes one of the most potent of American myths, what Donald Worster calls the principal myth of the West, "a story about a simple, rural people moving into an extraordinary land . . . and creating there a peaceful, productive life" (1992, 6). There is, perhaps, an echo of Henry Nash Smith's "Virgin Land" thesis to be found in *One Foot in Eden*: It could be argued that the elegiac tone of the novel—the doomed, lost land—shrouds the narrative in myth. In fact the central conflict in *One Foot in Eden*—the conflict between the yeoman existence and industrialized society—is also one of the central conflicts in the traditional myth of the West, as Nash Smith showed. Donald Worster asserts that rather than dismissing a myth as simple falsehood, "popular belief and historical reality are joined together in a continuous dialogue, moving back and forth in a halting, jerky interplay" (1992, 6). It is in this intersection that Rash operates and plays out his story. Even though Rash evokes the myth, he never succumbs to it. By allowing the characters to become fully human and three dimensional, the mythic aspects are undercut, and we are left with some of both. This is perhaps what the title connotes: one foot in a mythic agrarian Eden and one foot in harsh reality.

Rash also echoes the Nashville Agrarians, who lamented the booming industrialism, which they feared would eventually undo their rural society. In this way the established South saw itself as caught in a conflict of traditional values versus progress. It is this conflict that reverberates through Ron Rash's fiction, including *One Foot in Eden*. In the novel one can find a clear strain of the insistence on community and traditional society as opposed to ruthless progress, and one way to read *One Foot in Eden* is as an attack on the contemporary tradition of an ostensibly homogenous and progressive America.

The clash between the community's townspeople and farmers is embodied in Will Alexander, the High Sheriff, who narrates the first chapter, "The High Sheriff." His presence turns the first part of the novel into a murder mystery with Wild West echoes. Besides sharing his first name with Gary Cooper's legendary sheriff of *High Noon*, Will Alexander embodies several of the traditional western-hero traits. He is, however, also a typical southerner, burdened by both a personal and a historical past.

Will is living in a dead marriage, brought on by his wife's miscarriage and his own knee injury in college. He was a promising football player with dreams of teaching college, but the hospital bills killed his ambitions. To get away from it all, he joined the Marine Corps in 1941 and saw action in the Pacific. From his experiences in the war, Will brought home another burden to carry: "the glazed eyes of every Japanese soldier I'd taken the life from on Guadalcanal" (17). However, it was because of his experiences in the war that he got the job as deputy when he returned to Seneca. As the sheriff tells him, "If it comes to the have-to you can kill a man," the sheriff tells him (29). This ability places him in the company of western heroes such as Will Kane and Shane.

Will struggles morally with his profession. When he became a lawman, he moved from the family's tobacco farm in the Jocassee Valley into the town of Seneca. He thereby made the significant shift from farmer to thinker, estranging himself not only from his father and brother but also from part of himself. Will does not harbor any sentimental memories of the hard farming life; in fact his recollection paints a bleak picture of the farmer: "To farm a man did have to act like a mule—keep his eyes and thoughts on the ground straight in front of him. If he didn't he couldn't keep coming out to his fields day after day. ... Don't pretend you miss such a life as this," Will tells himself (15). Although respected in the community, Will still does not feel at home in the town where he lives. Looking at the sky to check the weather, he feels ashamed that he does not need to worry about that. He gets a "certain paycheck come rain or drought" (10). There is also the sense that a purer, more timeless world exists outside the town. Returning to town from a visit to the valley, Will glances at a newspaper and its reports of world crises: "But these events seemed somehow farther away than when I'd read about them this morning. It was as if being in Jocassee had taken me out of the here and now" (21).

As a result of his conflicting emotions, and realizing that he is "little more than a stranger" to his father and the family farm will "one day vanish completely as a dream," Will Alexander makes a moral decision: he will serve out his term as High Sheriff and then go back to farm on his family's land: "I'd farm this land until Carolina Power ran us all out and drowned these fields and creeks and the river itself. However long that was, it would give me some time to be a son and a brother again, maybe even learn how to be an uncle" (40). But Will's wife Janice does not share her husband's longing for the country. Their different class backgrounds have created conflicts that have led to a stranded marriage. Janice flinches when Will uses "hillbilly talk" (7), and she still plays "the role of the wealthy doctor's daughter" (41). She too has fallen prey to class prejudices and has been called "Mrs. White Gloves" by a town councilman, who jokes that she is probably "home teaching the sheriff the proper way to unfold a napkin" (41). Will is very much aware that his decision to move back to the farm will mean a divorce, since his wife will not move down the social ladder. But to Will, and in Ron Rash's fiction in general, place and kin mean more than prestigious titles, including that of "the doctor's daughter." The predicament echoes a central theme in American literature: the male flight to the wilderness away from civilizing women. But while Rash may play along with this theme, it is never reinforced or given credence. Any idea that "the wilderness" can offer solace is undercut in the novel by the constant awareness of the impending flooding and destruction of the rural community.

Rash succeeds in depicting Will Alexander as a three-dimensional and multifaceted character, but Will also embodies strong characteristics of the archetypal hero. Throughout the novel he must fight the elements to disclose the body Billy Holcombe has hidden. Will is also battling time: he must find the body before the valley is flooded and every trace erased. There is no doubt that Will is a competent match for the landscape surrounding him. In fact we should see him as someone who works with the land, sometimes against bad odds, to achieve his goal.

Like a modern Leatherstocking character, Will has an astute awareness of nature. We learn that he was baptized in the local river when he was ten years old. Already at that age he "hadn't been afraid" the long while he was held under water. "I had felt the power of that river and believed it nothing less than God Himself swirling around me," Will thinks (54), thereby infusing the landscape with a religious sense. In his adult life Will embodies a unique understanding of the landscape surrounding him. As murder suspect Billy Holcombe tells us, "He stood at the end of the row I'd been working, not looking at me but across the river. He looked like he was twice reading something to make sure it said what he thought it said" (146). This "reading" of the landscape links Will directly to Cooper's Leatherstocking and his countless western hero offspring, such as Hondo and Shane. Discussing Cooper's Natty Bumppo, Lee Clark Mitchell argues that the "capacity to see clearly, to hit the most distant of targets, to discover all but invisible signs of an enemy becomes at last a moral injunction, equated with the capacity to draw sharp ethical distinctions." This "ethical view of landscape" is, according to Mitchell, one of Cooper's strongest legacies to the western, in which "moral discernment is always signaled by a visual knowledge of surroundings" (29–30). This connection is also apparent in *One Foot in Eden*, and the idea is reinforced a few pages later when Will Alexander takes off his glasses to get a closer look at Billy, the murder suspect. This is how Billy experiences it: Will Alexander "just looked up and let his gray eyes fix on me like a hawk's eyes on a meadow mouse" (148). The allusion to Hawkeye, one of Natty Bumppo's many names, is probably not coincidental. Even when Will puts on his glasses, he is still compared to an animal: "They made his eyes bigger, not so much anymore like hawk's eyes as owl's eyes.... Wise eyes that don't miss a thing" (148–49). While the glasses may suggest a lack of vision, we are told that even without the glasses, Will's eyes are those of a hawk.

Will's function as a Leatherstocking character continues throughout the novel's two-decade span. The chapter titled "The Son," narrated by Isaac, the illegitimate child of Amy and Holland, takes place almost twenty years after the killing of Holland. Carolina Power has evicted people from the valley, and the flooding is about to commence. At the last minute Isaac decides to tell the truth and to reclaim his father's body with the help of his "father" Billy Holcombe. Will Alexander has not retired, as he promised himself—he is still High Sheriff. While this signals a minor weakness in Will, it also serves to strengthen his role as hero. Changes come and go in the community, but Will Alexander is the one constant.

When Will confronts the two men about their business, Billy admits that he killed Holland: "You can handcuff me if you want.... But I ain't going to run. I never figured to do that, even in the worst of it." Instead of pursuing justice to the very end, Alexander offers to ignore the twenty-year-old crime: "It's too late, Billy," he says in a gentle voice. He continues, "Let's get out of here, Billy. Whatever's been done has been done. We're too old to change it now. Let the water cover it up" (192–93). When Billy insists, Will agrees to help them recover the body. And once again his eyes indicate his intimate relationship with the land: He "looked at the water that covered the lower part of the field. His eyes followed it across the river bed and to the foot of Licklog. 'This isn't going to be easy. That river's deeper now'" (193–94). The small party moves out in a landscape mired in "a cold rain, the kind that soaked to your bones.... The clouds looked low enough to touch.... The rain suddenly came harder, like a big knife had slit the sky open" (195–96). After Isaac has found the few remaining bone pieces of his father, the party turns back, only to realize that the water has risen and that the river is very muddy, making it impossible to see where they step.

Once again Will Alexander takes control, his teeth chattering from the cold, and again tries to convince Isaac to leave his father's remains in order to prevent a murder trial. Isaac makes a moral decision and drops the sack of bones in the river's strong current. The party begins the river crossing, the cold water reaches their chests, and Will barks orders while holding the rope, but then everything goes wrong. Billy's foot gets caught in some timber and the current pushes him under. Amy goes under too and soon Isaac as well. He tries to save his mother, but the cold water quickly numbs him: "I felt the water cover me and for a few moments everything became dark and peaceful. Then I felt hands on me, strong hands, pulling me back to the surface, dragging me toward shore" (200). These are the strong hands of Sheriff Alexander, of course.

Waiting back at the farmhouse and unaware of what has just happened, the deputy sees "someone coming across what had been bottomland, carrying something in his arms. I couldn't put no face on him because the rain flailed down so hard it was like looking through a waterfall. That water he came plodding through was shallow, so shallow he looked to be walking on it, like he was a haint rising from the river" (206). The passage evokes images of both Christ and the iconic cowboy emerging out of the landscape at the opening of countless westerns. But this time it is the hero emerging from a landscape he has just defeated. This suggests an association with the particular link between man and landscape inherent in westerns, which is that "power" and "endurance" are the qualities inherent in nature that the hero must also possess (Tompkins 1992, 72). Even though the tone is not one of triumph—two people have, after all, lost their lives in the river—the depiction of Will Alexander as iconic hero remains obvious. And the fact that he is suffering from hypothermia and shock and still insists on going back to look for Amy and Billy only enhances the magnitude of his heroism. But let me stress that Will Alexander is only one of the narrators of the novel, and that he is in no way the main protagonist. Although Rash draws on some of the heroic imagery connected with the western hero and his relation with the land, Will Alexander never comes to dominate the plot. The novel is not structured as a story about a hero's fight against a villain. Instead the focus is on the small community around Seneca, its doomed agrarian lifestyle, and how these people deal with that situation.

Another character who embodies the clash between past and present, between the Old and the New South, and one who stands in sharp contrast to most of the other characters of the novel, is Widow Glendower, a "witch" who lives in a hollow upstream. She is both respected and feared and is the subject of many rumors and much speculation. The widow has served as makeshift doctor and midwife, and she is central to the action of the novel. After the widow's herbal and supernatural cures have failed to make Amy pregnant, she is the one who advises Amy to commit adultery. The widow also supplies the novel with an exotic and Gothic atmosphere, but just as important, she comes to represent another mountain tradition: the presence of the supernatural, which in this community is about to be exterminated in the name of technology and progress. One of the stories about the widow tells us how "once Lindsey Kilgore saw her rise out of a trout pool he'd been fishing, her body forming itself out of the water" (68). She is, in other words, a creature that is part of the landscape surrounding her. In Will's description of his childhood meeting with her, the mythic merges with the creature as well as a normal human being: "She was dressed in her black widow's weeds. That had made her white hair and her white skin more unsettling. She couldn't have been more than fifty, but to Travis and me she looked older than the mountains themselves" (44).

Ron Rash also uses the many landscape descriptions in the novel to outline the clash between the old and the new. The focus on the rural landscapes of North and South Carolina is a consistent trait in Rash's writing. He elaborated on this element in his fiction in an interview: "I think writers who write about a rural landscape are often viewed as being kind of provincial, but to me the natural world is the most universal of languages" (Bjerre 2007, 224). In many ways Rash's take on the southern landscape mirrors Ellen Douglas's landscape descriptions and the way she reasserts the landscape in order to, as Suzanne Jones puts it, "unburden it of Faulkner's mythic figuration" (2002, 134). As Jones argues, Douglas uses "specific localization" and detailed landscape description to distinguish her fictional place from the mythic landscapes already familiar to readers. By doing so, Jones notes, Douglas "resists her readers' inclinations to mentally conjure a generic southern place without registering the words that make it a very specific geographical locale" (135).

In *One Foot in Eden* the many landscape descriptions link the text to a certain place both geographically and historically. Will's descriptions of the Jocassee Valley clearly imbue the landscape with an inescapable sense of history and tradition: The word Jocassee "meant 'valley of the lost' to the Cherokee.... The road I followed had once been a trail, a trail De Soto had followed four hundred years ago when he'd searched these mountains for gold.... I took another right and passed fields where men once hid horses during what folks up here still spoke of as the Confederate War" (10–11). Apart from evoking a specific landscape, this passage demonstrates how Will's connection to the land is both strong and tied to a distinct sense of tradition.

The connection to the land and its history is so forceful that it creates one of the central conflicts in the novel, that between the Old and the New South. "Like almost everything up here," Will notes, "the road was little different than it had been in the 1860s. But change was coming, a change big enough to swallow this whole valley" (11). The coming change is also embodied in Will and the unresolved familial class conflict that leads him to move back to the farm. His decision is ultimately a wish to go back to his roots, to literally join history by becoming part of the land itself before it is too late. When he dies he hopes to be buried in the family grave "before they built the reservoir so when the water rose it would rise over me and Daddy and Momma and over Old Ian Alexander and his wife Mary and over the lost body of the princess named Jocassee and the Cherokee mounds and the trails De Soto and Bartram and Michaux had followed and the meadows and streams and forests they had described and all would forever vanish and our faces and names and deeds and misdeeds would be forgotten as if we and Jocasse had never been" (56–57). The intense merging of past and present and the insistence on place serve as a bulwark against the threatening historical amnesia that the flooding will bring. While Rash's landscapes are tied to history, they are distinctly unique, and the South of the geographical South Carolina of *One Foot in Eden* never feels like, say, the South of William Faulkner's Mississippi or the South of Flannery O'Connor's Georgia.

In line with feeling connected to the history that the landscape describes, the characters also express their emotions and experiences in terms of the natural world. This is especially true for Amy Holcombe, who narrates the second chapter, "The Wife." At first glance Amy Holcombe seems little more than a pretty face. Will Alexander describes her as "blue-eyed with yellow hair that fell to her waist, tall and slim but full-breasted" (27). But we soon realize that she is an integral part of the story, and her narration adds a crucial voice to the plot. Her chapter changes the tone of the story from murder mystery to domestic drama.

While Rash shows us the private side of Will Alexander, the most intimate sections of the novel deal with the relationship between Amy and her husband, Billy Holcombe. The two desperately want a baby but are unable because of Billy's sterility. Amy sums up the situation, explaining that after seeing her sister's children and experiencing how they filled "up the house with a happiness only children can bring," the contrast in her and Billy's house was startling. Their "house seemed quiet and empty. Billy felt it too. I knew he blamed himself. If I felt less a woman for having no baby, I knew he felt less a man for not being able to plant his seed in me" (64). Their intimate problem is enhanced by the pressure from the community; the older women say things such as "It's time you started your family," and the girls Amy grew up with "seemed to be saying to me I wasn't a woman till I had a young one of my own" (62).

Desperate to find a solution to her problem, Amy decides to visit the widow, despite her mother's warnings against the old woman: "If you and Billy ain't meant to have young ones it's the Lord's will" (65). By ignoring her mother's warnings and by going to see "the witch," Amy dismisses rational thought and belief in science and shows her faith in the irrational. But at the same time she is renouncing the Christian world, embodied by her mother and most of the community. She moves from a world guided by Christian beliefs and values to a secular and mystic world in which superstition and folk customs prevail. Once she has taken that step, it apparently also becomes easier for her to commit adultery. When the widow's herbs and spells do not bring results, the next step is to become pregnant with another man. Once Amy has made that decision, she is changed forever. Looking at herself in her mirror, she realizes that "there was something different about the face that stared back at me. Then I reckoned the differing. It wasn't the face of a girl anymore" (81). This is indeed a sinister initiation, one of many ominous yet seemingly inevitable turns in the novel.

Amy finally sleeps with Holland Winchester and becomes pregnant. At the very moment of the conception, with Holland on top and gasping, Amy feels "something deep inside of me, a kind of brightness welling up and spreading all through my body like spring water when it bubbles out of the ground. At that moment I knew certain as anything ever in my life that Holland's seed had took root inside me" (88). As the passage shows, Amy's language mirrors her close and almost supernatural connection with her natural surroundings.

Amy often expresses her emotions using a reference to the land and nature she will be forced to leave later in the novel. At the mention of sex Amy feels her "face blush up red as a moonseed berry." Later, when arguing with her husband Billy, she feels as if their "words was clouds gathering up for a storm." When she is talking to the widow, Amy experiences her words as "cold and hard as winter turnips." When she witnesses Billy shooting Holland, she sees "Holland's face white as August cotton bolls," and when she is making love to Billy, Amy thinks of their "bodies swirled together like two creeks becoming one" (72, 74, 77, 91, 96). In a relevant discussion of the writer Ellen Douglas's use of landscape in her novel *The Rock Cried Out*, Suzanne Jones argues that "the forces of nature take on an active role in the working out of the plot, reminding readers of nature's power and of the need for careful management of land and natural resources, but also that place is not just myth but also a reality" (2002, 136). She might as well have been discussing *One Foot in Eden*. Not only do the characters have an intimate relationship with the land around them, but the land plays an active part in shaping their lives, and the landscape plays a part in the plot as well. Holland Winchester's body is hidden in a tree for years, and it is the heavy rain combined with the flooding of the valley that causes the deaths of Amy and Billy at the end of the novel. Symbolically the flooding occurs simultaneously with Isaac's decision to reveal the truth about his real father, thereby disclosing twenty years of secrets and repressions. By indirectly comparing the consequences of Isaac's disclosure with the flooding, Rash enhances both the forces of nature and the power of human emotions.

Throughout the novel Rash instills his characters with a dignity that transcends any notion of good and evil. Billy Holcombe, who murders Holland Winchester and disposes of his body, never comes across as the villain Rash could easily have made him. Instead Billy is given his own voice and comes across as a full-dimensional character. As readers we understand his predicaments and the rough farming life he lives, and we sympathize with him. Will Alexander certainly sees him as an opponent, but Billy does not possess the meanness we would associate with a villain and a killer. Quite the opposite, as in many ways Billy is depicted as a "good old boy." He is a hard-working farmer who is perhaps more comfortable in the company of his horse than with his wife: "I'd been with Sam longer than I'd been with Amy. Even after me and her got married I spent more waking hours in the springs and summers with him than I had her.... I believed he'd had a reckoning of what I was saying.... That reckoning was me and him working together hard as we could to make a living from this scratch-ankle mountain land" (138). Rash's description of Billy reveals him as an honest, hard-working man who would not ordinarily kill another person.

Whereas Will knows the power of words and, more important, how to use words, the same is not the case for Billy. He considers words a danger best suppressed. His wife Amy is quite aware of this predicament. It is because of Billy's sterility that Amy sleeps with Holland Winchester. "I can't find a single living sperm," the doctor tells the couple (63). Billy is aware of their affair, but he has not commented on it, and Amy knows why. It is "as if it couldn't really be true without he made notice of it with his words, that silence could hide most anything between two people" (90). And Billy himself is aware of the reasons behind his silence: "I'd known once it was words something would come of those words" (117). To Billy words only complicate matters further, which is why he chooses silence. When he finally does use words and asks her whose child it is, Amy's answer leads to the confrontation and his killing of Holland Winchester.

Next to Will Alexander's strong and stoic masculinity, Billy embodies a frail and crippled masculinity. As a result of polio he walks with a limp, and he is unable to give his wife a baby. Billy also admits he is a coward when it comes to dealing with his wife's sleeping with Winchester. He compares himself to a farmer in the field "who sights a tornado hauling towards him and puts his head down reckoning if he don't look up and admit to its coming it might some-ways pass him by" (117). When he finally decides to face Winchester, he has grave doubts about his courage: "I didn't know if I was a brave man. . . . I didn't know if I could kill a man" (124–25). It becomes more and more obvious that Billy is not a typical villain. His imperfect masculinity does not serve to boost Will's masculinity or to reinforce Billy as villain. In fact, as the novel is narrated from five points of view, the dichotomy of good and evil, so often used in crime novels, is discarded. Instead both the sheriff and Billy are allowed to tell their stories, as is Billy's wife Amy, the deputy, and the son Amy had with Winchester. The result is complex and multifaceted characters that refuse to submit to preconceived and stereotypical notions of good and bad. One example is Amy's description of Billy, whom the other narrators see in terms of his handicap. Amy does not. After admitting that his legs were the first thing she noticed, she focuses on his upper part: "I saw the brown hair and gray eyes, the sun-browned face, high-boned and handsome. I saw the strength in his arms, the muscles that wrapped around his bones like muscadine vines. . . . You could tell those arms and shoulders was able for more heavy sweat than many another man's" (82). According to this description, Billy embodies a masculinity that also connotes physical strength and stamina.

Through several narrators we come to understand Billy's motives for killing Holland Winchester, and it becomes clear that he acts very much out of tradition and honor. Just as his profession as farmer links him to the land, so his actions link him to a long southern tradition. With a manhood already burdened by his being crippled from polio, the doctor's diagnosis of Billy's sterility is another blow to Billy. And when Amy shares the diagnosis with her mother, who then spreads the news in the community, Billy becomes livid. "Damn you to hell for talking of it with others," he scorns Amy, and "there was fury in his eyes for the women" and for Amy (66). So when Holland made love with Billy's wife, he challenged Billy's already fragile manhood to the breaking point and thereby set in motion an age-old plot, the outcome of which even Holland acknowledges. When Billy faces him with a shotgun, Holland grabs the barrel: "'Here,' he said, pushing the barrel against his chest. 'I'd have killed a man who done to me what I done to you.'" When Billy's hands shake, Holland steadies the barrel against his chest and challenges Billy: "Settle it now one way or another, Holcombe . . . because this here is the only way to keep me from claiming what's mine" (126). To understand the background of this behavior, we can turn to Bertram Wyatt-Brown's examination of honor and violence in the Old South.

In the antebellum South, Wyatt-Brown explains, the ritual of the duel was "a means to demonstrate status and manliness." He continues that almost all duels arose "because one antagonist cast doubt on the manliness and bearing of the other, usually through the recitation of ritual words—liar, poltroon, coward. The stigma had to be dealt with or the labels would haunt the bearer forever." While most southerners were opposed to the ritual of the duel, it was often excused on account of male honor. Wyatt-Brown gives a striking example of this paradox, in a quote from Sergeant S. Prentiss of Mississippi, who declared: "'I am no advocate of dueling, and always shall from principle avoid such a thing . . . but when a man is placed in a situation where if he does not fight, life will be rendered valueless to him, both in his eyes and those of the community,' then the only option was to fight" (353). So even though Billy has grave doubts about his abilities as a killer, especially when compared to a war veteran such as Holland (124–25), he still follows through and pulls the trigger because of the ingrained notion of honor. This does not justify it, of course, and both Billy and Amy struggle with the consequences of the killing for the remainder of the novel, with clear echoes of Dostoyevsky's *Crime and Punishment*. In this way Rash suggests that rather than a comforting history, tradition can be a domineering and suffocating force.

Jumping almost two decades in the narration, the chapter titled "The Son" is narrated by the eighteen-year-old Isaac, who comes to expose the dark family secrets behind his own conception. Holland's mother recognizes that Isaac is her grandson and establishes a secret relationship with him. Without saying it directly, she tries to pass on the truth to Isaac. It is also in Isaac's chapter, which takes place around 1970, that the community is displaced before Carolina Power's flooding of Jocassee Valley. Accepting the inevitability of their situation, the Holcombe family has moved into Seneca, where Billy has gotten a job at Dobson Mill. Unlike his parents and their generation, who are struggling to cope with the displacement, Isaac has a more cynical view on the situation: "I'd grown up knowing there was no future here, that Jocassee would sooner or later be covered in water, so I'd never let myself get attached to it the way Momma and Daddy had. . . . That's why I'd been in ROTC in high school instead of FFA [Future Farmers of America] and why I was headed to Clemson next fall on an ROTC scholarship" (168–69). On one hand Isaac embodies a positive take on the tragic displacement, and his decision to educate himself is a theme that resonates in Rash's later novels, primarily in *The World Made Straight*. In an interview Rash elaborated on the role of education in his writing: "I think education is the way you get out. Any minority culture knows that. . . . With Appalachia in particular, there are pervasive stereotypes about no one being able to read, no one having an education, and that's obviously not true. . . . As many intelligent people have come out of these mountains as from any other region" (Bjerre 2007, 220–21). So Isaac represents another, lesser known, more positive side of Appalachia, but on the other hand, it is hard not to read his determination in a tragic light. Isaac has lived his entire life without allowing himself to get attached to the land. In Rash's world, and in most southern fiction, that is no life at all.

Worst of all Isaac is also displaced when it comes to his own family. Homeless both spiritually and physically, he emerges as a potential Appalachian version of Camus' stranger, a helpless victim to an indifferent world. When Mrs. Winchester tells him that Holland is his father and that he was killed by Amy and Billy, Isaac's initial reaction is one of escapism: "I wanted to leave, not just her porch but Jocassee. . . . Then I'd be free of this place and her along with it once and for all" (175). Once again Rash emphasizes the link between the natural world and human emotions, as Isaac wishes that instead of the slow, steady rise of water in the valley, the water had "come like a flood and washed us all out so quick there wouldn't have been time for secrets that had been long hid in this valley to be revealed, secrets that should have been buried under this lake forever" (185). But when Mrs. Winchester begs Isaac not to "let the lake cover up your daddy's bones" (175), Isaac decides to act, to confront his parents with the facts, and thereby to embrace his destiny. As he tells himself, "It wasn't something I wanted to do but I knew I'd have to do it, because the not knowing was worse than the knowing" (182). He also realizes that no matter how hard he might try to ignore or escape the truth, "the truth had been trailing me like a bloodhound. Now it had a hold on me and wouldn't let go" (185). When Isaac confronts his parents with the truth and tells them that he is going to reclaim the remains of his biological father, he takes the final step in what Rash has built up as an inevitable Shakespearian tragedy. As described above, the rain-drenched trek ends with both Amy and Billy drowning in the frothing river.

The last chapter of *One Foot in Eden* is narrated by the deputy and takes place about half a year after Amy and Billy disappear in the river. Jocassee Valley has been flooded and turned into Jocassee Lake. The bodies of Amy and Billy do not rise. Instead the coffin with Widow Glendower's body comes to the surface. Determined not to have her reburied near his own kin, the deputy takes the coffin out on the man-made lake. "Sink straight to hell," he tells her and drops the bones in the water, having secured a permanent division between the two worlds that have clashed throughout the novel: past and present, Old and New South, superstitious mountain culture and rational technological progress. Hurrying back to shore, the deputy drives out of Jocassee and makes himself a promise, which also becomes the last words of the novel. "I wouldn't be coming back here to fish or water ski or swim or anything else like that. This wasn't no place for people who had a home," he thinks to himself. "This was a place for the lost" (214). The last sentence cements the clash between the Old and the New South as well as the inevitability of technology's victory over an agrarian era.

While *One Foot in Eden* is in part a nostalgic elegy to the lost land, it also becomes a testament to a specific time and culture. By writing the lost land back into existence, Rash insists on its importance, even today. This, again, points to the Agrarian vein in Rash's fiction that places him in the tradition of William Faulkner and Madison Jones. *One Foot in Eden* even emulates Madison Jones's *A Buried Land* (1963), in which an unwanted pregnancy leads to a crime that is covered up when the Tennessee Valley Authority floods the valley. Both novels display outrage at the destruction of the land and at the disgrace of having to remove coffins that were buried for centuries, thereby uprooting history. By raging against industrial progress and by re-creating a lost rural culture, Rash places himself in the tradition of Agrarians such as Andrew Nelson Lytle, who spoke melancholically of a lost era, a rural, backward-looking place of farms and small towns. But where Lytle's paradise was an elitist utopia, Rash's lost world is one of poor mountain people. This would not sit well with the Agrarians, who marginalized proletarian writers such as Erskine Caldwell.

Ron Rash depicts the contemporary southerner's struggle to maintain his or her roots in a time of rapid homogenization. As the title of the novel also suggests, the past is still there, in Rash's fiction, as in William Faulkner's "The past is never dead. It's not even past" (Faulkner 1957, 85). The inherent conflicts in his fiction are simultaneously a reminder of the necessity of living with one's past and a fierce attack on today's merciless industrialization. In *One Foot in Eden* Ron Rash has created a poetically beautiful yet tragically haunting work that resonates with the continuous changes of the South in the new millennium.

Works Cited and Consulted

Baldwin, Kara. "'Incredible Eloquence': How Ron Rash's Novels Keep the Celtic Literary Tradition Alive." *South Carolina Review* 39, no. 1 (2006): 37–56.

Bjerre, Thomas Ærvold. "'The Natural World Is the Most Universal of Languages': An Interview with Ron Rash." *Appalachian Journal* 34, no. 2 (2007): 216–27.

Faulkner, William. *Requiem for a Nun*. New York: Random House, 1951.

Jones, Madison. *A Buried Land*. New York: Viking, 1963.

Jones, Suzanne W. "I'll Take My Land: Contemporary Southern Agrarians." *South to a New Place: Region, Literature, Culture*. Ed. Suzanne W. Jones and Sharon Monteith. Baton Rouge: Louisiana State University Press, 2002. 121–46.

Mitchell, Lee Clark. *Westerns: Making the Man in Fiction and Film*. Chicago: University of Chicago Press, 1996.

Rash, Ron. *Serena*. New York: Ecco Press, 2008.

———. *Chemistry and Other Stories*. New York: Picador, 2007.

———. *The World Made Straight*. New York: Henry Holt, 2006.

———. *Saints at the River: A Novel*. New York: Picador, 2004.

———. *One Foot in Eden*. Charlotte, N.C..: Novello Festival Press, 2002.

———. "The Story behind the Book: *One Foot in Eden*." Marly Rusoff Literary Agency. N.d. [2002]. http://www.rusoffagency.com/fiction/foot_in_eden/behind _foot_in_eden.htm/.

———. *Raising the Dead*. Oak Ridge, Tenn.: Iris Press, 2002.

———. *Among the Believers*. Oak Ridge, Tenn.: Iris Press, 2000.

———. *Casualties*. Beaufort, S.C.: Bench Press, 2000.
———. *Eureka Mill*. Columbia, S.C.: Bench Press, 1998.
———. *The Night the New Jesus Fell to Earth and Other Stories from Cliffside, North Carolina*. Beaufort, S.C.: Bench Press, 1994.
Smith, Henry Nash. *Virgin Land: The American West as Symbol and Myth*. 1950. Reprint, Cambridge: Harvard University Press, 1970.
Tompkins, Jane. *West of Everything: The Inner Life of Westerns*. New York: Oxford University Press, 1992.
Worster, Donald. *Under Western Skies: Nature and History in the American West*. New York: Oxford University Press, 1992.
Wyatt-Brown, Bertram. *Southern Honor: Ethics and Behavior in the Old South*. New York: Oxford University Press, 1982.

Richard Ford ~ *The Lay of the Land*

ROBERT H. BRINKMEYER JR.

A Biographical Sketch

Richard Ford's trilogy about a man's life in New Jersey joins a number of other recent novels by southern writers who have chosen to set their work outside the South. Unlike southern writers of previous generations, who almost always set their work in the small-town or rural South, Ford and many other contemporary southern writers are traveling further afield, clearly less bound to the significance of place, particularly a southern sense of place. As I have discussed in my book *Remapping Southern Literature: Contemporary Southern Writers and the West*, the waning of regionalism and regional identity in the United States during an age of globalism has freed the southern literary imagination to explore new forms, issues, and settings, many of which are not at first glance distinctly or characteristically southern. Ford's fiction exemplifies this broadening. Of his six novels and two collections of stories, only Ford's first novel, *A Piece of My Heart* (1976), is set in the South; his other works take place in a variety of far-flung places, from Mexico to Montana to New England to Paris.

If Ford has a fictional home, it is one that moves, often being wherever he happens to be living when he is writing. In both his interviews and his fiction, Ford repeatedly downplays the significance of place as an active force shaping lives—an attitude summed up neatly by Frank Bascombe in *Independence Day*: "Place means nothing" (*ID*, 152). What Bascombe means, as Ford himself has pointed out in an interview, is that however much we might want a specific location to imbue meaning upon our lives, the only meaning that a place delivers is what we ourselves create for that place. Places by themselves are meaningless; what the human mind makes of these places is not. As Ford has put it:

> In talking about sense of place, or locatedness, or the importance of place, or how we feel about it, that figure of speech gets made perplexingly literal sometimes, and in that transaction personally responsible for how one feels, and what's important about place gets shed or lost. Therefore, my view is that anything you feel about a place, anything that you think about place at all, you have authored and ascribed to some piece of geography. Everything

that defines locatedness is then something that you yourself generate. So if it's a sense of place you experience, you're just expressing what you feel and which you say the place has created. (Guagliardo 2001, 142).

Ironically Ford's ideas about place in large part originate, as Elinor Ann Walker discusses in her fine book on Ford, in his southern origins and upbringing. Ford was born in Jackson, Mississippi, in 1944, to parents who had recently settled there; before that time the two had for many years enjoyed an itinerant existence, living on the road as Ford's father made his travels as a starch salesman. As Ford notes in a memoir, before settling in Jackson, his parents "had never had to choose a 'home,' a place to be in permanently," and it was only with his mother's pregnancy that the two decided to forego their transient life (Ford 1987, 46). Ford's childhood was a mixture of settledness and unsettledness. Although the family was now established in Jackson, his father continued working as a traveling salesman and was usually home only on the weekends. Contributing to the sense of instability was his father's declining health stemming from serious heart problems; and when Ford was sixteen his father suffered a second—and fatal—heart attack.

The Lay of the Land

"The permanent life" of impermanence, with all its complications, is precisely what Frank Bascombe struggles with in all three novels of Ford's trilogy, but his efforts are perhaps most charged and intense in *The Lay of the Land*, since his cancer has made him piercingly aware of his own precarious existence and of death's ever-present shadow. As in *The Sportswriter* and *Independence Day*, Frank develops various strategies, characteristically of avoidance, to survive the death of his son Ralph and the breakup of his marriage—crushing blows that tumble his life. In *The Sportswriter*, for instance, he repeatedly testifies to the value of ignoring what has come before and of leaving the past as far behind as possible. "I am a proponent of . . . forgetting," Frank forthrightly declares. "Forgetting dreams, grievances, old flaws in character—mine and others'. To me there is no hope unless we can forget what's said and gone before, and forgive it" (Ford 1986, 144).

In *Independence Day*, as the very title of the novel suggests, Frank affirms the independent life. He wants to live unbound from not merely the demands of and responsibilities to others but also from, as he characterizes the problems facing his son (and clearly Frank himself, too), "whatever holds him captive: memory, history, bad events he struggles with, can't control but feels he should" (*ID*, 16). Frank characterizes his life during this time as his "Existence Period," a midlife strategy in which he focuses almost exclusively on the future and the notion of becoming. He strives not to worry about how things used to be or now *are* but to keep alive instead the possibility of how they *might* be. In one of his most hopeful statements from his thinking during his Existence Period, Frank says at one point, "My own feelings were that since I'd jettisoned employment, marriage, nostalgia and swampy regret, I was now rightfully a man aquiver with possibility and purpose" (95).

Extended stays at the hotel in Little Rock, Arkansas, run by his grandfather, contributed to the unsettled nature of Ford's upbringing. Both before and after his father's death, Ford regularly lived at the hotel, usually during summers; and to these stays, during which he closely observed all the comings and goings, Ford attributes many lessons about life's tenuousness and vagaries. "To live in a hotel promotes a cool two-mindedness," Ford writes, "one is both steady and in a sea that passes with the tides. Accommodation is what's wanted, a replenished idea of permanence and transience; familiarity overcoming the continual irregularity in things" (Ford 1988, 38). As his words here suggest, Ford eventually saw life in the hotel as a model for life itself: a series of arrivals and departures, an ongoing interplay of the surprising and the routine in which the surprising eventually becomes the routine, an accumulation of experiences amassed, as he writes elsewhere, "not quite pointlessly. But not pointedly, either" (Ford 1987, 54).

Watching the extravagant variety of people in and around the hotel, people who would appear one day and disappear the next, perhaps never to be seen again, taught the young Ford that to see life summed up by any one person, idea, or place is merely a dream. "Life goes on with or without you," he writes. "Home is finally a variable concept." And he adds: "In the hotel there was no center to things, nor was I one. It was the floating life, days erasing other days almost completely, as should be. The place was a hollow place, like any home, in which things went on, a setting where situations developed and ended" (Ford 1988, 43). His time at the hotel, Ford notes, underscored the impermanence underlying—and belying—all notions of permanence; the only thing permanent about life indeed was its impermanence. For Ford this awareness was finally bracing, leading him to see that his life at the hotel, so different from his regular (and regularized) life in Jackson, was "not a stopover, a diversion, an oddment in time," but was instead what he called "the permanent life"—the life as experienced by us all. "Everything counts, after all," Ford says, concluding his essay on living at the hotel, pointing to the fact that the random and unexpected shape us as much as our efforts to order and exclude life's messiness. "What else do you need to know?" (Ford 1988, 43).

Richard Ford's *The Lay of the Land* (2007) concludes his magnificent trilogy on Frank Bascombe, a writer-turned-real estate agent living in suburban New Jersey, who struggles to find happiness and meaning in his everyday life. The first two volumes of the trilogy, *The Sportswriter* (1986) and *Independence Day* (1996), depict Frank's attempts at recovering from the two already mentioned devastating events that unmoored him: the death of a son from illness and the subsequent divorce from his wife. Both novels clearly illustrate the central concern in almost all of Ford's fiction, identified by himself in an early interview with Gail Caldwell: "I'm always interested in what happens after bad things happen. Most functioning, balanced people can put up with the terrible tragedies: a life ending, the death of a child. It's what happens afterwards that's interesting to me . . . because it's a proving ground for drama" (Guagliardo 2001, 46).

In *The Sportswriter* Frank navigates through what he characterizes as the geography of divorce, hoping to move beyond trauma into a more hopeful future; and in *Independence Day* Frank works to maintain his fiercely held and self-protective self-sufficiency while not completely cutting himself off from others, particularly his children. *The Lay of the Land* finds Frank five years past the time of *Independence Day*; now at age fifty-five, he is facing two new personal disasters: his second wife, Sally, has left him for her first husband, long presumed dead but now miraculously reappeared, and Frank has been diagnosed with and is being treated for prostate cancer. The relative stability Frank had finally established with his second marriage and his successful real estate career has come precipitously close to collapsing, and the novel follows Frank's attempts to find his way through a world that suddenly seems governed more by the random and the unexpected than by the conscientious efforts of Frank or anyone else.

By the time of *The Lay of the Land*, however, Frank, older, more experienced, and facing his own mortality, is not a man "aquiver with possibility and purpose"; and when the novel opens he has moved beyond the Existence Period into what he deems his "Permanent Period." By this new line of thinking, Frank now avoids thinking about and planning for the future to focus instead entirely on the present, accepting who he is rather than worrying about who he should be or who he was. Grounding himself in the here and now relieves Frank from "unwanted self-consciousness" and helps replace a "dimming fear-of-the-future" with "the permanent cutting edge of the present" (*Lay of the Land*, 160). How liberating it is for him to accept without guilt and remorse his present self and character; and at the same time, how liberating it is not to have to worry about where his life is going or how he might mess things up in the future. Frank notes that "one of the pure benefits of the Permanent Period—when you're as nose-down and invisible to yourself as an actualized unchangeable non-becomer, as snugged into life as a planning-board member—is that you realize you can't completely fuck everything up anymore, since so much of your life is on the books already. You've survived it" (75).

Frank apparently began inching toward what would become his Permanent Period at the end of *Independence Day*, when he joins the town's Fourth of July celebrations, suggesting his growing awareness that he needs to strike out from the isolation of the Existence Period and make himself part of a larger community. Frank was then coming to see that while his enforced emotional isolation provided him with psychological stability, it so diminished his interior life that he was close to being dead to the world and to himself. Frank had earlier in

Independence Day pointed to this danger when he commented on one of the strategies he often used to get through difficult times: "I try, in other words, to keep something finite and acceptable on my mind and not disappear. Though it's true that sometimes in the glide, when worries and contingencies are floating off, I sense I myself am afloat and cannot always feel the sides of where I am, nor know what to expect" (*ID*, 117). Ford himself has been even more explicit on the dangers, saying to Elinor Ann Walker that Frank's story in *Independence Day* suggests "the eventual sterility of cutting yourself off from liaisons with other people, from attachments, affinities, affiliations with other people. Finally the end of the line for independence is sterility" (Guagliardo 2001, 139).

Psychological death and emotional sterility still loom as dangers in *The Lay of the Land*, as do literal death and sterility. To combat his cancer Frank's prostate has been filled with radioactive titanium pellets and his penile control is, at best, distressed. As the novel opens, Frank faces the collapse of the stability and happiness he had achieved with his second marriage and his better relationship with his children. While he is generally more open to accepting others into his life, his health and marital crises pressure him to embrace a protective stance resisting deep involvement and deep self-understanding. This is a stance Frank had never completely given up, as evidenced in his words above about relishing unwanted self-consciousness and enjoying being invisible to himself. Whatever his change in perspective, regarding the self-definition of the Permanent Period, Frank still values keeping his life free from unwanted complications, particularly from the messiness involved in negotiating the presence of other people into his life. In some ways Frank models his life on the two activities he seems to enjoy most: selling real estate and working as a sponsor to those in need of advice. Both activities engage him with people, but only on superficial levels.

Selling residential real estate is particularly significant for Frank. He entered the profession during his Existence Period, in *Independence Day*, in part because the enterprise seemed to mirror his own perspective on life: realty, as he comments in *The Lay of the Land*, is "the profession of possibility" (34) and the standard bearer profession for the concept of *becoming* (52). Frank sees selling real estate as a modern-day manifestation of one of America's crucial cultural legends: the dream of the West, of picking up and moving on and starting over, of being hopeful that things can be made better simply by leaving one place for another. It is for this reason that Frank says that when people purchase new houses they participate in "a sort of minor-league Manifest Destiny" (90). "Sometimes a new vista, a new house number, a new place of employ, a new set of streets to navigate and master are all you need to simplify life and take a new lease out on it," Frank comments. "Real estate might seem to be all about moving and picking up stakes and disruption and three-moves-equals-a-death, but it's really about arriving and destinations, and all the prospects that await you or might await you in some place you never thought about" (336–37). By this configuration Frank as real estate agent serves as the pathfinder clearing the way for his clients' treks into the hopeful future.

Even though by the time of *The Lay of the Land* Frank sees himself as a Permanent Period "non-becomer," he nonetheless enjoys bringing possibility into other people's lives through selling them real estate. But he keeps his distance from his clients and resists becoming deeply involved in their problems. He is not totally isolated from the community, but neither is he totally active within it, as most of his interactions with other people involve the contingencies of business rather than life—and this is precisely how Frank likes it. At one point he happily describes his role as realtor and community member: "People are happy to see me, know that I'm thriving and will be there when the time comes, but still don't have to have me to dinner. In that way, I'm a lot like a funeral home" (267). People steer clear of him, in other words, unless they need him. Indeed Frank sees his job as realtor, particularly as a facilitator for clearing away difficulties and contingencies from contracts, as a model for his own effort at doing away with unwelcome annoyances from his personal life. He is most happy as a realtor, he says, when his work confers upon him "a pleasant, self-actualizing invisibility—the self as perfect *instrument*" (275); and clearly he is most happy in his personal life when he maintains a similar invisibility, in the sense of reducing his emotional life to the barest of essentials, of responding in simple ways to simple situations, without being plagued by problematic self-consciousness.

Along these same lines Frank often reduces the complexities of human emotion and action by configuring them in terms of real estate transactions—which he understands well and is good at putting together. At one point Frank thus equates the contingencies of a real estate contract with those of the marriage contract. "All marriages—all everythings—tote around contingencies whether we acknowledge them or don't," Frank says, adding, "There's a back door *somewhere* to every deal, and there a draft can enter. All promises to be in love and 'true to you forever' are premised on the iron contingency . . . that says, Unless, of course, I fall in love 'forever' with someone else. This is true even if we don't like it, which means it isn't cynical to think, but also means that someone else— someone we love and who we'd rather have *not* know it—is as likely to know it as we are" (231). Frank's comment seems perfectly reasonable, people do of course change their minds in relationships and marriages. Yet seeing life solely through the lens of business transactions is both reductive and cynical, despite his claims to the contrary.

Frank's work as a sponsor, even if he does not configure it this way, also points to what we might call his ideal of disengaged engagement. As Frank explains, as a sponsor he is a member of a network of individuals who visit people wanting to talk with someone about a problem. A sponsor listens and offers advice but shares nothing else other than his or her first name. Sponsor visits are brief, usually about twenty minutes with a one-hour limit, and a sponsor never visits the same person twice. "Sponsoring is not about connectedness," Frank explains. "It's about being consoled by connection's opposite. A little connectedness, in fact, goes a long way, no matter what the professional lonelies of the world say. We might all do with a little less of it" (96). As Frank makes clear, he thinks a good sponsor acts like a helpful sales agent, though the sponsor is not selling anything. At one point he says that he sees himself as "a natural Sponsor, since just like being a decent realtor, you have to at least harbor the suspicion that you have a lot in common with *everybody*, even if you don't want to be their friend." And at another he characterizes his sponsor visits as "more like a friendly stop-by from the bland State Farm guy, who you've run into at the tire store, asked over to the house to tweak your coverage, but who you then enlist you to help get the lawn sprinkler to work" (93–94).

Sponsoring, then, represents for Frank his ideal engagement with other people: he helps others, thus feeling good about himself, while strictly maintaining his independence from them. "Sponsoring has never actually produced a greater sense of connectedness in me, and probably not in others—the storied lashing-together-of-boats we're all supposed to crave and weep salty tears at night for the lack of" (96). The last thing Frank wants is to get deeply involved in other people's lives and for people to get deeply involved in his, particularly people he does not know well. At this point in his life, as Frank makes clear, he is not looking to make new friends, because that process would involve too much boring effort to catch them up with his already congested life, past and present. "When you meet someone who might be a legitimate friend candidate," Frank says, "the natural impulse is to start fading back to avoid all the yakkedy-yak, so that you fade and fade, until you can't see him or her anymore, and couldn't bear to anyway. With the result that attraction quickly becomes avoidance" (95).

As secure as he feels as a real estate agent and sponsor, and as secure as he feels nestled into the Permanent Period, Frank eventually comes to see that settling entirely into the present and into one's current self can be dangerous and stifling. As Frank comments, "permanence can be scary":

> Even though it solves the problem of tiresome becoming, it can also erode optimism, render possibility small and remote, and make any of us feel that while we can't fuck up much of anything anymore, there really isn't much to fuck up because nothing matters a gnat's nuts; and that down deep inside we've finally become just an organism that for some reason can still make noise, but not much more from that.
>
> This you need to save yourself from, or else the slide off the transom of life's pleasure boat becomes irresistible and probably a good idea. (76)

Permanence becomes even more scary for Frank when he comes face to face with his own mortality and with the fact that, in the face of time, chance, and fickle humanity, nothing is finally permanent. Indeed what most haunts Frank, and what stalks him throughout *The Lay of the Land*, is the opposite of permanence, which of course is *death*.

Death lurks everywhere in the novel, from the first page to the last. The event that opens the novel and that sets Frank's narration in motion is his response to a newspaper article describing a shooting during a nursing class at a Texas teachers' college. A disgruntled student had approached his professor, Sandra McCurdy, and with pistol raised to her forehead asked her if she were ready to meet her Maker. "Yes. Yes, I think I am," she replied, after which the student shot and killed her before turning the gun on himself (3). Like a protagonist from a Walker Percy novel, Frank is blasted out of his everydayness by the teacher's affirmation: "I just stood right up out of my chair, my heart suddenly whonking, my hands, fingers, cold and atingle, my scalp tightened down against my cranium the way it does when a train goes by too close. And I said out loud, with no one to hear me, I said, 'Holy shit! How in the world did she know that?'" (4). In pondering how he would have responded in Professor McCurdy's situation, Frank quickly realizes that unlike her, he is not ready to leave this world, not by a long shot. And he makes a resolution to reexamine his life, remaking it if necessary, in order "to get to where Ms. McCurdy was at her ending song, or at least close enough to it that if I was faced with something like the question she was faced with, I would give something like the answer she gave" (6).

So begins Frank's quest. During the week of Thanksgiving, a time when winter and its killing weather is moving in, Frank repeatedly comes face to face with situations highlighting the fragility of both existence and the cherished beliefs we ascribe to it. Death and loss are continually present. Early in the novel he attends the funeral of a friend, forcing him of course to ponder his own mortality. He later drives by a hospital where a bomb has exploded, killing an acquaintance. Much to his dismay Frank becomes a suspect in the bombing, with his life now threatening to become a Kafkaesque nightmare. He attends the implosion of a hotel, an event that calls into question Frank's hopeful ideas about the groundedness sustained by real estate. Frank learns later that the man he goes with, who is the father of a woman with whom he had once been involved, subsequently dies of a stroke on the Sunday after Thanksgiving. On the night before Thanksgiving, Frank's daughter is in an automobile accident and is arrested. And on Thanksgiving Day his next-door neighbors, the Feeneys, are killed in a home invasion. Frank himself is shot twice in the chest during that robbery. Throughout the novel, Frank thinks about the death of his son Ralph; and he also thinks of the loss of his wife Sally, who has moved to Scotland to be with her reappeared first husband.

In the few days that the novel takes place Frank tries to come to terms with the turmoil of what we might call "the lay of the land" of his existence. As he has in other stages of his life, Frank visualizes himself as a pioneer of sorts, a pathfinder moving through life's tortuous existential landscapes—for example, the geography of divorce. One of the models he sets for himself, as we learn in *Independence Day*, is the frontier hero Davy Crockett. In that novel he notes that a person must keep moving forward through life's terrain, sidestepping indecision and regret. "While it's bad to make a wrong move," he comments, "it's worse to regret in advance and call it prudence.... Disaster is no less likely. Better—much, much better—to follow ole Davy Crockett's motto, amended for use by adults: Be sure you're not completely wrong, then go ahead" (*ID*, 226). Also standing as a guiding model is James Fenimore Cooper's hero Natty Bumppo, whose presence is suggested when Frank and his son Paul, in *Independence Day*, take a trip to Cooperstown.

Frank continues to see himself as a frontier hero in *The Lay of the Land*, and he is joined by a fellow journeyman, the Tibetan Lobsang Dhargey—or as he is called in New Jersey, Mike Mahoney—who is a realty associate in Frank's agency. Frank and Mike represent another of the light-skinned/dark-skinned pairs of men in American literature who together traverse the wilderness, including Natty Bumppo and Chingachgook (in James Fenimore Cooper's Leatherstocking novels), Ishmael and Queequeg (in Herman Melville's *Moby-Dick*), and Huck and Jim (in Mark Twain's *Adventures of Huckleberry Finn*). Ford's pair traverses the suburban wilderness of New Jersey and its various geographies of emotional experience. Frank and Mike are mirror opposites of each other. Frank is a successful businessman drawn toward matters of the spirit; Mike is a Buddhist drawn toward material success. Working together Frank and Mike quietly influence each other, each drawing from the strengths of the other, so that both emerge as fuller and better men. For Mike this means tempering his overwhelming desire for wealth and all its trappings. Frank notes that as a convert to American capitalism, Mike has enthusiastically given himself over to the system "by turning himself into a strangely sharp dresser, by fine tuning a flat, accentless news-anchor delivery (his voice sometimes seems to come from offstage and not out of him), by sending his two kids to a pricey private school in Rumson, by mortgaging himself to the gizzard, by separating from his nice Tibetan wife, driving a fancy silver Infiniti, never speaking Tibetan (easy enough) and by frequenting—and probably supporting—a girlfriend he hasn't told me about" (16). Early in the novel Mike reaches a crossroads in his life: he must decide whether to continue as a real estate agent or to partner with a contractor to build a development of McMansions. Or in Frank's words he must decide if he wants to leave Frank's agency to "become a sleazy land developer" (195). Eventually Mike decides not to become a developer, following both his own heart—its Buddhist grounding—and the example of Frank. At the end of the novel he joins Frank as full partner of his, now *their*, real estate agency.

Mike's influence on Frank is less obvious, though no less significant, and it comes largely through Mike's Buddhism. Although Frank almost always breezily dismisses Mike's Buddhism, he nonetheless eventually moves toward a general acceptance of life, what Frank calls the "Next Level," which dovetails broadly with Buddhist thought. From the perspective of the Next Level, Frank sees that the previous stages of his life were not "forms of acceptance," as he once thought, but "forms of fearful nonacceptance" (357), strategies for denying rather than embracing what he calls the "responsibilities of the Next Level—that life can't be escaped and must be faced entire" (466). To face life entire for Frank means, most crucially, accepting the death of his son Ralph in all its finality. In a staggering moment of self-awareness, Frank acknowledges that he has never accepted that Ralph would never be returning: "That was my lie, my big fear, the great pain I couldn't fathom even the thought of surviving, and so didn't fathom it; fathomed instead life as a series of lives, variations on a theme that sheltered me. The lie being: It's not Ralph's death that's woven into everything like a secret key, it's his *not death*, the *not* permanence—the extra beat awaited, the mutability of every fact, the grinning, eyebrows-raised chance that something's waiting even if it's not. These were my sly ruses and slick tricks, my surface intrigues and wire-pulls, all played *against* permanence, not *to* it" (357).

Facing life entire, furthermore, demands that Frank live with compassion and an open heart. "I want to be upbeat and comradely—even if I don't feel that way," Frank comments. "We can, after all, always set aside our real feelings—which usually don't amount to a hill of beans anyway, and may not even be genuine—and let ourselves be spontaneous and bounteous with fast-flowing vigor, just as when we're at our certifiable best" (419). His new compassion brings him closer to all those around him, most particularly to Mike, his children Paul and Clarissa, and to Sally, who has returned after the suicide of her first husband and the Thanksgiving day shooting of Frank. Once aloof and self-absorbed, Frank emerges as a kind and gentle soul. Near the end of the novel, recovering from his gunshot wounds and happy with his reconciliation with Sally, Frank says that he has "begun to feel a growing sense of enlightenment." While he says that he has not become overly spiritual, he adds that he now sees "the best motivational question in the spirituality catechism" as "'Do I have a heart at all?' Do I see good as even a possibility? The Dalai Lama in *The Road to the Open Heart* argues I definitely do. And I can say I think I do, too" (476).

Armed with a "a practical acceptance of what's what, in real time and down-to-earth" (484), Frank gratefully embraces who he is and what he has done, thankful for all that he has been through, the good and the bad, the happiness and the suffering. Frank thus embraces the true spirit of the holiday around which *The Lay of the Land* revolves, Thanksgiving, which Frank says calls forth "the state of mind we enjoy best": "Acceptance—a spirit to be thankful for" (367). It is this spirit of acceptance that abounds in the novel's last scene, with Frank and Sally on board a plane filled with patients and loved ones heading for the Mayo Clinic. Rather than being glum and retreating into themselves, Frank and the others laugh and joke, making the best of their brief time together as companions on life's journey. Frank now understands that the expression "the lay of the land" has less to do with geography than with the human condition, has less to do with the American myth that by repeatedly moving one can escape one's troubles than it does with the universal condition, the trials and tribulations that we all, as creatures who will one day die, face upon this earth. It is this understanding that Frank points to in the novel's final words, spoken as their plane touches ground: "We resume our human scale upon the land" (485). In this glorious ending we see that Frank has evolved into a very different sort of pathfinder, less the Natty Bumppo–esque frontiersmen than the Buddhist seeker on the eightfold path toward enlightenment.

Whether we will hear anymore from Frank Bascombe or not, in telling his story in *The Lay of the Land* Frank has answered the question that began the novel: what does it mean to say that one is ready to meet one's maker, that one is ready to die (as Professor McCurdy had affirmed she was, when a gunman had leveled a pistol at her head)? By the end of the novel Frank now knows that were he in Professor McCurdy's situation, he too could—and would—answer, yes, I am ready, since he knows that in telling his story he has achieved what he says is "the final wish of all of us on earth": "To testify of our witness to wonders" (436).

That testimony lies at the heart of both *The Lay of the Land* and the entire Frank Bascombe trilogy, and it articulates the optimism undergirding Ford's imaginative vision. Anything but an unthinking hopefulness blind to human suffering, Ford's is a fully determined affirmation borne out of that suffering, what Tony Everett has called "tough-minded." "Bad things come to everybody," Ford said in the interview with Everett. "We don't get out of it. And the real important, the real interesting optimistic side of all bad things, is what we do in consequence of them" (Guagliardo 2001, 82). How people make do in the face of adversity—how we face the consequences—is finally the subject of Richard Ford's fiction; and nowhere is this more evident than in the magnificent novel concluding the Frank Bascombe trilogy, *The Lay of the Land*.

Works Cited and Consulted

Bone, Martyn. The *Postsouthern Sense of Place in Contemporary Fiction*. Baton Rouge: Louisiana State University Press, 2005.
Brinkmeyer, Robert H., Jr. *Remapping Southern Literature: Contemporary Southern Writers and the West*. Athens: University of Georgia Press, 2000.
Ford, Richard. *The Lay of the Land*. New York: Knopf, 2006.
———. *A Multitude of Sins*. New York: Knopf, 2002.
———. *Wildlife*. New York: Atlantic Monthly Press, 2000.
———. *Women with Men: Three Stories*. New York, Knopf, 1997.
———. *Independence Day*. New York: Knopf, 1995.
———. "Accommodations." *Harper's*, June 1988, 38, 42–43.
———. "My Mother, My Memory." *Harper's*, August 1987, 44–57.

———. *Rock Springs*. New York: Atlantic Monthly Press, 1987.
———. *The Sportswriter*. New York: Vintage, 1986.
———. *The Ultimate Good Luck*. Boston: Houghton Mifflin, 1981.
———. *A Piece of My Heart*. New York: Harper & Row, 1976.
Guagliardo, Huey, ed. *Conversations with Richard Ford*. Jackson: University Press of Mississippi, 2001.
Guinn, Matthew. *After Southern Modernism: Fiction of the Contemporary South*. Jackson: University Press of Mississippi, 2000.
Hobson, Fred. *The Southern Writer in the Postmodern World*. Athens: University of Georgia Press, 1991.
Walker, Elinor Ann. *Richard Ford*. New York: Twayne, 2000.

Cormac McCarthy ~ *The Road*

RICHARD GRAY

A Biographical Sketch

The Road is Cormac McCarthy's tenth novel. It is also the first of his novels to be met with almost unanimous critical acclaim. Those who were less than impressed with his ninth novel, *No Country for Old Men*, have greeted it with something pretty close to relief. Others—and these are so far in the majority among critics of *The Road*—have focused their attention, and their admiration, on what has been seen as a return to stylistic form and a return to the overwhelming questions that haunt so much of McCarthy's earlier work. In a time of literary minimalism, when so many writers seem intent on pursuing a style of scrupulous meanness, McCarthy has reverted in *The Road* to the rich and even baroque rhetoric of his novels *Suttree* and *Blood Meridian*. And at a moment when the notion of a grand narrative has been dismissed and deconstructed, McCarthy has chosen to continue his search in *The Road* for some answer to the overwhelming questions of life, death, meaning, and nothingness, and to address fundamental questions in what one critic of the novel has termed "a thought and feeling experiment, bleak, exhilarating (in fact endurable) only because of its integrity, its wholeness of seeing" (Mars-Jones 2006, 19). Like all novels—if we are to believe Bahktin—*The Road* is a curious hybrid. It is, like all McCarthy's fiction, haunted by the lives and writings of others; it is densely allusive and yet it is unmistakably the work of a fiercely original writer, swimming against the tide of literary fashion. It has the elemental quality of allegory and myth but also addresses issues that are ferociously contemporary, specific to the here and now. It declares the imminence, and perhaps the inevitability, of entropy, a world running down to inertia and oblivion, but it also offers a testament of faith in the will to meaning, the possibility of human intimacy and the simple, inextinguishable desire of the human animal to go on.

To take the allusiveness first: McCarthy has never made any secret of just how deeply intertextual he takes all texts, including his own, to be. "The ugly fact is that books are made out of other books," he declared once in a rare interview. "The novel depends for its life on other novels that have been written" (Woodward 1992, 36). One critic has called McCarthy "a literary hybrid"

(Ragan 1993, 15). Another has remarked that reading one of McCarthy's novels is "like strolling through a museum of English prose styles," adding that the border trilogy appears to have been written "by the illegitimate offspring of Zane Grey and Flannery O' Connor" (Pilkington 1997, 312, 318). There is a hint of criticism here, a sly suggestion that something is not quite right with a book that is a forest of allusion. Some commentators have gone beyond hinting and openly expressed offence. "Should a novel be quite so reminiscent of other novels as this one is?" one clearly exasperated critic asked of *All the Pretty Horses* (Doody 1993, 20). But such uneasiness or exasperation is surely beside the point. As a matter of principle, all literature is intertextual. McCarthy knows this. So, for that matter, do such otherwise different writers as the Kentuckian Wendell Berry and the Russian Joseph Brodsky. "All good human work remembers its history," Berry has pointed out. "The best writing, even when printed, is full of intimations that it is the present version of earlier versions of itself . . . it is a palimpsest" (Berry 1986, 192). "A good poet," observes Brodsky, "does not avoid influence or continuity but frequently nurtures them, and emphasizes them in every possible way. . . . Fear of influence, fear of dependence, is the fear—the affliction—of a savage, but not of culture, which is all continuity, all echo" (Brodsky 1999, 184). What matters is not the fact of dialogue between texts, since that is unavoidable, but the quality of that dialogue, what a writer adds to the existing monuments of literature, to use an Eliotic image, and how he reaccentuates the voices of his literary forebears in echoing them.

And McCarthy certainly, and decisively, reaccentuates the voices of his literary ancestors in *The Road*. The novel describes the journey of two people, a father and son, "moving south" across a bleak, devastated, and sparsely populated landscape because, as the father realizes, "there'd be no surviving another winter here" (4), where they begin their long trek. The structure of the narrative, a continuous series of discrete paragraphs undivided into chapters or sections, clearly repeats the rhythm of the journey, a series of short stages moving toward something like a destination. This recasts one of the iconic images of American literature, the journey. What the reader is confronted with here is not the open road of, say, Walt Whitman, John Steinbeck, or Jack Kerouac, but a route and a landscape on the point of vanishing. The journey here is not a linear progress, from the East to the West, a liberatory flight from the old to the new as in the classic American western. It is a turning back, from the North to the South, across an unobstructed space that triggers not a sense of freedom but a feeling of empty immensity. This is a landscape that denies definition, distinction, and it gives the sense that beyond the indeterminacy and vacancy of the immediate surroundings, the gray wastes that confront father and son in the course of their travels, there is only more vacancy, more empty space.

The echoes of Eliot, and of McCarthy's own earlier work, are inescapable here. The world has become a waste land. That image of the waste land recurs throughout McCarthy's earlier novels—in, say, his account of the "neuter austerity" (1989, 247) of the American West in *Blood Meridian* and his description of "the ancient road" across "mineral waste" (1992, 4) that the protagonist of *All the Pretty Horses* traverses. But it is reasserted more insistently and more powerfully than ever before here. *The Road* is set in some strange, post-apocalyptic landscape. There are no birds or animals left alive here. Most of the trees and many of the buildings have been destroyed, burned to extinction. And the air is filled with ash, requiring those who survive to wear face masks so as to filter the noxious air they breathe. Ash is everywhere—this is Scott Fitzgerald's Valley of Ashes universalized; ash is there at all times, even when it rains—as it does with great frequency. The foliage surrounding father and son "turned to dust about them" (10), we are told. Ashes, dust, and death are ubiquitous as the few human presences left on this darkling plain witness the death of both nature and culture. The reader is reminded, perhaps, not only of the T. S. Eliot poem but of the Christian funeral service that Eliot himself was echoing—although, in this case, there is no hope of recovery or resurrection.

The Road

"He . . . looked out over the wasted landscape," the narrator observes of the father, the protagonist of *The Road* at one point. What he sees is a world denied the possibility of survival or redemption. There is "no sign of life" (9) here. The land, covered in ash, is gray and barren; the foliage, what remains of it, is "black and twisted" (9); the houses, what remain of them, are empty of everything but "trash in the floor, old newsprint," appliances that no longer work, and furniture and fittings that are unused and falling apart. And "on the outskirts of a city," we learn, father and son come upon:

> a supermarket. A few old cars in the trashstrewn parking lot. . . . In the produce section in the bottom of the bins they found a few ancient runner beans and what looked to have once been apricots, long dried to wrinkled effigies of themselves. . . . In the alleyway behind the store a few shopping carts, all badly rusted. . . . By the door were two softdrink machines that had been tilted over into the floor and opened with a prybar. Coins everywhere in the ash. He sat and ran his hand around the works of the gutted machines and in the second one it closed over a cold metal cylinder. He withdrew his hand slowly and sat looking at a Coca Cola. (19)

What McCarthy transmutes Eliot's *Waste Land* into is a demythologized, dystopic space that is at once America after the fall and our world, wherever it may be, after the collapse from globalism into barbarism. The supermarket evacuated of goods and customers becomes here a paradigm of a depopulated America that enjoys no myth, no narrative, and no context, a place where signs carry advertisements for products that are not only gone but mostly forgotten ("What is it, Papa?" the son asks, when the father shows him the Coca-Cola retrieved from the gutted machine). In an earlier novel such as *The Crossing*, McCarthy's travelers encounter ruined churches and failed priests. In *The Road* they meet with a ruined monument to consumption, which is a measure of the transformation of the world from exchange into entropy. What is at stake here is not so much loss of faith as loss of function; there is not only no apparent spiritual meaning in this particular waste land, there is no discernible meaning or purpose of any kind. This is a world that makes no sense because the connections have gone and the signs no longer signify. The supermarket trolley is now used by the father and son to carry their few remaining possessions; the road is not so much one of the last vestiges of civilization as a place where small armies march, searching for the last few humans who have not been enslaved or eaten; books lie wet and rotting on library shelves; the map the father carries has been shredded into leaves. The small bits of narrative that are retained are runic—tattoos of spiders, skulls etched with paint, patterns of rock left by the roadside. Father and son have no name; they are mostly "the man" and "the boy." Nor do any other of the characters they encounter—apart from the nearly blind, cane-carrying "Ely," who, it turns out, is a chronic liar. If any of the old narratives that used to make sense of people's lives are recalled in *The Road* at all, they are recalled only to be subverted, flattened out into an absence of meaning. So Ely, in a sly reversal of biblical narrative, takes the antiprophetic course of declaring that God does not exist; advertisements, where they survive, are scrawled over with new messages warning of danger and imminent death; and an antebellum southern home that father and son enter at one point turns out to have a locked basement full of human beings kept as food. The son in *The Road* has no memory of the world before it was laid waste; the father has. But both are equally trapped in the vacancy of the present. This is a fictional landscape imbued with a sense of total and irrevocable loss, inscribing what it might be like to live after the fall.

For the reader this raises the question of what kind of fall has occurred. Many reviewers of the book have referred to the setting of *The Road* as postnuclear. It is easy to see why. A passage such as the following, describing a past moment dredged up from the father's memory, appears to describe a nuclear attack: "The clocks stopped at 1:17. A long shear of light and then a series of low concussions. He got up and went to the window. What is it? she said. He didn't answer. He went into the bathroom and threw the lightswitch but the power was already gone. A dull rose glow in the windowglass" (45).

The disaster that has visited this landscape is much more generalized, however, more allegorized than this passage read in isolation might suggest; and the general contours of the landscape through which father and son travel are those, after all, of surreal nightmare—a variation, not only on the Eliotic waste land but also on the darkness visible in the poetry of Dante and Milton and the prose of Céline. More prosaically, there are no signs of radioactivity, and none of the characters suffer from radiation sickness. The "event" that has reduced the United States—and, it is intimated, the rest of the world—to this deathly state remains resolutely unexplained. This might be the world after a nuclear holocaust or it might not be. Some other event might have turned the world to dust. The point is that McCarthy both says and remains silent. The unnamable remains unnamed, except in its human consequences.

The reason for this indeterminacy is simple. McCarthy is dealing with trauma, and in the first instance, with trauma of a very immediate kind. It is surely right to see *The Road* as a post-9/11 novel, not just in the obvious, literal sense, but to the extent that it takes the measure of that sense of dread that has seemed to haunt the West, the United States in particular, ever since the destruction of the World Trade Center towers. One possible way of interpreting the events of September 11 and their aftermath is precisely in terms of the traumatic—a recalibration of feeling so violent and radical that it resists but also compels memory, generating stories that have to be told. "Trauma," a word whose origins lie in the Greek word for "wound," was famously defined by Freud and his disciples in terms of an event the full horror of which is not and cannot be assimilated fully at the time but only belatedly. It is not "available to consciousness until it imposes itself again, repeatedly, in the nightmares and repetitive actions of the survivor" (Caruth 1996, 4): a "feature," Freud observed, "one might term *latency*" (1974, 84). The first step toward recovery is testimony to a listener, an "intellectual witness"—a concept that, as Geoffrey Hartman has explained, is "without generational limit" (1998, 37). This transformation of the traumatic event into what Cathy Caruth has called "a narrative memory" (1996, 153) allows the story not only to be verbalized and communicated but assimilated—the dispersed, and in most cases repressed, pieces of the event can be disinterred and delivered into some kind of sequence. The writer, acting here as both victim and witness, with the text both symptom and diagnosis, can, in the words of another authority on trauma and recovery, "see more than a few fragments of the picture at one time ... retain all the pieces and fit them together" into a meaningful story (Herman 1992, 2).

The determining feature of trauma is that it is unsayable. What is traumatic is defined by what Caruth has called "the impossibility of ... direct access" (1996, 4). And the mistake many writers trying to deal with the traumatic events of 9/11 have made has been precisely to pursue access of a very direct, very immediate kind. This is true of novels and stories as otherwise different as *Falling Man* (2007) by Don DeLillo, *The Good Life* (2006) by Jay McInerney, *A Disorder Peculiar to the Country* (2007) by Ken Kalfus, *Terrorist* (2006) by John Updike, *The Emperor's Children* (2006) by Clare Messud, *Twilight of the Superheroes* (2006) by Deborah Eisenberg, *Extremely Loud and Incredibly Close* (2005) by Jonathan Safran Foer, and *The Writing on the Wall* (2005) by Lynne Sharon Schwartz. Certainly what is notable about these texts is the presence of, and in fact an emphasis on, the preliminary stages of trauma, the sense of 9/11 as a kind of historical and experiential abyss, a yawning and possibly unbridgeable gap between before and after. "These three years past since that day in September, all life had become public," observes a character in *Falling Man* (2007, 182). Another character, in the lead story in *Twilight of the Superheroes,* echoes that observation. "Private life shrank to nothing," he reflects, "all one's feelings had been absorbed by an arid wasteland . . . one's ordinary daily pleasures were like dusty curios on a shelf" (2006, 36). The protagonist of *The Writing on the Wall* tries to find shelter from the storm of her feelings after the fall of the Twin Towers in an old—but not that old—periodical. "Global warmings, faulty voting machines, the elusive Pinochet—last month's magazine," she observes. "All from before. All these matters sound prehistoric" (2005, 145). And here is a character in *The Emperor's Children* looking at the cover of a new magazine that was his brainchild. It is the projected first issue, now scuppered, as in fact the whole project is, by the events of September 11: "Already with its vermilion, orange, and yellow graphic, a sunburst, a remarkable photograph of a sunburst, the idea having been that they were exploding upon the scene, illuminating truths, and different, down to the images, from the rest; already it looked out of date and faintly forlorn, like some child's abandoned artwork" (2007, 540).

It does not take a particularly subtle or intensive reading of this passage to see it as an act of recognition: that the old world has been turned upside down, altered ineradicably and the old literary forms and compulsions consequently are made to look "forlorn," immature and obsolete. The reader is possibly reminded of Henry James's claim, in his book on Hawthorne, that the Civil War "marks an era in the history of the American mind." "It introduced into the national consciousness a certain sense of proportion and relation," James explained, "of the world being a more complicated place than it had hitherto seemed, the future more treacherous, success more difficult . . . the good American, in days to come, will be a more critical person than his complacent and confident grandfather. He has eaten of the tree of knowledge" (1967, 135).

To that extent what we have here is a recurrent rhythm in the cultural history of the United States linking the national fate, at moments of crisis, with notions of innocence and the fall into a deeper self-consciousness, a darker knowledge. To point out that it is recurrent, however, is not to deny its significance. New events generate new forms of consciousness requiring new structures of ideology and the imagination to assimilate and express them. That is the intellectual equation at work here. And it begs the question of just how new, or at least different, the structures of these books are. The answer is, for the most part, not at all.

This is not an argument for simple change, always supposing such a thing were possible. What it is an argument for, though, is enactment of difference: not only the capacity to recognize that some kind of alteration of imaginative structures is required to register the contemporary crisis, to offer testimony to the trauma of 9/11 and its consequences, but also the ability and willingness imaginatively to act on that recognition. "Every age reaccentuates in its own way the works of its immediate past" (1981, 421) Bakhtin observed, and what is required by recent events is at the very least a radical reaccentuation. A book such as *The Emperor's Children* may acknowledge this by suggesting how "forlorn" texts written prior to the crisis appear to be, but it does not enact it. The irony is that, relying on a familiar romance pattern—in which couples meet and romantic and domestic problems follow and are concluded in reconciliation or rupture—books such as this and, for that matter, *The Good Life*, *A Disorder Peculiar to the Country*, and *Falling Man*, simply assimilate the unfamiliar into familiar structures. The crisis is, in every sense of the word, domesticated. "All life had become public"—that observation made by a central character in *Falling Man* is not underwritten by the novel in which it occurs, nor in any of these novels. On the contrary, all life here is personal; cataclysmic public events are measured purely and simply in terms of their impact on the emotional entanglements of their protagonists. In the early years of the American republic, Alexis de Tocqueville warned of the dangers of a cultural condition in which, as he put it, "each citizen . . . generally spends his time considering the interests of a very insignificant person, namely himself" (1966, 627). In a situation where "all a man's interests are limited to those near himself," he suggested, "folk . . . form the habit of thinking of themselves in isolation and imagine that their whole destiny is in their hands" (653–54). If anyone "does raise his eyes higher," all they see is either "the huge apparition of society or the even larger form of the human race." They have "nothing between very limited and clear ideas and very general and vague conceptions; the space in between is empty" (627). For all the limitations of his vision, Tocqueville hit on a point that is pertinent here, since many of the texts that try to bear witness to contemporary events vacillate in just this way between large rhetorical gestures acknowledging trauma and retreat into domestic detail. The link between the two is tenuous, reducing a turning point in national and international history to little more than a stage in a sentimental education.

    McCarthy's alternative strategy in *The Road* is not to domesticate but to defamiliarize. His way of telling a story that cannot but must be told is to tell it aslant, to approach it by circuitous means, almost by stealth. He translates trauma into a narrative memory that captures what it is like to live after the fall with the exactitude yet also the elusiveness of symbolism. A symbol, Carl Jung once suggested, is "the best possible expression of a relatively *unknown* fact" (Gray 1990, 137). If that is so, then *The Road* is a symbolic narrative, a powerful but also slippery tale of something, some trauma that seems to resist telling. That same slipperiness is at work in the staple idiom and even the setting of the book. Spare, even skeletal descriptions lead up to closing passages that are rhetorically and intellectually daring; the narrative voice, at first sight, appears to be the voice of the main character, the father, but as flow of thought and speech continues, that voice seems to segue into that of the author. So echoing Faulkner here, McCarthy manages to imbue the text with a sense of his own presence without deviating noticeably from a technique designed to suppress it: "He tried to think of something to say but he could not. He'd had this feeling before, beyond the numbness and the dull despair. The world shrinking down about a raw core of parsible entities. The names of things slowly following those things into oblivion. Colors. The names of birds. Things to eat. Finally the names of things one believed to be true. More fragile than he would have thought. How much was gone already? The sacred idiom shorn of its referents and so of its reality. Drawing down like something trying to preserve heat. In time to wink out forever" (75).

A passage such as this inscribes language as presence and absence—a presence made the dearer now by being only in memory, an absence made all the more harrowing as the world to which it gestures inexorably deteriorates, shrinks "down about a raw core." The author is, equally and analogously, there and not there, slipping through the verbal interstices. And a similar ghostliness or elusiveness typifies the world through which McCarthy's travelers make their way. At the beginning of the novel, for example, father and son are in an area of woods and mountains where the winters are too bitter to survive without shelter. As the two make their way south they encounter the remains of a dam and "a log barn in a field with an advertisement in faded ten-foot letters across the roofslope. See Rock City" (18), and "in the foothills of the eastern mountains" they journey across, father and son wake one morning to hear something coming. The ground is trembling; it is an earthquake (81–82). This is a landscape of nightmare, certainly, but it is perhaps also East Tennessee, the author's Appalachian birthplace. The journey down from the mountains occurs in a border territory, between substantial fact and surreal dream, where the author can negotiate fear. This is a map of that sense of dread, generated in the Western consciousness by 9/11 and its aftermath, which is precise in both its geographical and mental coordinates because it refuses the easy option of the immediate.

The intertextuality that is such a deep-rooted feature of McCarthy's work adds to our sense of a text as a border country. The voice of the author overlaps with the inner voice of the protagonist, and in turn the voices of McCarthy's literary forebears bleed into them; a vocal subtext resonates below the surface text, adding further dimensions of meaning. In effect allusion becomes a form of mediation, a means of layering the narrative, catching its drift or tenor but in a nuanced, partly hidden and quietly indirect way. *The Road* brims with significances that are only partially or tentatively disclosed because, among other strategies, the echoes of other writers act both to place and displace understanding. The echoes of Eliot are there not to pin down meaning but to multiply its possibilities. This is a waste land that is determinate to the extent that it is the consequence of some disaster. But the disaster remains unlocated and almost seems to be part of the nature of things, reminding us of what one critic said of all McCarthy's novels—that they appear to be a series of meditations on the unhomelike nature of our environment, the "scary disconnection of the human from the not-human that both Freud and Heidegger called the *unheimlich*" (Bell 1988, 33). The narrative certainly invites us, as I have suggested, to historicize its meanings, to connect it to that fear and sense of impotence that haunts the United States, and perhaps the West, in the early years of the twenty-first century. But it also compels us, through the multiple signification of the image of the waste land, to measure the gap that has perhaps always existed between the grounds of our existence and human acts and ceremonies; we are slipped the suggestion that to be human is, and always has been, to be stray and sightless, trapped in a landscape that is there in its bleak surfaces and yet not there in its deeper significances—abruptly at hand but also unseen. "We live in a world that is not our own, and, much more, not ourselves / And hard it is in spite of the blazoned days" (Stevens 1955, 383). Those lines of Wallace Stevens also seem to be echoed here in *The Road*, as in so much of McCarthy's earlier fiction, reminding us that it gestures toward both the historically specific (the world after 9/11) and the elemental and general (the world, and the human condition, at any given time). This is a historical work, albeit of a peculiarly symbolic, deeply mediated kind, but also a metaphysical one—or, to be more accurate, an argument against metaphysics.

Eliot's account of the waste land concludes, famously, with an attempt to shore some fragments from the ruins of culture and a desperate gesture toward the distant possibility of faith. McCarthy's conclusions, the fragments he shores against the destruction, are rather different. There is, first, the redemptive nature of craft, doing a task and doing it carefully and well. At one point, for instance, the father tries to repair the wheel mount of the supermarket trolley that carries their few possessions: "They collected some old boxes and built a fire in the floor and he found some tools and emptied out the cart and sat working on the wheel. He pulled the bolt and bored out the collet with a hand drill and resleeved it with a section of pipe he'd cut to length with a hacksaw. Then he bolted it all back together and stood the cart upright and wheeled it around the floor. It ran fairly true. The boy sat watching everything" (14).

Detailed, scrupulously attentive descriptions of work, activities requiring patience and skill, occur in all McCarthy's novels. They provide a still point in the turning, tumultuous world that his characters inhabit. And the echoes multiply beyond the author's own, earlier texts here. The care, the precision with which the actions of the father are described, echoes the care taken with the actions themselves. The father is absorbed in this moment and this activity; so is the prose, and so, as a consequence, is the reader. And the precision and attentiveness of action and style echo, in turn, other, earlier moments in works by McCarthy's literary forefathers (and they are nearly all fore*fathers* here): the description of the crew working on riveting and repair to the vessel in Joseph Conrad's *Heart of Darkness* (1902), the devotion of Nick Adams to the duties of the wilderness in Ernest Hemingway's *In Our Time* (1925), Cash Bundren's loving account of the process of building a coffin for his mother in William Faulkner's *As I Lay Dying* (1930). Skill does not offer redemption for father and son in *The Road*, but it provides a temporary shelter from the storm, a moment of almost ritualistic relief. The layering, the series of echoes here, within and beyond the text, supply a richly mediated portrait of work as, if not salvation, then a place of safety, a temporary stay against confusion.

"The Fire Sermon," the third section of *The Waste Land*, concludes with lines that appear to resonate throughout *The Road*:

> Burning burning burning burning
> O Lord Thou pluckest me out
> O Lord thou pluckest
> burning
> (Eliot 1936, 72)

The allusions here, as many commentators on the poem have observed, are to Buddha and St. Augustine, both of whom characterized lust of the flesh as a burning fire. St. Augustine in his *Confessions* singled out the eyes as filters to evil and rejoiced that God would pluck him from the snare they spread; Buddha gestured toward the prospect of all things burning free of desire with the result that the process of reincarnation would be exhausted. Fire in *The Waste Land*, as in the texts it echoes, is an agent of destruction but also of creation; it is a negative force, certainly, and at the same time a purgative and even redemptive one. Playing on this dense texture of allusion, McCarthy pursues a similar ambivalence. Fire destroys in the postapocalyptic landscapes of *The Road*, certainly. There is the body of a man struck by lightning that father and son encounter early on in the novel, "as burntlooking as the country, his clothing scorched and black. One of his eyes was burnt shut," we are told, "and his hair was but a nitty wig of ash upon his blackened skull" (42). There is the "burntlooking" landscape itself, where "the ashes of the late world" are "carried on the bleak and temporal winds to and fro in the void" (9–10). But fire also creates—or, if not that exactly, it offers another refuge: not the saving graces of occupation, care and craft, but the comforting hope of continuity, survival.

At several points in *The Road*, father and son comfort each other with the thought that, together, they are "carrying the fire." The reassurance they seem to gain from this is palpable, but it is not until toward the end of the novel that what they understand by this becomes clear. "I want to be with you," the son exclaims. "You cant," the father replies,

> You cant. You have to carry the fire.
> I don't know how to.
> Yes, you do.
> Is it real? The fire?
> Yes it is.

Where is it? I don't know where it is.
Yes you do. It's inside you. It was always there. I can see it. (234)

This fire is certainly "real" at certain moments in the narrative—for instance, after father and son light an oil lamp found in a deserted and derelict yard. The lighting of the lamp, described in meticulous detail, is another moment of ritualistic and redemptive labor, and the lamp itself offers a literal if feeble defense against a gradually darkening world. But beyond these intimations of the saving grace of craft, and this literal dimension, there is a further, symbolic layering at work here. The resonances that the image of fire possesses—in the lighting of the fire, the carrying of the fire—recall other, earlier writers from Shakespeare ("How far that little candle throws its beams! / So shines a good deed in a naughty world" [*The Merchant of Venice* 5.1]) to Wallace Stevens. And it is in this typically, densely allusive way that it offers not redemption but relief.

Stevens is perhaps the closest echo here, if we are trying to identify what carrying the fire or lighting the fire might suggest or promise. Eliot, with the tropes of fire and burning, reaches out toward the possibility of salvation; Buddha and St. Augustine, using the same tropes, turn possibility into promise. What McCarthy alerts us to is quite different: the chance not of being saved but of surviving. Fire in *The Road* articulates no more, and no less, than the sense of an innate human vitality, an ardency of heart, the simple, fundamental continuation of the spark of life in a world that otherwise seems irretrievably lost and dead. Here McCarthy seems to be echoing lines from one of Wallace Stevens's most famous and notable poems, "Final Soliloquy of the Interior Paramour." In the dark Stevens sees "light" as a miraculous influence on the obscurity in which we live. The highest light comes from God and from our imagination, which in the creation of where we can be together is one: "Out of this same light, out of the central mind / We make a dwelling in the evening air," and to dwell there together is enough (Stevens 1955, 524). These lines seem to echo, in turn, that moment in *King Lear* when the mad king finds temporary refuge from the storm in a bare, fire-lit hovel on a blasted heath. The layering of textual allusion here, back from McCarthy through Stevens to Shakespeare, invites us to find—not safety, still less salvation—but sufficiency in the simple human acts of hanging on and hanging together, passing on and passing around the will to live.

Craft, continuity, and community are what, for the most part, is "enough" in *The Road:* a source of light, however flickering and fragile, in an irreversibly dark world. That is until the end of the narrative; then, something curious happens. The father dies. The boy stays for three days by his "cold and stiff" body. Then, setting out again on the road, the boy encounters a figure that looks and sounds as if he had stepped out of legend: "The man that hove into view . . . was dressed in a gray and yellow ski parka. He carried a shotgun upside down over his shoulder on a braided leather lanyard and he wore a nylon bandolier filled with shells for the gun. A veteran of old skirmishes, bearded, scarred across his cheek and the bone stoven and the one eye wandering" (237).

The man assures the boy, "I'm one of the good guys," tells him that he has "a little boy" and "a little girl" (the boy, he adds, is "about your age. Maybe a little older" [239]), and promises that he and his family "don't eat people." The man then takes the boy into the woods, where his family is sheltering; there the boy is greeted with warmth and affection by a woman, the wife and mother in this small, nuclear family. "Oh," she tells the boy, "I am so glad to see you" (241). After this initial meeting, the woman, we are told, "would talk" to the boy "sometimes about God." The young man confesses that, when "he tried to talk to God," he found that "the best thing was to talk to his father." "The woman said that was all right," the narrator confides. "She said that the breath of God was his breath yet though it pass from man to man through all of time" (241).

What are we to make of this? It is possible that this is a bleaker moment than it appears to be. There may be the intimation here that humanity is about to start again along the same old road leading to disaster—a spiraling upward that will lead eventually to another spiraling downwards into apocalypse. There may even be the chance that when the man reassures the boy "we don't eat people" (239), he is simply lying; cannibals, after all, are not given to announcing their intentions. It is possible, but unlikely. The woman simply puts the notion of continuity, so subtly articulated in the image of fire, in a more emphatic and surely coarser register. She has the voice of the great mother, calm, generous, and accepting: "Oh . . . I am so glad to see you." The man, in turn, is a reassuringly paternal figure; with his weathered face, his assured carriage, the way he stands out from his surroundings, his bluntness of manner, and breadth of personal experience, he also recalls any number of American heroes from Natty Bumppo to Randle McMurphy. The family, with its "little boy" and "little girl," in their symmetry and the feelings of security they generate, seem to offer a way out, an emotional haven. It is as if, at this moment, McCarthy has withdrawn into the sheltering confines of American myth, a myth that is, in this case, a curious but not uncommon mix of the heroic and the domestic. The man is a reassuring blend of adventure and authority, the woman a source of inspiration and comfort; together, with their two children, they seem to rescue the boy from the dark passage of the road, taking him into the comforting womb of the woods and into the arms of an American form of the holy family. The whole novel could be seen, among other things, as a covert assault on American exceptionalism, but this moment temporarily drags the narrative back into the consolations of a separate and special national destiny. If this is an act of recuperation, and it certainly appears to be, then it does not work. On the contrary it is deeply unconvincing—not least, because it is at odds with just about everything that has occurred in the novel before.

After the brief account of the several conversations that took place between the boy and the woman "about God," there is only one paragraph left in *The*

Road. But it is a paragraph that returns us to the central narrative thrust of the novel, its richly mediated account of the harsh facts of the human condition and the humble shelters human beings try to construct to help them deal with or at least tolerate those facts. There is crisis here in McCarthy's account of the unhomelike nature of the world, especially now; but there is also a sense of continuity in his gestures toward how human beings nevertheless try to build a home for themselves, or the illusion of a home, even now. "Once there were brook trout in the streams in the mountains," the narrator recalls. "They smelled of moss in your hand. Polished and muscular and torsional. On their backs were vermiculate patterns that were maps of the world in its becoming. Maps and mazes. Of a thing which could not be put back. Not be made right again. In the deep glens where they lived all things were older than man and they hummed of mystery" (241).

Characteristically this could be a memory of the unnamed father or the elusive author or both. It hardly seems to matter. What matters is the series of tensions on which this passage, and the novel it concludes, are built: between the recognition of passing and the remembering of an ardent vitality; the specificity of a mapped and known world and the resonance of one that remains insubstantial, unknown, and unknowable; and the acknowledgment of human insignificance and the assertion of at least the will to meaning. The rhythms of fall and possible recovery mark these concluding sentences, just as they leave their traces on the book they conclude. In doing so they bear testimony to trauma but also intimate the chance of survival. That final phrase, "hummed of mystery," is a typically bold yoking together of the material and the insubstantial; the mysterious seems to take on, for a moment, bodily or at least vocal shape.

McCarthy's strategies for dealing with the ghosts that haunt the twenty-first century, particularly in the West and especially in America, may not be startlingly new. Formally what is at work here, after all, is the romantic belief in deferral (which accounts for the slipperiness of idiom), the symbolist commitment to what Mallarmé called "that part of speech which is not spoken" (1956, 21) ("the ideal is to suggest the object," Mallarmé said, because it is the "perfect use of this mystery which constitutes the symbol" [38]), and the modernist conviction that the use of what Frank Kermode called "the Image as radiant truth" might lead to the creation "out of a number of words" of "a single new word which is total in itself and foreign to language"(1961, 2, 43). But McCarthy has reworked those strategies to address contemporary pain, offering a realistic measure of its extraordinary scope, the sense of apocalypse that now seems to haunt the West, and in doing so neither minimizes that pain nor surrenders to it. The experience and the knowledge flowing from it that McCarthy maps are potentially annihilating, defying speech. But McCarthy is not reduced to silence; neither do his characters surrender to despair or simply accept annihilation. In the process *The Road* surely echoes, in its structure of feeling, if not literally, Samuel Beckett's attempt to name *The Unnamable*: "I don't know, I'll never know, in the silence you don't know, you must go on, I can't go on, I'll go on" (1960, 418).

Works Cited and Consulted

Bakhtin, Mikhail. "Discourse in the Novel." *The Dialogic Imagination: Four Essays by Mikhail Bakhtin*. Trans. Caryl Emerson and Michael Holquist. Austin: University of Texas Press, 1981.
Beckett, Samuel. *The Unnamable* (1958). *Three Novels*. London: Calder, 1960.
Bell, Vereen. *The Achievement of Cormac McCarthy*. Baton Rouge: Louisiana State University Press, 1988.
Berry, Wendell. *The Unsettling of America: Culture and Agriculture*. San Francisco: Sierra Club Books, 1986.
———. *Standing by Words*. San Francisco: North Point Press, 1983.
Brodsky, Joseph. "A Footnote to a Commentary." Trans. Jeremy Gambrell and Alexander Summerkin. *Rereading Russian Poetry*. Ed. Stephanie Sandler. New Haven, Conn.: Yale University Press, 1999. 184–99.
Caruth, Cathy. *Unclaimed Experience: Trauma, Narrative and History*. Baltimore: Johns Hopkins University Press, 1996.
———, ed. *Trauma: Explorations in Memory*. Baltimore: Johns Hopkins University Press, 1995.
DeLillo, Don. *Falling Man*. London: Picador, 2007.
Doody, Margaret Ann. "Where a Man Can Be a Man." *London Review of Books* 15 (December 16, 1993): 20.
Eisenberg, Deborah. "Twilight of the Superheroes." *Twilight of the Superheroes*. 2006. Reprint, London: Picador, 2007.
Eliot, T. S. *Collected Poems, 1909–1935*. London: Faber & Faber, 1936.
Farrell, Kirby. *Post-Traumatic Culture: Injury and Interpretation in the Nineties*. Baltimore: Johns Hopkins University Press, 1998.
Foer, Jonathan Safran. *Extremely Loud and Incredibly Close*. New York: Houghton Mifflin, 2005.
Freud, Sigmund. *Moses and Monotheism: Three Essays*. Trans. James Strachey. London: Hogarth Press, 1974.
Gray, Richard. *American Poetry of the Twentieth Century*. London: Longman, 1990.
Hartman, Geoffrey. "Shoa and Intellectual Witness." *Partisan Review*, February 1, 1998, 37–48.
Herman, Judith. *Trauma and Recovery*. New York: Basic Books, 1992.
James, Henry. *Hawthorne*. 1879. Reprint, New York: Macmillan, 1967.
Kalfus, Ken. *A Disorder Peculiar to the Country*. 2006. Reprint, London: Simon and Schuster, 2007.
Karlin, Wayne. *Lost Armies*. New York: Henry Holt, 1988.
Kermode, Frank. *The Romantic Image*. 1957. Reprint, London: Penguin, 1961.
Lee, Chang-Rae. *Native Speaker*. New York: Riverhead, 1995.
Lukács, Georg. *The Meaning of Contemporary Realism*. Trans. John and Necke Mander. London: Merlin Press, 1963.

Mallarmé, Stephané. *Mallarmé: Selected Prose, Poems, Essays and Letters.* Trans. Bradford Cook. Baltimore: Johns Hopkins University Press, 1956.

Mars-Jones, Adam. "Life after Armageddon." Review of *The Road. Observer,* November 26, 2006, sec. 25, p. 19.

McCarthy, Cormac. *The Road.* New York: Alfred A. Knopf, 2006.

———. *No Country for Old Men.* New York: Alfred A. Knopf, 2005.

———. *Cities of the Plain.* New York: Alfred A. Knopf, 1998.

———. *The Crossing.* New York: Alfred A. Knopf, 1994.

———. *All the Pretty Horses.* New York: Alfred A. Knopf, 1992.

———. *Blood Meridian.* New York: Alfred A. Knopf, 1989.

———. *Suttree.* New York: Random House, 1979.

———. *Child of God.* New York: Random House, 1973.

———. *Outer Dark.* New York: Random House, 1968.

———. *The Orchard Keeper.* New York: Random House, 1965.

McInerney, Jay. *The Good Life.* London: Bloomsbury, 2006.

Messud, Clare. *The Emperor's Children.* 2006. Reprint, London: Picador, 2007.

Pilkington, Tom. "Fate and Free Will on the American Frontier." *Western American Fiction* 37 (1997): 312–24.

Ragan, Paul. "Values and Structure in *The Orchard Keeper.*" *Perspectives on Cormac McCarthy.* Ed. Edwin T. Arnold and Dianne C. Luce. Jackson: University Press of Mississippi, 1993.

Schwartz, Lynne Sharon. *The Writing on the Wall.* New York: Counterpoint, 2005.

Stevens, Wallace. *Collected Poems.* London: Faber & Faber, 1955.

Tocqueville, Alexis de. *Democracy in America.* Trans. George Lawrence (1835, 1840). New York: Harper & Row, 1966.

Updike, John. *Terrorist.* 2006. Reprint, London: Penguin, 2007.

Woodward, Robert B. "Cormac McCarthy's Venomous Vision." *New York Times Magazine,* April 19, 1992, 28–31, 36.

CONTRIBUTORS

Marcel Arbeit is associate professor in the Department of English and American Studies, Palack University, Olomouc, Czech Republic. His main fields of research are contemporary southern literature, American and Canadian independent cinema, and popular culture. He is the author of a monograph on the novels of Fred Chappell and Cormac McCarthy published in 2006 (in Czech) and the main editor of the three-volume *Bibliography of American Literature in Czech Translation* (2000). His recent publications have focused on Fred Chappell, Harry Crews, Richard Ford, Lewis Nordan, and the American South in film. He also coedited *Vypravěči amerického jihu* (Southern Narrators, 2006), a Czech anthology of classic twentieth-century American southern short fiction. He is the current president of the Czech and Slovak Association for American Studies.

Edwin T. Arnold is professor of English at Appalachian State University in Boone, North Carolina. He has published widely on southern writers, including William Faulkner, Cormac McCarthy, Erskine Caldwell, and Donald Harington. Arnold is presently editor of the *Faulkner Journal*. His most recent publications are the essay "Doctor's Son," included in the collection *White Masculinity in the Recent South* (2008) edited by Trent Watts, the foreword to John Sepich's *Notes on Blood Meridian: Revised and Expanded Edition* (2008), and his book *"What Virtue There Is in Fire": Cultural Memory and the Lynching of Sam Hose* (2008).

Thomas Ærvold Bjerre is a lecturer at the Center for American Studies at the University of Southern Denmark. He recently finished his doctoral dissertation, "Cowboy Crackers: Echoes of the American Western in Contemporary Southern Fiction." He has contributed to the books *Larry Brown and the Blue-Collar South*, *Perspectives on Barry Hannah*, and *Madison Jones' Garden of Innocence*. He has published articles and interviews on various southern writers and aspects of southern culture in *Mississippi Quarterly*, *Appalachian Journal*, and *American Studies in Scandinavia*. Bjerre has coedited a special issue of *Mississippi Quarterly* on Lewis Nordan and he has cowritten *Cowboynationen* (2009), a book in Danish on the American western. Apart from southern literature, his research areas include American literature and film, the American Civil War, and masculinities studies.

ROBERT H. BRINKMEYER JR. is Emily Brown Jefferies Professor of English and professor of southern studies at the University of South Carolina. He is widely published in twentieth-century and contemporary southern literature and culture, with books on Catholic writing in the South, Flannery O'Connor, and Katherine Anne Porter, along with *Remapping Southern Literature: Contemporary Southern Writers and the West* (paperback 2007). Professor Brinkmeyer received a Guggenheim Fellowship to complete his most recent book, *The Fourth Ghost: White Southern Writers and European Fascism, 1930–1950* (2009), which won the Warren-Brooks Award for excellence in literary criticism.

JEAN W. CASH, professor of English emerita at James Madison University in Harrisonburg, Virginia, has published articles and presented numerous papers on southern writers. She authored a biography on Flannery O'Connor, *Flannery O'Connor: A Life* (paperback 2003), and with Keith Perry she coedited and contributed essays to a collection of essays on the life and work of Larry Brown, *Larry Brown and the Blue-Collar South* (2008). Her current project is an authorized biography of Larry Brown, forthcoming.

THOMAS E. DASHER is professor of English at Berry College in Rome, Georgia. He served as provost at Berry from 2000 to 2007. Before coming to Berry he spent seventeen years at Valdosta State University, eleven as head of the Department of English and six as dean of the College of Arts and Sciences. Dasher began his academic career at Georgia Southern College (now University) after completing his doctorate in 1978. He has a bachelor's degree in English from Davidson College, a master's in English from the University of North Carolina at Chapel Hill, and a doctorate in English from the University of South Carolina. He is the author of *William Faulkner's Characters: An Index to the Published and Unpublished Fiction* (1981) and has published widely on southern literature.

OWEN W. GILMAN JR. is a native of Maine, which does not happen to be a southern state, but after encountering the South in Uncle Sam's army (Fort Gordon, Georgia) and in graduate school (University of North Carolina in the southern part of heaven, Chapel Hill), he explored diverse features of southern culture, including the collected work of Barry Hannah. In his *Vietnam and the Southern Imagination* (paperback 2008), for example, one chapter is devoted to exploring ways in which Hannah's fiction incorporates the Vietnam War experience. He contributed a chapter, "The South," to *The Columbia Companion to American History on Film: How the Movies Have Portrayed the American Past* (paperback 2006), edited by Peter C. Rollins. He is professor of English at Saint Joseph's University in Philadelphia, where he has been teaching for the past thirty years.

JOHN GRAMMER is professor of English at the University of the South in Sewanee, Tennessee, where he also directs the Sewanee School of Letters, a summer graduate program in literature. His book *Pastoral and Politics in the Old South* was published in 1997 and won the C. Hugh Holman Award, given annually by the Society for the Study of Southern Literature for the year's best scholarly book on southern literature. His essays and reviews have appeared in *American Literary History*,

Mississippi Quarterly, Southern Literary Journal, and other periodicals. A native of Texas, he was educated at Vanderbilt University and the University of Virginia.

RICHARD GRAY is the first specialist in American literature to be elected a fellow of the British Academy. Professor of literature at the University of Essex and a former editor of the *Journal of American Studies*, he has published sixteen books and more than fifty articles on American literature. His books include *The Literature of Memory: Modern Writers of the American South; Writing the South: Ideas of an American Region* (winner of the C. Hugh Holman Award); *American Poetry of the Twentieth Century; The Life of William Faulkner: A Critical Biography; Southern Aberrations: Writers of the American South and the Problems of Regionalism* (2000); *A History of American Literature* (2004); and *A Web of Words: The Great Dialogue of Southern Literature* (2009). He recently edited *A Companion to the Literature and Culture of the American South* (2004) and co-organized a colloquium on the American South held in Vienna; the proceedings were published as *Transatlantic Exchanges: The American South in Europe-Europe in the American South* (2007). A regular reviewer for the *Times Literary Supplement* and the *Literary Review* and a regular broadcaster for the BBC, he is currently working on a second and abridged edition of his *History of American Literature*, a book on the idea of America, a book on the immigrant encounter in the South, and a television documentary on Edgar Allan Poe.

JAN NORDBY GRETLUND is chair of the Center for American Studies, University of Southern Denmark. He is the author of *Eudora Welty's Aesthetics of Place* and *Frames of Southern Mind: Reflections on the Stoic, Bi-racial and Existential South*. He is the editor of *The Southern State of Mind* (2010) and *Madison Jones' Garden of Innocence* and the coeditor, with Karl-Heinz Westarp, of *Walker Percy: Novelist and Philosopher; The Late Novels of Eudora Welty; Realist of Distances: Flannery O'Connor Revisited;* and *Flannery O'Connor's Radical Reality* (2007). And with A. J. Badger and Walter Edgar he has coedited *Southern Landscapes*.

M. THOMAS INGE is the Robert Emory Blackwell Professor of Humanities at Randolph-Macon College in Ashland, Virginia, where he teaches and writes about southern literature and culture, American humor and comic art, film and animation, Asian literature, and William Faulkner. He is the editor of *The Greenwood Guide to American Popular Culture* (2009). Recent publications include *William Faulkner: Overlook Illustrated Lives; The Incredible Mr. Poe: Comic Book Adaptations of the Works of Edgar Allan Poe;* and *Literature*, volume 9 of the *New Encyclopedia of Southern Culture* (2008). He is a founder of the Southern Studies Forum of the European Association for American Studies, and in 2008 the Society for the Study of Southern Literature honored him with the Richard Beale Davis Award for Lifelong Contributions to Southern Letters. With Ed Piacentino he has edited *Southern Frontier Humor: An Anthology* (paperback 2010).

CHARLES ISRAEL grew up in upstate South Carolina. He holds degrees from Wofford College, Emory University, and the University of South Carolina. He has taught literature and writing at Clemson University, the University of South Carolina, South Carolina State University, and Columbia College. He has published journal articles on American literature and southern literature. He wrote biographical-critical entries in the *Dictionary of Literary Biography* on Barry Hannah, George Garrett, Louis Simpson, and Gwendolyn Brooks, and he is coauthor of a history of Columbia College. He has published short stories in journals and magazines. He is a life member of the Board of Governors of the South Carolina Academy of Authors.

CLARA JUNCKER is associate professor of American literature at the University of Southern Denmark, where she has directed the Center for American Studies. She has published widely on both sides of the Atlantic within the fields of nineteenth- and twentieth-century American literature, African American studies, southern literature, composition studies, and literary theory. Her books include *Through Random Doors We Wandered: Women Writing the South* (2002); *Transnational America: Contours of Modern U.S. Culture* (2004); and *Circling Marilyn: Text, Body Performance* (2010). In the fall of 2008 she was lecturing and writing in Korea and China, negotiating cultural differences on a daily basis.

KATHRYN MCKEE is McMullan associate professor of southern studies and associate professor of English at the University of Mississippi. Her areas of scholarly interest are southern literature, nineteenth-century American literature, writing by women, film studies, humor studies, and global South studies. She has published articles in *Legacy, Southern Literary Journal, Mississippi Quarterly, Southern Quarterly, Studies in American Humor,* and *Studies in the American Renaissance,* and she recently coedited a special issue of *American Literature* called "Local Literatures, Global Contexts: The New Southern Studies." She is also coeditor of *American Cinema and the Southern Imaginary* (2010).

TARA POWELL is assistant professor of English and Southern Studies at the University of South Carolina at Columbia. Her research interests include New South verse memoirs, Waldensian-American life in Appalachia, and literary representations of southern intellectual labor. Her essays and poems have appeared in *Mississippi Quarterly, South Atlantic Review, Southern Poetry Review, Southern Quarterly, storySouth, Tar River Poetry, Weber Studies,* and other journals.

SCOTT ROMINE is associate professor of English at the University of North Carolina at Greensboro, where he teaches courses in American and southern literature. He is the author of *The Narrative Forms of Southern Community* and *The Real South: Southern Narrative in the Age of Cultural Reproduction* (2008). He contributed essays to several volumes, including *South to a New Place; Look Away! The U.S. South in New World Studies* (2004); *Perspectives on Barry Hannah* (2006); and *Thomas Dixon and the Birth of Modern America* (2006). Currently he is at work on a project exploring literary representations of the Reconstruction.

HANS H. SKEI is professor of comparative literature at the University of Oslo, Norway. Skei has written and published extensively on southern literature, beginning with two books based on his doctoral dissertation, *William Faulkner: The Short Story Career* and *William Faulkner: The Novelist as Short Story Writer.* He organized an international Faulkner seminar and edited the proceedings in the book *Faulkner's*

Short Fiction: An International Symposium (1997). He published *Reading Faulkner's Best Short Stories* (1996) and *Faulkner and Other Southern Writers: Literary Essays* (2004). He coedited, with Jakob Lothe and Per Winther, *Less Is More: Short Fiction Theory and Analysis* (2008). He has also published widely in Norwegian on subjects ranging from literary history and theory to crime fiction.

CARL WIECK has degrees from the University of Louisville, Northwestern University, and the University of Paris and has been a Fulbright student in Berlin as well as a Fulbright teacher in Ivory Coast. In addition to Morehouse College, he has taught at the University of Louisville, University of Abidjan, University of Jyväskylä, and University of Tampere. He has written for publication only in recent years because teaching has always taken priority and he decided early on not to publish from motives not his own. His two books, *Refiguring Huckleberry Finn* (paperback, 2004) and *Lincoln's Quest for Equality: The Road to Gettysburg* (2002) are thus products of long gestation, as is the article in this collection, which is beholden to the teaching and reflection permitted by those earlier years.

INDEX

Literary works are indexed under the author's name, not the title.

Allison, Dorothy, 105; *Bastard Out of Carolina*, 112
Anderson, Sherwood, *Winesburg, Ohio*, 216
Angelou, Maya, 1
Aristotle, *Ethica Nicomachea*, 167

Bahktin, Mikhail, 260, 265–66
Balzac, Honoré de, 79
Barthes, Roland, *S/Z*, 79
Bauman, Zygmunt, "From Pilgrim to Tourist," 194–95
Becker, Ernest, *The Denial of Death*, 219
Beckett, Samuel, *The Unnamable*, 273
Bell, Madison Smartt, 22–23
Bell, Vereen, *The Achievement of Cormac McCarthy*, 268
Berry, Wendell, 21, 261
Bjerre, Thomas Ærvold, 218, 221
Blakely, Diann, 108
Blount, Roy Jr., 5, 11, 201
Bly, Robert, *Iron John: A Book about Men*, 226
Bogue, Barbara, *James Lee Burke and the Soul of Dave Robicheaux*, 150
Brinkmeyer, Robert H., Jr., *Remapping Southern Literature*, 248
Brodsky, Joseph, 261
Broncano, Manuel, 222
Brown, Larry, 105–17, 136; *Dirty Work*, 105; *Facing the Music*, 105; *Father and Son*, 106, 113, 115; *Fay*, 106–17; *Joe*, 106–107, 113–14, 115; *A Miracle of Catfish*, 105

Bryant, Bear, 140
Buddha, 269, 270
Buddhism, 256–58
Burke, James Lee, 148–62; *Crusader's Cross*, 150–62; *Half of Paradise*, 148; *The Neon Rain*, 148; *White Doves at Morning*, 148
Butler, Jack, 204
Butler, Pierce, 61–62

Caldwell, Erskine, 114, 210, 246
Calhoun, John C., 63
Camus, Albert, *The Stranger*, 245
Canakis, Costas, 34
Caruth, Cathy, 264
Céline, Louis-Ferdinand, 263
Chappell, Fred, 204, 217
Chitwood, Ava, 21
Civil War, 6, 19–28, 30–42, 45–56, 148, 265
Cobb, James, 11
Conrad, Joseph, *Heart of Darkness*, 268
Cooper, James Fenimore, and Natty Bumppo, 237, 256, 258, 271
Crews, Harry, 105, 106
Crockett, David, 256

Dante, Alighieri, 263
Darwin, Charles, journal entries, 22
Defoe, Daniel, *Moll Flanders*, 106, 111–13, 116–17
DeMarr, Mary Jean, 51
Descartes, René, *Discourse on Method*, 208

282 Index

Dickens, Charles, 140; *A Tale of Two Cities*, 61
Dickerson, James, 108, 110
Dostoyevsky, Fyodor, *Crime and Punishment*, 244
Douglas, Ellen, 106, 239–40, 241–42; *Can't Quit You, Baby*, 48; *The Rock Cried Out*, 242
Dreiser, Theodore, *Sister Carrie*, 106, 111–13, 116–17
Durban, Pam: *All Set about with Fever Trees*, 58–59, 60–61; *Cabbagetown Families*, 58; "Keep Talking," 61; *The Laughing Place*, 59, 61; nonfiction, 59; "Rowing to Darien," 61; *So Far Back*, 59–72; "This Heat," 58

Earley, Tony, 174
Edgar, Walter, 62
Edgerton, Clyde, 174–88; *The Bible Salesman*, 175–87; *Raney*, 144, 174–75; *Walking Across Egypt*, 144
Ehrenreich, Ben, 76, 84
Eliot, T. S., 261–62, 267, 268; "The Preludes," 143; *The Waste Land*, 262–63, 269
Ellison, Ralph Waldo, 1, 78; *Invisible Man*, 84
Emerson, Ralph Waldo, 27; family of man, 7–8; global village, 7–8
Evans, W. McKee, 30
Everett, Percival, 1, 73–87; *American Desert*, 74; *Erasure*, 76–87; "F/V: Placing the Experimental Novel," 79; *I Am Not Sidney Poitier*, 75; "Signing to the Blind," 76; *Suder*, 74; "The Appropriation of Cultures," 75; *Walk Me to the Distance*, 74; "Why I'm from Texas," 75
Everett, Tony, 258

Faulkner, William, 9, 13, 41, 68, 106, 159, 191–92, 204, 212, 239, 240, 246, 266; *Absalom, Absalom!*, 4, 47, 48, 60, 137; *As I Lay Dying*, 268–69; *The Hamlet*, 226; *Light in August*, 106, 111–13, 116–17; *The Reivers*, 213, 217; *The Sound and the Fury*, 51, 136, 217; *The Unvanquished*, 216
Fields, Mamie Garvin, 29

Fitzgerald, F. Scott, 108, 262
Flagg, Fannie: *Fried Green Tomatoes at the Whistle Stop Café*, 144
Ford, Richard, 1, 248–59; *Independence Day*, 248, 249–52, 256; *The Lay of the Land*, 249–59; *A Piece of My Heart*, 248; *The Sportswriter*, 249, 250–51
Forster, E. M., 196; *Howards End*, 201–202
Foucault, Michel, 77
Frazier, Charles, 19–28; Chinese poetry 24–27; *Cold Mountain*, 20–28; *Thirteen Moons*, 20
Freud, Sigmund, 221, 264, 265, 268

Gaines, Ernest J., "Just Like a Tree," 70
Gay, William, 105
Gibbons, Kaye, 43–57; *A Cure for Dreams*, 45; *Ellen Foster*, 43; *Frost and Flower*, 44; *On the Occasion of My Last Afternoon*, 44–57; *Sights Unseen*, 44; *A Virtuous Woman*, 43
Gilman, Caroline Howard, 1
Gilman, Charlotte Perkins, *Women and Economics*, 112
Gingher, Marianne, 110
Glendenning, Karin, 107
Goodspeed, Edgar J., *The Bible: An American Translation*, 186
Grant, Gavin J., 133
Green, Nancy, as 'Aunt Jemima,' 52
Gretlund, Jan Nordby, 41
Guagliardo, Huey, ed., *Conversations with Richard Ford*, 249, 251, 258
Guinn, Matthew, 92

Halberstam, Judith, 36
Hamilton, Alexander, 4, 5
Hamilton, William L., 128
Hammett, Dashiell, 150
Hannah, Barry, 9, 106, 107, 135–47; *Geronimo Rex*, 135; *Long, Last, Happy*, 146; style, 135; *Yonder Stands Your Orphan*, 137–47
Han-shan (Chinese poet), 24–27
Harington, Donald, 23–24, 203–15; *The Architecture of the Arkansas Ozarks*, 204, 210, 211; *The Cherry Pit*, 203, 205; *The Cockroaches of Stay More*, 207, 210, 212;

Ekaterina, 204, 207, 210; *Enduring*, 204–15; *Lightning Bug*, 203–204, 205–206, 209, 210, 212, 213; *Rose of Sharon* (work in progress), 207, 213; self-referencing, 211, 212; *Some Other Place. The Right Place*, 210; *When Angels Rest*, 209, 210; *With*, 210, 212
Harris, George Washington, 172
Harris, Trudier, *From Mammies to Militants*, 51
Hartman, Geoffrey, 264
Hawkins, Gary (film maker), 105
Hawthorne, Nathaniel, 265; *The Scarlet Letter*, 141
Hegel, G. W. F., 78, 167
Heidegger, Martin, 167, 268
Hemingway, Ernest, *In Our Time*, 268
Hendricks, Robert G., 25
Hennis, R. Sterling, 174
Herman, Judith, 264
Hewlett, Lynn, 108
Homer, *Odyssey*, 21, 22
Hood, Mary, 60; *Familiar Heat*, 9
Hoover, J. Edgar, 177, 182
Hovis, George, 175
Howells, William Dean, 176
Humphreys, Josephine, 29–42; *Dreams of Sleep*, 29; *The Fireman's Fair*, 30; *Nowhere Else on Earth*, 29–42; *Rich in Love*, 30

I'll Take My Stand, 138–39, 140
Irving, John, 203; *The Cider House Rules*, 140

Jackson, Andrew, 63
James, Henry, 265
Jefferson, Thomas, 4, 5
Jocassee Valley, SC, 233–46
Jones, Anne Goodwyn and Susan Donaldson, *Haunted Bodies: Gender and Southern Texts*, 37–38
Jones, Madison, *A Buried Land*, 246
Jones, Suzanne, 239–40; "I'll Take My Land," 242
Joyner, Charles, *Down by the Riverside*, 54
Joyce, Kathryn, 172
Jung, Carl, 266

Keats, John, "Ode on a Grecian Urn," 68, 161
Kemble, Frances Anne, 64; *Journal of a Residence on a Georgian Plantation in 1838–39*, 61–62
Kermode, Frank, 272
Ketchin, Susan, 175
Kirchner, Ernst, 80
Klinger, Max, 80
Knole, Paul, 22
Koon, William, 13
Kooning, William de, 83
Kreyling, Michael, *Inventing Southern Literature*, 2–3

Ladd, Joseph Brown, 1
Laqueur, Thomas W., 221
Lee, Harper, *To Kill a Mockingbird*, 2, 19, 51
Lewis, C. S.: *Great Divorce*, 190, 199, 200, 201; *Screwtape Letters*, 190
Lowell, Robert, "For the Union Dead," 55
Lumbees, Native Americans, 29–42
Lytle, Andrew Nelson, 246

McCarron, Bill, 22
McCarthy, Cormac, 22–23, 106, 174, 260, 262–74; *All the Pretty Horses*, 261, 262; *Blood Meridian*, 260, 262; the critics, 260–61; *The Crossing*, 263; defamiliarize, 266; intertextuality, 264–65, 267; *No Country for Old Men*, 260; *Orchard Keeper*, 203; *The Road*, 262–73, "the ending," 270–72; *Suttree*, 260
McElya, Micki, *Clinging to Mammy*, 52
McKee, Kathryn, 3
McLaurin, Tim, 105
Mallarmé, Stéphané, 272
Marquez, Garcia, *One Hundred Years of Solitude*, 211
Mars-Jones, Adam, 260
Marx, Leo, *The Machine in the Garden*, 235
Mason, Bobbie Ann, *In Country*, 145
Melville, Herman, *Moby-Dick*, 256
Miller, Arthur, *Death of a Salesman*, 117
Mills, Jerry Leath, 107
Milton, John, 263; *Paradise Lost*, 181, 187

Mitchell, Lee Clark, *Westerns: Making the Man in Fiction and Film*, 237
Mitchell, Margaret, *Gone with the Wind*, 2, 6, 19, 23, 46–47, 51, 140
Morrison, Toni, *Playing in the Dark*, 50–51

Nabokov, Vladimir, 210; *Lolita*, 204, *Pale Fire*, 204
Nashville Agrarians, 21, 235, 246
New Criticism, 7
New Southern Studies, 3–4, 19
Newton, Isaac, 85
Nordan, Lewis, 216–30; *The All-Girl Football Team*, 216; *Boy with a Loaded Gun*, 217; *Lightning Song*, 217–30; *Music of the Swamp*, 216, 217; *The Sharpshooter Blues*, 217; *Sugar among the Freaks*, 216; *Welcome to Arrow Catcher Fair*, 216; *Wolf Whistle*, 216, 217
Novel, the; *Bildungsroman*, 110, 113, 186, 217–30, 233–34; and biography, 7; endings, 23, 270–72; and film, 2, 30, 74, 148, 235, 237; Post-9/11 novels, 264–65

O'Brient, Dan, 107, 110
O'Connor, Flannery, 8, 62, 106, 133, 140, 176, 182–84, 190, 240; "The Artificial Nigger," 184; and Eudora Welty, 2; "Good Country People," 182–83; "A Good Man Is Hard to Find," 183; *Mystery and Manners*, 1, 8; *The Violent Bear It Away*, 116, 182–83; *Wise Blood*, 116
Offutt, Andrew, 120, 127–28
Offutt, Chris, 105, 119–34; "Blue Lick," 128–30; film career, 119–20; *The Good Brother*, 120–33; *Kentucky Straight*, 119; memoirs, fantasy, and comic book writing, 119; narrative technique, 129–30, 132; themes, 126–28
Orwell, George, 161
Oxford American (magazine), 214

Palmer, Pauline, 38
Park, Mungo, *Travels in the Interior of Africa*, 54
Pascal, Blaise, 123

Percy, Walker, 15, 65, 255
Perry, Carolyn, and Mary Louise Weaks, *History of Southern Women's Literature*, 29, 35
Phillips, Jayne Anne, 1
Piacentino, Ed, 21–22; *The Enduring Legacy of Old Southwest Humor*, 166

Ramsey, William, 76
Ransom, John Crowe, 5
Rash, Ron, 233–47; *Among the Believers* (poems), 233; *Burning Bright* (stories), 246; *Casualties* (stories), 233; *Chemistry and Other Stories*, 234; *Eureka Mill* (poems), 233; *The Night the New Jesus Fell to Earth* (stories), 233; *One Foot in Eden*, 234–46; *Raising the Dead* (poems), 233; *Saints at the River*, 233; *Serena*, 234; *The World Made Straight*, 233, 244–45
Rauschenberg, Robert, 83
Ravenel, Shannon, 106, 107
Robertson, Ben, *Red Hills and Cotton*, 169
Rubin, Louis D., Jr., 43; *The Edge of the Swamp*, 137–38; *The History of Southern Literature*, 1
Ruppersburg, Hugh, 196

St. Augustine, *Confessions*, 269, 270
Sanchez-Arce, Ana Maria, 85
Sartre, Jean-Paul, *Being and Nothingness*, 167, 169, 171
Schwartz, Matthew, *In Defense of Homesickness*, 194
Sexton, Patricia Cayo, 225
Shakespeare, William: *King Lear*, 143, 270; *Macbeth*, 234; *The Merchant of Venice*, 270; *The Tempest*, 146
Shavers, Rone, 84, 85
Singleton, George, 165–73; *Novel*, 165; southern festivals, 171; southern politicians, 169–70; *These People Are Us*, 166, 168; *Work Shirts for Mad Men*, 166–73
Simms, William Gilmore, 138
Simpson, Lewis P., 9
Smith, Henry Nash, *Virgin Land*, 235
Snyder, Gary, 25, 26, 27
South, the: the community, 36–42, 143–44, 192–93; the concept of time,

8, 41, 45–56, 59–71, 161, 205, 207, 211, 212, 213, 246, 263; gender issues, 30–42, 46–55, 63–71, 94–103, 108–17; identity, 2–5, 6; the political situation, 137, 160, 234–35; racial issues, 9–11, 29–42, 45–56, 59–71, 76–85, 95–103, 138, 191–92, 196–99, 216

southern literature: alcoholism, 94, 114, 136, 149, 153, 162–72, 204; the canon, 4–5; crime fiction, 148–50, 157, 159, 160, 234; existentialism, 14–15, 235–37, 240–46, 249–58, 262–73; the family, 112–15, 174–87, 234–35, 262–63, 269–72; the grotesque, 12, 140; humor, 11–12, 130–32, 165–72, 175–87, 204–14; landscape, 9, 240, 242–42, 261–63; the literary microcosm, 44–57, 59–71, 93–103, 120–33, 150–61, 166–72, 175–87, 189–202, 204–14, 216–30; place, 248–50, 255; poor whites, 93–103, 111–17, 139–40, 165–72; religion, 13, 142–43, 174–87, 175–87, 271–72; sex and violence, 14, 95–103, 115–16, 141–42, 145–46, 204–205

Southern Renaissance, 4
Southwestern humorists, 12, 171–72
"Stagg R. Leigh," 81–85
Starr, William, 73, 74, 75, 84
Stevens, Wallace, 268; "Final Soliloquy of the Interior Paramour," 270
Stewart, Anthony, 73, 84
Stono Rebellion, 62
Styron, William, 211; *Set This House on Fire*, 203

Tate, Allen, "Ode to the Confederate Dead," 14, 55
Terr, Lenore, *Too Scared to Cry*, 222–25, 227
Tocqueville, Alexis de, 266
Tolstoy, Leo, *War and Peace*, 23
Tompkins, Jane, *West of Everything: The Inner Life of Westerns*, 239
Trefzer, Annette, 3
Tucker, Susan, *Telling Memories Among Southern Women*, 49
Turner, Nat, 53, 62–63
Twain, Mark, 1, 9, 172; *Adventures of Huckleberry Finn*, 120–33, 256; *Adventures of Tom Sawyer*, 121; *Following the Equator*, 76; "Jim Smiley and His Jumping Frog," 12; "Notebook 35," 125
Tyler, Anne, 1

Vesey, Denmark, 62
Vietnam, 149
Voltaire, *Candide*, 177, 181

Walker, Alice, *The Color Purple*, 51, 80; "Everyday Use," 64
Walker, Kara (visual artist), 52
Wallace-Sanders, *Mammy*, 52
Walter, Brian, *The Architect of Stay More* (documentary in progress), 211
Walton, Katharine, 108
Warren, Robert Penn, *All the King's Men*, 4
Watson, Burton, 24, 25, 26, 27
Weaver, Richard, 5
Welch, Rodney, 110
Wells, Kitty, 151, 152, 161
Welty, Eudora, 2, 174; *The Optimist's Daughter*, 70
Whitmire, Tim, 24
Wilcox, James, 189–202; Catholic world view, 190–91; *Heavenly Days*, 191–202; *Hunk City*, 191; *Miss Undine's Living Room*, 190, 191; *Modern Baptists*, 189, 191, 197; *North Gladiola*, 189–90, 191, 192, 195, 196; *Polite Sex*, 190; *Sort of Rich*, 190
Winfrey, Oprah, 43, 82
Wittgenstein, Ludwig, 74
Worster, Donald, *Under Western Skies*, 235
Wright, Richard, *Native Son*, 80
Wyatt-Brown, Bertram, *Southern Honor: Ethics and Behavior in the Old South*, 243–44

Yaeger, Patricia, *Dirt and Desire*, 38, 53
Yarbrough, Steve, 91–104; *The End of California*, 92–93; *Family Men*, 91; *The Oxygen Man*, 93–104; *Prisoners of War*, 92; *Safe from the Neighbors*, 93; *Visible Spirits*, 92

www.ingramcontent.com/pod-product-compliance
Lightning Source LLC
Chambersburg PA
CBHW030610230426
43661CB00053B/1926